SEX & DRUGS & ROCK'N'ROLL:
The Life of
IAN DURY

RICHARD BALLS

OMNIBUS PRESS
LONDON · NEW YORK · SYDNEY

Cover designed by Phil Gambrill
Picture research by Nikki Lloyd & Richard Balls

ISBN: 0.7119.8644.4
Order No: OP 48235

Exclusive Distributors
Music Sales Limited,
8/9 Frith Street,
London W1D 3JB, UK.

Music Sales Corporation,
257 Park Avenue South,
New York, NY 10010, USA.

Macmillan Distribution Services,
53 Park West Drive,
Derrimut, Vic 3030,
Australia.

To the Music Trade only:
Music Sales Limited,
8/9 Frith Street,
London W1D 3JB, UK.

Extracts of lyrics printed with kind permission of: Mute Songs,
Palan Music, Oval Music, Heathwave Music, London Publishing House/
Mautoglade Music Ltd, Warner Chappel Music Ltd.

Front cover photograph by Harry Goodwin
Back cover photograph by Patrick Ford/Redferns

Every effort has been made to trace the copyright holders of the photographs
in this book but one or two were unreachable. We would be grateful if the
photographers concerned would contact us.

Typeset by Galleon Typesetting, Ipswich.
Printed and bound in Malta by Gutenberg Press.

A catalogue record for this book is available from the British Library.

Visit Omnibus Press on the web at www.omnibuspress.com

*In accordance with the late Ian Dury's wishes, 25p for every copy of
this book sold will be donated to Cancer BACUP. Further donations to
Cancer BACUP can be made by phoning 020 7696 9003*

For Anne

Contents

Acknowledgements

I decided to write this book about the life and music of Ian Dury towards the end of 1998 after attempting to find one and discovering that none existed. It was always my intention for this to be an independent book in which Ian's story would be told through those who knew him best. Consequently, the basis for this biography lies in original interviews with more than 50 people conducted between March 1999 and February 2000, and only where necessary have I used previously published material. Despite being an 'unofficial' biography, Ian Dury took a most generous attitude. Towards the latter end of my research, I met him at his home and discussed the book with him, and at no stage did he seek to prevent me from writing his story. Although he did not give an interview himself, he gave his blessing for me to talk to family members and friends and, knowing I was a fan, made it clear that he did not want the book to be a "hagiography". For his co-operation, I am sincerely grateful.

To meet and talk with those who knew Ian during his 57 years was never work; it was quite simply a privilege. Without exception, they showed me kindness, sharing their thoughts, memories and, in some cases, treasured possessions with me. They also displayed great patience with my tiresome demands for the dates, places and other minutiae which all go to make up this fascinating, never before told, story. Most importantly of all, they spoke candidly and with great honesty.

My sincerest thanks and appreciation go to the following people: Barry Anderson; Terry Day; Mickey Gallagher (good luck to The Little Mothers); Charlie Gillett; Russell Hardy; Chaz Jankel; Wilko Johnson; Andrew King; Chris Lucas; Gordon and Andra Nelki; Steve Nugent; Humphrey Ocean; Geoff Rigden; Denise Roudette; Charlie Sinclair; Ed and Linda Speight; Stuart Spencer; Johnny Turnbull; Molly Walker; Norman Watt-Roy; Wreckless Eric.

I would also like to express my thanks to the following people, who also kindly gave interviews for this book: Jo Bexley; Mick Blake; Peter Blake; Baxter Dury; Glen Colson; Jenny Cotton; Alan Cowderoy; Germaine Dolan;

BP Fallon; Chris Foreman; Hamish Halls; Mick Hill; Ian Horne; Derek 'The Draw' Hussey; Anne Ingle; Jona Lewie; Laurie Lewis; Lene Lovich; Pippa Markham; Stephen Monti; Davey Payne; Rainbow George; Merlin Rhys-Jones; Mary Ritchie; Fred Rowe; Chris Miller (Rat Scabies); Peter Sedgwick; Brigid Slevin; Max Stafford-Clark; Paul Tonkin; Shirlie Watts; Kate Young.

My research was assisted by other people to whom I am also indebted, specifically Roger Dopson at Diamond Recordings; Tony Judge of the 'Be Stiff' official web-site; Noel Slevin at the Finn Valley Voice, Donegal; Chailey Heritage Old Scholars' Association; Mrs Taylor whom I met in Front Lane Community Centre, Cranham; Upminster Infants and Junior Schools; The Royal Grammar School, High Wycombe; Eugene Rae, archivist at the Royal College of Art; The *Western Mail & Echo* Library; The Royal Court Theatre, London; The Haymarket Theatre, Leicester; The Shakespeare Birthplace Trust, Stratford; Len and Lenka Hooper; and my friend and fellow hack Steve Gedge. Jamie Spencer, of East Central One, was an important point of contact for Ian Dury. Also, hello to Jayne Burchell (who probably got help from her mum).

Special thanks also go to Alison Balls, my sister, and Mark Tierney, for allowing me to treat their home like a hotel during my frequent visits in London, my father and mother, John and Sylvia, and my colleague, *Eastern Daily Press* photographer Bill Smith, who scanned some of the photographs. I am also grateful to Chris Charlesworth, the editor at Omnibus Press, who showed great enthusiasm for this book from the beginning and was always available to provide advice and support.

Most of all, I want to thank Anne Parton, who first encouraged me to write this book and has regretted it ever since. She displayed patience beyond the call of duty during the 12 months in which this book was written and researched and assisted in its preliminary editing.

Richard Balls, February 2000

Prologue

The London Palladium: 9.10pm, Sunday February 6, 2000.

Through the fine gauze curtain. six dimly lit figures can be seen emerging on to the stage. A huge roar goes up in the theatre and, as the house lights go down, The Blockheads start tuning up for the anthem which has opened every one of their live shows for more than 22 years – 'Wake Up And Make Love With Me'. The screen rises, revealing large vases of cut flowers along the front of the stage and a shimmering silvery backdrop. Above the band hangs a banner with the boxer dog in boxer shorts from the cover of the band's latest album *Mr Love Pants.* Suddenly, the warm-up comes to a halt and the song's unmistakable opening notes pour out from Chaz Jankel's piano. A heavy funk rhythm cascades through the speakers, cueing the entrance on stage of one of Britain's most charismatic performers.

From the wings, Ian Dury takes to the stage with the aid of a walking stick and two towering chaperones. He is dressed for the show – billed 'New Boots and Panto' – in a pale blue jacket, black trousers, dark red Dr Martens boots, his trademark white scarf and a grey Trilby hat. Noise swirls around the dark, Edwardian venue and the audience jump to their feet to salute their hero. Looking thin and gaunt, Ian is helped onto a large box and gazes out on the sea of faces through a pair of dark glasses. Smiling sardonically, he raises his hat, his acknowledgement to the crowd; slow, measured, every inch the seasoned performer. Pulling the microphone towards him, he sings in his trademark croaky voice: "I come awake, with the gift for womankind/You're still asleep, but the gift don't seem to mind", and the gig bursts into life.

But tonight the evening is tinged with sadness. In the bars, the stalls and galleries of the Palladium is a collective sense that this may be the last time Ian Dury will ever publicly perform this great sex anthem. Tonight, you can't help feeling, a great English showman is bowing out.

Ian Dury's very own 'Sunday Night At The Palladium' would be a fitting finale. As a teenager, his mother had brought him here to see Fifties crooner Johnnie Ray and he had watched in amazement as women flocked to the stage with huge bouquets of flowers. Later, he returned to the famous theatre on assignment for *London Life* magazine for which he did some illustrations. The young art graduate sketched the faces of the stars at the 1965 Royal Variety Show including Peter Cook, Dudley Moore, Dusty Springfield, Peter Sellers, Spike Milligan and – topping the bill – Tony Bennett. The Palladium, which first opened as a theatre in 1910, has played home to the kind of music hall acts who so influenced Ian's songwriting and performing. In line with the venue's variety show traditions, several acts are performing tonight, but this time it is Ian Dury's turn to top the bill in the theatre where he has seen the greats perform.

It is an emotional occasion, but above all, pure entertainment. In a box beside the stage, Government minister Mo Mowlam is jiving and singing along to 'Billericay Dickie'; in another, Ian's five-year-old son Billy is jumping up and down excitedly and drumming his hands on the ledge. Behind him, Ian's eldest son Baxter, his daughter Jemima and wife Sophy look on, full of smiles. Everyone here can feel the significance of the occasion – even The Blockheads have dressed smarter than usual in keeping with the venue. Ian, too, is aware of his surroundings, but is unimpressed. "I want to bring a bit of low-life into these walls. Oi Oi!" he yells. "Danny Kaye is listening, Bing is listening," he jokes to roars of laughter from the crowd.

Many of his friends, including former managers and musicians, are in the audience. Tonight, they are party to a classic Dury performance of songs old and new: 'Wake Up And Make Love To Me', 'Clevor Trever', 'The Passing Show', 'What A Waste', 'Billericay Dickie', 'Itinerant Child', 'Mash It Up Harry', 'Spasticus Autisticus', 'Bed 'O' Roses No 9', 'Reasons To Be Cheerful (Part 3)', 'Sweet Gene Vincent', 'Hit Me With Your Rhythm Stick'. His two escorts return to the stage, standing one each side of Ian and yelling 'Hit Me' into the microphone. But as the song thunders triumphantly to a close, Ian and the band are greeted by a barrage of calls for an encore and his minders leave the stage without him. "We're not into going off for a cup of tea and then coming back again. We'd rather sit out here and soak it all up," Ian says. Then, from Chaz's guitar, comes the first few notes of one of Ian's most famous songs. He stops, and then restarts the instantly recognisable tune, teasing the audience, before launching into the entire opening sequence of 'Sex & Drugs & Rock'n'Roll' and sending his fans delirious. When it finishes, Ian thanks the crowd, his voice cracking with emotion, but the evening ends on a light note. As Ian is led slowly away, 'I've Got A Lovely Bunch Of

Coconuts' plays over the speakers, while The Blockheads throw flowers into the stalls. And then, he is gone.

It was in 1977 – the Queen's Silver Jubilee Year – that Ian Dury first blended his music-hall mannerisms and Cockney rhyming slang with the American funk rhythms of Chaz Jankel. In doing so, the pair created a look and sound that was unique. Even as punk raged around him, *New Boots And Panties* – Ian's audacious début album – left listeners open-mouthed in shock. His chart topper, 'Hit Me With Your Rhythm Stick', sold in excess of one million copies and has been described as "the first British funk record".

Rarely has an artist moulded a persona as engaging as that created by Ian Dury or written lyrics as distinctive and devoid of cliché. Tellingly, his popularity with the British public remained undimmed over 20 years. The London Palladium holds more than 2,000 people, but Ian Dury and The Blockheads' one-off show sold out weeks in advance, as fans clamoured to see him for what would prove to be the last time. Even when his profile in the UK's fickle pop scene waned during the early Eighties, Ian and the band continued to pack out venues and headline international festivals. He maintained a cult following that spanned the entire social spectrum and cut across all age groups.

Ian Dury's relevance to pop is far greater than his chart record of three Top Ten hits, including one number one, might suggest. He wore a razor-blade in his ear and scared the pants off people long before pasty-faced punks were gobbed on by pogoing mobs. Kilburn & The High Roads – his alarming group of misfits – were breaking all the rules of conventional performance in the early Seventies when the first shoots of US punk were just showing through in the shape of The Stooges and The New York Dolls. Johnny Rotten had studied Ian's hobgoblin stance from the sticky floors of London pubs long before he appeared as the green-toothed, snarling vocalist in The Sex Pistols. The Kilburns' strange music and eccentric appearance also inspired the formation of Madness, one of the English success stories of the Eighties.

Ian's unforgettable first solo record – 'Sex & Drugs & Rock'n'Roll' – became an anthem in a Britain which was falling apart at the seams and its title has become generic. 'Reasons To Be Cheerful' also found its way into the modern language and is further proof that Ian Dury's contribution has been as an originator, rather than a copyist. As an artist, he had a keen eye for image and was alert to the importance of presentation before pop videos ever played a marketing role. He saw himself, not as a singer or 'pop star', but as an all-round entertainer.

Ian Dury was as British as the flag he once embossed on his teeth. Not surprisingly, he never cracked the American market. It was always on home ground that Ian Dury would be a 'household name'.

So polished was his performance, that it was hard to imagine that it was just that. Cockney wide-boy, diamond geezer – man of the people. He looked tough and, like many of his characters, spoke in rhyming slang – "I've forgotten me lemon curds [words]" – he laughed at The London Palladium. But his roots did not lie in working-class England at all. Ian Dury had a privileged post-war upbringing and his rough facade was born not out of his home life, but rather his experiences in hospitals and schools as a polio sufferer. From the age of seven, he had to build up physical and mental defences just to survive and this resilience helped him in his battle with cancer. Behind the prickly exterior, however, was a kind, caring and emotional man, as close friends testify.

Having been raised in a strongly matriarchal household, the women in Ian's life shared that single-mindedness that he knew as a child. His treatment of women was not always exemplary and no one would ever have described him as a feminist, but his charm always endeared him to women.

More than anything, his disability shaped the person he later became. As one of his aides once said: "Whatever is wrong with Ian happened 45 years ago and we aren't going to solve it now." Many of those close to him were of the same mind. Far from attempting to exaggerate his physical disabilities, Ian originally tried to hide them on stage. But inevitably his pronounced limp and his need for a helping hand going on and off stage became an integral part of his public image – he was as synonymous with polio as he was with a cloth cap, tangled white scarf and Essex laddism. The release of 'Spasticus Autisticus' – his protest against the International Year Of The Disabled – was a brave move, but he took few risks when it came to his carefully crafted persona. From the bowler-hatted magician who made his solo début at High Wycombe Town Hall in 1977 to the singer in the hat and shades who walked out at the London Palladium in 2000, the concept never changed. Journalists loved the 'loveable rogue', who unlike other more pretentious rock stars, spoke the 'language of the street'. He became the darling of the quality broadsheet press that his early fans grew up to read.

But it was not just in the music papers and live music venues that the name of Ian Dury was written large. The anti-establishment rebel had his ego massaged in the company of some of Britain's most revered actors and he continued to command respect among the cream of society. His acting work, his missions for the children's charity UNICEF and his television commercials introduced him to a new generation of fans. From *New Boots*

And Panties to *Mr Love Pants*, Ian Dury became one of our most endearing and inventive performers.

For a crippled youngster with the odds stacked against him, his life was one of achievement born out of adversity. But like all life's 'clever bastards', as Ian would have agreed, he "probably had help from his mum".

*"No-one said you must be as good as gold,
it's what you haven't done that matters when you're old."*

– 'Cacka Boom'

1

UPMINSTER KID

"My mum got the milk train down to Truro because they told her I wasn't going to make it. It was in Nissen huts barrack huts, an RAF-type hospital, and they let her come to the outside, and they turned the light on over my bed – you know, she saw my little white face on the pillow: a four o'clock in the morning job. But I was still there the next morning."

– Ian Dury

"Good Evening, I'm from Essex, in case you couldn't tell," Ian growls, prompting roars of approval from the audience. "My given name is Dickie, I come from Billericay, and I'm doing very well." A few jaunty notes on the piano and Ian Dury and The Blockheads carry their fans off on a carousel ride of music hall and Essex laddism, courtesy of one of Ian's best loved lyrical creations, 'Billericay Dickie'. From his earliest dalliance with rock'n'roll through to his very last gigs, Ian became universally identified with his characteristic stage persona. Off stage, in interviews and conversation, he cultivated a roguish image and his liberal use of the vernacular reinforced the public perception of him as a 'working-class hero'.

But Ian Dury was no "lawless brat from a council flat" like 'Plaistow Patricia', no East End barrow boy or Cockney street kid. Contrary to his Pearly King persona, his roots were set firmly in middle England. In many ways his upbringing could even be regarded as privileged. Ian played up his 'diamond geezer' image, but his start in life was cut glass. 'Billericay Dickie', 'Clevor Trever' and his other characters have brought him deserved acclaim as a sharp-witted social observer and ingenious lyric writer, but the rough-and-ready urban Britain to which they belong are a far cry from his own affluent childhood. While he was renowned for his openness and blunt talk in interviews, the reality of his upbringing remained firmly in the shadows.

Ian Robins Dury was born on May 12, 1942, at 43 Weald Rise, Harrow Weald, in Harrow, in the county of Middlesex. His mother, Margaret Cuthbertson Dury (formerly Walker), worked as a health visitor, and his father, William George Dury, drove buses for London Transport. As required, the couple registered their first child two days after his birth in the district of Hendon, in north west London. Such details might seem inconsequential 58 years on, but from the moment that Ian Dury set foot on a stage, his place of birth has been consistently and widely misstated, the vast majority of commentators assuming that he was born in the Essex town of Upminster. Those close to Ian knew him as a stickler for detail, be it about dates, occurrences, clothes or jazz and rock'n'roll minutiae, and it is not clear why this fundamental fact has been falsely documented with such regularity. The most likely explanation, however, is that Ian felt that Upminster – the last stop on the London Underground's District Line and the place where he spent most of his childhood – sat more comfortably with his wily Essex-lad image than did Harrow, a north west London suburb most commonly associated with a posh public school.

An early profile of his first rock'n'roll band, Kilburn & The High Roads, published by *Melody Maker* in 1973, confirms that when the press first came calling, Ian preferred to promote his Essex associations. 'Born: Upminster, Essex, but declines to give the date', the question-and-answer-style article read. Not only was the singer coy about his origins, he was also sensitive about his age. The genealogy of Ian Dury and The Blockheads, painstakingly researched in Pete Frame's *Rock Family Trees*, for which Ian provided much information, stated in 1979: "Ian Dury was born in Upminster, Essex (in case you didn't know)." Such has been the proclivity of both the media and his fans alike to connect Ian with the Essex landscape of his songs, that the US–produced *Rough Guide To Rock* claims he was born in Billericay, while even the 1998 edition of *The Encyclopedia Of Popular Music*, scrupulously collated over eight volumes by Colin Larkin and widely regarded as the definitive source for rock'n'roll knowledge, states that Ian was born in Upminster. The myth was perpetuated in all but one of the obituaries which appeared in the press the day after his death. In reality, the backdrop to Ian Dury's childhood and adolescence was a million miles away from the working-class roots of his largely absent father, which he chose to emphasise in favour of the middle-class background of his mother who raised him.

The home in which Ian grew up was a matriarchal one and his childhood and teenage years were dominated by strong-willed women. The 'Walker women' grew up as wealthy Irish Protestants, whose impressive homestead was in the wilds of County Donegal in the Irish Republic. When Ian came into the world in the middle of the Second World War, it was his mother, with the support of his two aunts and his grandmother, who took over his upbringing and made the key decisions about his future, often in difficult circumstances. His mother, known as Peggy, and his aunts – Betty and Molly – were well-spoken and well-educated, and had responsible jobs in health and education. It was against this secure, middle-class backdrop that Ian set out in life. When he found fame, he frequently talked about his father and was keen to impress his working-class credentials during interviews. But it was his mother's background as a member of a privileged land-owning family which held the most sway over Ian's childhood.

The family seat in the matriarchal line that produced Ian Dury is called Kilcadden House and is situated in a lush 189-acre dairy farm in the Finn Valley, County Donegal. A rambling Georgian mansion with no fewer than 32 apartment rooms, it stands imposingly on an isolated back road between Crossroads and Ballybofey, and was originally built for John Walker, Ian's great grandfather. John Walker's own father had been given a farm close to the site of Kilcadden House during the time of the great famine in Ireland in 1848, but after his wife and some of his children died, all at a young age, Ian's great-grandfather found himself orphaned. John Walker was raised by an aunt and when he was old enough to manage the dairy farm, the aunt had Kilcadden House built for him. When it was completed she set about organising the rest of his life. She disappeared to Scotland for a few weeks, visiting old friends, and on her return presented him with a list of 'suitable' girls for him to marry, ordering him to make himself known to each of their families. It is believed that at his very first port of call, he met the girl who later became his wife and whom he brought to live in his grand new home. According to Ian's aunt Molly Walker, when the future Mrs John Walker arrived at Kilcadden for the very first time, she is said to have turned to her husband-to-be and said, "Well John, I think we'd better have a fair sized family or we shall look rather foolish."

In common with Irish couples of their generation, they did just that. In all, they had ten children: James, John, William, Cuthbert, Arthur, Andrew, Robin (who died as a young boy), Janet, Louise and Violet. As the owners of a large dairy farm, the Walkers enjoyed a good social standing in this windswept and rugged region of north west Ireland, selling milk to the 'Twin Towns' of Ballybofey and Stranorlar. All the children grew up at Kilcadden and five of the six boys eventually married and emigrated, mostly across the Irish Sea to Britain. James, the eldest son, married and settled in London, where he was later appointed to the prestigious post of Law Editor of *The Times*. He and his wife did not have children of their own, although they would send generous gifts to their various nieces and nephews. Andrew also moved to England where he worked as an inspector of technical colleges and he and his wife had several girls and one boy.

William qualified as an engineer and lived for a time in Canada where he worked on the railways. But he returned to Kilcadden House years later to marry the local girl he had always loved. They also remained childless. Cuthbert became a doctor, got married in England and the couple kept up Kilcadden traditions by having a baby daughter.

John Walker married Mary Ellen Pollock, a Protestant Irish girl from a large farming family who owned two large farms on the other side of the Donegal border in what would become Northern Ireland after partition in 1921, and she had one brother, James, and two sisters, Eva and Betty. John, like Cuthbert, also trained as a doctor and shortly after the couple married in Ireland they moved to the peaceful and picturesque fishing village of Mevagissey in Cornwall, where he set up his medical practice.

However, the three Kilcadden girls never married, and this simple fact has been part of Walker legend ever since. Molly Walker, Ian's aunt, explains the ancient Kilcadden fable: "A few generations ago, one of the Walkers had three children – two boys and a girl – and they saved some money up for the older boy to go on this 'royal tour' around Europe, which was the fashion in those days. He didn't take it up because he didn't want to go, but his younger brother was very pleased to do so. He used that money, made a fortune, spent it, married a fairly well off girl and then spent her money as well. The sister had the poor taste – as her family saw it – to marry a Catholic in one of the Catholic cathedrals, and her father was so angry about this that he was supposed to have put a curse on the Walker women. From that day, no Walker woman married, and this went on through several generations."

The home of Ian's grandparents – John and Mary Walker – could not have enjoyed a better location in the tiny village of Mevagissey. The eight-bedroom house, which had been specially built for them and contained a doctor's surgery and waiting room at the rear, sat on top of a cliff, from where a steeply meandering path led down to the beach below. It was named 'Pentilly', the original name given to Mevagissey, in a gesture which the couple hoped would help to keep the name alive. The meadows which enveloped the large family home provided an idyllic environment for their four children, William, Elizabeth, Margaret (Ian's mother, Peggy) and Mary, who was known as Molly.

For a brief time, the family moved to the Lancashire town of Rochdale, north of Manchester, after some high drama at 'Pentilly'. When John Walker's partner in the practice married a local woman, some of those who knew him had warned his wife-to-be that he was simply after her money and, not long after the marriage went ahead, they separated and her finances went to him. Angry and embarrassed about his partner's behaviour, John

Walker felt he could not stay in the village and sold his practice, moving with his wife and three eldest children to Rochdale. Molly was born during this time, but two years later the First World War broke out and John joined up after arranging for somebody to look after his new practice. By now, Elizabeth was attending a boarding school in Derry and William had been sent to a preparatory school on the Welsh border. Molly and Peggy were meanwhile despatched to Kilcadden, where they were looked after by their grandmother and their aunt Janet. Arriving in the bleak landscape of Donegal in 1915, the two sisters lived there for about a year before their father came to collect them and took them back to the house in Mevagissey to which the family had now returned. When the schools broke up for the summer, the two young sisters were reunited with William and Elizabeth, the brother and sister from whom they had been separated.

After the summer holiday, Peggy, who had now reached school age, was sent to a small private boarding school in the nearest town of St Austell, while Molly, who was two and a half years younger, was enrolled at the infants school in the village.

The Walker household then – like that in which Ian would later grow up – was a literary one and Peggy and Molly were both good readers by the time they went to school. "We all used to read quite a lot because we had a great big bookcase in the drawing room at Pentilly and we decided that we would see which of us would read all of the books in that bookcase first," recalls Molly. "It was rather difficult because it kept changing and people kept putting new ones in, so we never quite settled that, but I can't remember a time when I couldn't read."

As literate as they were, when it came to music, the Walkers were a dead loss. Molly laughs: "The thing that was always said about the Walkers was, 'It's no good talking to the Walkers about singing because they haven't got any sense of sound and they'll never sing in tune. They're an absolutely hopeless lot.' We were brought up to think that and we lost all our confidence, but that hasn't been inherited by Ian and his family."

Education and professional training had always held an important position in the Walker household and it was no surprise when Peggy decided to follow in the footsteps of two of her uncles and receive medical training. An American aunt of hers was a qualified doctor – a rarity in the late Twenties and early Thirties – and she immediately encouraged Peggy to pursue her goal and offered to assist with her college fees. Shortly after completing her education, Peggy moved to London and, finding she did not enjoy her initial studies very much, began training as a health visitor. In the meantime, Molly had been to Montpellier in France to work as an au pair and when she returned to England, her father suggested that she, too, should continue her studies. She enrolled at University College London, which Elizabeth was attending, to read French, and at Peggy's invitation, moved into the flat she was renting near Camden Town. The three sisters remained extremely close during their college years and Peggy and Molly later shared rooms together in Swiss Cottage, near St John's Wood. At around this time Peggy, now in her early twenties, went back to Kilcadden for a holiday during which an event occurred which would be talked about for years afterwards.

Molly remembers: "Peg heard that her uncle Arthur, who was then running the farm and the house, was going to a house which they had lived in up a mountain somewhere, and she said she would awfully like to go with him to see it. So they went off together and the story goes that whatever she did up there, she managed to get this curse taken off the Walker women. Anyhow, the fact is that some months after that she married and several of our girl cousins also married."

Whatever the truth behind the intriguing 'legend of Kilcadden', there is no doubt that shortly after Peggy returned from her vacation in Donegal, she got married. Her husband, William Dury, was a bus driver and one-time boxer whose background had little in common with Peggy's prosperous middle-class upbringing in rural Cornwall. Raised in London, he was just 13 when he left school and was employed by London Transport when they met. Information about his family background is thin on the ground, although it seems his own father had died after a long illness before William's marriage to Peggy. It is thought Ian's parents first met in a social club and soon after they married they moved, with Molly, to 43 Weald Rise, Harrow Weald, a non-industrial area of north west London with a suburban character. Peggy was then working as a health visitor, while Molly was employed at the College of Nursing, where she and a former matron were charged with collecting the names of those who had left nursing and whose skills were urgently needed following the outbreak of war. When Molly's colleague retired, the work was taken over by London Borough Council and she was moved to the County Hall building. Molly remembers Peggy and Bill as a happy couple at this time.

"He was a very nice chap, I liked him," she says. "They used to go off on holidays. Once they went off to South Wales and picked up a rather lovely old sheep dog. He'd been born on the farm and he was so lovely as a puppy, they'd all spoilt him and they said, 'Well he's no good really for keeping sheep and if you'd like to have him then you can have him', and so they bought him."

At the beginning of the Second World War, as thousands of children were being evacuated from London and other major cities, Peggy decided to take in a boy and girl from central London whom she had heard about through her work. Whereas many children were despatched to the homes of strangers in far-flung places under extensive Government programmes, this was a private arrangement organised by Ian's mother. Many such arrangements were made by middle-class families during the war and this eventually caused a problem for the Government as homes were often already full when children arrived on official schemes. In total, three million people were evacuated from towns and cities in the UK, and children from the London area are remembered for singing 'The Lambeth Walk' as they were herded off to the country. Peggy would look after her two evacuees until the bombs finally fell silent. But by then, the Durys would have a child of their own.

Although Molly had moved out of the house in Weald Rise some time before and gone to live with a friend in Oxford, she believes she was staying with her sister when Ian was born. "I was up in London off and on because the chap who was my boss had been made head of Nuffield College in Oxford," she says. "He went back to that and then Winston Churchill or somebody decided he'd be a good person to send out to America and so he was sent off there and while he was getting ready to go, I was in London for a few months. I have certainly got this memory in my mind of Peg going into labour and the midwife who was with her came out and called over the stairs to my mother, 'Oh Mrs Walker, come up, you've a lovely grandson'." In an interview for *Mojo* magazine in 1998, Ian joked that he was "conceived at the back of the Ritz and born at the height of the Blitz!"

When Ian's birth was registered two days later, his father was described on the certificate as an "omnibus driver", but he was ambitious and soon expanded his horizons. He embarked on a training programme with Rolls-Royce which would open up a more fulfilling and lucrative career as a chauffeur for affluent businessmen. After obtaining his certificate, William Dury, or Bill to his friends, began to spend more and more time away from his wife and infant son and the marriage suffered. As the bombs continued to rain down on London, Peggy moved away from Harrow and, with her son and the two evacuees, went back to her mother's house in Mevagissey.

"I remember that Peg was teaching the other children who were school age, but Ian wasn't, he was about three," says Molly. "She thought that she couldn't just leave Ian wandering about the house, so she brought him in one day and gave him a book to look at. He took this book and he looked at a word and he said, 'I think I know what that is'. It was a book of nursery rhymes or something like that, and then Ian looked at the next one and read a whole line. It was the kind of nursery rhyme with a good deal of repetition in it. So he said, 'Mum, I can read, I can read' and it almost happened like that. It didn't take long for him to be reading."

At the end of the war, Ian and his mum moved again, this time to Switzerland where his dad was chauffeuring. Later, Billy Dury would work for the Western European Union, but at this time he was driving for a rubber millionnaire. Ian, although only a small boy at the time, retained some memories of this period and the family clearly lived in style. "My mum said dad got the sack for cavorting with the geezer's missus – my dad was a bit of a chap. We lived in a little village called Les Avons, near Montreux," he told *Mojo* in 1998. "Noel Coward went to live in the same place in 1958 and I think it was the same house, called the Villa Christian. I was there 10 years before Noel Coward! He probably found some of my notes and knocked out a couple of musicals on the strength of it, the old bastard!"

In 1946, Ian and his mum returned to an England still bearing the scars of the war and settled into the rural village of Cranham, which bordered the "garden suburb" of Upminster. They moved into a cottage owned by his Aunt Betty, who was working as a doctor with a health authority, and the three of them lived together. By this time, his parents' marriage was effectively over – although they were still in contact – and the bulk of the time Ian spent with his dad in Essex was during arranged visits. "It wasn't a sudden break-up," says Molly. "Obviously he had to get a job and because he'd got this special training from Rolls-Royce, he tended to go for people who had that sort of car, and so they were, inevitably, separated."

The couple were from opposite ends of the social spectrum and this had caused friction between them from the start. Intellectually they were incompatible and whenever arguments erupted during the early days of their marriage, Peggy won hands down, leaving her husband frustrated and belittled. Asked in the BBC2 documentary *On My Life*,[1] televised on September 25, 1999, whether his mother's family felt that she had married beneath herself, Ian confirmed that such sentiments had been voiced at Kilcadden. But he was quick to defend his father.

"My old man's dad was a bus driver, I think his granddad was a bus driver, at a time when a bus driver was seen for a working boy as a very good gig, which it probably was. I know my dad was very proud of his skills as a bus driver and, after that, as a chauffeur. He didn't think it was a demeaning occupation, although he never let anyone call him Billy, it always had to be Dury."

On the failure of his parents' marriage, Ian said: "He was, I think, quite angry about not being educated when he should have been educated; he was very bright, very aware, very alert. I think there was a point when my mum, because she was at university and she had this middle-class upbringing, she could dig him out with the verbals to the extent that he would lose the plot and he would get very angry. I think that created quite a bit of the old tension that existed between them. My dad and my mum split up . . . it didn't spring off as a natural relationship."

Cranham was a quiet backwater in the Forties. Cornfields dominated the surrounding area, although the cottage in which Ian lived, number 90 Front Lane, overlooked the inauspiciously named Bedlam Cottages, which are still standing today. Next door was The Plough, a Charrington's pub run by the Andersons, which had been in their family for 200 years. The pub, then located in Plough Rise, was later demolished and rebuilt further down the road, where it remains a landmark. Nowadays, neat little signs bearing such addresses as 'Pond Walk' and 'Green Banks' serve to remind passers-by of Cranham's agrarian past. Shops and other businesses dominate the busy street, which begins at the junction of St Mary's Lane and eventually joins the A12. The cottage at number 90 Front Lane has been demolished and replaced with two modern red brick semi-detached houses with tarmac driveways. Ian Dury would not be the only number one songwriter to emerge from Front Lane. Another one-time resident was Micky Denne, who with Kenny Gold composed the evergreen 'You To Me Are Everything', a chart-topper for The Real Thing.

Cranham may not have been so attractive and peaceful had plans for a sprawling development gone ahead. In the mid-Thirties, Cranham Hall Farm was earmarked for a large housing scheme covering 400 acres which would have blurred the Upminster-Cranham boundary. But the outbreak of war and a reform of British planning laws in 1947 combined to stymie the erosion of this slice of lush countryside and the border with Cranham running south of St Mary's Lane – where Upminster Infants and Junior Schools were situated – survived to mark the end of urban London and the beginning of rural Essex.

The Upminster that Ian Dury would have seen for the first time was heavily scarred by the war. Large areas of East London and Essex were flattened during ferocious Nazi bombing expeditions and the devastation in the Upminster area is recorded in a number of local books.

'The Blitz' that began on July 10, 1940, represented the first stage of Hitler's planned invasion of Britain, and Essex was at the eye of the storm. RAF camps were singled out for attack and bases at North Weald and Debden were bombed on August 16. Eight days later, Hornchurch Air Field was hit and more than 80 bombs fell on South Hornchurch and Rainham, both close to Upminster. To begin with, Upminster escaped attack, but it was only a matter of time before the town suffered a similar fate to those befalling other suburban districts. At 8pm on Sunday October 20, 1940, a stick of bombs fell on Upminster, claiming its first victims and devastating a number of streets, including Waldegrave Gardens, a wide and pleasant road lined with detached and semi-detached houses where Ian and his mother would later live.

One bomb landed in the entrance to the Infants School, wrecking cloakrooms, but leaving the rest of the building without heavy damage. Upminster got away lightly in the months that followed during which the Germans dropped incendiaries instead of high explosive bombs and zoned in on areas outside the capital. In March 1941 there was a renewal of the Blitz, but following an intensive raid on May 10, the Essex town enjoyed a period of respite which was to last almost three years. During this lull, the RAF requisitioned a piece of land for its 6221 Bomb Disposal flight and it became known colloquially as 'Upminster Bomb Cemetery'. A Nissen hut was built on the site for the convenience of the airmen occupied on these dangerous duties and the facility was also used by the Army Bomb Disposal Units.

The peace was finally shattered in January 1944 when bombs rained down once more on Upminster. In this renewed offensive, the effects were to be particularly bloody. In June, the Germans launched their first V1 flying bombs and, in all, four landed in the town. Within weeks, however, a more deadly weapon was unleashed on its terrified residents – the V2 rocket. The missile had been launched on its deadly course from The Hague/Duindigt area of The Netherlands and took four minutes to reach Upminster. But because it was impossible to predict where it would land, most people were sleeping in their beds and not in garden shelters when it exploded in the front garden of number 63 Waldegrave Gardens after midnight on March 12, 1945. The occupant was absent that night, but the rocket killed five people in neighbouring houses, and injured others. Families living opposite in the quiet street had narrow escapes: a telegraph pole flew down the road and lodged itself in a bedroom wall at number 54, while the occupants of number 50 were sucked out of the bedroom and onto the front lawn, still in bed. Eleven properties were demolished or seriously damaged in the blast. Five days later, another V2 was directed at Upminster, but came to ground in a field near a farm. It proved to be the last device to fall on the town. The nightmare of the Blitz was finally over.

The absence of a census during the war years means there are no firm figures for the population of Upminster, but by 1951 it had reached 13,000, double the level in 1931. During the Thirties, the 'Garden Suburb' had been promoted by selling agents as "an Essex beauty spot" and was clearly targeted at the middle classes. Its expansion was largely fuelled by the arrival of families from other parts of "Essex in London" such as Ilford, Barking, East Ham, Upton Park and Forest Gate, who wanted to exchange their built-up surroundings for a more peaceful environment. The extension of the London Underground's District Line from Barking to Upminster in 1932 made it doubly attractive to house-buying commuters.

Ian was five years old when he started at Upminster Infants School in St Mary's Lane in September 1947. Local parents and children knew the school simply as 'The Bell' as it stood opposite The Bell Inn, a popular watering hole that dominated the busy crossroads in the main street. Starting on the same day at Upminster Infants was his neighbour from Cranham and his closest pal, Barry Anderson, whose family ran The Plough pub. Just six weeks younger than Ian, Barry lived above the pub with his parents, his older brother John and sisters Jean and Janet. Ian also became friendly with John, who was of a more artistic bent than Barry and who went on to become a fashion designer to The Queen. But it was Barry from whom Ian was inseparable, racing dirty-kneed through the fields and farms of Cranham, scrumping apples and causing such mischief as little boys are duty bound so to do.

Barry, who now lives in Switzerland, recalls these early missions with his best friend. "When we were four years old, he had all the books," he says. "He could read so much better than me so he would read me stories. Even at that age, I wasn't up to his standard. I used to let him out of his window in the evening so we could go scrumping for apples. My parents were running the pub, so I could get out whenever I wanted. There was a front door with two big bay windows each side and Ian's room was the left-hand window which had a sloping garden up to it. I used to put some kind of truck wheel against it, he'd open the window and he'd come out in his pyjamas. Ian was the one who said, 'Get me out. Come and collect me at seven o'clock, I'll come out the window,' and we did whatever we did. He was old even when he was young."

Ian's precociousness, however, came at a cost. Initially he had refused to go to school and, concerned about his erratic behaviour, his mother had taken him to see three psychiatrists by the time he was five. "My mum was a totally brilliant mother," said Ian on Radio 4's *Desert Island Discs* in 1996.[2] "She steamed into me from a very early age and taught me to read before I went to school, so I think by the time I went to school, I didn't want to go there, I didn't see the point."

Ian was bright for his age and did well at school, although his early school days were disrupted by prolonged bouts of illness, according to Molly. Chicken pox, measles and other such viruses were, of course, common among children, but Ian was beset by such ailments and missed the best part of an entire term as a result.

Ian's young life was far from typical of the era and was in many respects more liberal and cultivated than most. Although his father paid regular visits, his home life was shaped by the well-educated Walker sisters. Much of his spare time as he grew up was filled with trips to theatres in London's West End and other cultural excursions. "His mother used to take us to places like The Old Vic," says Barry. "We saw Richard Burton playing Richard III and we had seats in the front row. I was excited by what was happening on stage, although everything else was above me, but it wasn't above Ian. We went to see *West Side Story* when it first opened and his mum also used to take us to pantomimes."

For most children living in Greater London after the Second World War, a day trip to Brighton or Southend would have been the highlight of the year. Ian, meanwhile, was setting out in first-class train carriages, bound for what must have seemed to him like a palace in the hills of Donegal. He was first taken to Kilcadden at about three years old and again when he was six. Memories of these and later holidays inspired him to write 'O Donegal', a song which he recorded in 1992. "We'll meet at the cross on the Rathmullen Road/Where the sight of Lough Swilley is a beauty bestowed/As we're counting our blessings away from the throng/We will hear the wild birds sing their Donegal song," he wrote.

Other childhood holidays were spent at his widowed grandmother's home in Mevagissey and later at the smaller house she bought at Veryan Green in the village of Veryan, also on the Cornish coast. Barry observes: "I think Ian's grandfather was Lord Lieutenant of Cornwall at one time. It always made me laugh when he pretended to be a total Cockney, which his father was, because he was from a middle to upper-class background."

His mother's family background was not a subject upon which Ian would dwell when he became famous. Few journalists would spend time in his company without hearing about his "old man", the bus driver who had gone on to drive the rich and famous, or how Ian had ducked and dived with the local mob in his teen years. They never heard stories of the country house and estate in Donegal where he was taken for school holidays or of his well-to-do relations both there and in Cornwall. To his adoring fans, oblivious of his well-heeled past, Ian Dury was an ordinary geezer from the streets.

At the time of Ian's first visit to Ireland in 1948, his great uncle Arthur and great aunt Janet were running the family business, aided by tenant farmers. For a six-year-old child from a suburb in Essex, this grand house and breathtaking countryside provided a real adventure.

But his unorthodox upbringing was not lost on Ian, as he made clear in the BBC2 documentary for which he made a nostalgic return to Kilcadden House in 1999. "My mum and my auntie lived in the same house. You could describe them as being early feminists; three sisters all went to university in the late Twenties and early Thirties and all got grants, all very bright. I was very lucky to grow up in that environment of such open-minded, wide ranging and intelligent people, 'cause it rubs off on you, even if you are being Harry the rebel," he said.[1]

Ian's father paid regular visits to Cranham and it wasn't just his son who ran out to see him. No longer a bus driver, Mr Dury was a smartly dressed chauffeur with a peaked cap and he would glide up to number 90 Front Lane in style – in a glistening Rolls-Royce. In the late Forties, he was like royalty.

"You can imagine a Rolls-Royce turning up at an old pub, which the Plough was, and he used to take us out for a ride," says Barry. "He just drove us to Southend and back, but in a Rolls-Royce, and nobody had a car then. For us this was just growing up."

He adds: "Ian was always making up dirty rhymes when he was young and he used to read everything he could find. His father used to bring us *Esquire* and we used to gaze at the pictures of women and God knows what."

Years later, Ian would write 'My Old Man', a touching and disarmingly matter-of-fact tribute to his dad, which featured on his first solo album *New Boots And Panties*. "My old man wore three-piece whistles/He was never home for long/Drove a bus for London Transport/He knew where he belonged/Number 18 down to Euston/Double-decker move along, double-decker move along/My old man," he sang. Recalling his dad's later driving assignments for rich businessmen, Ian wrote poetically: "Later on he drove a Roller/Chauffeuring for foreign men/Dropped his 'aitches' on occasion/Said 'Cor blimey' now and then/Did the crossword in the Standard/At the airport in the rain/At the airport in the rain/My old man."

Records at Upminster Junior School state that Ian began there on September 7, 1949, and that his last day was on September 10, 1950. But Ian never actually attended the school, for on a sweltering August day in 1949, his life suddenly and irrevocably changed. That day, Barry's mother took the two pals on the train to the seaside at Southend, a popular destination for Essex children. While they were there, the boys went for a swim. There were plenty of children in the open-air pool that day and the two friends splashed about together in the water, enjoying the warm weather. Without thinking about it Ian doubtless swallowed water from the pool. So, probably, did Barry.

"In a rural time, the highlight of our lives was to go to Southend," says Barry. "We didn't actually go on the beach, we went in the pool. There used to be an open-air pool, I think it might still be there, on the front of Southend towards Westcliff, and we went in there."

About six weeks later, little knowing the serious repercussions that day trip would have, Ian and his Aunt Moll headed off on the train to Cornwall, for a fortnight's holiday at his grandmother's house in Mevagissey. Molly had been planning to visit her mother and Peggy had asked if she would mind taking her seven-year-old son, as she was working and she was worried he'd be bored spending the rest of his school break in Cranham. Hand in hand with his aunt, Ian set off for his Cornish holiday and when they arrived, his grandmother suggested that Molly and Ian sleep in a small building in the garden which had been built to house guests when the house was full. In the evenings, Ian's aunt would read him a chapter from a story book and after a few days, he astonished her by finishing one of the books by himself. But his happy holiday was about to turn into a nightmare which would haunt him for the rest of his life.

Molly describes what followed: "We were there a little while and one day he didn't look at all well. He said, 'I've got a rotten headache' and he didn't really want to get up. So I said, 'Well don't get up yet,' and I went in to speak to my mother about it and I said, 'I really think I ought to have the doctor because it looks to me as if he's got a temperature.' So she said, 'Well, bring him in.' She had got a bed in a room which we really used as a dining room, but there were a lot of people in the house at that time and she had put a bed down in that room, so we brought him in and put him in that bed. The doctor came and he said to Ian, 'What's the matter?' You know what kids are like, Ian said, 'It just hurts,' and the doctor said, 'Well, where does it hurt?' and Ian said, 'I don't know.'

"The doctor said to me, 'Well he certainly doesn't seem well, although I can't quite make it out. If he doesn't seem any better by the end of the day ask me to come back and I'll have another look.'

"So he wasn't any better and I asked the doctor to come back, and when I went in to see how they were getting on I saw the doctor testing the reflex in his knees and I thought, 'Oh my God, he must think he's got polio.' Polio was much on our minds and we had always had a lot of polio in that area, although Ian didn't catch it there. The doctor came out and he said, 'I'm afraid it looks to me as if it is polio and he'll have to go straight off to hospital. Where's his mother?' I said, 'She's in Essex,' and he said, 'Well, can she possibly get down here? If she possibly can, she ought to come.' I immediately phoned for an ambulance to take him up to Truro which was the nearest big hospital and I said, 'Do you think I can go with him?' and he said, 'I think you could, yes.' So I rang Elizabeth and told her this and said, 'If she [Peggy] can possibly get the night train down, she should come to Truro.' It was very tricky because there were two trains that went, one from Paddington and one from Waterloo, but anyhow she got there and she came down.

"They were very good to me, they said, 'Come on, come and sit with him,' so I sat there and he was sort of drowsy and wasn't saying much at all. We got to the place and they said, 'Well you just go and wait in there,' and I waited and I waited and nobody appeared and I said, 'What's happened to that boy.' I began to think he'd died and been taken off to the morgue. It really was an awful moment. But then they said, 'You can come up and see him' and by that time he had been taken upstairs and put to bed. They came in and gave him some jab or other, although I don't think it did him any good.

"In the morning Peg turned up just as he was being moved to the isolation hospital. It was all very fraught, it was terrible, but he was so calm. He never went into a tantrum or anything, he was absolutely wonderful in that way, I must say. I remember that there was a woman in the next room and she kept crying out, 'Oh, I'm so ill and no one will come to me,' which didn't make it any more cheerful. I went along to see if I could find some of the nurses to say, 'For God's sake, do come and do something for this wretched woman,' and they said, 'Oh, she keeps on like that all the time.' Peg saw Ian and she went to the other hospital with him and she said to the Sister, 'Look, I've got nurse's training, I'll come and work with you, if you'll allow me on the ward,' but she said, 'I'm sorry, we can't do it.' So she just had to leave him there which was terrible really."

In the book *A Summer Plague: Polio And Its Survivors*,[3] Ian said: "My mum got the milk train down to Truro because they told her I wasn't going to make it. It was in Nissen huts, barrack huts, an RAF-type hospital, and they let her come to the outside window, and they turned the light on over my bed – you know, she saw my little white face on the pillow: a four o' clock in the morning job. But I was still there the next morning."

Both of Ian's arms were rendered immobile, as well as his legs, but he maintained movement in his right hand. By 1949, medical staff were only too aware that polio could twist and warp a victim's body like a corkscrew and doctors at the Royal Cornwall Infirmary in Truro put Ian in a plaster cast which covered his legs, arms and torso. He spent a torturous six weeks imprisoned in this shell and his ability to grip a dinky toy in his only free hand was the only pleasure he was afforded.

"And you were fucked if the nurse didn't like you . . . Oh yes, prisoners to hot milk in the morning, this bloody little jug thing coming towards you; it looks like a teapot but it's for pouring into people's mouths – 'Wah, wah, don't want this'," said Ian.[3]

Back in Cranham, Barry was anxious about his friend. He had been kept in bed at the pub for three days with flu symptoms after news of Ian's illness reached his parents, but the fickle hand of polio had not touched him on that innocent afternoon swim. The seven-year-old boy had sensed his own parents' worry, "... but they didn't tell me at the time, and I wondered what had happened to Ian," he says. It would be more than a year before he would see his friend again. It was ironic that Ian developed polio in Cornwall which had been a black-spot for the disease. The reaction of local people to the drama in Mevagissey says a great deal about people's attitudes to polio and the paranoia it created at that time.

Molly: "People say the most extraordinary things. I remember people saying, 'Well, you can't really be so worried because wouldn't it be much better if he died because what sort of life will there be for him?' What happened in Mevagissey was their answer to all this trouble about a child getting polio. It was all over the village as you can imagine, and they immediately had the town hall re-cleaned. Actually, he hadn't even been in the town hall, but I dare say it didn't do the hall any harm."

After six weeks encased in plaster, Ian was transferred, on a stretcher, to Black Notley Hospital, just outside Braintree, in Essex. There he was put on a large ward where all the children were at one end and the naughty ones were wheeled up to the other end where a man in an iron lung watched them in the mirror above his head. Few people could ever imagine the trauma felt by Ian, a seven-year-old boy paralysed overnight, wrenched away from the mother to whom he was so close and thrust into a hospital surrounded by other sick children, many of whom were in excruciating pain. He would be there for a year and a half.

"Every Tuesday and Thursday they put you in this manipulatory situation," said Ian.[3] "Obviously, they thought they were doing you good, stop you ossifying or whatever the word is. But I mean, this geezer used to get hold of my left ankle and my left thigh and kkkkkrrr, pull my heel up to my arse – keep it loose, fucking hell. It was called the screaming ward and you could hear people screaming on the way there, and it was you when you was there, and you could hear the others on the way back – I imagine. I can't really remember, I've blocked it out."

Of his feelings towards other children on the ward, Ian said:[1] "When you're a kid, you're very open to whatever's going on, you're with a peer group, you're with other people who are just the same as you or in different states or even worse or whatever. You don't consider 'em anything different from what's normal, whoever they might be, whatever condition they're in. You ain't judging whether they're a nice person or not and there's some real shockers and there's some really smashing ones and sometimes the really smashing ones can't even communicate at all. I was in bed next to a geezer who had a device where he could turn the page of the book and he was in very bad pain and everybody liked him. He hardly communicated with anyone, but everyone liked him, everyone thought he was a top geezer. At night, the pain used to make him cry and scream and you would get used to that and because you liked him you didn't resent it. Now, there was other people in there you didn't like, who were horrible people, who might be crying and screaming and you fucking hated them, I mean really loathed them for that, for doing that."

It was during the summer of 1947 – two years before Ian had stepped fatefully into the pool in Southend – that polio had last struck in Britain, casting a ghastly shadow over the country. At lakes, pools and at the seaside, the virus indiscriminately entered the healthy bodies of children and young adults, paralysing some and taking the lives of others. The epidemic was sudden, its effects devastating, and those struck down by it during the years immediately following the Second World War would later feel the aching injustice that the scientific victory over polio had come too late for them. Ian Dury was one such child.

The scourge of poliomyelitis had first been reported in the UK in the mid-nineteenth century and the father of Neville Barnes Wallis, the inventor of the bouncing bomb, was among those who contracted the disease. By the 1920s still little, if anything, was known about polio and other cases certainly went unreported. Ignorance about polio among doctors and scientists also led to some incidences of polio being mistaken for other illnesses, although an epidemic is thought to have taken place during the years following the First World War. But it was in the United States that the disease showed its deadly power in 1916, with New York suffering a massive epidemic.

Polio is no respecter of class and among those left crippled in 1916 and in the following years was future US President Franklin Delano Roosevelt. He was on a vacation from Washington with his wife Eleanor and his five children on the island of Campobello, off the coast of Maine and New Brunswick, in a beautifully warm August 1921, when he caught the disease. Then aged 39, he was on his way from Washington to his holiday retreat, when he stopped off at a boy scout rally at Bear Mountain in his capacity as president of the Boy Scout Federation of Greater New York. He was exhausted when he arrived, but he immediately flung himself into swimming, sailing and other outdoor pursuits. While out sailing on the afternoon of August 10, the family spotted a forest fire on a nearby island

and they beat it down using brushwood before plunging into the water and racing each other to their holiday home. That evening, as Franklin Roosevelt sat down to open the post, he began feeling the first effects of the disease which, like so many others, had infected his body during his playful swim. He suffered a terrible chill which lasted almost the whole night and by daylight the muscles of his right knee were losing their strength. That evening the left knee also weakened and by the following morning he couldn't stand and was suffering from a high temperature. On the third day virtually all the muscles from the chest down were affected and he was also finding it difficult to use a pen. Soon, his wife Eleanor was nursing him constantly, giving him enemas to empty his bowels and using catheters to draw off his urine, and eventually he was removed to a New York hospital. The Roosevelts' marriage was later said to have been strengthened by the torment of the initial onset of his polio.

Roosevelt was left partially paralysed by the disease, but he stoically continued in public life and in 1924 he amazed onlookers as he strode forward with leg braces and crutches to make his 'Happy Warrior' speech nominating Al Smith for the presidency. It was the first time he had been seen in public since becoming ill and it was at this rally that he was first told about Warm Springs, in Georgia, by George Foster Peabody, a Wall Street financier. A young man named Louis Joseph was rumoured to have made a biblical-style recovery from the paralysis which had crippled him since he was a child and Roosevelt, who believed his political fight-back depended on his being able to walk without aids, was prepared to try anything. Roosevelt's spirits lifted visibly after bathing in the pool and he was instrumental in setting up a 'Hydrotherapeutic Center' there. Spurred on by his enthusiasm and his unerring belief in the healing qualities of Warm Springs, it quickly became a place of pilgrimage for thousands of polio sufferers.

In 1928, Roosevelt's dramatic assent to power was signalled when he was elected governor of New York and he was re-elected two years later. In 1932 he received the Democratic presidential nomination and the following year he became the 33rd president of the US, remaining in the White House throughout the Second World War, until his death in 1945 aged 63.

In Britain, incidences of polio crept upwards slowly following the First World War and rarely exceeded 1,000 in any one year, except in 1938 when just under 1,500 cases were noted. But the summer of 1947 was to change all that; suddenly polio tightened its invisible grip. By the end of that year, the tally was 7,776 and the attack rate in England and Wales was 18 per 100,000 – on a par with the 1916 epidemic in the US. In response to the ensuing panic, the *British Medical Journal* told readers on August 16, 1947: "Throughout history certain diseases have caused widespread panic . . . Today poliomyelitis is arousing widespread anxiety among the public, out of proportion to the low morbidity and mortality rates among those infected."

The rapid and unexpected arrival of polio surprised a medical profession which was largely inexperienced at treating those affected by it. As the Senior Medical Officer at the Ministry of Health, Dr W.H. Bradley, told delegates at the National Foundation's First International Conference in New York in 1948: "During the 1947 epidemic in Great Britain when we had nearly five times as many cases as ever before in our history; when the disease killed four times as many people as diphtheria; and when we suddenly realised that poliomyelitis was our most important problem at the time, we had to do a great deal of letter writing and telephoning to experts all over the world to get advice."

By now, polio had truly taken hold and between 1947 and 1958 it affected 58,000 people, 35,000 of whom – like Ian – suffered some degree of paralysis. On average, the death toll was 360 per year and the majority of victims were young adults. Vaccination with the 'killed' Salk vaccine began in the UK on a very small scale in 1956 and because of the numbers still contracting the disease, an intensive programme was launched two years later. The vaccine had been developed by US microbiologist Jonas Edward Salk at the University of Pittsburgh, where he and a team cultured viruses from all three strains possible for polio. From these, Salk produced a formaldehyde-killed mixture of the three strains in a mineral-oil emulsion and announced his vaccine in 1953. After animal tests and preliminary clinical trials had been successfully completed, the first large-scale Salk vaccination programme was carried out in 1954. The following year, some children were injected with faulty vaccine and contracted polio, but mass vaccination went ahead despite this setback.

In Britain public acceptance of the vaccination was slow and it took the death of England footballer Jeff Hall in the spring of 1959 to motivate people to attend the clinics. Polio cases then fell rapidly, until another outbreak occurred in Kingston-upon-Hull, and this time the Sabin polio vaccine, taken orally in the form of a sugar lump, was employed to halt the disease. Albert Bruce Sabin was a Polish-born microbiologist who had developed his vaccine using live viruses which had been rendered harmless by laboratory treatment, in contrast to Salk's killed vaccine. Initial vaccinations were conducted in the Soviet Union where it proved safe and was easily administered. By the Sixties it had replaced the Salk vaccine around the world.

In a propaganda film broadcast in the United States after the Second World War by the National Foundation for Infantile Paralysis, or 'March of Dimes' as it was known, polio was portrayed as 'The Crippler' – an ominous shadowy figure leaning on a crutch and stalking its victims. 'And I'm especially fond of children' warned the voice-over as a little boy wilted in his father's arms and a small girl raised a hand to her fevered brow.

Like many such children, Ian Dury was left paralysed by polio and his figure would forever be twisted. But, in one regard, he could be considered more fortunate than some. Prior to the Education Act of 1944, handicapped children were particularly isolated; most were housebound and only a very few of those with comparatively slight disabilities received a normal education. But under this legislation, every child had to continue their schooling until the minimum school-leaving age of 14, and arrangements for handicapped children were introduced at schools and other learning centres. Also, while contracting polio must have been deeply traumatic for a child, those who were affected later in life often encountered more problems in coming to terms with their disabilities.

In *The Polio Story* by P.J. Fisher, the author observed: "The extent to which the life of a person is disrupted by the paralytic type of poliomyelitis depends primarily upon individual reaction. This, in turn, can be conditioned by the age at which the illness is contracted, the severity and site of the paralysis, and by the family background and income. The older the victim, the more difficult is the psychological adjustment, and because paralysis in any form increases the reliance of the patient upon others, the psychological problems increase in ratio to the maturity and the degree of independence in the nature of the victim when he became disabled."

The physical and psychological battle that lay ahead for Ian would mould his personality for life.

2

BLACKBOARD JUNGLE

"Ian had a very liberal life – he had the rule of the roost really. I think he had the breeding of a little aristocrat, with all the benefits . . . He made up for his disabilities by being the one who got the records, the first one to know what rock'n'roll was."
– Barry Anderson

Chailey Heritage was a school and hospital for children with a broad range of disabilities, brimming with positive thinking and good intentions. But a centre for young offenders could barely have toughened up Ian Dury as much as the three and a half years he spent within its bleak Victorian confines. Disfigured and severely disabled children were left to pick themselves up off the floor when they tumbled over and death cast a terrible and constant pall over its young community. It was here that Ian quickly discovered "the law of the jungle reigned". 'Men Made Here' reads a sign over the door at Chailey today, and the hard lessons Ian learned at the hands of its staff and residents would play no small part in the protective, sharply observant and singularly determined person he would later become.

"Even though I was very young, I didn't get no aggro from anybody older than me because I was quite able to divert that. I was good at the verbals, you know, and sussing things out. Also, I always happened to be with somebody who could hardle themselves, a mate," said Ian.[3]

Ian was almost nine years old when he arrived at Chailey Heritage Craft School in East Sussex in 1951. The school was made up of three units: a boys' hospital, a residential centre for disabled boys called St George's, and a separate unit for the girls. It struck a peculiar balance between a hospital and a public boarding school, and was once described by an editor of *The Times* as "the public school of crippledom". Set in a lush part of the county between Haywards Heath and Lewes, Chailey Heritage had been established in 1903 when charity worker Mrs [later Dame] Grace Kimmins and her friend Alice Rennie brought seven crippled boys down from London to teach them boot-making, printing and other trades from which they could earn a living and gain independence. The establishment was an off-shoot of the Guild of the Brave Poor Things, founded in 1894, and much of its philosophy derived from Mrs Kimmins' husband, Dr C.W. Kimmins, an educational psychologist with the London County Council.

Fading photographs of Chailey when it first opened conjure up images of Charles Dickens' novel *Oliver Twist*, and the building where the children were housed had actually been a Victorian workhouse. But Chailey had quickly expanded, a girls' school was opened, later named The New Heritage, and a new residential unit called St George's was opened by the Prince of Wales in 1932. Following the foundation of the Welfare State in 1948, control of the hospital passed into the hands of the National Health Service, but the school retained its independence and responsibility for teaching patients. For a brief time, there was a seaside branch of Chailey Heritage at Newhaven, East Sussex, known as Tidemills, but the Second World War prompted its closure.

Disabilities among those living at Chailey ranged from minor diseases to severe deformities. For a child like Ian, who had already attended an ordinary school as a healthy child, it must have been particularly distressing. He found himself alongside other polio sufferers and children with TB, and also boys and girls with startling deformities and diseases which, in some cases, would kill them before they reached adulthood. In the 1999 newsletter for Chailey's Old Scholars' Association, Mrs Quibell recalled working at the hospital in 1948 (then as Staff Nurse Roake) together with Sister Ruth Gorrie. Her memories give a glimpse into the bleak world which the already traumatised Ian Dury was sent. "Antibiotics were still in their early stages and many of the patients were destined for years of treatment with plaster casts and surgery," she wrote. "Many would have deformities such as crooked backs or short limbs or stiffened joints. They needed splints and spinal jackets when they became ambulant. Poliomyelitis was still with us, with crippling results. We also had short-term patients whose health was generally poor after whooping cough perhaps or due to Fibrocytis disease." She added: "The overall memory of Chailey in the early days is: rustic and rural; the dawn chorus; the nightingales; the fires on the common and the gentians [flowering plants]; the absolute blackness at night."

Polio had paralysed the left side of Ian's body and withered his left leg and arm. But his disabilities were put into perspective by the terrible physical deformities suffered by other children there. He told the *Independent* in August 1998:[4] "You know, there were kids there with fingers coming out their shoulders, still, they played ping-pong. They were fucking lunatics." Ian also drew reference to a disturbing side of the ostensibly caring establishment, adding: "A lot of the staff were pervs. No buggery, but a lot of enforced wanking."

One of the children Ian met at Chailey was Stuart Beeton (later Spencer, following his mother's re-marriage) and at one time they slept in beds next to each other in the hospital wing. At first, Ian spent much of the time lying or sitting in bed and his mobility was limited, although he had learned to walk again. Stuart clearly remembers: "Ian was a lad, he was lively. He was a young chubby lad sitting up in bed as brown as a berry and part and parcel of ward life." However, their own personal reflections on Chailey are markedly different. Stuart had known nothing else and the deformed and lame figures around him were his normality. Born in nearby East Grinstead, Stuart was admitted to Chailey with TB in 1941 when he was just 18 months old, and he remained there until his 16th birthday in 1954.

"One of the children was in an iron lung and later, others were thalidomide, so they were quite severely handicapped," recalls Stuart, who regularly attends reunions at Chailey and edits the Old Scholars' Association newsletter. "Amongst ourselves we didn't worry because we all grew up around disabilities, but there was reaction because I can recall an occasion when a party of us was taken from Chailey to a nearby village fete. A bus-load of us arrived and the ladies of the village were sitting down to watch a show and when they saw all these youngsters arriving with callipers and sticks, they suddenly all got up out of their seats and didn't want to be near us. It was contagious as far as they were concerned. Some people couldn't handle it and they still can't today."

He adds: "Ian's polio wasn't as bad as some of the children. He had one good leg, compared to others who had lost the use of lower limbs completely; some of them could just fold their legs up around the back of their neck and tie them in knots and roll like a ball because the muscles had just gone."

Nowadays, Chailey does not have a hospital and the NHS facilities used by the school pupils and many outpatients are provided by South Downs Health (NHS) Trust. Located on one site, it has a nursery, pre-school and primary department building, six custom-built residential bungalows and a swimming pool, which was opened in 1997 by TV presenter and former England striker Gary Lineker. But back in 1951, children were there to stay. Separated from their parents and siblings, they had to adjust to a life, the routine of which was not dissimilar to that of a prison, and glimpses into the outside world were few and far between. Their reality was not that of other children; Chailey was their life.

Stuart explains: "We used to have parents' days, usually on a Sunday, and by the time they got to Chailey at around 2pm from wherever they lived, they got two hours and then they were on their way back again. Ian's dad used to come and visit him and afterwards Ian used to tell me that his dad was a chauffeur and drove a Humber Supersniper or something. My father did similar work; he did bus driving in London and then he used to drive a Daimler.

"Ian's father came whenever he could. It was one long ward and we could see from the window all the people piling off the bus when it came. You used to say, 'Who have I got today?' and if there was no one for you, you burst into tears because you got no one. It was a bit cruel, but you knew nothing different. You lived in that sort of atmosphere and couldn't compare it with anything else. Everybody looked forward to it when they had relations coming because they brought things from outside."

Ian's friend Barry, whom he had last seen on that ill-fated trip to Southend and who had evaded the crippling disease, was also brought to see him in his strange new environment.

"I didn't see him until I was taken to Chailey by his mother," says Barry. "I went to Chailey three or four times. His mother used to have an old black Ford Popular which was one of the perks which the health authority gave her." Asked what Ian said to him on these visits, Barry replies: "He asked me to get him out. 'Let's go,' he said."

Before Ian arrived at Chailey, medical provision had been the direct responsibility of the senior staff. Stuart recalls this changeover and one particular conversation he had with one of his nurses when he was only six years old.

Stuart: "We found that as children we took sides, so that if somebody said, 'I support Arsenal' and somebody else supported Blackpool, you thought, 'Well, it seems 16 of them like Arsenal, so I'll be an Arsenal supporter as well. So, when they were talking about this National Health Service, I said something like, 'I reckon it's a good idea that we have a National Health Service,' and this sister snapped at me and said, 'What a load of rubbish, you haven't got a clue what you're talking about. It's the worse thing that could ever happen.' "

The regime at Chailey was strict and the children were kept busy. Although there were no examinations, pupils were graded at the end of each term and taken through each subject to see how much they had remembered. Chailey children were also taught printing, shoe-making, leather-work and carpentry and other practical trades. It was a regimented lifestyle.

"Things ran to a pattern," says Stuart. "The bell to get you up rang at 6.45am and you had your breakfast. On the school side, those who could walk walked to school and one or two who couldn't were taken by car. We went backwards and forwards across the common for dinner and at tea-time you would come home and 6.45pm was the bell time. During my days there was only the radio on and that went off at about eight o'clock. The only time I can ever recall it staying on longer was if there was a boxing match."

The common close to the school was a source of exercise and adventure for the youngsters and their handicaps did not preclude them from taking part in outdoor games. In fact, staff encouraged them to get as much fresh air as they could.

"We used to go across the common to meet the girls," remembers Stuart. "There was a dividing line and so we used to meet on the boundary. It was a lovely place; it was open heath land, with ferns and bracken and gorse, and still had remnants from the war. There were a lot of trenches and a lot of live ammunition lying around. We used to use the trenches as camps, put bracken roofs over them and build dens, and waylay the local baker and get loads of bread off him. We played football, cricket and tennis, and even the ones on sticks and crutches were still on the field, kicking the ball, chasing after it with their crutches and shoving you out of the way. You weren't bored, you made model aircraft with the old balsa wood kits. The majority of children went home at Christmas, although I didn't go home for several years. That was a turning point for me when I went home. I was about ten and I was sitting on the bus and I said, 'Oh look, fire engines' like a youngster. I simply hadn't seen these things before."

The ethos of Chailey Heritage School was to make the children as independent as possible and the majority of medical staff adopted a tough line regarding their treatment. More than 50 years on, some of the methods employed sound cruel for children with such severe disabilities. But in the eyes of the staff at Chailey, it was their very vulnerability and dependence on others which dictated their treatment. Children in the hospital were wheeled outside in their beds as a matter of course, whatever the weather conditions. On hot days, they were parked on the shady side of the building. Cot beds had high screens at the head and the young patients were smeared in calamine which they thought looked like war paint. In the winter, the nurses went round with cod liver oil cream, spreading it on hands, faces and ears to prevent chilblains. The diet was plain and healthy and often featured goats' milk.

Stuart clearly remembers Chailey's 'alfresco' policy: "You stayed there all weathers, whether it rained or snowed. If it was really bad, they pulled the covers down, but generally you were out there. I can remember waking up at about four o'clock in the morning in the summer, light had already come about, and they would whip all the bed clothes off and roll them down the bottom so you were there in the cold, just shivering. The warmth of the sun hadn't even got up then and it used to come up from behind a big chapel there, but until it reached above that, you were freezing. It hardened you up."

Many of the children, including some TB and polio sufferers, had to learn how to walk at Chailey and again the message was uncompromising – if you fell down, you had to get yourself back up without any help. This no-nonsense approach to medical treatment and the stern discipline meted out by members of staff left Ian with memories which would never leave him. The harsh environment also required Ian to fight his own corner and it instilled in him some tough attitudes of his own.

In 1973, Ian gave a candid interview to the adult magazine *Penthouse* under the headline 'You Don't Have To Have A Leg Iron, But It Helps'.[5] In the article by Steve Fuller, Ian displayed an anger towards Chailey, depicting it as a miserable, cold place. For the three and a half years he was incarcerated in Chailey, he was living in "Marat-Sade" and was "very unhappy", he said. The analogy he used was disturbing. Ian was referring to an early 19th century play in which a group of lunatics, under the direction of the Marquis de Sade, put on a play about the death of Marat, the French revolutionary leader who was stabbed to death in his bath.

"Being in that place is one of the reasons I talk the way I talk," said Ian.[5] "Before that I talked not quite BBC. A third of the kids there were funny in the head as well as being disabled. It was a very tough place, very cold and very brutal. I was there until I was twelve and a half. The situation was that from within you got very strong, but also you got coarsened. The law of the jungle reigned in that place. There was a lot of fighting. If you fought a kid who wore two leg braces – I only have one – then you sat next to him on a bench and started beatin' fuck out of each other like that. I could use one leg and one hand, so I usually won. I put the boot in. There was a lot of behaviour that just don't happen in the outside world. Later, you pretend to be arty about it but when I was there, I was just there, it was real. Thinkin' about it now, I realise it was fuckin' heavy. It was like a hospital in one way, like a school in another way, and like a prison in another way. It was very uncomfortable. Guys would die there."

On one occasion, Ian saw a disturbed child receive a beating for not getting into line properly. "He was in another world anyway, but he got well done, he got thrashed by this cane-bearing second-in-command."

Another boy who was treated at Chailey during Ian's time there was Peter Sedgwick, who had heavy metal braces strapped to both legs and attended the school from 1949 to 1958. In past interviews, Ian talked of tangling with him at Chailey, and although Peter does not remember these fracas, memories of the harsh regime have never left him. With hindsight, he now sees the benefits of the Chailey 'do-it-yourself' way.

"Chailey was primarily a place which concentrated on promoting, demonstrating and encouraging independence," says Peter. "In my days, it was a place where wheelchairs were banned. If there were any students who couldn't walk fast, the message was, 'Well start off earlier and you will get there at the same time as everyone else.' It was very practical, down-to-earth guidance. I remember my own first experience with this. Each dormitory had an adjacent bathroom with three baths and half a dozen wash bowls and I wanted a bath and asked the attendant to lift me into the bath and he said, 'No, I'll show you how to get in the bath,' which he did, and he stood by me while I got in the bath. That was from ground level and into a full-sized bath and it was that principal that they applied, which quite honestly gave total independence to people who were there during that era.

"It was an establishment which, I think, had a bad side effect in so far as when you were at a young age, you weren't able to turn to your parents or brothers or sisters to confide or to unload emotion, you bottled them up. Certainly my wife accuses me of not showing emotion in life generally and that is probably a drawback of Chailey. You were there for three terms a year, with a one-day parent visit at half term and that was it. You were at the establishment all the time. You could develop friendships to whom you could chat about anything and everything, but it wasn't the same as being able to unload emotions when you were down.

"There was a hierarchical structure at Chailey with dominants and submissives. It was hard work to the extent that you had friends and played with your friends as you went to school and you sought to beat the system. A lot of us smoked, but we weren't allowed to, so we were seeking to beat the system by ensuring that you could get hold of these cigarettes and smoke without being caught. When you became a prefect, which I later became for two years, there was less pressure under the hierarchical structure, because you were at the top and you had responsibilities as well for a dormitory and life was easier from that point on."

Many of the stories told of Chailey during the Forties and Fifties could as easily be reflections from pupils of any boarding school in England. Chailey had its serial escapees who were eventually picked up miles away at various locations around the country and Ian also went missing on occasions. The slightest opportunity for adventure or insurgency was seized upon and some of the boys replenished their supplies of cigarettes by befriending soldiers camped out on the common on their way to manoeuvres. One of the ward orderlies, a Mr Hargreaves (thought to be a Chailey old boy), instilled a chilling fear into the boys. Although time has dimmed the memory of other former pupils, Ian never forgot the abject humiliation he suffered at the hands of Hargreaves.

Ian said:[3] "He was a bastard. He had a large boot − a boot that big − clunking in, and he'd blow the whistle, ring the bell, whatever. One night I shit the bed. I woke up enough to shake the shit out of my pyjamas and fall asleep again. In the morning, you had the sliders went out first, who would slide on the lino on a blanket, who couldn't walk without appliances: the sliders went out − I was a slider then − and then the walkers . . . As the sliders were coming in from these low washbasins, the walkers would go out. And the walkers were going out when somebody spotted that I hadn't moved, right, and Hargreaves said: 'Why haven't you moved yet?' Ooo-ooh, he got everybody round the bed, all the sliders up on adjacent beds and all the walkers all round, everybody, the prefect, all gathered round the bed. He said, 'Roll over,' and I rolled off. And everybody saw the shit and they went, 'Waa-aah'."

The vision of the Army-style orderly bearing down on children in their beds also left an indelible impression on Stuart, although he did not witness Ian's degradation.

"He [Hargreaves] had a disability and wore a big boot and he used to walk around with this leather strap with buckles," he recalls. "It was one of the little leather straps they used to tie the callipers around the leg joint. He was always carrying it and he used to flick it at the kids − give them a clip around the ear. I didn't think much of this until I was showing a picture to Ian when we met up a couple of years ago and Ian said, 'Tell me, is Hargreaves still there, whatever happened to him?' I said 'Didn't you know? He committed suicide. He took himself up to one of the dormitories, into the attic, and hanged himself.' And Ian said: 'Made my bloody day, that has'."

But in Hargreaves' defence, Stuart says: "He was not sadistic, but he was authoritarian and that might have been part of building us up for life afterwards. Life outside of that place was going to be a struggle for most of them anyway."

Inevitably, some of the children sent to Chailey died there, but it seems that the hard approach taught at the school helped the survivors to accept such tragedies. At the age of 11, Ian had a tendon transplant in the operating theatre in the girls' wing and he was taken over there with a boy of 17 called Brian, whose leg was being amputated below the knee. There were only three beds in the ward and in the middle of the night, the screens went up around the empty bed and a girl of eight or nine called Wendy was brought in.

Ian said:[3] "She never stopped moaning and we had to read to her; and we were cursing her out really. When we got back to the main boys' hospital, this nurse was riding past on her bike and she said that poor little Wendy had died two days after we'd gone. The incredibly intense guilt we felt for not liking her when she was moaning – I remember that strongly. We both felt really bad."

Stuart also remembers tragedies occurring at Chailey: "I can recall about three children who died, but it didn't make a big impression. The first one was a young lad called Peter Coe during the early Forties. This lad was in constant pain. You just had to touch a limb or a sheet on the bed to create pain and in the end he just disappeared. He went silently and I suspect that was euthanasia. Later on, there was a lad called Bobby Sutch. I don't know what his disability was at the time, but he fell forward going up some steps and hit his knees on these concrete steps and that caused a dreadful disease of brain inflammation and he died. I think that another lad called Reggie Cooper had bad lungs and he died."

When Ian was asked about Chailey in the 1999 BBC2 documentary about Chailey, it seemed that his feelings had mellowed. Previously, he had painted a bleak picture of the place, but here he chose to dwell on its positive aspects.

"Chailey was basically a good place. It was a trade school really and they taught you cobbling, print-making or carpentry. That is one of the reasons you used to be able to go into cobblers' shops, I'm talking about 15 years ago, and every cobbler you ever saw was disabled, 'cause they were trained to be cobblers. Chailey made me strong physically and mentally."

He went on: "The spirit of that place was absolute. There was no despair, there weren't any suicides as far as I recall. It was a good place in many ways. It wasn't a good place in terms of education. My mother thought that 'rather than him being a cobbler, I'd like him to go to Grammar School and become a lawyer'."

Peggy was extremely anxious for Ian to attend a proper school as his illness had already kept him out of regular classes for five years. Even before contracting polio, Ian had fallen behind his peers because of illness, but although he passed his eleven-plus exam, his mother was finding it difficult to secure him a place at an appropriate school. It is understood that she had hoped to enrol Ian at Christ's Hospital because it had a school doctor and was attended by other children with polio. She was turned down, however, on the basis that her salary, combined with that of her husband, was too high. Feeling frustrated at the educational opportunities that her son was missing, she asked the staff at Chailey to give Ian some extra help, while she sought out a grammar school that would take him. Instead, they moved him into a class of less able children so that he could help them.

In the end, it was Aunt Moll who resolved the problem of Ian's schooling. She was employed by the education authority in Aylesbury, overseeing the education of 'special needs' children, and she recommended the Royal Grammar School in nearby High Wycombe. She had always taken an active interest in her nephew and believed that this school would provide a supportive environment and an excellent academic grounding for him. Essex County Council, meanwhile, awarded him a grant to attend the school in Buckinghamshire. But for all his aunt's good intentions, Ian's time there would be hell.

"I said I thought I might be able to get him into Wycombe Grammar because I knew they'd had another boy there for the last year who was an invalid. I thought perhaps that would be all right and I knew the head quite well, but it wasn't awfully good. It wasn't a very good choice," admits Molly.

The Royal Grammar School was a vestige from another era. Standing large on Amersham Hill, the stately looking neo-Georgian buildings which formed the grand facade of the school had been built in 1915 and could house as many as 300 boys. The school had been located in Easton Street in the town, but was transferred to the attractive 22-acre site on the hill after it became a properly funded establishment in 1902. It was this striking architectural sight – another Victorian institution for Ian to rebel against – which greeted him on his first day at the school where he would board for five years. The history of the RGS – where academic excellence, old-fashioned moral values and rugby were highly prized – dated back nearly 400 years, making it one of the oldest schools in Britain. It was founded by an obscure local charitable organisation during the reign of Elizabeth I, and officially registered by charter on July 21, 1562. But throughout most of its history, the RGS struggled to survive and it was not until the turn of the century that the school won the kind of reputation for which it had been striving for hundreds of years.

The man largely responsible for the turnaround was the then headmaster G.W. Arnison. He spearheaded the transfer of the school to Amersham Hill and, in 1909, began an Officer Training Corps, instituting Captain F.W.L.G. Norton-Fagge as the first commanding officer. Rugby was meanwhile established as the main winter sport for pupils. Among the teaching staff for one term during this watershed period was T.S. Eliot, who apparently hated it. He left for a bank job in London which gave him more free time to write and it is suggested that his poem 'The Wasteland' was about the school. According to an official history of the school, the minutes of the prefects' meetings in the last years of Arnison's time in charge "reflect a self-confident group of senior boys who revel in the responsibilities they have been given over the younger pupils. They have an engagingly serious attitude to running the school and a slightly old-fashioned, pompous way of recording their business."

Now, the RGS has more than 1,100 pupils and enjoys the academic reputation it strove for years to attain. Ian Dury is just one of a long list of its former pupils who rose to prominence in public life. The roll call includes: Professor Roger Scruton, writer and philosopher; Professor Michael Zander, professor of law at the London School of Economics; Lord McIntosh of Haringey, Labour peer; David Ashby, Conservative MP for Leicestershire North-West; Peter Fry, Conservative MP for Wellingborough; Howard Jones, pop singer; England rugby players Matt Dawson and Nick Beal; and Richard Hickox, composer and conductor.

In the summer of 1954, when the unsteady figure of Ian Dury first arrived in his grey flannel shorts and red blazer, an authoritarian was at the helm. Edmund Ronald Tucker, known around the school as 'Bertie', was a scholar of Jesus College, Oxford, where he had read Classics before taking charge at the RGS in March 1933. A patriotic Welshman, he was a Church of England lay-preacher, a local magistrate, an avid sports fan, and a disciplinarian who was determined to maintain the school's growing reputation for academic achievements. He was to make Ian's life there a misery. His wife, who was also Welsh, ran the school dining room and kitchen and she would also have reason to remember Ian's name during the formative years he spent there. For a rebellious youngster with a developing passion for rock'n'roll, such a staunchly traditional grammar school was the last place on earth he wanted to be. He was 12 and a half when he arrived, a year older than most new boys, but he went into the first year and not the second. This, combined with his disability, meant he stood out.

Commenting on his time there,[1] Ian said bitterly: "Couldn't say I was happy there. I was the most miserable I ever was in my five years there. I didn't fit in there and I wouldn't have fitted in there if I hadn't have had polio, I'd like to think. God forbid, I might have been a bank manager."

In the 1973 *Penthouse* magazine interview,[5] it was clear that his disability earned him unwanted attention and played a part in his difficulties at the school. "When I went to grammar school I became a right little cunt. They used to call me Spastic Joe, so I had to get up a whole defence mechanism against that. It got to my head. I was an odd case. I was just an outlaw and it was like that until I was 17," he said.

Ian did, however, find a soul mate in 'Uplyme' boarding house who shared his growing passion for music. Edward Speight was born in Sheffield and had moved to Aylesbury with his parents in 1953. He started at the RGS when he was 11 and stayed on in the school sixth form. But before he left he was already an accomplished jazz guitarist and, like Ian, would go on to enjoy a career in music. His friendship with the Upminster dissident with the calliper on his leg endured right up to Ian's death.

Ed remembers: "The first time I saw Ian was on my first day there and he was walking up the corridor ahead of me. I can't remember how we first got talking. It was odd in those days because we all had to wear short trousers and they wouldn't make an exception, even in his case. The next year they did allow him to go into long trousers, although you weren't supposed to go into long trousers until the sixth form."

High Wycombe in the mid-Fifties was typical of many small conformist English towns at that time, when the Second World War was still fresh in people's minds. It was also home to a large US Air Force base and because the servicemen tended to dominate the centre of the town, especially in the evenings, the locals felt a certain antipathy towards them. This manifested itself in various ways and youngsters who had their hair in a James Dean-style crew-cut were seen to be somehow aligning themselves with the Yanks.

Ed: "Ian and I both had crew-cuts and we got into trouble with the headmaster for it. But about a year or so after that, probably after Ian left, the Colonel of the local American air force asked the headmaster if they could use our playing field to put on their American football, with cheerleaders and all that, and for some reason he said yes. It was great because they just took over. They erected pylons, they had a group playing on a portable truck with a transformer, cheerleaders, and hot dog vendors. Jayne Mansfield came with her escort in a pink Chevrolet and actually drove all over the rugby field and churned it all up. The headmaster was so blinded by all this he didn't seem to be upset. It was amazing."

As pupils roamed the corridors of the Royal Grammar School in the wintry days of 1954, Britain was preparing to "shake, rattle and roll" to Bill Haley & The Comets; the rock'n'roll revolution was on its way. Ian adored music and, as 1955 dawned, he was in heaven. Awe-inspiring rock'n'roll records were being released by the week and the rate of new singers was hard to keep pace with. Rock'n'roll also represented a whole new attitude after the austerity of the immediate post-war period. When Haley's 'Rock Around The Clock' blared from cinema screens at the start of Richard Brooks' movie *The Blackboard Jungle*, rock'n'roll took on a new anti-establishment role. As youngsters settled down in their seats, they were greeted by the following prologue: "Today we are concerned with juvenile delinquency – its causes – and its effects. We are especially concerned when this delinquency boils over into our schools. The scenes and incidents depicted here are fictional. However, we believe that public awareness is a first step toward a remedy for any problem. It is in this spirit and with this faith that *Blackboard Jungle* was produced."

Ironically, or perhaps intentionally, this adrenaline-building cocktail of loud music and marauding hoodlums was a call to arms for teenagers from Los Angeles to London, who bopped, sang along to their new icons and slashed cinema seats. The following year, the film *Rock Around The Clock* was released in a bid to capitalise on Bill Haley's immense popularity. Even in the quiet of High Wycombe, the RGS was not immune to this new fever.

Edward Speight saw little value in rock'n'roll as his peers gyrated ecstatically to Little Richard, Fats Domino and other American rockers. But he did share Ian's other musical passion – jazz. They spent hours listening to artists such as Ornette Coleman, Archie Shepp, Charlie Parker and John Coltrane, although no one at the school could possibly have predicted the direct influence that these black American musicians would have on the crippled boy from Upminster.

Ed: "I never particularly went for Elvis Presley. I remember that we went to the local picture house in Desborough Avenue in High Wycombe – or desperate avenue – for a matinee performance of *Rock Around The Clock*. I'd been reading about all this jiving in the aisles and 'Teddy boys' with flick knives. I just sat there and listened with the arrogance of youth, and because at that time I was listening to Charlie Parker, I thought, 'This is dreadful rubbish – this is the end of music.' Even then I knew that these seemingly middle-aged men running around the floor with checked suits and short hair were good players, that they had to do this to get a gig and that they were jazz players by nature. They were having to play this dreadful watered-down blues music which didn't compare in any way with the Chicago electric blues of the Forties which we'd heard. So, in an inverse way, we thought 'whities' had got hold of the black man's music and it was never going to be the same again."

Carefully planned escapes from the confines of the boarding house at RGS presented opportunities for the boys to hear more of their beloved jazz, or in Ed's case, to actually play it. "I was going out and playing the banjo three or four nights a week in local art colleges and crawling into the boarding house at two o'clock in the morning, having briefed people to leave windows open for me to climb in. We would break into the signals hut of the Combined Cadet Force which was run by psychopaths who had this kind of principle of making the most psychopathic sixth former a head prefect or sergeant. Our protest was to break in and listen to *Voice Of America Jazz Hour* on the radio receiver – one made one's protests where one could. It was a golden era for music. From the mid-fifties on, there was a lot of jazz and blues and a lot of records were being released or re-released in England: early blues players as well as all the New Orleans jazz. Bear in mind that Charlie Parker didn't die until 1955.

"Then there were rock'n roll singers like Gene Vincent. Amongst the musically minded people at school, we listened to quite a broad range of music and the headmaster did allow people to form groups. He didn't do the usual thing and try and say it was the 'devil's music' and was broad-minded in that respect. He must have been or he wouldn't have let the Americans drive across his treasured rugby field. Ian and I got involved in a group [The Black Cat Combo Skiffle Group]; one guy played a tea-chest bass, I played guitar and Ian played washboard."

Meanwhile, Ian's dislike for the school was growing. His spiky personality led to frequent confrontations with Mr Tucker and other teachers. This was no surprise bearing in mind the traumatic events of his childhood and his experiences at Chailey, although it is doubtful that he would have welcomed the school with open arms had he been able-bodied.

Even at the age of five, Ian had refused to go to school and his mother had sent him to see psychiatrists. As she had taught him to read before he arrived at school, he didn't seem to see the point of going there. At Chailey, Ian had been among the literate elite and the other children had queued up for him to write letters for them on Saturday mornings. But at RGS, Ian was a small fish in a much larger pond. Although one boy at the school had cerebral palsy and was far more severely disabled than Ian, he was very bright and went on to become an Oxford scholar. Ian simply felt self-conscious and rebelled.

"That was the first time I became aware there was something wrong with me, when I went there, not when I was at Chailey because there was plenty worse off than me there," said Ian.[3] "I was aware of my position in the society of the Royal Grammar School, High Wycombe. Yeah, I entered the RGS as a chubby little mascot. That did feel like a weird environment, and it was – I still think so. It was the Round Table – you know, grocers' sons and stuff."

He went on: "They were over-helpful at first, and then they realised I didn't need that much help – by which time I was a villain for taking advantage of it. It's quite a difficult thing knowing what you're supposed to do, anyway."

More often than not at the school, the name Ian Dury spelled trouble. He refused to conform to the school's ways and didn't attempt to hide his loathing of the place. He was frequently disciplined and made himself unpopular with teachers and some of his fellow pupils. Even today he is not well remembered by the school and some of his peers. One former boarder, who asked not to be named, said of Ian: "He wasn't really academic. He was rebellious and obnoxious from day one and one suspects that he did not want to be there in the first place. He was in trouble a good deal of the time. Mr Tucker was a very academic type and wanted academic excellence and clearly Ian Dury didn't fit into that picture whatsoever. So he brought a lot of trouble on himself and went out of his way to get under people's skin."

Killed with kindness during the first six months at the school, until they realised that the crippled boy could do most things for himself, Ian was never bullied because of his disability. However, it led indirectly to some unpleasant experiences.

"They thought that the slipper didn't hurt me, they thought that polio meant you didn't feel pain," recalled Ian.[2] "I had 16 prefects meetings in half a term and then they went to the headmaster and said, 'Look, he doesn't feel pain, can we mess his head up?' Well they didn't actually say that but they asked, 'Can we give him some poetry to learn and essays to write instead please as a punishment for his misdemeanours?' So the headmaster gave them permission and I had to go in a box room where all the suitcases were stored and learn 80 lines of *Ode To Autumn* by Keats. If I got a word wrong they would add that on to the end of the sentence. After five nights of this, my head had definitely gone and I was walking down the corridor and I burst into tears. A very nice man, I can't remember his name, but he was the house master of another boarding house, came out, saw me blubbing in the corridor. Because he was a father and had some kids at the house and everything, he did the fatherly thing and put his arm round me and said, 'What's the matter?' and I said, 'They've got me, they've got me' and he went and put a stop to it. Mind you, I probably deserved it."

His disability was the cause of uncomfortable moments outside the Royal Grammar School, as well as inside it. One day, his Aunt Molly – who always took a great interest in her nephew's progress – took him to see a specialist because Ian's mum was concerned about the discomfort caused by his heavy leg-iron. "When it came to his turn to be seen, the man turned to the person who was working with him and said, 'Now, this is that boy with the terribly interfering mother who keeps rushing forward asking for this and that, isn't it?' " recalls Molly. "I thought, 'That's a very fine way to speak before a boy in his teens. Whatever is he going to think?' I was absolutely horrified. It was a perfectly reasonable thing to ask, you can imagine getting in and out of a car with a stiff leg like that. I noticed that Ian never went to that man after he left school."

Holidays, especially those long summer breaks, brought welcome respite from High Wycombe and it was these times that Ian remembered very fondly. When he was 13, Ian returned to the mountains and streams of Donegal for the first time since he contracted polio. Barry accompanied him, becoming the very first in a long line of chaperones who would mind him during his life. Supervised by Ian's mother, they travelled first class by train from London to Morecambe and then took the night boat from Heysham to Belfast. From there, they caught the train to Strabane in Northern Ireland and then on to Derry, where they were picked up in a taxi by Ian's relatives. The two boys stayed at Kilcadden House for three weeks and spent their time cycling up and down the winding country lanes, with Ian riding a tricycle. Two years later, Ian's mum and the two boys spent a second vacation in the nearby village of Rathmullen.

"When we went to this mansion [Kilcadden House], it was like going back in time," remembers Barry. "It was a palatial place, but run down and they had tenant farmers. Once, we were going across this little brook in Donegal and he was leaning across this fence on a wooden bridge and he fell in. It wasn't deep, but he went daft and screamed at me to pull him out, which was very difficult to do."

Ian had great memories of his holidays in Ireland: "Great aunt Janet, she went to Dublin only once in her life to get some false teeth in 1901 and the last time I saw her was in 1969. Fanny the maid, the one who was quite severely, religiously one-minded, would come out of the dining room and bang the gong and you would troop in there and you had Lucozade and cucumber sandwiches."[1]

Ian's mother had maintained close contact over the years with Brigid Slevin, whose husband had worked for the Walkers, and on these later visits Ian played with her sons Barney, Noel and Danny. Brigid remembers seeing Ian for the first time with the calliper on his left leg. "Ian coped with it very well; he used to laugh about it and he used to bring a boy with him [Barry] and they called him his 'helper'. He would pick him up when he would fall. There was a swing between two chestnut trees at our old house and he used to swing on that."

In letters to Brigid many years later, after Ian's rise to fame, his mother often expressed her relief and joy that her only child had survived polio. "They didn't really expect him to live at all, he had been through an awful lot," says Brigid. "I remember his mother saying when the rock'n'roll thing started that she didn't care what he did. Whether or not it was the sort of thing the family would have wanted him to do, I don't know, but she said she didn't care what he did so long as he lived. They were so glad he had lived through the polio that as long as he was happy, that was all that mattered."

Holidays back home in Upminster offered Ian the kind of excitement he was really looking for as a teenager. Here he roved with a gang of teenagers invigorated by the cult movies such as *The Blackboard Jungle* and *Rebel Without A Cause*. During a showing of *Rock Around The Clock* at the ABC in Romford, they tore out cinema seats and were thrown out by ushers. At the Romford Odeon, where Barry's uncle was a manager, they slipped in to watch rock'n'roll bands, and they usually managed to get served in local pubs. It was away from the boarding school, which was out of synch with his desired image as a hard-nosed tearaway, that Ian was at his happiest. In Upminster, he talked about his records, girls and clothes and exchanged crude jokes. Most importantly of all, he was part of a gang to which he could truly relate. Years later, in one of his very first songs, 'Upminster Kid', Ian evoked the exciting days of his adolescence: "When I was 15 I had a black drape jacket and sideboards to my chin/I used to drive around in a two-tone Zephyr with a mean and nasty grin."

Chailey had affected the way Ian spoke as he tried to fit in with the other kids. But it was on the streets of Upminster that Ian first heard the Cockney rhyming slang that he would import into his songs and his everyday banter. "I grew up in Upminster with a local accent and I've savoured it," he said.[2] "One day I heard a bloke in Upminster say, 'Cor look at the state of his Barnet,' and I went, 'What's that?' He goes, 'It's Barnet Fair – your hair,' and I found that very amusing. Ever since then I've hung around with people who enjoy it as well. I worked with Roger Lloyd Pack [English actor] on a project a few years ago and he came in one day and said, 'Oh, I'm having terrible trouble with my April.' I said, 'April, you've got me there Roger, what is it?' and gave me this long answer. Your Aris is your bottom and it goes 'Aris, Aristotle, bottle, bottle, and glass/Arse.' I go, 'Tell me. Is April in Paris? Ah, okay.' It's just funny."

But when he had to return to High Wycombe, bitterness and frustration were back on the timetable. "In the summers I would be movin' with a team of roughnecks, working boys, like 30 or 40 of us, going to the pictures and tearing up the seats. Then I'd have to go back to grammar school. That was weird," Ian recalled.[5] "When I was 14 and randy, when I was at boarding school, I ached for a piece of crumpet. I would trace out of pin-up books, ladies, the first one with her clothes on, then I'd trace it again with less clothes on. On the first page with the first drawing I would type the first stanza of a poem, then the second stanza on the second page would be hornier and by the fourth page she'd be completely nude and the poem would be really horny. Then I'd have a wank and tear it all up and throw it away."

He added: "With ladies, there was always aggravation. I'd try to mind-fuck 'em. I was very unhappy until I was 15. I was so into ladies, I thought I was a repressed homosexual. I thought, 'Perhaps I'm a repressed homosexual! Who cares. Wow, look at them ladies!' Like that."

During a school holiday in Upminster, Ian had his first sexual encounter. "I had some kinds of extreme shyness, but also an associated who-gives-a-fuck, devil-may-care, what's-the point-of-worrying-about-it attitude," he said.[3] "I remember the first experience of sex I had was with this girl in a rain hut in Upminster Park. She was sitting on my right-hand side and my left hand couldn't undo her blouse. So I said: 'Would you mind coming and sitting on this other side, please?' She went, 'That's a weird one,' and moved over, though she didn't quite know why. She wouldn't see me again because I was too fresh. I was quite young, I was 14."

Towards the end of 1949, Ian's mother and his Aunt Betty had moved from Cranham to a more salubrious address in Upminster. Number 12 Waldegrave Gardens was a large detached house with bay windows, four or five bedrooms and an attractive enclosed rear garden. The quiet street was about two minutes' walk from the Upminster Underground stop in Station Road and just around the corner from Roomes Stores Ltd, an eye-catching building which had opened as a drapery in 1927 and expanded into a department store in May 1937. The Roope Hall church community centre was also nearby.

The Walker home was always full. Ian's aunt, although still single, had adopted two children of her own, Martin and Lucy, both of whom were younger than their cousin Ian. In post-war Britain, it was common for children to be adopted or taken in and, although she was single, his aunt's work with the local health authority would have made her an ideal adoptive parent.

"Elizabeth always said if she reached a certain age and hadn't got married she would adopt," says Molly. "So she adopted Martin and we said, 'Well, you can't just have one child, you'll have to have two' and then she adopted Lucy. They thought the world of their mother." Other residents in the extended Irish household included Ian's grandmother, who was now very elderly and had moved up from Cornwall, while an au pair called Hansi helped to look after Ian's cousins. The house was so full that Peggy bought a Bluebird caravan so her son could live in the garden and have some privacy. Such was the extent of the garden and orchard, that three houses have since been built on the land. Armed with his cherished collection of jazz and rock'n'roll records, his girlie magazines and sketch pads, Ian vanished into his mobile home, which he remembered cost £404. Here, in the epitome of middle-class suburbia, the indulged 14-year-old smoked cigarettes, turned up the volume on his wind-up gramophone and partied with his mates. "We had great fun in the caravan. I had parties in there with 15 people sometimes. The joint was rocking," said Ian.[1]

Recognising her son's nascent interest in popular music, his mother took him to jazz and pop concerts from 1958 onwards. He watched in awe as Count Basie led his band at The Royal Festival Hall, and was knocked dead by the drumming of Sonny Payne. He also witnessed the crooner Johnnie Ray at The London Palladium and remembers the girls bringing bunches of flowers to the stage. Deaf in his right ear, Ray performed with a hearing aid and contorted his body as he sang. His unusual singing style probably left its mark on Ian.

Barry, who was by now attending Gaynes Secondary School in Upminster, was struck by the easy-going attitude adopted by Ian's mother. "My father would say, 'Go to bed' if I dared get out and he caught me," he says. "It's not that he would slap me or anything, but I was under the thumb. Ian had a very liberal life – he had the rule of the roost really. I think he had the breeding of a little aristocrat, with all the benefits. He was far more intelligent than anybody I have ever known at that age. To me, he was an old person and that is why I stuck with him. He made up for his disabilities by being the one who got the records, the first one to know what rock'n'roll was. He was knocked out by 'Blue Suede Shoes'. We used to sit outside the caravan and smoke, because that was the big thing, and play these records. I didn't appreciate Fats Domino at that time, but Ian knew about him. Ian was a rebel and he wanted to be the rebel without a cause. He would be the first one in blue jeans, he would be the first one to look for Levis, that was the thing to do at that time. He talked about Wilson Pickett when nobody had ever heard of Wilson Pickett, so he knew his onions at a very young age."

One of the very first 78s to hit the turntable of Ian's gramophone was his mother's favourite, Frank Crumit's 1927 recording of 'Abdul Abulbul Amir'. Ian knew all the words off by heart and the song was among the eight Desert Island Discs he selected for the Radio 4 programme in 1996. The others were: Bobby Charles, 'Small Town Talk'; Dean Martin, 'That's Amore'; Gene Vincent, 'Woman Love'; Taj Mahal, 'Music Keeps Me Together'; Alma Cogan, 'Naughty Lady Of Shady Lane'; Ann Peebles, 'I Can't Stand The Rain'; Ornette Coleman, 'Ramblin''. But to the teenage Ian Dury, there was no one to beat Gene Vincent.

Says Barry: "We used to hang out in the Regent Cafe in St Mary's Lane, where we used to discuss rock'n'roll. Everybody went for the popular figures like Elvis, but Ian was convinced that Gene Vincent was the top rock'n'roller."

In his interview with *Penthouse*,[3] Ian spoke in detail about his early musical influences and explained his particular fascination with Vincent. "With me, it's been since rock'n'roll started, since I started hearin' it, it's just been music I got off on. I was listenin' to Charlie Parker and Jelly Roll Morton, all those ones. I never listened to long hair music. I always listened to jazz 'cause lots of the kids at school had jazz records. Free jazz, all kinds of jazz. I was listening to rock'n'roll too. *Blackboard Jungle* started it all over here, that was a big scene. When Lonnie Donegan made 'Rock Island Line', that was the start of the skiffle thing in England, which ended up with The Beatles and the Stones. I was in a couple of skiffle bands. I even bought pop show tunes in those days like 'Cross Over The Bridge' and selections from *Guys And Dolls*. I started collecting records, 78s, around 1955. I'd buy Louis Armstrong, I'd buy Gene Vincent, I'd buy Elvis. I remember hearin' 'Heartbreak Hotel' and 'Blue Suede Shoes'. I bought every Elvis record and every single by Gene Vincent until he stopped making them. 'Be-Bop-A-Lula' really got to me. I'd cry and get right off on it.

"Gene Vincent got to me more than anybody; he was in a special little category because he was what I wanted to be as a singer. The way he could fly about! I didn't know he was crippled at the time, so that didn't have anything to do with it. It was his head, the shape of his head because it was opposite from mine. That was before he was Mr Leather, I never liked him when he became that. It was when he was wearin' plaid and had pale blue hair. The face, the beauty of it. He's in a film, *The Girl Can't Help It*, singin' 'Be Bop A Lula'. Eddie Cochran's in it too and Jayne Mansfield. Fuckin' incredible. The greatest rock'n'roll film of all time, in full colour. There's a lot of crap in it too. Little Richard is singin' 'The Girl Can't Help It' and Phil Silvers' glasses splinter. It was his thinness, his wastedness, Gene Vincent. His face, his music and his singing."

Back in the stuffy confines of the RGS, however, the aspiring rock 'n'roller's recalcitrant attitude continued to cast him in the role of trouble-maker and in his last year there he was embroiled in a controversial incident. Versions of the story vary, but Ian always insisted he was innocent.

Molly describes Ian's original version of events and what followed. "Mr Tucker had a tiresome wife, who was always interfering in things," she says. "She knew that there had been a bit of a to-do about fish and one day she said, 'Now, there is to be no more of this, you'll all sit down and eat your fish properly' and she shut the door and went out. A few minutes later she came back in and as she opened the door a fish flew across the room and hit her on the face and she, for some reason or other, decided Ian had done it. That was really an awful lot of nonsense when one came to think of it seriously, because for one thing, his arm wasn't anything like strong enough to throw the fish like that and he didn't know she was coming in at that moment. The whole thing was a lot of nonsense. Anyway, she stormed off and saw her husband and said the boy had been disgraceful and he would have to deal with him. He snatched him out of the room and gave him six of the best. Then I think he felt that wasn't a very wise thing to do and I said to him, 'Would you let me take him out', which I would do occasionally while he was at Wycombe, 'and have a talk to him?' So, he said yes, because I think he thought then that he had better be a bit on the soft side and I said to Ian, 'It may seem silly, but men do get awfully worked up about their wives, and started to tell him the facts of life.' Ian said, 'Well, it's all very well Aunt Moll, but I didn't throw the damned fish,' and I said, 'Well in that case, the whole thing is very silly indeed.'

"The next thing was that I happened to be going down to see Elizabeth in Upminster that same weekend and Ian suddenly turned up. That was a bit startling really, because he didn't usually take journeys of that nature. He had thought, 'Well damn this man, I'm not staying here,' but he'd been annoyed by other things too. Peg said to him at once, 'The first thing you've got to do is to ring the head and say you're here, because he'll be getting slightly agitated that you've disappeared from school and he won't know where you are, and that won't do. Ring him up and tell him you're here.' Ian wasn't very keen on that, but he did it and I said, 'Well look, I'll bring you back on Monday morning. Tell him that.' And that settled it in a way."

Ed Speight also recalls the 'fish incident', but his version suggests that the story which Ian told his aunt may have been altered for her benefit. "Ian and the headmaster's wife had a mutual loathing," remembers Ed. "One day Ian wouldn't eat the fish and the headmaster's wife was on duty, supervising and making sure that everybody emptied their plates. Ian just said, 'I'm sorry, I'm not going to eat that, I can't, it's horrible.' I think she tried to pick up the plate and he pushed it away and some of the fish fell on her and she immediately misinterpreted this and went whingeing to her old man. She accused 'this boy' of throwing his plate of fish at her. The headmaster went ape-shit and hit Ian and sent him flying across the room and he landed on his arse.

"Immediately the headmaster realised what he'd done, because for any person in authority, even then, to strike a child, but particularly someone like that, was quite serious. But Ian didn't do anything, he didn't make a report. He talked to his aunt about it and they said to him, 'Look, if you want to report it, this would be a serious charge,' but he never did. He just thought 'I'll let the bastard live in fear.' It was a way of taking revenge because from that moment on the headmaster knew he had to be careful.

About a year afterwards this boy, Warwick Prior, said to the headmaster, 'If you ever touch me like that again I'll lay you out,' and he laid off. The two incidents were kind of linked."

When Ian was interviewed by Sue Lawley on *Desert Island Discs*, he said he had been expelled from the school in the wake of the alleged fish throwing. To this day, however, his aunt has no knowledge of this. She clearly remembers driving him back to the school after the incident and says he completed his final term. Neither the Royal Grammar School, or anyone who attended at the same time, recalls Ian being thrown out. There is no doubt that the school was pleased to see the back of him and would not have been keen on him staying on in its sixth form. But he certainly stayed in the school after the fish incident and was also allowed to take his 'O' Levels. Ian's claim that he was expelled may well have been part of his lifelong attempt to portray himself as a dissenter who stuck two fingers up to authority at every turn.

Quite apart from Ian's spat with the headmaster's wife, his Aunt Molly was dissatisfied with the standard of education he was receiving at the RGS. Ian's mother, who had strongly felt that a grammar school education was what Ian needed, was also uneasy. Shortly after arriving at High Wycombe, the Stoke Mandeville Hospital, near Aylesbury, had invited him to attend exercise sessions there one afternoon a week, in order to keep up the strength in his weakened limbs. Ian had agreed, but his mother and aunt felt that the school should have provided him with additional tutoring to help him replace the lessons he would miss.

Molly: "Some of my colleagues in the office said to me, 'Are you really happy about Ian being at the Royal Grammar School, because they're a bit tough there you know?' I said, 'I don't know. As far as I know he's all right.' I know that they had a game in which they would take Ian in his wheelchair up to the top of a pile of coke in the playground, leave him there and let him slide down. But he seemed to be quite agreeable to that, although he did fall out once or twice and it wasn't very good for him. I didn't think that was what was worrying him really." But she adds rue-fully: "Ian didn't have a happy time there and I felt rather responsible for that."

Despite being miserable, Ian did leave with 'O' Levels in English Literature, English Language and Art and the latter was to be his calling. Before completing his exams, he had attended an interview at Walthamstow College of Art and was offered a place on its painting course. For years he had been sketching, regularly drawing naked women, and an art course seemed the perfect antidote to the academic and inflexible environs of High Wycombe. The school did not actually have a full-time art teacher, but Ian had put it down on the list of subjects he wished to study at 'O' Level and his single-mindedness was to pay dividends when he passed the exam having had no formal tuition.

At Walthamstow Art College, Ian Dury would find not only personal freedom, but a new bohemian way of life.

3

PENCIL SQUEEZER

"Peter Blake's message was 'Paint the things you like or that you are interested in' and Peter was into rock'n'roll. Ian was into rock'n'roll, but he was also into dolly-birds, so he would do drawings and paintings of dolly-birds with knickers and titties."

– Terry Day

Pop Art was all the rage as Britain rushed headlong into the Swinging Sixties. A two-fingered salute to the abstract expressionism of painters like Jackson Pollock and Marc Rothko, Pop Art took humdrum objects and icons of popular culture as its subjects and represented them as realism personified. The cult of celebrity had developed fast with the rise of television in the Fifties and in Pop Art, movie idols such as Laurel & Hardy, Marilyn Monroe, James Dean, and rock'n'roll heroes like Elvis Presley, were faithfully captured in vivid paintings and bright collages. Spurning still-life, landscapes and interiors – traditionally the bread and butter of 'serious' artists – this radical group of painters took their inspiration from science fiction, sport and other forms of popular entertainment. They seized on absolutely anything with mass appeal and produced arresting pictures and sculptures to which ordinary people could relate. Andy Warhol's 'assembly-line' images of Coca-Cola bottles, Campbell's soup cans and idols such as Chairman Mao, produced through silk-screening techniques, have proved the most enduring images of the American Pop Art era. In Britain, artists such as Joe Tilson, Richard Smith and Eduardo Paolozzi played an important role in the appearance of Pop in the late Fifties and early Sixties. However, it was Peter Blake who became the leader of the group. His work, and his refreshingly down-to-earth approach to art, would animate many young artists – among them Ian Dury.

Ian's decision to take up painting could not have come at a more exciting time in the worlds of art and music. Free at last from the constraints of boarding school, he entered a more casual, non-conformist world where he could draw and paint the singers, musicians and actors who dominated his thoughts. At art school, he had the first opportunity to interact with the kind of creatively minded and liberal people who would surround him for the rest of his life. When, on October 16, 1959, Ian walked through the gates of South West Essex Technical College and School of Art in Forest Road, Walthamstow, Northeast London, so began one of the happiest periods of his life. While Britain underwent a popular culture revolution, Ian Dury had 'never had it so good'.

"I sort of thought I'd like to be a painter one day, it was the way of life that appealed to me; it was freedom, the style, the glamour of not being normal," said Ian.[1]

The threat of another world war was looming when the college opened in 1938 and its extravagant architecture drew some criticism. Lavish columns adorned its classic facade and a long flight of stone steps led up to the main doors of the building, which in total cost £166,000 to build. As it turned out, the college was a valuable asset to the war effort, training people in activities ranging from radio communications to espionage. Today it is known as Waltham Forest College and comprises eight schools: Applied Science; Arts; Language and Teacher Training; Automobile Engineering; Business and Computing; Health Studies; General Education; and Tourism, Hospitality and Hotel Management. Ian's friend Barry Anderson enrolled on a course in Hospitality and Hotel Management at the same time as Ian started his art course, the two pals having chewed the matter over together during a final school holiday. But in this vast building, with its winding, airy corridors, the artists stood apart from the rest, and in the autumn of 1959, Ian Dury – ever the attention seeker – found himself the centre of a group of people who were turning heads. Some, like Ian, were also destined to find fame, including film-maker Peter Greenaway and The Bonzo Dog Doo-Dah Band's comic originator Vivian Stanshall.

The scruffy band of painters had much in common. Many had already attended the South East Essex Technical College and most hailed from Ilford, Romford, Dagenham, Barking or Walthamstow itself. Their chatter was punctuated with local slang and the group was not short of good story-tellers, with Ian being no exception. Occupying rooms on two floors of the building in Forest Road, this artistic troupe made their presence felt in every part of the college and some students found them fascinating and, at times, intimidating.

Mary Dawe was doing a secretarial course at Walthamstow and came to know some of the art students when she began dating her future husband Alan Ritchie, who had failed his exams at the South East Essex Technical College and was modelling there. She later studied art herself at Walthamstow.

"The art department there ruled the roost really," Mary recollects. "They thoroughly enjoyed their 'art' status and if you went up to the refectory at tea-time, the art department had the very front tables. Everybody else had to queue, but I suppose if they had Life Classes, they could just leave a bit early. So they were always very established and they just used to chat us all up; they would sit watching everybody coming in and they would chat up all the new ones. They were very intriguing because I had just come from school, completely naive, and I couldn't understand a word any of them said. Partly they were talking in hip talk and also quite a lot of rhyming slang, which probably came from Ian because he loved all that. They would say things like, 'Cor, I like your barnet' and I just didn't know what they were talking about. Really, they used to terrify me at first and then I started going out with Alan and got to know them."

Seventeen years old and still relatively inexperienced sexually, Ian made a strong impression on women from the moment he arrived at Walthamstow. His pronounced limp and misshapen body invariably caused some people in the college to stare at him. But his mop of dark tangled hair, his unsettling gaze and his unabashed attitude towards sex were more than enough to attract the kind of female attention he craved. Girls who encountered Ian in his early college days remember a mischievous rogue, babbling incessantly with his friends, telling lewd jokes, calling out after them – anything so long as all eyes were on him. If he felt self-conscious about his disabilities and was attempting to compensate for his physical limitations, his behaviour gave no indication of any such insecurity. Quite the reverse. Ian seemed at ease with his handicap and quickly identified the benefits it could bring.

Anne Ingle went to study at Walthamstow at the age of 19 and although not in the painting department, she came into contact with Ian. "He would be the one with the courage to say the outrageous thing and behave outrageously and not care," she says. "I wouldn't say he was very nosy exactly, but he would be charting any romances that were going on in the college and he knew I had been out with a particular person and he wanted to know all the ins and outs of that, everything. That was the way he was, very upfront and salacious. He was a very sexual kind of guy."

Aside from Ian's physique, his clothes were also striking. A ragged gypsy neckerchief, which looked like it needed a wash, was tied around his neck and he regularly wore waistcoats over his good-quality American jeans. But it was the glint in his eye suggesting he was up to no good which accounted for his appeal with the girls.

Anne explains: "He had a great wit and he was big into sex – well most men are – but he was not afraid of saying it and letting you know it. Whether he thought he wasn't going to live very long and was going to make the most of it or maybe he thought he wasn't attractive to women, I don't know. There was an aura around him and he knew everything that was going on, like who slept with who if they did anything like that at that stage, which the arty types tended to do. He stood out from the crowd for a number of reasons. He didn't have the inhibitions which the rest of us had because he had to live with the way he was and he just went for it."

One day, when she and Ian were talking, he confronted her in a way that she found uncomfortable. Although he did not say so directly, he made reference to the way he looked and he knew that the directness of his question would put him in control. His disabilities, Ian had quickly discovered, allowed him to be more direct with other people than they would be in response. The intention was not to be nasty, but to put himself in a position of power.

"Ian just asked me outright, 'Would ya take me home to your parents, would ya?' and that threw me and upset me," says Anne. "I would say there is a streak of wickedness in him, because he knew he was putting me on the spot by saying that. Maybe I was going through this very socialist phase at the time and had been spouting this stuff and he wanted to put me in my place and he certainly did, because I have remembered it all these years. It couldn't have hurt me more, because I knew I had to say, 'No, I wouldn't'. He took no notice of it and carried on talking, it meant nothing to him. If he had seen where I lived he wouldn't have been wanting to go home with me. I was trying to be so bloody trendy and with it and he knew really I was just a conventional little person."

Neither was the magnetism of Ian's personality lost on Mary. "He was very up-front with women and I don't know whether his disablement brought out mothering instincts, I don't know how it works, but he was very attractive. There is a definite charisma; he has these deep brown eyes and a lot of twinkliness about him."

One student at Walthamstow, Hilary Horpike, was crazy about Ian and he exploited this, teasing her relentlessly. She once told a fellow student how Ian had crept up behind her in the corridor with his stick, put his face against her ear and growled, 'Hello little girl', giving her a terrible fright. Without a doubt, Ian simply loved the fascination he held for women and he milked the extra appeal of his disability.

It was not just at Walthamstow that the long-haired Ian Dury was making himself known. He was also drawn to the bohemian bars and hang-outs of Soho, particularly the Partisan Café.

Ian said: "I met this geezer there called Larry, an amazing bloke, who had a pension from the Burma railroad; he was a habitué. And he said a true thing – though I think it's less true now – he said, 'If a disabled girl comes in here, all the geezers will look away from her. If a disabled guy comes in, all the girls will look at him.' Plus, if you're an art student and you've got long hair and you've got a bad limp, you're a romantic figure in a way."[3]

Of the deep friendships Ian developed during his four years at Walthamstow, one was to prove highly consequential. Terry Day was a 'likely lad' from Dagenham who had studied painting at South East Essex, but aside from his precocious artistic talents, he was a gifted free-form jazz drummer. His own father had been a drummer and his older brother Pat was a child prodigy, who had been playing with prestigious jazz musicians such as Graham Bond from a tender age. Pat's achievements had been a source of much pride and inspiration for Terry, who began drumming himself when he was 15 and when Ian met him at college, he was playing regularly. On Friday nights and at weekends, he drummed with bands at pubs, weddings, dances, bar mitzvahs and socials at working clubs in Dagenham. But his appetite for jazz was satisfied in a variety of night-time hangouts, including The Bell in Walthamstow and The Plough in Ilford, where, along with Ian, Joe Snowden and Alan Ritchie, he saw the Johnny Burch Octet featuring Ginger Baker on drums, Jack Bruce on bass – both of whom were later in Cream – and Graham Bond on alto sax. Terry was a regular visitor to Ian's garden caravan listening to records on his wind-up gramophone. Terry gave Ian his first drum lessons.

"Ian and I used to drive everybody crazy by using paint brushes as drum sticks and tapping out rhythms on the corridor window ledges," Terry remembers. "At Walthamstow, we used to paint and draw in the corridors on the top floor so the noise from our drumming would carry throughout the building to the bottom floors. One day a lecturer from the ground floor came up the stairs screaming at us, 'You ought to be locked up in a lunatic asylum,' and I shouted back, 'You don't know how right you are.' Ian liked my response. We did drive them mad with our incessant beats, day in, day out, week in, week out. The lecturer was right, we probably should have been locked up. Maybe that's where 'It's nice to be a lunatic' [Hit Me With Your Rhythm Stick] comes from?"

It was in the corridors of the college and the nearby streets that Ian first came across an expression with which he would later greet his audiences and subsume into his everyday language, according to Terry. "Instead of 'Morning mate' or 'Hello', all the blokes would greet each other with 'Oi Oi'. This expression was definitely in street use, so I don't think anybody could claim to be its originator. As with other phrases, jargon and collo-quialisms, Ian acquired it and made it part of his vocabulary. The good thing about 'Oi Oi' was that you could greet each other from across the street and grab your mates' attention from down the end of the corridor."

Few could have known at this time that Ian would find fame through music. He took his art seriously and worked diligently on honing his drawing techniques. He was no natural musician, as he would happily admit himself; he had little or no understanding of musical keys and couldn't carry a tune in a bucket. But that didn't stop him, and thousands of other kids who were jumping around their bedrooms to Chuck Berry, from joining skiffle groups. After all, the beauty of such collectives was that anyone could play. A 'do-it-yourself' style of music, it originated in the US and involved the use of home-made instruments like comb-and-paper kazoo, tea-chest bass, saw, washboard, spoons, or any household object with even the slightest rhythmic potential. Early groups were given a host of descriptions including jug, skittle, spasm or spaz bands, and many of them combined their makeshift instruments with guitars, banjos, trumpets, clarinets or harmonicas.

The skiffle craze hit Britain in 1957, fuelled largely by Lonnie Donegan who, accompanied by Beryl Bryden on washboard, went to number eight in the UK charts with the Leadbelly number 'Rock Island Line'. His later novelty hits 'Does Your Chewing Gum Lose Its Flavour' [no 3 in 1959] and 'My Old Man's A Dustman' [no 1 in 1960] were, meanwhile, reminiscent of the music hall era of which Ian was so fond. Through Donegan, skiffle enjoyed immense popularity with teenagers who, although not musically talented, could experience being in a band. John Lennon was playing skiffle at a church picnic in 1957 when he and Paul McCartney first met and The Quarry Men, the forerunner to The Beatles, owed much of their sound to skiffle. In Upminster Park, Ian Dury and his friends clattered their way through songs of this kind.

Barry Anderson recalls: "We put a skiffle group together when we were about 19. We had one girl, Jo Dobson, who was from Cranham, there was a guy from Derbyshire, I played guitar and Ian played the tea-chest. Occasionally we used to play to different people in Cranham Village Hall. We weren't very good, I have to tell you. Ian used to do all these whoops and noises, like he does on his records, and I used to tell him to shut up and tell him, 'That's not how "Freight Train" goes'. We had an Austin Seven which we painted lilac, which belonged to a guy called Richie, who lived in St Mary's Lane. It had curtains and no brakes, but we used to put the stuff in there and then go to the park and play."

Irrespective of Ian's musical limitations, Terry Day sensed that the Upminster rock'n'roller was destined to put his name in lights. "I wasn't from a rock'n'roll background, I'm from a jazz background and I could smell it then, he wanted to be a rock'n'roll star. It was almost written that fame was going to come his way," says Terry.

In the early Sixties the British music scene went through a sea change. From Chubby Checker's 'Let's Twist Again' to The Beatles' 'Love Me Do', a new energy and confidence was injected into popular music and art schools were breeding grounds for future stars in music and other areas of the arts. In London and the south east, Eric Clapton, Ray Davies, Pete Townshend and more were soon to graduate from art school to the pop charts. Unlike these contemporaries Ian, despite musical leanings, his long hair and beatnik clothes, would have to wait almost 15 years before he rose to prominence.

Nevertheless, the social scene at Walthamstow was nothing short of paradise as he luxuriated in two of his biggest passions – art and jazz. Along with Terry Day and other jazz devotees, Ian haunted such venues as the fashionable West End jazz club, Ronnie Scott's, and the Elm Park Jazz Club in Essex where he saw musicians such as Terry Lightfoot, Chris Barber and Acker Bilk. He even established his own jazz club in the college along with Barry Anderson and others, and booked some of his heroes.

"We could have had Tubby Hayes or The Beatles," said Ian.[1] "I mean, we could have had The Beatles for £400, but we thought, 'No, let's have Tubby Hayes.' I was a big fan, so we got the Tubby Hayes quintet for the price of a quartet."

Barry recalls: "We used to pay something like £40 for Acker Bilk. Another friend said to me that The Beatles were the best thing they'd ever heard and I said, 'You must be joking.' "

One evening, Ian and Terry went to see the jazz saxophonist Roland Kirk playing at Ronnie Scott's and sat directly beneath the blind player. They were so impressed by his playing that they went up to him after the gig. "Ian said, 'God bless you and thank you man,' " says Terry. "Even though Roland was blind, he knew who we were. 'You're the cats in the front, right next to the mike,' he said. I shook Roland's hand and he said I had nice warm hands."

Walthamstow itself was a hot-bed of talent during this burgeoning era and several of the students who tramped the corridors of the art department would go on to win acclaim in their chosen fields. Peter Greenaway was one of them.

Born in Newport, Wales, in 1942, he had decided at the age of 12 that he wanted to be a painter. In 1959, he also arrived at Walthamstow. Ironically, the Royal College of Art turned down his application to join its film-course and instead he learned his craft at the Central Office of Information where he spent 11 years cutting short, off-beat films. It was not until 1982 and *The Draughtsman's Contract* that he was hailed internationally as one of the most innovative and thought-provoking directors of his generation. Using startling imagery and richly decorated sets, he went on to serve up other equally sumptuous offerings such as *Belly Of An Architect*, *The Cook, The Thief, His Wife and Her Lover* and *The Pillow Book*.

Laurie Lewis, another close friend of Ian's from Walthamstow, remembers the young film-maker. "Peter Greenaway and I both used to work in the corridor and one year they introduced this mural course. I didn't want to do it and I managed to get off it, but Peter stayed on and he spent over a year doing just one painting which went up the corridor and around the stairwell. I didn't like it much, but it was epic."

More creative genius was to emanate from the art school in the form of Vivian Stanshall, the wildly eccentric character behind The Bonzo Dog Doo-Dah Band. Described by DJ John Peel as "the court jester of the underground rock scene in the Sixties", he emerged as one of the most surreal comic performers ever seen in Britain. A Londoner who had been evacuated with his mother to Oxfordshire during the war, he had grown up in Walthamstow and later Southend-on-Sea in Essex. At home, his father tried to teach him to speak BBC English, but once outside he reverted to the language and dress code of the local Teddy boys. After leaving Walthamstow he found fame with the Bonzo Dog Doo-Dah Band, who scored a Top Ten hit in November 1968 with 'I'm The Urban Spaceman'. As his humour teetered on the brink of insanity, so he lived life on the edge, bingeing on drugs and alcohol. It was during this mayhem that he and Keith Moon – The Who's drummer and legendary party animal – once famously paraded around the West End of London dressed as Nazi officers. In the late Seventies Vivian lived with his second wife Ki (Pamela) Longfellow-Stanshall on a boat moored on The Thames where he wrote *Rawlinson End* and the semi-autobiographical *Teddy Boys Don't Knit*. They relocated to a ship in Bristol after their other home sank and he continued writing and collaborated with Steve Winwood. In 1994, he made an appearance in the video for Pulp's hit single 'Do You Remember The First Time?' but on the morning of Sunday, March 5, 1995, he died in a fire at his third-floor flat in Hillfield Park, Muswell Hill, in north London. In common with Ian and Peter Greenaway, Viv Stanshall was a one-off, whose unique gifts rendered comparisons with other artists and performers meaningless.

Laurie Lewis says of the college's impact during the early Sixties: "Walthamstow was absolutely wild. It was bursting at the seams, so most people used to paint in the corridors because there wasn't enough room to get in the lecture rooms. It was just an exceptional time because different art schools would measure their success by how many students they would get into the Royal College of Art. If they got one or two students in, they felt good about it, but across the three years I was at the Royal College there were 33 students from Walthamstow, and that speaks for itself. I was in the film school and there were only nine places and four of them were from Walthamstow, but Walthamstow didn't even have a film department."

The arrival of Peter Blake had a significant impact on the art department and, for Ian Dury, it was a watershed. In the autumn of 1961, when Peter arrived at the college, he was busy establishing his name in the Pop Art movement. Acclaimed by the critics, he won first prize in the John Moore Exhibition in Liverpool later that year for his 'Self Portrait With Badges', in which he stood holding a book about Elvis, adorned with badges decorated with flags and other motifs. In the BBC's Monitor film *Pop Goes The Easel*, broadcast in 1962, presenter Huw Wheldon gave the following definition of the man and the movement: "Pop Art, the world of the popular imagination, the world of film stars, the twist, science fiction, pop singers. The first, and I suppose in some senses the leader of the group, is Peter Blake."

Peter Blake was from Dartford in Kent and had studied at Gravesend Technical College and School of Art before being accepted by the Royal College of Art in 1950. His studies were interrupted by National Service between 1951 and 1953, but on his return to college he met Joe Tilson and Richard Smith and began exploring the themes which would later appear in his work. At the same time, a collection of artists based at the Institute of Contemporary Arts in London had formed the Independent Group, a discussion forum which was looking at science fiction, American magazines, cars and advertising, as legitimate subjects for artists. Peter Blake developed a fascination for circus acts, comics and badges. He also recreated images from his early childhood. After graduating from the RCA in 1956, he toured Europe for a year studying popular art, funded by a Levenhulme Research Award, and his travels inspired the collages, pin-up photos and paintings with which he made his name. These works were to come to epitomise Pop Art in Britain. He also painted his favourite rock'n'rollers, Bo Diddley, The Everly Brothers, Little Richard, Chuck Berry, and big screen actresses such as Kim Novak and Tuesday Weld. So it was no accident that Ian Dury chose similar icons of the 20th century for his own creations.

Reminiscing with Peter Blake about these halcyon days in the BBC documentary *On My Life*,[1] Ian said: "One of the first things we learned from you was to become personally involved with the subject of our paintings, rather than just going out and doing some bland old boozer in Leyton or something. You said, 'Well, do you actually care?' I remember that as soon as you began teaching us, you said, 'Do you like boxing?' and it was when Cassius Clay had just started firing up and various interesting wrestlers were around like Sky High Lee."

At 29, Peter Blake was closer in age to the students than many other teachers and in their eyes he was 'cool'. He was a natty dresser, often wearing tweed or herringbone jackets, and had a neatly trimmed goatee beard and 'college boy' haircut. Deeply knowledgeable and enthusiastic about music, he had spent much of his youth in London's trendy jazz and Be-Bop joints like The 51 Club, The Flamingo, The 100 Club and Club Eleven. At the time he began teaching at Walthamstow, his work was beginning to attract serious attention. But such critical acclaim didn't pay the bills and he was earning his crust at three different colleges – St Martin's, Harrow and Walthamstow – where he taught three different forms of art on three separate days of the week. On a Wednesday morning in 1961, shortly after his arrival at Walthamstow, he was sent to find his group of students who were out sketching.

Peter describes the scene: "I had just started teaching at the college and they had explained that my role would be to take them on outdoor drawings. The person I was reporting to said they'd gone off somewhere and he gave me directions. So I started to walk there and on the way I went into a pub for a drink and there was Ian and one of the other kids. So instead of saying 'Come on lads, off you go', we had a drink together and then walked up to the college. Ian took the project really seriously and worked very hard at it and our friendship developed from there."

Of his teaching ethos, Peter says: "What I gave them was carte blanche to paint what they were interested in, instead of imposing ideas on them. Then I started bringing in magazines. If they were painting wrestlers, I could bring wrestling magazines in or whatever, and I could feed them information and encourage them. It was very good academic art teaching at Walthamstow. They were taught to draw well and they were very enthusiastic teachers, but the element that I added was opening a door for them."

Ian responded well to Peter's ideas and began merging his love of rock'n'roll, jazz and films, with his painting skills. Like Peter, he took to using lettering in his pictures, sometimes to form a background against which his subject would stand out. He also surrounded black and white images with bright colours and in one such creation, the faces of Laurel and Hardy were placed at the bottom of a seascape painting. But Ian had one very real preoccupation – women.

"The girls he painted were usually of a pin-up kind," says Peter. "Certainly in the RAF where I had been not very long before, there was this culture of pin-up girls painted on aeroplanes or you would do pin-up girls for the sergeants' mess or for the other men, so that was part of my background, but for me to say to the students, 'It's all right to do it' was a breakthrough I think."

Terry adds: "Peter's message was, 'Paint the things you like or that you are interested in,' and Peter was into rock'n'roll. Ian was into rock'n'roll, but he was also into dolly-birds, so he would do drawings and paintings of dolly-birds with knickers and titties. So he more or less followed that Pop Art philosophy and that came directly from Peter."

The Walthamstow artists were conscientious about their art and took their studies seriously. Although Ian now admits he was not very good at art initially, he says he "became good by dint of effort". And despite the late nights at jazz clubs and boozy sessions in The Bell, adjacent to the college, art remained his prime focus.

Laurie Lewis says he has never worked as hard as he did at Walthamstow and remembers it as an "incredibly productive" time. "We used to do a full day and then we would do an evening class, which meant hanging around for an hour, and this would go on until about 10pm," he says. "You would think that would be enough for normal people, but after we were thrown out of the building, we would climb back through a little window we had left open, pull down these World War Two blackout blinds and then work all night. There were a couple of guys who used to sleep in the forest because they had nowhere to live. One particular character used to spend his whole grant on the first day on artists materials and for the rest of the year he'd bum dinner tickets from the fashion department girls who were worried about their figures and never ate anything anyway, and that's how he lived."

Ian's four years hard grind at Walthamstow were richly rewarded when he was accepted on the painting course at the Royal College of Art. Essex County Council awarded him a grant for his three-year, post-graduate course and on October 2, 1963, he arrived 'team-handed' with members of the Walthamstow group, including his friends Stanford Steele, Joe Snowden and Bill West. Gaining admission to the RCA was no small achievement and Ian was proud that he had the chance to add his name to its prestigious roll call. One year after his arrival there, his mentor Peter Blake began teaching in the painting school and the two, who were firm friends at this stage, were reunited.

The RCA was founded in 1837 as a school of industrial design and later renamed the Central School of Practical Art. In 1863 it relocated to Exhibition Road, in Knightsbridge, south London, but it was not until 1896 that it was christened "The Royal College of Art" by Queen Victoria.

During the 20th century, it produced such renowned artists as Henry Moore and David Hockney.

While Ian was there, he was surrounded by talented painters, sculptors, photographers, film-makers and musicians. In common with his time at Walthamstow, Ian retained happy memories of this period. Many of these were associated with a large house at 144 Elgin Avenue, Maida Vale, which he initially shared with Terry Day, Alan Ritchie, Dave Parfitt and a sculpture student from Gants Hill in east London named Derek Woodham. Later, another acquaintance, Frank Dolphin, moved into the basement. While he was living at this archetypal student lodging house Ian first met another close friend – Russell Hardy. Russell was not an artist, had no connection with either Walthamstow or the RCA, and was about as different from Ian as anyone could be. But it was to be Russell with whom Ian would enjoy some of his most important musical collaborations.

The story of Ian Dury's rise to fame in one of Britain's most extraordinary bands is littered with little coincidences and connections. Ian's personal magnetism and his ability to connect with people from any background drew many engaging characters towards him and it was from these assorted friendships that Ian's motley 'rock family tree' grew. Back in 1960, Terry Day had strolled into The Plough in Ilford to see a jazz band and recognised Russell who was sitting in the bar. Russell was then working as a lab technician in the Radio and Television department of South East Essex Technical College in Barking, which Terry had attended, and had just started playing jazz music with his work colleague Terry Holman, who had a bass guitar. But the hippie technician with the wispy beard was excruciatingly shy and had never performed in public. Instead, he sought refuge in the college's empty hall where he could practise on the grand piano without people listening. When the effervescent drummer spotted him on his own at the jazz session, Russell reacted with typical embarrassment and self-consciousness.

Russell describes the occasion: "I was terribly shy in those days and never used to speak to anybody, I just used to go bright red if anybody spoke to me. Terry was one of those very with-it blokes and a sharp dresser, although he was an absolute wreck, and he used to pull chicks all the time. I was always slightly in awe of him because he had this terrific persona about him. He said to me, 'I didn't know you liked this sort of thing,' and I sort of looked at him and said, 'Well I've been drinking for quite a long time'. Later it occurred to me that he meant the jazz."

Russell was born in Huntingdon on September 9, 1941, and educated at Vanburgh Castle School and then Greenwich and Warren County Secondary School in Chadwell Heath, Essex. He had had some training in classical music and learned the rudiments of modern piano playing from a teacher in Ilford. But he had virtually no experience of playing with other people when he bumped into Terry in The Plough. The very thought of performing publicly would have been enough to give Russell nightmares. But Terry – with his laddish swagger and self-confidence – was the perfect antidote. Along with Russell's friend Terry Holman, they formed a jazz trio, rehearsing at the college, and eventually Terry Day persuaded the self-conscious pianist to take the plunge and entertain some of the students with their jazz standards. Stuck for places to rehearse, the trio eventually found the ideal solution.

Russell says: "All these pianos from around east London had been collected up and stored in the back of two or three cinemas. There were hundreds of grand pianos, all standing on their ends behind the screens, with these huge great speakers. We used to just go in on a weekend in the mornings before the cinema opened and that is really where I got my introduction to music."

Ian was not involved in these earlier sessions, but he and Russell struck up a close friendship after they met towards the start of Ian's spell at the RCA, forging an unlikely double-act. Ian was loud and unruly, yelling out song lyrics, swearing and leering at women, while Russell was painfully introverted and malleable. He was also Ian's unofficial chauffeur and would drive him and his friends around London and to parties. When Ian fell over in the street, Russell was there to pick him up and dust him down. Russell's docile nature seemed to bring out a manipulative side of Ian's character. But while Ian took advantage of the kindness of his latest 'helper', he in turn coaxed Russell out of his shell and opened him up to an exciting world which he would otherwise have missed.

"They cottoned on to me because I was easy-going and I had a car, which was the major item for Ian in those days," explains Russell. "I used to have a Mark I Ford Consul and if we were going along and Ian would see some nicely dressed girls walking down the street, he would wind down the window and gob all over them. I used to think, 'That's disgusting', but he was so funny. He was always a bit scruffy, very studentish. At parties, he would make an impression one way or another, either by doing a lot of talking or he would create a rumpus and then expect everyone to get him out of it. I used to have to carry him on my shoulders and if there were stairs I would give him a piggy-back upstairs. Ian was good fun, but I hated parties in those days.

"At some parties I was all right. But if there was a lot of people there I didn't know I would go in and then go out and sit in the car. I would wait for them all night and go to sleep. Then, at about two or three o'clock in the morning they would come out and say, 'Come on, wake up Russ, we're going home.' I was like a chauffeur. I never found Ian's disability a problem to deal with, because he always just got on with it and never made a big thing about it, although the horrible callipers he had to wear in those days were pretty ghastly. He always had nice girlfriends. He was one of the sort of blokes you wouldn't want to be near first thing in the morning, because he used to wake up like a bear with a sore head and I think his girlfriends got the brunt of that."

Mary Ritchie believes this "ruthless side" of Ian's psychological make-up was born out of his disability and that he had learned to manipulate people as a means of survival. His natural way with people and his sense of fun, meanwhile, meant that people went along with him and put up with his sometimes unreasonable demands.

"I remember once, Ian wanted to score some dope and he had taken us off into some pretty ghastly area and Russell was driving this black Zephyr full of people," says Mary. "It was a dodgy situation to be in and Ian went traipsing off down these steps. He wasn't the sort of chap you could allow to go on his own into a dodgy situation, so the others were obliged to go along with him and be his bodyguards. But he wouldn't think twice of getting anyone into situations like that. Ian just sort of expected that really, so there was always that slightly unattractive side to him. But it's the way he had to survive.

"I remember going to the laundrette once with Ian and he'd got this mass of disgusting washing, a lot of it being great big handkerchiefs, and it ended up with the ladies milling around helping Ian and doing it all for him. It was just like that, at the drop of a hat, and it was just very typical. He didn't know how to work the machines, he was dropping his disgusting washing all over the floor and they just rallied round, helping, and he was laughing and chatting to them. Obviously for him it was difficult, but it didn't seem to bother him and he just got on well with them."

Aside from Bill, Stan, Terry and Joe, all of whom he knew from Walthamstow, Ian had another close friend at the RCA – Geoff Rigden. The two had met at the entry examinations in the summer of 1963 and when the course began they carried on where they had left off. Geoff, a native of Taunton in Somerset, was bowled over by the "leery" types from east London and Essex who seemed to fill the college, and found it difficult to make out what they were saying. Ian, who had greeted him simply as 'Taunton' when the two met up again at the start of term, had an aura which Geoff found hard to ignore.

"My first recollection of Ian was as a rocker," says Geoff. "He had a leather jacket, which I probably envied. He looked kind of beaten. At the

Royal College, you couldn't help being fashion conscious because it was part of the era. American clothes were big and in those years there was only one place you could get them. It was a shop in Shaftesbury Avenue and as soon as people got their grant, they would dive down there and get an imported button-down collar shirt. Ian knew all about that sort of stuff and about Soho."

Just as Russell frequently found Ian's behaviour amusing, Geoff also noted the range of tricks he had up his sleeve to grab people's attention. "At lunch-time people would go off to the common room and because Ian couldn't get around, I used to hang about with him, and we would go down to the pub or to the V&A [Victoria and Albert Museum] canteen," says Geoff. "Ian used to get old pennies and he'd say, 'Oi, watch this,' and then flick one all the way down Exhibition Road. We used to stand and watch people wondering, 'What's that?' He used to embarrass me – I just thought, 'Oh 'streuth.' "

Ian revelled in stirring up situations and then standing back and watching from a safe distance. In the evenings, Ian, Terry, Alan and Geoff, often blagged their way into art exhibition openings where they could get free wine and champagne and such functions were perfect settings for Terry, an incorrigible 'ladies man', to turn on the charm. Ian, for his part, loved goading his friend into chatting up glamorous women. The results were hilarious.

Geoff describes one such incident: "Terry would say, 'Look at that bird over there' and Ian would say, 'Go on, Tel, go on.' One evening, Terry went over to this Asian girl and said, 'Excuse me, do you live in London?'

"Girl: 'No, I'm only staying here for two or three days.'

"Terry: 'Oh, are you really, where are you staying?'

"Girl: 'I'm staying at a nice hotel, The Savoy.'

"Terry: 'Oh, are you really? That would be in The Strand. Do you know London at all? I could show you around, you know?'

"Girl: 'Actually, I'm here with a friend who is showing me around.'

"Terry: 'Oh yeah. Your friend, now would it be a gentleman?'

"Girl: 'Yes.'

"Terry: 'Oh, is he?. Where is he?'

"She pointed to a corner and it was Marlon Brando.

"We all went, 'Oh Christ,' and Terry said, 'Oh that gentleman over there. Oh well, it was nice to meet you.' " Mortified, they beat a hasty retreat.

By the mid Sixties, popular music in Britain had undergone a metamorphosis. A new breed of groups had arrived on the scene, many of which had former art school students in their ranks. Their popularity coincided with the widespread use of LSD, cannabis and amphetamines. While American kids tripped out to Bob Dylan and the Velvet Underground, in the UK, The Beatles, The Rolling Stones, The Who and The Yardbirds burst onto the airwaves and into the national consciousness. Flower power, free love and Woodstock were on the horizon, and the nature of British popular culture was changing before people's eyes.

Through his art studies, Ian found himself rubbing shoulders with celebrities of the time, among them Charlie Watts, drummer with The Rolling Stones. Charlie's girlfriend Shirlie, whom he had met in 1962 at the first rehearsal of the Alexis Korner Band, had become friendly with Derek Woodham while studying at Hornsey Art College in north London. One year after joining the sculpture department at the RCA, Shirlie and Charlie became friendly with his flat-mates from Elgin Avenue, Ian and Terry.

Shirlie: "Ian was great, a lot of fun, and he certainly had some rough edges. He and Terry had come from Walthamstow Art School and were like real working-class boys. Charlie came to know them because he had always been more of a jazz musician than a rock'n'roller and he got pretty friendly with them, particularly Terry. We used to hang out together and we still saw them after Charlie and I got married in 1964 and left. Getting married got me thrown out of college, because the professor of sculpture ran a very tight ship and he didn't want girls there anyway. This was in the bad old days and he made sure he got rid of us as soon as he could. It was after that student power came into being."

By now, Terry had established himself as a free jazz drummer and was in close contact with the Rolling Stone. "I first met Charlie Watts coming out of one of the cinemas in Shaftesbury Avenue," says Terry. "Alan Ritchie and I had gone to the pictures that night and that's how we met Shirlie and Charlie. We all got on a bus, I paid his fare, and we went up to Baker Street where he had a flat. After that we just talked about drums and he became interested in the music I was making. By 1965, I was established musically and was working with The People Band and he was interested in that. I described the band to him and he said he would like to do a recording."

In 1968, Charlie produced *The People Band* album at Olympic Studios in Barnes, and Ian, Laurie and Geoff all dropped in to watch the sessions. A chameleon-like project, The People Band lived up to its name and the list of those who went through its ever-revolving door reads like a 'Who's Who'. Film director Mike Figgis of *Leaving Las Vegas* fame, Smiths' producer John Porter, and guitarist Chris Spedding were among the contributors. However, the self-titled album was to be the only recording made by the band which broke up shortly afterwards.

Among Terry's other acquaintances was the artist Ozzie Clark – as Russell Hardy discovered at a party one night. To Russell's enduring embarrassment, the encounter was a brief one. "I was terribly green in those days and didn't have much clue about people or anything, but I went to a party round at this house," says Russell. "I was never too much of a party-goer because I was too shy, but I had the car at the time and when I said I was going home, Terry said, 'Could you give Ozzie a lift?' It was one of those funny things, because Terry said, 'Look, he's gay, but he's perfectly harmless. He's a very nice bloke.' By this stage, Ozzie was standing by the car and I said, 'Okay, I'll give you a lift,' and he said, 'I won't be a minute, I'll just nip in and get my things.' Of course as soon as he did, I shot off up the road because I was totally freaked out that he was gay."

At the RCA, as in all other times in his life, scantily clad women featured prominently in Ian's art work. Friends describe him working on large thickly drawn pictures of girls in various states of undress which would virtually cover an entire wall of his spacious ground-floor bedroom at Elgin Avenue. 'Flo Diddley' – a picture which he submitted as part of his degree show – depicted a black girl with her knickers down, set against a tartan background, with a tartan frame. In 1964, Ian painted a 10ft by 8ft picture of Billy Fury for a youth club in Mornington Crescent. But his college thesis was not about sex or rock'n'roll – it was about the gangster, Al Capone.

In his interview with *Penthouse* magazine,[4] Ian gave a detailed insight into his long-held fascination with gangster films and violence. "I like James Cagney films when he's not going completely crackers. *Key Largo* is an incredible film. The forties American gangster films are my favourites. *Kiss Of Death* with Richard Widmark and Victor Mature. The first time I saw *The Wild One* just took my head apart. Marvin's incredible in that, he never blows it. Paul Newman's another one, *Somebody Up There Likes Me* is great. There's a knife fight on a roof with Steve McQueen. *The Magnificent Seven* is another incredible film. Tony Curtis is another one I really dig. *The Vikings* – fucking 'ell.

"I did a drawing of a wiped-out looking Mitchum in that movie *El Dorado* where he's a drunken sheriff. He's really pissed in it and he's wearin' this filthy old vest. In the drawing, I put this beautiful shiny horse lookin' over Mitchum's shoulder. I posted it to him and a couple of weeks later it comes back, signed, with this: 'Dear Ian, we'll have to shoot the horse.' "

Ian always had a girlfriend on the go, one of whom was Patricia Few. She was from London's east end and didn't attend the college. It is understood that she was from Plaistow, although it is not known whether she was the inspiration behind 'Plaistow Patricia'. She frequently accompanied him to jazz clubs and stayed with Ian at the bachelor pad at Elgin Avenue. But it was in his own art class that Ian would meet the girl he would go on to marry.

Betty Rathmell was a quiet and attractive woman from Caerleon, a village just outside Newport, in Gwent, South Wales. Born in Leamington Spa, Warwickshire, on August 12, 1942, exactly three months after Ian, Betty's parents Thomas and Lilian Rathmell were both artists. The couple also had two older girls, Celia and Miriam. With her strongly artistic family background, it was no surprise when Betty entered her local college in Newport to study painting and went on to win a place at the Royal College of Art.

Her Cheshire-born father Thomas had taught art at Liverpool College of Art and subsequently at the RCA. During the Second World War he had been based in Leamington Spa, working with the Industrial and Naval Camouflage Unit. In 1947, he and his family moved to south Wales, where he got a job teaching at Newport College of Art. His influence on the painting school was an extremely positive one. He succeeded in attracting a lot of talented artists to Newport which became renowned in Wales for its painting department during the post-war period. In recognition of his contribution, he was appointed vice-principal of the college.

Thomas Rathmell's own figurative paintings and occasional works of the local area put him on the map as a gifted artist in his own right. In 1969, he was commissioned by the Welsh Office to record the investiture of the Prince of Wales at Caernarfon Castle. His picture, measuring six feet by five, depicted the whole of the interior of the castle and captured the moment when the Queen held hands with Prince Charles. It was displayed in the conference room of the Welsh Office in Cardiff, although illness prevented Mr Rathmell from attending the unveiling ceremony on December 18, 1970, attended by the then Welsh Secretary Peter Thomas. His reputation as a painter in Wales brought him further portrait commissions from educational institutions and authorities and his work was exhibited in museums and galleries around South Wales. He died in 1990 at the age of 78.

Betty entered the RCA in the autumn of 1963. Her work, like that of her father, was largely figurative and very human, and her talents were recognised when she was awarded the David Murray Travelling Scholarship during her time there. Betty is thought to have arrived in London with her tall, dark-haired boyfriend Dave Parfitt, with whom she had studied in Newport. Towards the end of their time at college, however, Betty broke off their relationship and began seeing Ian.

Ian said:[1] "Betty was a very good painter, a much better painter than me.

She wasn't at all overt or trendy or anything like that. She was a proper painter, did it because she wanted to do it. She didn't do it to be wearing this hat or that hat, she was wonderful."

Betty and Ian graduated from the RCA on July 8, 1966, both with a 2:1 ARCA Diploma, and moved in together. The following year they were married at a registry office in Barnstaple, Devon. A reception was held afterwards at a large house in the nearby hamlet of Brockham, to where Ian's mother, his Aunt Betty and her children had moved from Upminster some years before. Ian's father and mother, his two aunts and his cousins were at the ceremony, along with Betty's parents and sisters. Surviving photographs of the occasion are said to show the couple and their families celebrating outside a local pub. Few of their college friends attended the wedding, but they do remember the Durys' first home together – Cara Lodge in the Bedford Park area of Chiswick in west London. At the turn of the century, the area had been an artistic community and the property – which Peter Blake found for them – was a purpose-built studio. It was an unusual and bohemian home in which a minstrel's gallery overlooked a spacious room which was divided up by screens. For the young newly-weds it was economical and perfectly suited their artistic endeavours. Around the same time their finances were helped when Ian took part-time work as an art teacher at Luton College of Further Technology.

Soon after they were married, however, in March 1968, Ian's life was devastated by the death of his father. William Dury, whose working-class roots Ian so admired, died suddenly aged 62. "He spent nine hours at Heathrow Airport in the rain, smoking too many fags, talking to the other chauffeurs, waiting for his boss to come back from Belgium, and he died that night of emphysema, in a little lonely bed-sit up in Victoria," Ian said in an interview with the *Daily Telegraph* in July 1998.[6]

"They took him to Caxton Hall Registry, you know, the morgue, and I had to identify his body. So there's my old man lying on this purple velvet slate with a lovely stained-glass window with this strange smile. I knew he didn't look quite right. I didn't realise until I cleared his room out that he hadn't got his teeth in. I went and knocked on the door of the bloke next door and I said, 'Did you know my dad?' I said, 'Would you mind . . . his shoes and his teeth? I can't handle it. I can't touch 'em.' He got rid of them. Everything else was all right. But I couldn't touch his fucking teeth."

Ian and Betty had little money of their own when William Dury died but with the £2,000 that he left them, they decided to start a family of their own. Ten months later, on January 4, 1969, Ian's daughter Jemima was born.

Fatherhood didn't impinge on Ian's socialising. He continued to go out with his male friends and the casual attitude which friends saw him adopting to his domestic responsibilities was to set the tone of his marriage to Betty.

Russell observes: "When Jemima was born things carried on as normal, we would still go out on the piss. Ian never actually let anything like that get in the way of what he wanted to do, if he had a bee in his bonnet about the direction he was going in. He liked all the nice things; he had a wife and a baby, but it never actually became his life. Most people settle down, but for Ian that was just one side of it and the direction he wanted to go in was a completely different thing. He would never let his marriage or anything like that interfere with what he was doing. Betty put up with an awful lot.

"I would go into the house, quite often with Terry Holman, and Ian, and Betty would be there and Jemima would be going to bed or had just woken up as we came in at some ungodly hour of the night. She would suddenly pop up out of her cot with this fantastic beam on her face. She was only a little tiddler in a jump suit – she was great."

Peter Blake, whose wife gave birth to a daughter named Liberty just six weeks before the birth of Jemima, was working as an illustrator and had painted the famous cover for The Beatles' 1967 album *Sergeant Pepper's Lonely Hearts Club Band*. In Ian's third year at the RCA, Peter had helped him pick up work as an illustrator with *London Life* magazine. The *Sunday Times* magazine had also published pencil drawings of Ian's, usually of celebrities such as Tony Bennett and Ella Fitzgerald, and Geoff Rigden occasionally accompanied him to newspaper's offices to deliver his work. One magazine feature about movie icons, entitled 'The Immortals', displayed 40 sketches by Ian (they misspelled his name 'Drury'). Among those he drew were Omar Sharif, Al Jolson, Rudolph Valentino, Errol Flynn and Buster Keaton. For a magazine article marking the 900th anniversary of the Battle of Hastings, Ian did drawings of its famous adversaries, Harold and William, against brightly coloured backgrounds. But Ian "didn't want to make a living doing that" and let it lapse. Like Ian, Geoff was also finding the financial rewards of his art studies paltry. He was living with his wife Pam near Olympia in Kensington and they also had a little daughter, Kate. Consequently, the college friends continued to spend time together.

"We would go down there for a meal and they would come to us once a week," says Geoff. "We didn't have any money, none of us had any money. I used to see Ian during the day and we used to hang out. He had a small billiard table – he always had a gimmick – and so we used to spend the day pissing about playing billiards. Both of us were still painting."

By now, Betty was working at The Paul Mellon Foundation, an academic institute for research into British art which was established by the celebrated American philanthropist. She worked as a picture researcher in the archive section of its offices in Bury Street, close to the British Museum. In 1970, the Foundation closed and was replaced by the Paul Mellon Centre for Studies in British Art which remains today in London's Bedford Square.

Geoff had written off to dozens of colleges without any luck, but eventually landed some teaching work. He had been doing some interior decorating at Kensington Market when it first opened and one of the carpenters working there suggested that Geoff write to Canterbury College of Art, where his son was a student. Geoff, a talented abstract artist, applied to the college and struck up an immediate rapport with Tom Watt, a straight-talking Scot who was then head of the painting department. Almost immediately upon his arrival at Canterbury, a conversation took place which would have lasting repercussions for Ian. ·

Geoff: "Tom Watt asked me if I could recommend anybody for part-time teaching and I said, 'Yeah, Ian Dury,' and from that he went to see Ian. I think he probably preferred Betty's work, but because of the sheer force of Ian's personality, or whatever, he recruited Ian, and that's when we went to the college regularly. We would both go down on the train together and Ian used to come and stay at our house the night before. We were both very diligent. Ian had to have his hair washed and Pam would do that for him. Our flat was a bit ramshackle and we had to set up some arrangement whereby he could turn out the light after he had read his book."

Ian's arrival in September 1970 made an indelible impression on students and fellow teachers alike. At 28, he was younger than most of the staff and his shambling appearance was more in keeping with the students than other members of the faculty. With his long and unkempt curly hair, his outlandish collection of baggy cardigans and his halting walk, he was an unmistakable figure around the college, located in the heart of the medieval city. His outspokenness and unfaltering enthusiasm for his subject also made him impossible to ignore.

Hamish Halls, who still teaches art history at the college, was struck by Ian's decidedly odd persona and suspected that he was playing up the laddish Cockney image which owed so little to his upbringing.

"I remember his walk which, of necessity, was a bit of a rolling gait, but I sometimes wondered if he accentuated it a bit," he observes. "There was this Essex lad theme in his songs and there was a sense in which he played that, because you tend to play the parts that you can play. Maybe, like

[Toulouse] Lautrec, he felt there was a bit of society in which he could be inconspicuous. Stuart Durrant [a lecturer] was once in Ian's studio and Ian was out making some coffee or something. The telephone rang and he answered the phone and a cultivated female voice asked to speak to Ian. I think he said, 'Hold on a minute, madam,' because she had that kind of voice. 'Who shall I say wants to speak to him?' and the answer was, 'His mother.' He then wondered what was Ian's real background and who was this very refined-sounding woman claiming to be his mother?

"I came to the college as an art historian and art history had been imposed almost by act of Parliament. The new diploma of art and design had to have 20 per cent of art history and complementary studies. If you were running a very successful painting or sculpture course and you were told to get rid of 20 per cent of it to make way for something else, it caused resentment simply because it removed people's budgets and handed them over to other people. There was also a distrust in those days between the perceived intellectuals and those artists who didn't feel the need to talk about it. Some people believed that an artist was a person with a belly full of beer and some good gestures and felt that if you had to start philosophising about it, then you were lost. Certainly, there was a lot of truth in that. There was this stand-off at the highest levels and when assessment time came around you had two external assessors at daggers drawn.

"At lunch-time there were all these pubs around the old building and every group went to a different one, even the students went to different cafes. The graphic designers were clean and went to the Cherry Pie Cafe and the fine artists went in their paint-splattered clothes to the coffee lounge. The college had no real common room then, but a little later we acquired a coffee room, by renting some medieval building which became the canteen for those who didn't mind a little bit of squalor and didn't want to go to the cafes, and they used to meet in there. Ian would sway up to you with his leg irons very much on show and give you this friendly tap, which sent you reeling across the room, accompanied by, 'Oi Oi'. You didn't quite know how to answer it and I would say, 'Oh hi Ian, come and have a cup of tea'. He was always friendly, but there was this continuing kind of un-spoken joke going on. I realised, and it was only confirmed later when his songs became popular, that he had a lot of knowledge and a lot of wit and it was such a waste that we didn't get him in and involve him in the college more."

During his two years teaching at Canterbury, Ian occasionally sat in on interviews, along with Tom Watt, for places on the college's foundation art course. Following some personnel changes at the college, there had been a strong tendency to recruit students from the north of England and

Scotland for this course and relatively few students from Canterbury's art history department were accepted. This resulted in some antagonism between tutors at the college.

Hamish: "People who were interviewed here sometimes had Ian Dury and they would ask me, 'Who is this bloke Ian?' and I would say 'Ian Dury, why?' They would say, 'Well he just sat there chewing gum looking at me and finally the chairman of the selection panel said, 'Anything you want to ask, Ian?' and he would go on looking at you and then just say 'No.' Somebody else in the same situation had come from St Albans and the chairman asked if Ian had any questions.

"Ian: 'Where are you from then?'

"Student: 'St Albans.'

"Ian: 'Get much aggro that way?'

"Student: 'No.'

"Ian: 'Great, great.'

"That was it. Those were his questions. Maybe he thought it was just a complete waste of time or he was subtly seeing how this person would react to the unexpected. I think the established echelons of the college thought Ian was a bit of a liability, but he is somebody who is remembered with an affection and respect which goes beyond the fact that he became famous."

Kate Young, who taught at Canterbury at this time and still lectures there in history of art and cultural studies, remembers the marathon drinking sessions for which the painting department was legendary. Ian was invariably in a drunken stupor by the end of the afternoon and had to be poured onto the train to go home.

"I used to see other teachers dragging Ian along on the train station like a sack of potatoes," she remembers. "His foot would be hanging out behind him and he would be dragging it along. The way they did it was very pragmatic and purposeful, but very unceremonious. This was often in the early evening, if they had got into the bar at lunch-time and stayed drinking in the afternoon. I don't think much teaching got done.

"Ian wasn't famous then, but he did have a reputation and people would take notice of him. He was certainly special, even then. In those days, fine art departments were like they are in novels. Lots of young tutors came down from London. The head of fine art used to keep all his paper work in his fridge, usually with a decayed cheese sandwich and a bottle of scotch on the desk. This was the person who employed Ian, so with that sort of ethos he fitted in. The fact that tutors drank all afternoon didn't really matter.

"I think they all abdicated any sort of adult responsibility when they shut their front doors and set off on the train to come down to Canterbury.

They were all very laddish and did a lot of drinking and other things and were very much in with the students. This was in the days before political correctness and all these rules governing relations with students and all the paper work that binds us now. It didn't exist then so it was much freer. It was like a community of artists, rather than a strict distinction between tutors and students."

Although they were part-timers and heavy drinkers, Geoff and Ian were nevertheless extremely conscientious about their teaching responsibilities at Canterbury and came to be seen as father figures by some of their charges. Such was his commitment to the course that Geoff moved his family to the village of Woolage Green, eight miles out of the city on the old Roman Road. He would routinely call to the homes of his bleary-eyed and often hung-over students in order to get them to come to his classes. Some mornings he would also have to wake Ian, who stayed with him in order to avoid an early morning train journey to Canterbury. But although a popular double-act, their contrasting painting styles led to some lively clashes in the college studios. Ian's work was largely illustrative, while Geoff favoured abstract painting and their respective classes often found themselves embroiled in heated debates.

Paul Tonkin was one of Ian's students at the time. "Ian was very popular because he told funny stories and was like one of the lads and Geoff Rigden was even more so and so they made a good team really," he recalls. "Ian's paintings were very proficient, painstaking copies of photographs, portraits of people; photographs he had taken himself and carefully copied using water colours. From my point of view, they were too precise and mechanical, although the results were good. What Ian and I were doing was absolutely poles apart, but he had an instinct for recognising something that had your personality in it. One day we were having a general discussion and it became a stand-off with Ian on one side and Geoff Rigden on the other. There was this quite heavy debate over 'What is the point of abstract art?' "

Germaine Dolan also found herself under Ian's tutelage in her first year at Canterbury and she was impressed by the natural charm with which he won people over, including the more traditional, conservative lecturers. She also remembers Ian's preoccupation with drawing naked women and says her sister Genevieve posed for him on a couple of occasions.

"What Ian lacks in physical mobility he makes up for with one of the greatest mouths around," says Germaine. "He is very good at charming everybody, however disparate they are, because I think he has developed an incredible skill in sussing people out because it's his main way of getting around. He had some fairly gruesome experiences in his youth, going to all these weird schools and I think he has learned from those experiences how to get through difficult times. And he is very charming and very clever and erudite in lots of ways.

"He has always allowed millions of people into his dressing room and I think he likes to meet the public; they are his material, that's where he gets his ideas. He always used to say that everything you do is for somebody, every song you write, every painting you do, and I think there is a lot of truth in that. It is part of your emotional life as well as your artistic or poetic life and that's why you do it really. Ian does get intensely involved with people and that is why he has such volatile relationships. He does tell the truth quite a lot which is often hard to take."

Despite the obvious rapport he had built up with his students and his flair for painting, Ian was starting to be pulled in a very different direction. Rock'n'roll had been a source of stimulation for Ian since he was at school. Gene Vincent & The Blue Caps had held a special place in his affections ever since he had first heard gems like 'Blue Jean Bop', 'Be-Bop-A-Lula' and 'Woman Love' as a teenager. Back then, the glamour of American singers such as Vincent and Elvis Presley seemed a million miles away from his caravan in suburban Upminster. But his friendship with musicians like Terry and Russell and his flamboyant personality always kept alive the possibility that he too might play in a rock'n'roll band. Indeed, before he ever taught at Canterbury, Ian had come up with a name for his very own group.

It had come to him one day as he and Russell cruised through Kilburn towards Cricklewood in north west London in the pianist's Mark I Ford Consul. Pubs, bookies, take-aways and old-fashioned Irish dance halls, such as The Galtymore, lined the main drag that led, eventually, to Staples Corner and the beginning of the M1 motorway to the north. It was an ever-evolving thoroughfare inhabited by thousands of Irish immigrants lured by the promise of construction work and big boozers full of familiar faces and accents in which to spend their money and exercise their fists on Saturday nights. Although he had no specific reason to visit Kilburn, Ian often gazed on its passing parade during spins around London with Russell. Thanks to him, this prosaic London address would soon be springing up on bill-posters and in the trend-setting pages of the music press. Russell says: "Me and Ian used to go up to Kilburn a lot in the car and he just came out with it one day. He said: 'I've thought of a great name for the band. What about Kilburn & The High Roads?' "

4

PLAYING THE FOOL
IN A SIX-PIECE BAND

"We thought that we would make a couple of records, get rich, buy houses in the country and paint. That was the master plan and it is incredible to think that we actually believed that."

– Humphrey Ocean

As the eventful Sixties came to an end, popular music was at a crossroads. The Beatles were no more, the Stones were tax-exiled in France and major acts like The Who, Pink Floyd and Led Zeppelin were becoming increasingly detached from their audience. The fan unity that had been established by The Beatles and their contemporaries was breaking down as rock and pop subdivided into styles and modus operandi. While The Faces were raucous and David Bowie was refined, middle-of-the-road groups like The Carpenters, The New Seekers and Dawn, and singers like Neil Diamond, set a more mellow tone. Number one hits in the early months of 1970 included such sentimental offerings as 'Wand'rin Star' by Lee Marvin, 'All Kinds Of Everything' by Dana and 'Bridge Over Troubled Water' by Simon & Garfunkel. Meanwhile, progressive rock, its grandiose pretensions epitomised by Emerson, Lake & Palmer, was looming ominously on the horizon.

Whatever was happening in the mainstream – as reported in the columns of *Melody Maker* – was of scant interest to Ian Dury. Jazz and rock'n'roll records were still on Ian's turntable and his vision of performing in his own rock'n'roll band was closer to being realised. Together with his old Royal Grammar School friend Ed Speight, Ian had been encouraging Russell to try out rock'n'roll numbers on the piano. Russell lacked Ian's insatiable appetite for rock'n'roll, but he hesitantly agreed to practise some of the songs which Ian hollered out. In the upstairs bedroom of Alan Ritchie's council house in Eastern Avenue, Newbury Park, in Essex, where Russell was lodging at the time, the three got together and hammered out a bizarre collection of Fifties songs. And so began one of Britain's oddest musical troupes.

Russell: "Ian wrote to someone like Chappell Music and got a load of peculiar song sheets with things like 'The Cat Came Back' which we were mucking about with. Ted Speight was a scientist at the time, but he could read music and he was a semi-professional musician. He had been having guitar lessons for years and could read music like a book. Ian would ask, 'What's this song Ted?' and Ted would strum out the melody. I will never forget, Ian came up to me one day, quite out of the blue, and said, 'Here Russ, how would you like to be a millionaire?' and I said, 'Well, I wouldn't mind, why?' and Ian said, 'Well, I'm going to form this rock band and we are going to become millionaires.' I just said 'Oh really, right.'

"Ian loved jazz, but the thing he always really liked more than anything else was rock'n'roll. He liked jazz and he listened to jazz, but the thing he always went on about was Eddie Cochran and people like that. Whenever we were out in the car, he would be sitting there thumping out a rock'n'roll song and I think that's why he wanted to become a rock'n'roll singer. He really wanted to be another Eddie Cochran. I said to him, 'But Ian, I can't play rock'n'roll' and Ian just said 'Oh, that don't matter, you'll soon pick it up.' I didn't really pick it up. We got Ted Speight round and I went through the motions of doing it and it sounded all right, but I knew I hadn't got the feel for it and it took me years and years of playing it to get it right."

In the winter of 1970, as Ian, Ed and Russell continued to resurrect Fifties juke-box favourites and musical curiosities from their youth, it was decided to commandeer some experienced jazz musicians to rehearse the songs properly. Terry Day had already shown his talent for free-form jazz percussion, while saxophonist George Khan had also played with The People Band, as well as with such blues legends as Ben E. King and Screaming Jay Hawkins. The line-up was completed by Charlie Hart, a softly spoken and extremely accomplished bassist who had played with both Terry and George in The People Band and The Battered Ornaments respectively. Born into a well-to-do family in Oxford, Charlie had studied economics at Kings College in Cambridge before abandoning academia for music. He had seen Ian around, knew he was not a musician, and was initially sceptical about his plans to form his own band.

Charlie remembers: "Everybody was saying to me, 'This guy Ian, he's great', and I had met Ian before, ligging around at the 100 Club, a sort of jazz groupie. My first impression when I met him was, 'Oh, I'd better give him a lift home because he can't walk properly,' and when he asked me to play, I thought, 'This is never going anywhere, but I'll do it.' "

George Khan was then managing the Jubilee rehearsal studios in Covent Garden, and in November 1970, armed with a decidedly offbeat collection of songs, the group went there to practise. The day of the first rehearsal coincided with the Lord Mayor's Show and Russell was late after being held up in traffic, by which time the saxophonist had fallen asleep. When they started playing, this embryonic Kilburns line-up rattled out rock'n' roll numbers including Freddie Cannon's 'Tallahassee Lassie', 'The Walk' by Jimmy McCracklin, 'Lucille' by Little Richard, 'Twenty Flight Rock' by Eddie Cochran, and 'I'm In Love Again' and 'I'm Walking' by Fats Domino. Anyone within earshot of this cacophonous stomp down memory lane would have been aghast. As well as the rock'n'roll tunes of Ian's childhood, their choice of covers included Alma Cogan's whimsical 1955 hit 'Twenty Tiny Fingers' and 'The Naughty Lady Of Shady Lane', a song which she had recorded, but which was a Top Ten hit for both The Ames Brothers and Dean Martin in the same year. Ian's fascination with the bizarre also led them to play 'A Ballad Of Davy Crockett', the novelty song which Russell had taught Ian on a 'pixie-phone' (a toy xylophone).

The rehearsals in Covent Garden didn't last, however. The band soon adjourned to Alan Ritchie's house where they jammed on Sunday afternoons and by Christmas the sessions had been abandoned. Before ever making it to a public stage, this earliest incarnation of Kilburn & The High Roads had drifted apart. But while it was clear that Ian Dury was no conventional singer, he had got his first taste of being a rock'n'roller. He could also sense that for all his musical limitations, he had the personality and sheer front to entertain people. With British pop music at a low point, Ian knew he could offer something better.

Ed Speight: "It never really got past me and Russell trying to get Ian around to the idea of relative pitch, in terms of high and low. It was quite heavy weather and quite hard going. It's odd because when he used to sing in a kind of Mario Lanza voice, which he quite often did, he used to sing every note perfectly in tune. When Ian sang in his own voice, that's when the relative sense of high and low was not there. Ian said himself: 'If I can do it and front a rock'n'roll band then surely anyone can do it and jazz players should find it easy to play rock'n'roll'."

The rehearsals lasted long enough for Russell to make a telling observation. "Musically it was really interesting. It was a bit untogether, but it was a fantastic line-up, because they were all really good musicians and it just worked somehow. But it wouldn't have worked in the end, because they were all too much up their own arses and thought so much of themselves. There were too many different types of people with their own various ideas and Ian wouldn't have been in charge of it. That was the overriding factor, that Ian wouldn't have been able to control it."

Despite this brief flirtation with rock'n'roll, Ian was still teaching art and simply saw the band as a way of "subsidising my painting activities".

Certainly he threw himself into his teaching at Canterbury and he showed both an ability to connect with his students and a canny eye for unorthodox people; those who socialised with him in the pubs and cafes in the town were guaranteed a highly entertaining time. In the spring of 1971, Kilburn & The High Roads was still merely a dream in the mind of its instigator. Charlie Hart and Terry Day were still playing odd jazz gigs while George Khan and Ed Speight had drifted away from the picture. But by the autumn, Ian and Russell had begun to lay the foundations on which a revitalised Kilburns line-up could be built. One day, the 'Pied Piper' of Canterbury led a motley crew of musicians into a vacant college room and kick-started the group.

Keith Lucas, then aged 21 and a student of Geoff Rigden, had already gained some experience as a guitarist. Born in Gosport, Hampshire, on May 6, 1950, he was raised in Cornwall, and had attended Truro Secondary School until his family moved to Malta, where his father was stationed with the RAF. He was 16 when he began his musical apprenticeship with the 'Pentagon Beat Group' while attending school in Malta and he also played sporadically with The Graduates. On his return to England, he studied for one year at Salisbury Art School and then enrolled at Canterbury College of Art where he joined the ridiculously named local band Frosty Jodhpur. Long-haired and with a penchant for multi-coloured shirts and trousers, Keith was an eye-catching and valuable asset for Ian's group. His musical influences were wide ranging, taking in Toots & The Maytals, Sly Stone and Fats Domino, and like many students he enjoyed playing the Rolling Stones and other classic rock riffs. During rehearsals in the college and the nearby university, Keith would career maniacally around the room, swinging his guitar dangerously close to microphone stands and other band members. Even better for Ian, Keith was a great guitarist, although any formal training had amounted to little more than some tuition from Ed Speight.

Chris Lucas, who was in the second year of his studies and another student of Geoff Rigden's, was also invited into the fold. No relation to the guitarist, he shared a house with Keith and other students in Northgate, one of the medieval areas of Canterbury. Their lodgings were directly opposite Slick Dicks, a health food restaurant run by Canterbury University law student Ian Smith where musicians and artists congregated, and a pub called The Jolly Sailor. Chris had played drums for about a year, although his musical influence amounted to little more than half-baked impressions of Charlie Watts. But Ian and Chris shared something much greater than an interest in music. They had both had polio.

"The first time I met Ian was hilarious," Chris remembers. "It was his first day at Canterbury and I had been there a year already. The old art school was a purpose-built studio with skylights and these long corridors. I came around the corner of one of these corridors and Ian was at the other end and we walked towards each other. He was limping this way and I was limping that way and before we reached each other we were both in hysterics. It was an instant thing because we were the only two gimps at the art school and from that moment on we were mates."

Discarding the old jazzers with whom he had experimented a year earlier, Ian recruited young Canterbury students who would let him take the reins. "Ian likes being in control," says Chris Lucas. "He was like that as an art lecturer as well as a rock'n'roller, but with the first band it wouldn't have been like that because they were all serious musicians who had been playing for ten years already and they knew what they were doing. They weren't going to listen to Ian who had never been in a band and had never played music. I think it was part of Ian's strategy that once that hadn't worked he was going to get a bunch of young guys in and he would be able to call the shots. I think that's how it was really.

"When the band first started, me, Keith and Ian Smith all lived in the same house and we had a drum kit, bass guitar and a load of amps and so when Ian was in Canterbury for three days in a row, he would stay at our place. We would stay up all night listening to music and smoking dope and Ian would crash out on the sofa."

Humphrey Butler-Bowden was one of Ian's painting students. Polite, well-spoken and very tall, with long hair, Humphrey was busy working for his degree, painting pictures which he knew would be liked by the establishment in art colleges. But secretly he was working towards becoming a successful portrait and figurative artist, painting individualistic pictures of Cadillacs and people. Humphrey's musical ability was virtually nonexistent, but he had recently bought a green Gretch acoustic guitar from a shop in Canterbury. Aware of the striking visual aspect he would bring to the band – and his new instrument – Ian told him he wanted him in the group. He agreed and joined as rhythm guitarist.

Humphrey Ocean, as he was later christened, describes the first time he encountered Ian: "He walked in on the Wednesday when we had only been at Canterbury for two days. There were various bods teaching there who all seemed older than God to us, but then Ian walked in and he was a bit more our age. He was very distinctive looking because of his 'Mrs Kelly' cardigan. Ian had taught at Luton and had a student called Kelly, whose mum made these amazing Fair Isle cardigans using any bits of Day-Glo coloured wool – they were fantastic things.

"I just remember thinking, I want to know more about him. He walked around and he said later that he spotted me over in the corner because I looked like Robin Hood, with long hair and tight green jeans. Everyone else was wearing flares and I used to have ice-blue jeans because they were what the rockers wore in the Sixties. I also think Ian was interested in me because I was one of the few people there who was not doing American abstract expressionist art. They were all enthralled by America and were doing these big colour field paintings and looking at Rothko and Maurice Lewis. Of course, that was very much part of my training, but I was swimming the other way and painting recognisable people and things."

Coincidentally, Humphrey had started a painting of Gene Vincent, who was one of his heroes, although he hadn't mentioned this to Ian. But the pair would soon have a reason to talk about the inspirational rocker. Gene Vincent died suddenly on October 12, 1971, at the age of 36, and it was this tragic news that motivated Ian to re-ignite the band which had sputtered to a halt the previous winter. A few weeks after the death of his hero, Ian approached Alan Upwood, the social secretary at Canterbury Art College and said that if he wanted "a good assessment" he should put Ian's band on the bill for the Christmas dance. Sensibly, he agreed, and Kilburn & The High Roads were booked to appear with Skin Alley & The Magic Rock Band. In the meantime, the group was offered another gig and as a consequence it was on December 5, 1971, at Croydon School of Art in south east London that Kilburn & The High Roads played their first gig. That night they opened up for another bunch of oddballs, Thunderclap Newman, who had lately enjoyed a number one hit with the Pete Townshend produced 'Something In The Air'. Those who took to the stage with Ian Dury for his first public rock'n'roll performance were Chris Lucas (drums), Keith Lucas (lead guitar), Humphrey Ocean (rhythm guitar), Ian Smith (bass), and Russell Hardy (piano). Stepping into the breach as the group's first roadie was art student Colin Thomas alias 'Larry Lilacs'.

"The gig was on the third floor and we had to carry a piano up the stairs. Ian had four other guys carry the piano up and down the stairs while he sat in the dressing room putting on his make-up," says Chris.

The stress of the group's first public performance weighed heavily on Russell Hardy, who had never played a rock'n'roll gig before, although Thunderclap Newman made his evening by asking if he could borrow his piano.

Russell says: "I will never forget the feeling of sheer terror of having to go up on stage – it really was the most frightening thing I have ever done. I just wanted to be anywhere but in that place. It had never really bothered

Keith, but I had been so introverted and so critical about my own playing, and I always thought it was a load of shit. But it went down a storm; it was actually amazing."

About a week later, the band were paid £40 to open the end-of-term Christmas party at Canterbury. Here, their ranks were swelled by Geoff Rigden on harmonica, Paul Tonkin on out-of-tune violin, and Tony Edwards on bongos.

"I suspect it was quite awful because in those days we were doing a lot of Fifties covers and Fats Domino and Gene Vincent songs – old rock," says Chris. "It was badly played and Ian was the worst vocalist you had ever heard in your life. He couldn't sing, he couldn't hold a note, he couldn't come in on a beat, he was just a crap vocalist really. But he had something and people liked it."

Humphrey says of the occasion: "Musically, it was probably appalling, but there is no doubt about it that spiritually it was the point of no return – something had happened. We thought that we would make a couple of records, get rich, buy houses in the country and paint. That was the master plan and it is incredible to think that we actually believed that."

By this time, Ian, Betty and their baby daughter Jemima, had long since left their flat in Chiswick. Their new home was an old vicarage in Wingrave, a quaint and very conservative village in Buckinghamshire. The dilapidated rectory had been found for them by Ian's aunt Molly, who lived nearby, and the monthly rent was low enough even for a struggling artist with a family. An isolated building, with draughty rooms and its own land, it was in dire need of refurbishment and the initial months were spent decorating the house and tidying the overrun garden, where Ian unearthed piles of empty VP sherry bottles, presumably a legacy from an earlier clerical occupant. It was a world away from the London flats they were accustomed to and it was an idyllic setting to paint and raise a family. It was also an attractive retreat and rehearsal space for the Kilburns, their ever-changing girlfriends and college friends. Russell, who had been renting a room at Alan Ritchie's flat in Maida Vale, moved to Wingrave at Ian's invitation and set up a piano in his bedroom. He also helped to transform the front room into a semi-sound-proofed rehearsal room, by sticking egg boxes and mattresses to the walls and door. Assuming his usual subservient role, Russell was also kept busy collecting timber, stocking the fire and driving Ian around.

It was at Wingrave on December 18, 1971, that Betty gave birth to the couple's second child, Baxter. While a midwife assisted with the birth in the couple's upstairs bedroom, astonishingly the group crashed about in rehearsal below. Ian broke off briefly from the session to see his wife and rushed back into the room announcing, 'It's a boy, it's a boy'. The band then resumed where they had left off.

Russell recalls: "About half an hour after she had Baxter, Betty actually came downstairs on her own and told us to shut up because she couldn't get any sleep. We were mortified really because we hadn't given it a second thought."

With Russell permanently on hand, Ian began writing songs in earnest. He spent hour upon hour in his room scribbling out lyrics on pieces of paper, emerging to show them to his in-house composer. It was in this rural, tranquil setting that Ian put his urban experiences into perspective and onto paper.

"The way that Ian wrote things, some of the lyrics you could associate with some kind of feeling and other ones like 'Upminster Kid' were like a story," says Russell. "But the way he had written that fitted a sort of 12-bar blues type of thing. At that time I didn't actually realise it was that sort of thing because I didn't know much about rock'n'roll, I was a jazzer, which is a completely different emphasis. That's probably why they came out in such a quirky manner. Some songs I just used to find incredibly funny."

At weekends, the vicarage was invaded. The Kilburns would catch the train from Canterbury and tumble into the station at Wingrave, attracting stares of disbelief from the conservative, tweed-clad villagers. Invariably, after rehearsals, the troupe would be spotted trundling around Wingrave in whatever car Russell had at the time, usually destined for the local pub.

Chris: "Everyone else in the village was a retired colonel or post-mistress. This band of freaks would turn up every Friday, ramble around the village on Sunday afternoons and go to the pub and order green Char-treuse because somebody had read that Charlie Parker drank green Chartreuse."

Canterbury student Germaine Dolan and her sister Genevieve had danced frenetically on stage during the band's inaugural gig at Croydon and a handful of subsequent shows at the college in home-made costumes. They too had come under the spell of the charismatic Canterbury lecturer and had been christened 'The Roadettes'. Their performances inspired Ian to write one of the group's earliest songs 'The Roadette Song' ("Action's very bad but her friction's double rich/Brazen little huzzy, rock'n'rollin' bitch/When it comes to business, she take off like a jet/Rockin's her voca-tion, she's a very high roadette").

"Ian was always very dressy and he had his own exact ideas about what he was going to wear," says Germaine. "He wrote the word 'Roadette' in a sort of slanting script which I cut out and sewed on to these matching vests and I think we had little scarves around our necks. The dancing was completely frantic, we used to be totally wiped out and in the end we decided it was too hard."

Ian later insisted that he was not seeking fame as a singer at that time, but it was clear that the Kilburns was becoming a semi-serious endeavour and that there would be only one person at the helm. Ian constantly tinkered with the group's line-up and could be ruthless towards those who failed to meet his exacting standards or simply didn't fit in with the definitive picture which existed in his mind. Ian Smith lasted a month before being fired by Ian (a short spell even by Kilburns' standards) and replaced by Charlie Hart, unquestionably a more proficient bass player. Terry Day, who had given Chris Lucas drum lessons, returned to the fold in May 1972 to usurp his pupil. In typical fashion, however, no one protested at his dismissal or tried to save Chris's place in the group, including Chris's flat-mate Keith. Ian called the shots and no one dared challenge his authority.

Chris: "There was a crucial rehearsal one weekend at Wingrave and we had a couple of gigs coming up. I had this new girlfriend who I was smitten with and I went to London on my way to Wingrave, met up with this girl and never got out of London. On Monday, Ian sacked me. He said, 'It's completely unprofessional – we're never going to get anywhere if you don't come to the fucking rehearsals.' And what was really galling was that Ian decided that's how it was and nobody said, 'No, you can't throw Chris out.' It was my Thames van that was driving the band around, but he had made up his mind and that was it.

"I was a pretty basic rock'n'roll drummer, whacking the snare drum. But what led to my demise was a personal thing with Ian, rather than my drumming. I had polio at a similar time to Ian and I was always quite confrontational with Ian. I had learned to manipulate people in a particular way to do things that I couldn't do and because Ian was more afflicted than me, he had become a fucking master manipulator of people. I could see it all the time before other guys in the band, he was an emotional blackmailer. He would get to you – he would get to your weak point.

"Russell was Ian's stooge. Even before Ian was a star, he had gofers and minders, years before he needed them. When we met, Russell was his number one man. He drove him around and he picked up the band. At Wingrave, Russell chopped the firewood, he kept the fire going, fixed anything that went wrong with the house and Ian swanned around like Lord Muck. Russell was shy and withdrawn, so Ian could get him to do stuff. Somehow, Ian could get him to write the kind of song that Ian felt he could do. With me, he couldn't do that, because I would say, 'Ian, don't come that with me,' and Ian thought, 'Fuck it, I don't need this.' "

Shortly after Chris's departure, a drifting and extraordinarily volatile figure emerged on the scene. He was Davey Payne. Born in Willesden, north west London, on August 11, 1944, he attended White Hart Lane Junior School, Tottenham, and then Pathfields Secondary Modern in Clacton-On-Sea, Essex. He first played his saxophone publicly when, as a 15-year-old, he entertained people at the Shangri-La Caravan Camp in Clacton with his rendition of 'I'm Forever Blowing Bubbles'. After moving from Clacton to London, he began taking lessons, going to jazz clubs and listening to John Coltrane, Ornette Coleman, Chico Hamilton and Fred Katz. After giving up the sax for a while, he began playing soprano sax at mixed media events in the late Sixties at Middle Earth. He was eventually drawn into The People Band, with whom he moved to Holland, and first met Ian when he returned to London in 1970. "He thought I was a junkie. I thought he was an idiot," Davey remarked in Pete Frame's *Rock Family Tree* of Ian Dury & The Blockheads. Davey then adjourned again to Holland and it was on a return trip to England that he caught the Kilburns doing an all too infrequent gig in Canning Town with The People Band.

Davey recalls his initial introduction to Ian: "There was this free-form jazz group with Ian Dury who was doing Little Richard numbers like 'Tutti Frutti' and a few originals. Ian said to me, 'Why don't you join Kilburn & The High Roads?' and so I did. I didn't really know what blues was, but I was speaking to Mike Figgis, a trumpet player in The People Band, and he said, 'Oh it's just a root fourth and fifth.' I knew scales, so I worked out a few blues keys and mixed it with free-form jazz and Keith Lucas was saying, 'Yeah, great man, Frank Zappa.' "

Davey had a violent temper and could fly off the handle at any given moment. But although this put the band members on their guard, it gave the group's live shows an exciting edge. Although no one knew it then, his crazed saxophone solos would play a central part in the music of Ian Dury for more than 25 years.

Charlie: "When Davey came into the Kilburns, he was a brilliant player, but he was completely unschooled and the idea of having a rock group with somebody like that in it was pretty revolutionary and brilliant. For wild, off-the-wall creativity, Davey was great. He was actually the foil on stage to Ian."

During the spring and summer of 1972 gigs were thin on the ground. Among the handful of bookings the Kilburns did receive were Medway Art College, Luton Airport Social Club and Wing Youth Club, a few miles from the vicarage, where the audience consisted of farmers and other curious villagers. The group also played at a party at St Anne's College in Oxford, where Charlie Hart's mother was a don.

"Ian had a few drinks and about half-way through playing 'Johnny B.

Goode' he passed out and collapsed in a heap on the floor," says Charlie. "We all carried on, as one does, and waited until someone revived him. Then somebody pulled him up from the floor and stuck his leg back together. Ian shook himself and said 'What song is this?' Somebody said, 'It's Johnny B. Goode,' and he just grabbed the mike and carried on."

But if anyone else doubted whether this shambolic ensemble would ever make it, Ian remained focused. Charlie and other band members could only admire his unflinching belief that fame was just around the corner.

"When we used to rehearse in Wingrave, we had hardly done any gigs at all. The band was pretty chaotic musically, and with hindsight, it seemed a pretty long shot really," comments Charlie. "We were a chaotic rock'n'roll band, playing this strange stuff with a singer who couldn't sing. I remember saying to Ian, 'Look, it's about time you learned the notes of the scale', but there was no chance. But even at this early stage there was an earnest discussion in the kitchen at about two o'clock in the morning about how we were going to divide up the first million pounds of publishing money which was going to arrive. I remember thinking at the time, 'This is ridiculous.' In retrospect, I can see that if you can visualise the thing you are aspiring to, then you can get there."

In an attempt to secure more live shows, Ian and a number of band members took off to Holland in a Morris Traveller and descended on booking agencies. The People Band had targeted Holland in the late Sixties and found gigs in abundance, but the Kilburns' excursion was less fruitful. Humphrey's Grundig tape-recorder failed to work properly when it was plugged in at offices around Amsterdam, causing the tapes to play at half speed, and, not surprisingly the bookings didn't come. When they got back, things got worse. Humphrey contracted viral meningitis, the consequence, he believes, of staying in damp houses and squats on the Amsterdam trip, and his illness prompted yet another schism in the fragile ensemble.

"When we came back, I was in hospital and Ian actually got very alarmed about that and felt responsible for me," says Humphrey. "His way of showing that he cared was to fire me, although he did it in the nicest possible way. He wrote me a very nice letter suggesting that I should pursue my studies and finish my last year at Canterbury, and so I was out."

As the Romany party which was the Kilburns worked its way towards London at the end of 1972, the airwaves were shuddering to the rock anthems of Slade, The Sweet, Mud, Mott The Hoople and Gary Glitter. In direct contrast to the Kilburns' 'War On Want' wardrobe, these glam bands shared a garish uniformity, dressed in ankle-twisting boots, brightly coloured flares and make-up. Back-stage dressing rooms looked more like theatrical costume departments and record company executives were excitedly pouring cash into this outlandish fashion parade. But in pubs around north London, a new movement was being born which was the antithesis of glam rock. Here, beneath the frothy waves of the music industry was an undercurrent where shallow image-making had no place and opportunities lay in abundance for groups who were simply burning to play. A burgeoning circuit for rock bands was emerging, due largely to the vision of promoter Dave Robinson, a straight-talking Irishman, who was then managing Brinsley Schwarz. Robinson knew a number of bands who were writing good songs and had been concerned at the lack of outlets for the kind of raw music they were playing. The Sixties London club scene, through which emerged The Rolling Stones, The Who, The Yardbirds among others, had died and been replaced in part by jazz. Initially, Robinson had set out to find venues for Brinsley Schwarz, but his appeals to pub landlords had prised open doors for other groups.

As Kilburn & The High Roads started gigging in London, regulars at north London boozers were already raising their pint glasses to the likes of Bees Make Honey, Eggs Over Easy and Brinsley Schwarz. The latter [Nick Lowe, Ian Gomm, Bob Andrews, Brinsley Schwarz and Billy Rankin] had a residency at the Tally Ho in Fortess Road, Kentish Town, where they were trying to recover from the fallout of a publicity stunt almost two years earlier that had gone horribly wrong. Robinson's management company, Famepushers Ltd, had flown a crowd of journalists and *Melody Maker* competition winners out to see the band at the Fillmore East in New York, where they were supporting Van Morrison and Quicksilver Messenger Service. But when the flight was delayed, most of the guests missed the Brinsleys' set. The public relations nightmare had become legend and left the group heavily in debt, but they stayed loyal to Robinson and went with him to the Tally Ho. The vocalist in the band, which took its name from the lead guitarist, was Nick Lowe. "We would have followed Dave through shark-infested waters," Nick told *Vox* magazine in 1991.[7] "He seemed to be this unstoppable figure exuding a tremendous amount of confidence."

Ducks Deluxe, which was formed when singer Sean Tyla teamed up with guitarist Martin Belmont, were also regulars at the pub, along with New York bar band Eggs Over Easy. Members of this group were living around the corner and wangled their first gig there by convincing the couple who owned the pub that their music qualified as jazz. As punters poured into the Tally Ho, word spread to other pubs and a beer-soaked network of rock venues slowly emerged. Driving down the Holloway Road one day, members of Ducks Deluxe spotted a promising venue, The Cock, went in, and twisted the landlord's arm into letting them do a set.

Ian in 1970. *(Joe Gaffney/Retna)*

CERTIFIED COPY OF AN ENTRY OF BIRTH   GIVEN AT THE GENERAL REGISTER OFFICE

PAS A 515472/99

Application Number

REGISTRATION DISTRICT	Hendon	
1942 BIRTH in the Sub-district of	Harrow	in the County of Middlesex

Ian's birth certificate.

Ian's grandparents, John and Mary Walker, the
parents of his mother Peggy.
(Courtesy Molly Walker)

Ian's mother Peggy, pictured relaxing in her
native Cornwall.
(Courtesy Molly Walker)

Ian's father, William Dury.
(Dury family archives)

Ian, aged about four, with grandmother Mary
Walker and a cousin in Mevagissey, Cornwall.
(Courtesy Barry Anderson)

Ian with his mother and father.
(Dury family archives)

Barry Anderson (left) and Ian on the rocks at Cornwall in 1948. A year later Ian would be crippled by polio. *(Courtesy Barry Anderson)*

Ian at the gate of his home at 90 Front Lane, Cranham, aged about six. *(Courtesy Barry Anderson)*

Ian in his calipers, aged about 10. *(Dury family archives)*

Ian at The Royal Grammar School, High Wycombe. *(Dury family archives)*

Ian showing early signs of rebellion – a greasy
quiff – at High Wycombe.
(Dury family archives)

Teddy Boy Ian at Walthamstow Art College.
(Dury family archives)

Ian in the canteen at Walthamstow.
(Terry Day)

Betty Rathmell, whom Ian married in 1967.
(Dury family archives)

Examples of Ian's artwork from the late Sixties. *(Dury family archives)*

Drawing by Ian Drury # The Immortals

Movies had their heyday when Metro-Goldwyn-Mayer could boast on its studio payroll 'more stars than there are in heaven'. The times have toughened, and films with them. Neo-realism, cinéma-vérité, hard-ticket spectaculars: the vocabulary swells. But the magic endures. Movies deal in myths, endlessly unfolding in the plush darkness. They reflect life, but they are larger than life. They traffic in ideas, and boost the sales of iced lollies. Often they are made by no-brows for low-brows. Sometimes, perversely, they spawn a masterpiece. This issue scans the film scene of the 1960s. It is a landscape haunted by its past, and harassed by its future. First, on these pages, we survey the ghosts. They were stars, and now they are immortals. They belong securely to the legends they helped to create. If memory has mislaid their names, turn to page 42

Ian with Kilburn & The High Roads in 1974. Clockwise from top: David Newton-Rohoman, Davey Payne, Charlie Sinclair, Ian and Keith Lucas. *(Joe Gaffney/Retna)*

In a domino effect, the proprietors of the nearby Lord Nelson, The Hope & Anchor, in Islington, and The Torrington in Finchley agreed to give these bands a stage and the vibrant rock'n'roll scene imagined by Robinson was under way. Small pubs were transformed into rocking venues which shook with the sounds of bands who had previously been starved of outlets. Audiences crowded around tiny stages, often dangerously close to teetering microphone stands, while musicians were forced to change their clothes in freezing lavatory cubicles out the back. What had been a desert for bands, was now an oasis, and Kilburn & The High Roads became part of it. All except Terry Day, that is.

Terry was fired in January 1973. Although he was close to Ian, Terry was a jazz percussionist and his natural style had little in common with the sound for which Ian was striving. "When I first started playing with Ian, people said to me, 'What are you playing with that man for?' and I said, 'Well, because he's a friend and he's asked me to play drums' and they'd say, 'But you can't play rock'n'roll' and I'd say, 'Yeah, but I'm learning.' I wasn't a rock'n'roll drummer, I was a free drummer. They reckon the best rock'n'-roll drumming I ever did was when I broke an arm and played with one arm and I think that might be true."

Ian's replacement for Terry was truly inspired. He had spotted David Newton-Rohoman, a black percussionist who needed crutches to get on and off stage, playing with the Magic Rock Band at Canterbury College. A stylish dresser and charming man, with a weird and wonderful family background, he was the perfect addition to an already startling cast. He was born in Guyana, South America, on April 21, 1948, and went to the Bourda Roman Catholic Comprehensive until his parents moved to England when he was 14. There, he went to the Grange Secondary Modern School in Aylesbury, Buckinghamshire, and later studied commerce at Slough Technical College, where he first started playing in groups. His mother, who worked as an NHS nurse, was also an 'obeyah woman', who practised a form of African witchcraft at their Camden Town home. When the Kilburns arrived to collect David for rehearsals and gigs, they would find her stretched out on her downstairs bed with a queue of people waiting for private sessions. By the time her son joined Ian's group, he was a respected musician on the live circuit, having played with The Interpreters, Ray Williams & The Grenade, Kripple Vision and The Magic Rock Band, where he spent three years. He needed the support of two crutches in order to walk to and from the stage, reportedly as a result of an accident when he was a baby.

As Kilburn & The High Roads launched its assault on London, both the visual and aural impact of the new line-up was unforgettable. Humphrey stood like a statue on one side, often in a flared white suit, and Russell sported a wispy beard behind an old beat-up piano. In the middle, the stooped and usually black-suited figure of Ian clutched at the microphone for support. Keith, in an effort to grab the limelight, moved jerkily around the stage, Davey hovered menacingly and the drummer crashed energetically around his kit, his muscular arms more than making up for his redundant legs.

In November 1972, the Kilburns wandered into The Speakeasy, the trendy West End hang-out of rock stars such as Eric Clapton, Jimmy Page and Keith Moon. Calling in at the club off Oxford Circus one afternoon, they got a glimpse of the more glamorous side of rock'n'roll when they found Leo Sayer rehearsing for a show. "He had all this amazing Fender equipment, sparkling away. We asked the geezer who ran the club for a gig and he gave us one for £15. We knew that Pete Townshend and Keith Moon were in the club that night, but when we played, we expected to get ignored."

They weren't. During the interval, Dave Robinson and songwriter Nick Lowe walked into the dressing room and advised Ian to join the London pub circuit. Dave then introduced him to Martyn Smith of the Iron Horse Agency, who was booking all the major pubs, and the Kilburns were booked to play at the Tally Ho.

The first couple of gigs drew small audiences, but after a favourable review appeared in *Time Out*, interest in the group increased. Ian's moon-lighting, however, cost him his day job in Canterbury. "I was on a tasty earner down there. It was the equivalent to £100 a day nowadays," he said.[7] "I got the sack for non-attendance, so I thought, 'Well, it's the Tally Ho – that's my new career' – and then I only got a shilling out of it that night."

Dave Robinson took over the band's affairs and encouraged them to play other London watering holes. Said Ian:[7] "We had a four-month period of hammering it out because Robinson said it would get our act in shape. The Kensington was £16 and the landlord Matt would give us another fiver. Always gave it to Davey Payne. The sax player always copped the extras. And in a pub, you always get a free drink."

One of the regulars at The Kensington was Ian Stewart, an old art school friend of Ian's. After one gig he went up to Ian and said he knew plenty of famous people who wished they were playing pubs. But the singer was unimpressed.

"At the time we was doing it, we wanted to be in the Royal Albert Hall," said Ian.[7] "We fuckin' hated the pubs. We hated getting on the fuckin' stage, and we hated the fact there was no dressing room. I hated that I had to go behind the speaker to take my shirt off. There was this bird in The Cock who used to grab my bollocks every time I went in there and shout, 'Oi, are you going to play Crippled With Nerves?' I'd say, 'You fuckin' lunatic, spilling beer on my feet. Get off.' There was that incredible closeness, which was great, looking back on it."

The Hope & Anchor in Islington was at the forefront of the pub rock scene, hosting The Kursaal Flyers from Southend, and Dr Feelgood from nearby Canvey Island, and others on the circuit. The Kilburns' first gig at the legendary venue was on March 23, 1973, but the occasion was memorable for all the wrong reasons. Said Ian:[7] "We bought a new van at the British Car Auctions. It was maroon with 'Danger – Inflammable' written on the front, and it had been carrying dangerous chemicals around. We were driving down from Aylesbury, where we were based, and as we came off the motorway the big end fell out. Fred Grainger, guv'nor of the Hope, came and rescued us. When we got there, there were about seven people in the audience and eight on stage. It was still a good crowd."

Ian had borrowed £500 from his mother to buy the van, but repair bills now threatened to stop them playing. When news of their plight got out, Dave Robinson rounded up Brinsley Schwarz, Bees Make Honey and Ducks Deluxe, and on May 3, 1973, staged a benefit night at Camden Town Hall. Three hundred punters turned up and £130 was raised for the repairs.

But for all this, Kilburn & The High Roads were only playing one gig a month. Fed up with playing grotty old pubs and getting nowhere, the Kilburns decided to come off the road and take stock.

As pub rock took hold of the London scene, a young music fan called Charlie Gillett was hosting a show called *Honky Tonk* on BBC Radio London. Along with his dentist friend Gordon Nelki, he had just returned from Louisiana with a bunch of Cajun songs which he wanted to introduce to a British audience. But they had been unable to find an outlet for their proposed compilation and their plan to establish a small record company was in limbo. As the pair contemplated their future, an American student named Steve Nugent contacted Charlie and alerted him to Kilburn & The High Roads, suggesting that he feature them on his programme. Charlie did nothing about it, but soon afterwards, Dave Robinson called to his home. A Cajun song Charlie had played on his show, 'Promised Land' by Johnnie Allan, had grabbed his attention, he told him. But the real reason for contacting Charlie was to get some radio play for Brinsley Schwarz and other groups from the growing pub rock circuit. In passing, the promoter also recommended an amazing new group on the scene – Kilburn & The High Roads.

Once again, Charlie didn't act immediately on the tip-off, but one night he finally decided to see the group for himself and headed for the Tally Ho. The venue wasn't packed, as Ian's group was still fairly new to London's pub scene, but he was transfixed by what he saw on stage.

Charlie: "There was this motley collection of people on stage with this gruff-voiced bloke who was kind of lurching about the stage a bit, and it wasn't immediately apparent he was disabled. And there was nothing about the band that suggested that they were a band. Normally, there is some-thing about musicians when they come together as a unit, they look slightly alike, they are wearing similar clothes, or they are the same age as each other. At the very least, there is something about them that suggests that they know each other, but these people looked like they just met at a bus stop and decided to walk into a pub and start playing together. There seemed to be a big age range, although it wasn't as great as it seemed at the time. Ian was about 30 or 31, the keyboard player would have been a similar age, but again people of that age can either try and look younger or they don't, and there was nothing about these people in their early thirties that they were trying to look like they were in their early twenties. If any-thing, they looked how they were going to look in 20 years time, it was very weird.

"The saxophone player looked demented and the guitarist looked like he was still in school. When the band came off at half-time, the drummer didn't; he just stayed behind his kit, and you were left wondering whether he was a social outcast or what. They would go back on stage and the songs they were doing were a completely bewildering mixture, because again, as much as bands tended to look like each other, so a repertoire of songs tended to be fairly predictable. When you had heard two or three numbers you sort of knew how it was going to go, but with this lot you didn't.

"They did 'Tallahassee Lassie' by Freddie Cannon, 'The Walk' by Jimmy McCracklin and 'Twenty Tiny Fingers' by Alma Cogan, which was one of those songs which would make you turn the radio off. The idea that someone was reviving this horrible thing was incredible. In the middle of it, the saxophone player would be playing free jazz, the piano player didn't seem to be doing anything, so it was bewildering and exciting because you didn't know what was going to happen next.

"The singer was saying all sorts of vaguely scurrilous things between the songs and the lyrics were . . . 'I'll have you down behind the bike shed' and 'When I was 15, I wore a black drape jacket, sideboards to my chin.' I thought, if I could write songs, these are the kind of songs I would like to write."

When the band finally went off stage, Charlie Gillett was further astonished by what he saw. The drummer clumsily got to his feet and hobbled off stage on crutches. He had hardly any control of his feet, leaving the top half of his body to do all the work. But, afterwards Charlie realised that this accounted for the sense of looseness which helped to make the Kilburns' sound so refreshing.

Charlie: "I came back from that gig and on the radio show I said, 'There is this band that you have all got to go and see.' I went to see them again and came back saying, 'There is no band in town remotely like these people, in looks, sound, attitude, or anything.' Every reason for liking pop music or jazz or rhythm and blues or New Orleans music was all together here. Then on the third or fourth time I saw them at the Tally Ho, during the interval the singer came up to me and said, 'Oi, you keep saying these things about us on the radio, why don't you manage us?' I didn't know what managing meant. It was one thing to sit in your office and produce some records you liked and that was about as close as I wanted to get to being a record label. But I couldn't think of why not. Gordon Nelki and I had got nowhere with our first plan and so there we were managing Kilburn & The High Roads."

Naive as they were in the business of rock management, Charlie and Gordon were organised. They bought a van in which the band could travel to gigs, another one for their gear, waged them at £8 a week and set about finding their new charges a suitable place to rehearse. Gordon lived with his wife Andra and their three young children, in a large house in Stockwell, and the couple managed to persuade the vicar at St Matthew's Church, Brixton, to let them use his crypt. As a 'thank you', the Kilburns performed at the church fete.

Better still for Ian and his cohorts, the Nelkis' was an open house, where they could doss down for the night and get fed and watered. The easy-going couple's home overflowed whenever the band returned from their rehearsals and a small loft above the family's garage became the living quarters of the group's roadies, Paul Tonkin and Mick Hill. Ian frequently slept on the floor at their home, while other band members were put up at various times above Gordon's nearby dental surgery. Their three children found their colourful house guests entertaining and Ian came to be viewed as a kind, if rather spiky, uncle. Once, Gordon's son Julius, then aged about seven, treated the Kilburns to a puppet show about "how good it was not being on the dole". These were educational times for all.

But almost as soon as the writer-and-dentist duo took over the band's management in the spring of 1973, they were exposed to a side of Ian which was to become all too familiar. Gordon explains: "After the second day's rehearsal at the crypt, Ian came back to the house before the others and there was already a vibe – Ian could really vibe a place out – and then the others appeared. Suddenly he turned round and said that Charlie Hart was out. The others had all been bubbling away together, plotting the future and talking about riffs and whatever else, and there was complete astonishment at this. But to Ian's amazement, more people went with Charlie Hart and suddenly it was not just Charlie Hart that was out – this band was splitting up and Ian wouldn't relent. I think Ian thought Charlie Hart was pulling it in the wrong direction, it was too jazzy and not enough of what Ian wanted. There was always a power struggle. Ian was nervous of the musicians who had too much control because he wasn't a musician, and I think Ian wanted Humphrey back."

Charlie Gillett also believes that Ian's desire to dominate the situation lay at the root of the decision. "Charlie Hart was by far the most knowledge-able musician in the band; he knew how to do arrangements, what key things should be in and what chords to play, and I think that was the problem. To him there were rules and he had the temerity to think he knew what ought to happen. But in Ian's world, it was for Ian to decide what should happen and for the rest of them to do it."

Charlie Hart gives his own version of events: "Ian fired Terry, who was my mate, so that upset me. Although Terry wasn't the ideal drummer, I didn't like the way he was just pushed out. Also, I think I had done my bit from Ian's point of view. I had played regular bass for a while and he was going back to getting in art students like Humphrey, who had great ideas but were probably less experienced as musicians. I think he fired me when I was probably walking away anyhow. It was when Charlie and Gordon took over the management formally that Ian fired me, so probably he felt secure enough to get rid of me at that point. That's how people run groups.

"When I am in a group, I do like to have an influence on the way things are and if people don't let me then I do lose interest. In a way, Ian didn't really want my input that much; he wanted to control it all and I am not that easy a person to control. I went off and joined Ronnie Lane's band after that and that was more my cup of tea, because although Ronnie wasn't a musicians' musician, he had a great interest in the fabric of sound. Ian was difficult to get on with, of course he was, but conceptually he was doing interesting things, which ultimately is the test."

At Ian's suggestion some months earlier, Humphrey, who had forgiven Ian for dumping him from the band earlier, had gone out and bought a bass guitar. Despite some rudimentary tuition from Ian, Humphrey's bass playing wasn't even close to the standard set by Charlie Hart, but Ian was determined to re-introduce him to the band.

"I found a Fender jazz bass advertised at the back of *Melody Maker* at an address in Lordship Lane, Wood Green," remembers Humphrey. "I went round there and there was this chap with a skimpy towel around his waist who had just come out of the bath and I was thinking, 'Please don't let the towel fall.' He took me into his front room and there was a bass on a sofa with fun-fur cushions laid across at jaunty angles as if that would immediately make me say, 'Oh, yes.' Of course, I was gullible and I did say, 'Oh yes,' and bought it for £120. After his bath, this chap had been splashing Denim or Brute all over himself and the whole place smelled like a kasbah. So when we went gigging and the place got hot, this bass would start smelling of after-shave.

"I used to go up to Wingrave a lot with Ian, I would paint there and he would play drums, and he just got me off the ground with the bass. We would stand there playing 'Tea For Two' for about three hours and then we would start playing utterly free form jazz bass and I thought, 'God, I'm good,' although it sounded awful. But it loosened me up and then Charlie Hart came back from Holland where he had been playing with a band. I remember him walking in and we both absolutely blushed to the roots, because there I was, the usurper, the painter who had been moved in, and there he was, a serious musician with a brand new bass. It was a tricky moment and it was almost as if I had got the girl he had been chasing."

Humphrey's return, like the arrival of David Newton-Rohoman, enhanced their stage presence and media potential. One afternoon at Groveway, Andra covered the garden wall with a white sheet and the mismatched musical troupe lined up for a photograph. In the resulting picture, taken by roadie Mick Hill, Russell was reading a newspaper, Humphrey was performing a mock curtsy in the smart white suit which he regularly wore on stage, and the others stood nonchalantly in dark overcoats and jackets. The photograph – inspired by Charlie Gillett's observation that the band looked as if they had met in a bus queue – appeared in the pages of the music papers and became the group's trademark picture. The visual impact of the Kilburns was now stronger than ever, but a new name had to be found for Humphrey, as Butler-Bowden was considered inappropriate.

Charlie: "Gordon heard him say his name and said, 'You can't use that,' and he walked around the room for a minute and then looked at him and said, 'Humphrey Ocean.' Everybody else said, 'Humphrey Ocean, that's it,' and he has been Humphrey Ocean ever since."

Humphrey felt at home at the Nelkis' and their relaxed nature provided a refreshing contrast to the stressful world of pub rock. "Gordon and Andra seemed hugely unlikely," he observes. "It was the opposite of what we did get plenty of and more – seedy basements, dank carpets, piss, going into clubs at 3 o'clock in the afternoon to set up the gear which smelled of beer and vomit – anywhere where there had been fun the night before. Metaphorically, it was the stains on the sheets, you had missed the fun and you had to crank it all up again."

By mid-1973, the Kilburns' reputation as a live act had spread beyond London. They were helped by promoters Paul Conroy and Nigel Kerr of Charisma Artists, and the set included more and more of Ian's songs. 'You're More Than Fair' was a humorous reggae-style number which Ian crooned in a mock Jamaican accent. One of the very first songs written by Ian and Russell, it sent a ripple of laughter around the audience with its opening line: "You're more than fair, you've got a gorgeous bum/Why don't you come to my house and meet my mum". It was an instant hit, along with 'The Call Up', a calypso number which inspired audiences to do the conga around the room. Tongue-in-cheek songs typified the party atmosphere of a Kilburns' gig and made the group stand out from the other acts on the circuit. For the most part, pub rock was made up of musicians dressed in lumberjack shirts and blue denims and reliant on country and blues rhythms. Ducks Deluxe, Brinsley Schwarz and Bees Make Honey played good-time music and had plenty of life, but they didn't have the Kilburns' sense of theatre.

"We had this policy in the Kilburns of never playing the same kind of song in a row," Ian said in the sleeve notes of the CD compilation *Reasons To Be Cheerful*, released in 1996. "That was more important than what we were playing. We used to go and see these bands and every bloody song was the same as the one before. I'd get really bored watching bands play each song in the same rhythm and the same key. So we had a policy of changing the key and the style of the music."

Ian's lyrics were also unlike those of other songwriters. Other Dury originals which started to feature in their shows then included 'I Really Got My Eye On Your Cheesy Pie', 'Okay Roland' and 'Rough Kids', an infectious urban anthem which owed its aggressive edge to Ian's growling vocals and Payne's rousing saxophone bursts. 'Pam's Moods' was a slow cocktail number, loosely inspired by Geoff Rigden's wife. "A life of broken china, sneering yellow hate" sang Ian in an oblique reference to a messy incident in the couple's home in Canterbury.

"I used to live with Geoff and Pam in Woolage Green in Kent, where Ian used to come and stay sometimes before he was teaching," explains Mick Blake. "I went in there one morning and there was not a sound, there were doors open and things, but there was no one there. I went upstairs to have a look and there was Geoff in bed with sheets over him. When he pulled them back he was covered in yellow paint. When me and my family lived there, we never witnessed any shouting matches, but apparently they were famous for it."

But it wasn't the only slow song in the Kilburns' varied set. In 'Crippled With Nerves', Ian sang uncharacteristically in tune, crooning above a lilting guitar, gentle sax playing and accompanied by female backing singers. Russell admits: " 'Crippled With Nerves' was a song that Ian actually wrote about me because I was so frightened about playing in public."

The compelling spectacle of Ian and his strange entourage, combined with Ian's unusual lyrical style, was attracting more and more attention from the music press. Following a gig at The Kensington, west London, on July 13, 1973, Geoff Brown of *Melody Maker* wrote of Ian: "Either he was propping the mike stand up or it was keeping him upright, but the guy certainly had style and the pose was clearly Gene Vincent's. Ian Dury is rather like a modern Vincent with a touch of Beefheart's growl and a hint of Bryan Ferry's mannered delivery. You've guessed it, Dury is really an original." A few weeks later, in a review of a Kilburns' gig at Dingwalls in Camden Lock, Brown observed: "The few golden old 'uns they play are given life by new, idiosyncratic arrangements, but it's the self-penned material that's the best."

On September 1, 1973, *New Musical Express* writer Nick Kent lavished the band with praise in an article headlined: 'Hardened Criminals Plan Big Break Out' and concluding 'At Least That's The Way They Look, But They're Going To Be Big'. The band's latest champion had been won over at a gig in the 100 Club in Oxford Street and he offered the following description of Ian: "He looks like a greased back, squat Lou Reed, but even Lou Reed never looked quite as oppressive and sinister as this. One side of his body is paralysed but this never seems too overt up on the small stage. His suit is probably from Brixton Market and his shirt and tie may just as easily have soup stains on them as not. He wears black leather gloves just like Gene Vincent used to, chews gum constantly and never opens his eyes. He is simply the most charismatic figure I've ever seen on a small British stage. Seeing Kilburn & The High Roads that night was the most exciting performance I've yet witnessed. It was rather like seeing The Who in some small club just after they'd changed their name from The High Numbers, and watching Townshend thrashing his equipment into fragments, or more appropriately witnessing the original version of Them, complete with a juvenile Van Morrison rough housing in a Belfast pub. It was that exclusive thrill of being there, almost accidentally, just as something great is going through its vital embryo stage. And make no mistake, both despite and because of their various eccentricities, the Kilburns are great."

As with other onlookers, this reviewer was captivated by the visual side of the Kilburns. Keith Lucas was described as "a juvenile Keith Richards crossed with Anthony 'Psycho' Perkins" dressed in "a black top and liquorice patterned drainpipe slacks". Humphrey was likened to "a refugee from a Kentucky Fried Chicken advert complete with ludicrously baggy white gangster suit and earring", while Russell Hardy was said to resemble "an original beatnik, a curious facial amalgam of Graham Bond and Fagin, wearing a red Panama hat instead of a skull-cap".

Time Out devoted a page to the Kilburns on August 3, including the photograph taken by Mick Hill, and hailed them as "one of the most exciting new London bands". Writer John Collis observed: "They must have been a bunch of toughs assembled from the rougher end of Kilburn, used to playing the sort of pub where women fight as well as the men, and now trying to broaden their choice of venues. The gum-chewing singer, using the microphone as if it was some form of surgical apparatus, sported a curious Mohican haircut and a battered drape jacket. The other members of the band appeared to be wearing sacking. One hesitated to push through the crowd to indulge in boot-splashing in case a group of enthusiasts were comparing flick knives in the stalls. It turned out that the singer was an art teacher and the band was made up of his students and friends. This knowledge doesn't weaken the impact of the band, now that they are back in circulation."

He concluded: "Ian Dury's idiosyncratic lyrics and Russell Hardy's melodic and rhythmic ingenuity provide a new form of rock'n'roll: tight dance music infiltrated by Latin inflections and New Orleans sensuousness. Plus humour. You can listen to the Kilburns, you can bop to them, but either way you're bound to be grinning."

Charlie and Gordon were meanwhile acquainting themselves with the spit and sawdust conditions which prevailed in London's boozers. "There wasn't that many venues and there were never that many people at the gigs," says Charlie. "Now, everybody in the world says they went to see Kilburn & The High Roads, but they bloody didn't, because we were counting the door money and there wasn't much to go round.

"It was people just going out for a night's drinking, mostly in their late twenties and mid thirties and some of the same people who might have gone to a jazz gig. It was never hip, it was teachers, college students, whatever. With clubs these days, it is what you are wearing which dictates whether you get in the door or not, but it was not remotely like that. Everybody was pretty scruffy looking. There was a bit of dancing in front of the stage and basically it was a beer drinking, cigarette smoking scene, no drugs, just a pub scene. There were horrible changing rooms, if there was anything at all."

Aside from putting each of the Kilburns on a wage, the new management team also lined up recording sessions at a number of studios, including Jack Jackson's in Rickmansworth and The Majestic in Clapham. Charlie and Gordon were keen for the group to be picked up by Atlantic Records, but the recording sessions never produced a demo good enough to interest such a major label. Bottling the Kilburns live sound proved an impossible task.

Charlie: "It was too eccentric, too London and Ian Dury wasn't a good singer by any of the normal criteria and he would be having trouble reaching the notes in the songs he was trying to go for. Tom Waits was doing something parallel in America, although I don't know if Ian made any connection with that at the time, but in America the idea of there being a maverick thing with Ry Cooder and Randy Newman and those kind of people was allowed. They weren't commercially viable and Warner Brothers nurtured those and recorded them without really recouping the cost of making the records. Nobody was going to take that line here."

Of the early attempts to record the group, he adds: "We never came close to catching the best of the live sound. It was partly because the drum sound was pretty loose. Recording is very ruthless, but at a gig you can get carried away by all sorts of extraneous factors, including the fact that you are dancing to it, you have had a drink or two, and the general atmosphere of it. But in a studio, a microphone is pretty unforgiving."

An extraordinary development was about to take place, however. Out of nowhere, Kilburn & The High Roads were invited to play on a small British tour which included the kind of rock venues they could only ever have dreamed of playing. More unbelievable still, the headline act was The Who – then embarking on a UK tour to promote their new album *Quadrophenia*. Even now, there is some confusion as to what prompted the invitation.

According to Russell Hardy, Roger Daltrey had seen the Kilburns' gig at The Speakeasy, the same gig at which they had been spotted by Dave Robinson. A year later, when the British leg of The Who tour was being planned, Daltrey made contact with the group and invited them to be the warm-up act. But Gordon says the origins of the tour have always been a mystery, and that Ian had tried desperately to find out how it had come about. Either way, it was a fantastic break.

Gordon recalls: "The Who had three huge Pantechnicans [tour lorries] and we had a little Commer van with a piano in it. The van only came up to the height of the wheel of one of their things – it was a remarkable sight."

The Who's *Quadrophenia* album was released on November 3, 1973, a conceptual story-line album which told the tale of Jimmy the Mod, based loosely on 'Irish' Jack Lyons, an old Mod fan and friend of the group from Shepherd's Bush. Following the tour, the album went on to become The Who's third biggest selling album, reaching the number two spot in the UK and the US. By 1973, The Who enjoyed god-like status and had notched up a series of hits since 'I Can't Explain' had first put the band on the map in February 1965. Stories of Pete Townshend and Keith Moon destroying guitars and drums, sound equipment, dressing rooms and hotel suites were well worn by the mid-Seventies, but the *Quadrophenia* tour was not without fresh moments of controversy.

The tour opened on Sunday October 28, 1973, at Trentham Gardens, Stoke-on-Trent and proceeded to the Civic Hall, Wolverhampton, the following night. On November 1 – the third night of the tour at Kings Halls, Belle Vue, Manchester – Kilburn & The High Roads joined the party. Up to this point, the Kilburns' live experience had been art schools, colleges, pubs and clubs, but this was another world. Dodgy amplifiers, unroadworthy vans, second-rate guitars and dank changing rooms, were still fresh in the memory when they walked on to the vast stage at the 5,000-seat venue within the Belle Vue amusement park. This was the largest capacity venue on the tour and the two consecutive shows by The Who were sold out.

Humphrey: "I remember Daltrey said to David Rohoman, 'Are you ready, are you excited?' and Rohoman said, 'I'm shitting myself man. It's easy for you. I mean, you just go out there and they all love you, but for us it's different.' And Daltrey turned round and said, 'Don't you believe it, they just watch for us to make one slip and we've got all that way to fall.' The first night we walked into the dressing room at Belle Vue, there was booze everywhere. I drank a bottle of Pernod after the gig and the walls were kind of moving and I thought, 'Yes, I have had rather a lot of Pernod'. But in fact, the walls really were moving because it was a made-up dressing room with panels and screens and The Who had finished their gig and the crew were pushing it away."

For the audience, *Quadrophenia* also represented a new experience because the sound effects swirled the music eerily around the venues. "This is an album called *Quadrophenia*," Daltrey told the audience "and it's the story about a kid who goes down to the rock in the middle of the sea and looks back on a couple of weeks when he leaves home and a few backwardly nostalgic glimpses . . . Anyway, it starts off with the sound of the mighty sea – in quadraphonic. So open up your three left ears and experience quadraphonic for the first time." The first of three nights at the Odeon Cinema, Newcastle, was a fiasco. Inevitably, Townshend was at the centre of the uproar. When the backing tapes malfunctioned, the guitarist screamed abuse at the soundman Bob Pridden, grabbing him around the neck, pulling him over the mixing desk and throwing him towards the centre of the stage. With astonished fans looking on, he smashed his guitar on the stage and started tearing down the backing tapes and equipment. The curtain was dropped and the audience was left in darkness for about 10 minutes, before the foursome returned and the gig continued.

But the finale was to cause more upset for fans. Townshend demolished his second guitar of the night and hurled one of his amps to the ground, while Keith Moon ploughed through his kit, sending things flying across the stage. Subsequent newspaper reports were not complimentary. The Newcastle *Journal* condemned his antics as "a ridiculous display of unwarranted violence witnessed by thousands of easily influenced teenage pop fans". Moon and Townsend agreed to appear on the local TV show *Look North*, but simply laughed off the incident.

Russell Hardy, the Kilburns' shy and retiring pianist, was distinctly unimpressed with the behaviour of The Who, both on and off stage. "Keith Moon had a particular temper. It would start off with kicking his drums over and throwing them about because of his frustration and eventually it became part of the set. At one point they nailed his drum kit to the floor. They were just something else," recalls Russell. "Roger Daltrey would come in and have a chat with us and we would always get our couple of cases of liqueur brandy and scotch and beers. They always had this ritual of smashing all the plates and everything. When you came into the dressing room where they were they would smash everything up to get themselves psyched up. Eventually they gave them paper cups and plates. Keith Moon had headphones on and things for timing because his counting wasn't too good, and there were other gimmicks. It was definitely an eye-opener, but it was a bit disillusioning."

In truth The Who's 1973 *Quadrophenia* tour was, by their standards, something of a disaster. Obliged to rely on extensive backing tapes to reproduce the musical textures of the album, The Who lost the vibrant spontaneity that had carried them to the peak of their profession. Time and time again the troublesome backing tapes frustrated the band, hurling them into a tailspin from which they never truly recovered.

Roadie Mick Hill adds: "I can remember Roger Daltrey turning up in Manchester and he shouted up to David Rohoman, who was on stage, 'Oi, no pogo sticks?' Another night Keith Moon crawled out across the back of the stage and under David Rohoman's chair to see how he played the drums. Basically David wobbled on his seat, his arms were twice the size of anyone's thighs and he had these little legs that dangled down. He'd been advised to take up drumming to help his leg muscles."

The British leg of the *Quadrophenia* tour concluded with three shows at The Lyceum, in The Strand, London, but this old theatre proved an unsuitable choice for The Who's ambitious project and many fans complained that having paid £2.20 for tickets, they couldn't see the stage. In contrast, the Kilburns were back on home turf and went down a storm in front of some regulars from their pub residencies. As the tour came to a close, the Kilburns' camp was buzzing with excitement. Pete Townshend had been chatting with Ian during some of the shows and had now invited the band to accompany The Who on their American tour which began a week later. On November 20, The Who were due to play The Cow Palace, San Francisco, before going on to arenas and auditoriums in Dallas, Atlanta, St Louis, Chicago, Detroit, Boston, Philadelphia and Maryland. The 12-date tour also included a show at The Forum in Montreal, Canada. For a band with no record deal to its name and more accustomed to playing in the back rooms of pubs, colleges and social clubs, this was an astonishing opportunity.

Charlie and Gordon immediately began making arrangements for the trip, but there was a hitch – none of the Kilburns possessed a passport. With the first US date just days away, it was a race against time. Andra zipped into action, telephoning the passport office near Victoria Station and alerting the staff that an unlikely looking mob of musicians would be descending on the office that day. The scenes at the passport office were chaotic.

"When we got there, and all these people were behind their tills waiting to deal with this band, this enormous row broke out because Ian decided to fire Paul Tonkin – sack him just at that moment," remembers Gordon. "This guy had just gone all the way to Southampton on the first available train and was told, 'You're not coming to America.' He had played violin on the very first gig eve, although I don't think he could pay violin, but he had tripped over something, or not put something down properly at the last gig. The passport officials could not believe what they were seeing and then another fight broke out because someone said, 'Well I'm not going if he is out.' I was watching in disbelief and I think that was close to when I pulled out. I said to Charlie, 'I'm not going on with this, even if they're as big as The Rolling Stones, I'm not interested.' "

Precisely what happened next is unclear, but the Kilburns never went to America. Many of those involved had their suspicions as to whether it had ever been a possibility, except in the mind of Ian, and Gordon was among the sceptics. "The band got their passports, but then we found out that there was this band Lynyrd Skynyrd, who were already booked to tour

America, and there was never any question of the Kilburns going. Ian had been talking to Pete Townshend and maybe they were both drunk and he had come back to Charlie and I and said they were on this tour. We had to go ahead as if it was happening, but it was definitely never going to happen." The confirmation of Lynryd Skynryd as support suggested politics may have played a part, as they were on MCA, the same record label as The Who. But, whatever the reason, Ian was deeply disappointed.

In the sleeve-notes for the *Reasons To Be Cheerful* compilation,[8] Ian recalled: "Pete (Townshend) kept asking us if we'd come to America with them, and I think they wanted us on Tracks Records. But we didn't get to America. We queued up for days to get our visas and then we didn't go, and that was a bit of a blow."

The Who debacle was followed by another major blow. Humphrey, one of Ian's closest allies, quit the group. The sensitive painter had become deeply disaffected with the tawdry rock'n'roll lifestyle and the back-stage shenanigans he witnessed on The Who tour pushed him too far. Ian was upset at the decision, but Humphrey was adamant. "I didn't like the life, I didn't like slumming it in bed-sits," explains Humphrey. "I didn't mind what I did for painting, but somehow I did for being a musician and my first reaction to not painting was that I began to feel ill for not having done what I wanted to pursue. On the other hand, The Who loved lying around on the floor and shitty dressing rooms and the whole life and I realised it was not what I wanted. I wasn't having a breakdown or anything, but I felt like I was going mad. As a loner I found it very difficult, delegating and being part of a six-man team. At that time, what I liked about painting was that I could do it any time of day or night, and with the band it drove me mental waiting for someone to turn up.

"My granny had died about a year before and I was left £300 and I thought, 'Well, now I can afford to stop.' I was trying to work out how many eight pounds a week that made, because that was what we earned in the Kilburns. It was very odd to be so pulled in one direction by a love of the people in the Kilburns and eventually hating what I wasn't doing. It was quite inevitable that I left. I was never clearer about anything and there was no way that anybody could persuade me to stay. Peter Blake tried. 'So few people make it as a painter, don't do it,' he said, as he was puking up over a Porsche outside Dingwalls. I was holding his forehead and he was saying, 'Don't leave the Kilburns – blaaaagh.' But I was unmovable."

All in all, 1973 had been a highly eventful year for Ian Dury. Within 12 months, his group had transformed from a dreamy art school project to a serious rock'n'roll band and from changing their clothes in the filthy toilets of the Tally Ho pub, the Kilburns had graduated to trendy London hangouts and had supported The Who in some of the biggest venues in the country. But while Ian's music career had taken off, his marriage had collapsed. The lure of London's bright lights and his drive for success had proved too powerful a distraction from his wife and children, and as Ian basked under the stage lights of Dingwalls, a trendy new night spot in Camden Town, he attracted increasing attention from women. Ian admitted the group had brought his marriage to an end, "but not because I was out there getting drunk, drugs and groupies, because I was never there basically".[1]

There can be no question that Ian was flattered by the female adulation which accompanied his growing profile and the temptation was proving too great.

In an interview with the *Guardian* in June 1998,[9] Ian said: "I never thought I was handsome and here I was getting told I was handsome. It was the first week Dingwalls opened, and the women . . . that did tipple my head. I was 30 years old and I was getting smothered in 'em, smothered. Everyone was going, 'Ello babe' and touching me up as they went by, and I was looking at myself and thinking, 'Why are they all doing this to me?' " Asked whether he was tempted, he replied: "Wasn't I ever? Then I met someone who I ended up living with, and split up with my wife. There was a period when I was absolutely fuckin' mental with the birds. It was weird being told I was gorgeous, and I believed it."

His break-up with Betty does not appear to have happened suddenly and the couple maintained an extremely close and loving relationship throughout the years that followed. However, some of those who lodged with them during their three years in Wingrave testify to the kind of pressure which had been slowly building in the old vicarage. In 1973, as Ian jammed with his pals in his makeshift rehearsal room, polished his photographic skills and got more and more live bookings, Betty was struggling to make ends meet. Those who spent time in their home during this fraught period in their marriage paint an unhappy picture.

Mick Hill describes the scene at Wingrave: "I was in bed one day and little Jemima came in and said, 'Mick, dad says could you get up because Betty's broken all the china.' I know them now, wives of people that are going to be successful musicians and all that, but where's the kids' food on the table? When I moved there, Baxter had just been born, he was a few months old, and Jemima used to sit in a big armchair watching television. The vicarage had huge rooms, a big croquet lawn, an allotment and a big brick-domed, hand-pump well. It was right by the duck pond in the village. There was a music room set up there that was covered in egg boxes and loads of Ian's paintings on the wall, nudes with sequins and beads stuck on them. The local bobby came round one night and there was low-key lighting and he was standing there shining his torch on these nudes and he said, 'What, is this some sort of nightclub then?' Ian was most impressed that he had made a vicarage look like a nightclub."

Chris Lucas, the group's dismissed drummer, sympathised with Betty's plight: "We would go to Wingrave with all the gear and rehearse for the weekend and it must have been a nightmare for Betty. We would pitch up there and there were always extra people, various girlfriends and hangers-on and we would take over the house for the weekend. They had little kids and Betty just kept out of the way. After a while, Ian got Russell to soundproof the best room in the house by nailing mattresses and egg boxes to the door and we would all rehearse in there. We were all notorious dope smokers and Ian would have to get everyone up in the morning for rehearsals. I think it reached a point where she just said, 'Fuck this, I'm not putting up with it.' Even though Ian might say he was subsidising his painting, we never actually made any money because we spent it in the bar before we went home. Betty must have been thinking, 'Well, he's not here for three days and he's coming back with a fiver. Meanwhile, I'm bringing up the kids and trying to be a painter.' "

Russell also witnessed some uncomfortable scenes in the Dury household and he points to a side of Ian's character which was unapologetically single-minded.

"Ian decided we needed to be in London to operate as a band and I think he just made the decision that the band was more important than anything. He basically said to Betty, 'We're moving to London and there is no room for you and the kids.' "

5

CATSHIT MANSIONS

"We did this song called 'I Made Mary Cry' which was about a psychopath cutting a girl up in a bus shelter and it was a really quiet waltz which got really loud and ended up with a Dury scream. We did a gig in Windsor barracks for some regiment which was going overseas to Hong Kong and this very well-spoken officer comes up and says, 'Your songs are disgusting, but they're rather amusing.'"

— Charlie Sinclair

Denise Roudette was still in her teens, tall and stunningly beautiful when idle curiosity took her into the dingy back room of a north London pub and into Ian Dury's life. Within months of accosting the 31-year-old singer as he hobbled off stage dripping with sweat, the pair were in love. By the following spring, they had set up home together in south London in a spartan flat which enjoyed a paradoxical panorama taking in the Oval cricket ground on one side and Kennington Gasworks on the other. 'Catshit Mansions', as it was nicknamed with characteristic Ian bluntness, was far from the most romantic setting, but it was in this run-down block of flats that their roller-coaster and sometimes violent relationship would be played out and where Ian would write some of the songs which would make him a household name. Although their partnership would not survive Ian's rise to prominence, Denise was to be a source of support and encouragement to him over a period of six years.

Denise, who now lives in London with her three children, says: "It was an interesting relationship. Ian taught me a lot about life and having a creative life, which is quite hard to do. He has this way of bringing people around him, a bit like a tree in that respect — he stays in position and everyone comes to him. He has a way of talking very directly and giving you his full attention. I was attracted to him and to his charisma and I understood straight away what he was trying to do."

Denise was born in Darlington in the north of England to a Jamaican father, Rudi, and English mother, June. She was just five years old in 1959 when the family moved to Lagos in Africa, and during what was a very happy time there, she received a rich musical education. She vividly recalls the groups of drummers, ranging from small boys to grandfathers, who would play from sunrise to sunset. The little girl's musical education was further enriched at an open-air cinema where she watched Ray Charles, Louis Armstrong and other jazz greats. On the family's return to England around 1964, they settled in Poulton-Le-Fylde, a village just outside Blackpool and it was here that Denise spent her formative years. Music continued to be a dominant force at home where Denise, her older brother and younger sister, were treated to calypso, jazz and other musical styles. Her father's other passion was cricket and he regularly hosted end-of-season benefit parties for West Indies cricket stars, including the legendary Gary Sobers. At the age of 13, Denise got her first taste of live rock music when she and a school friend bought tickets to see Jimi Hendrix at the ABC in Blackpool.

"I really wanted to meet Jimi and my friend went around to the stage door and said, 'We've come to get Jimi Hendrix's signature,' and the doorman said, 'Who?' " recalls Denise. "Hendrix came down about 10 minutes later and said, 'No one has ever asked for me before,' he was really excited. He asked me, 'How old are you?' and I said, 'Thirteen,' and he laughed and just said, 'Okay sister,' and gave me his autograph."

Denise was oblivious to Kilburn & The High Roads when she and a friend strolled into the Lord Nelson on the Holloway Road for a drink towards the end of 1972. As they stood at the bar, Denise was fascinated by a band playing on a television set on the wall. When the penny dropped that they were performing in a room in the pub, she went for a closer look. Back home in Lancashire, Denise had seen dozens of rock bands and musicians, but she had never clapped eyes on anything like this before; especially the menacing singer with the close-cropped hair, dark suit and black leather gloves. His charisma and intense stage presence made him even more seductive.

"They came off stage and had just finished doing 'The Roadette Song' and my name was Roudette. I went up to Ian and said something crass like, 'Did you write that song for me?' " she remembers.

Within weeks, Denise, who says she was 19 at the time, was turning up at venues where the Kilburns were playing, including Dingwalls, and Ian was besotted. He visited her on a couple of occasions at college in Bristol, where she was studying dental hygiene – and in the New Year – halfway through her second year – she dropped out and moved to London to be with him. It is not clear exactly when Ian left his wife and two young children, but he was still spending time with Betty when he and Denise met. When the lease at the old vicarage expired and the church asked them to vacate the property, Betty moved with Baxter and Jemima to Aylesbury. By this time, the Kilburns had already launched their London offensive and Ian had upped and left for the capital, bedding down at Charlie Gillett's home in Clapham and Gordon and Andra's house in Stockwell.

Davey Payne says bluntly: "We were doing 'The Roadette Song' and he met Denise Roudette dancing or something, and he was with Betty then. Denise was dead beautiful and that's really why he left Betty."

It was while Ian and Denise were sleeping on a mattress on the floor of the Nelkis' sitting room, around the spring of 1974, that Ian acquired a more permanent base. Clive Davies, a reporter friend of Ian's, was vacating his flat on the third floor of Oval Mansions, in Kennington, and offered it to Ian and his teenage girlfriend: they gratefully accepted.

"It was a one bedroom, no bathroom flat, with an incredible outlook from the top floor of Oval Mansions," says Denise. "You had the Oval cricket ground spread out before you and the gasworks behind you, which was dramatic. We spent about a month doing it up which was great because although we were on and off the road, there was not a lot happening at that time. He taught me basic decorating skills and was a hard task master. I spent hours and hours sanding and watching him paint – he had to put the gloss on.

"We would start the day off with either doughnuts and coffee or Rivitas and cheese and coffee. We were either on the road and coming back at three or four in the morning, if it was a local gig, or if there wasn't a gig happening, Ian would tend to be writing lyrics. He would write down lines, titles of songs. He always had songs on the go, probably 150 or something. He would come to me and say, 'I've got a great couplet.' He was quite mechanical in how he would write. He was always talking and recounting stories, making fun. The thing about Ian is that he never forgets anything. He is a hard task master, whether it is working out a song with a band, writing a lyric or designing the cover for an album."

Money was tight at 40 Oval Mansions. Neither Ian nor his girlfriend signed on and usually blew their weekly wage from the Kilburns at Ronnie Scott's on a Friday night. Ian was irrefutably a night person and would sit up into the early hours talking to Denise and close friends about jazz, rock'n'roll, the history of music, or working his way through his record collection. During the day, the couple would wander happily around Brixton market, buying food and second-hand clothes, and sometimes Ian would help Denise run her own clothes stall at the markets in Portobello Road and Club Row. Overall, theirs was an unconventional lifestyle.

While Ian's domestic arrangements changed, Charlie and Gordon had been working hard to secure a record deal for the band. The Kilburns, who could have easily been mistaken for vagrants, were not the easiest band to peddle in the plush offices of the major record companies in London. Eventually, however, they were offered a contract by Raft, a small division of the major US label Warner Brothers, where artists included Linda Lewis. The deal was attractive, with an advance which included new sound equipment and a five-figure lump sum. Ian was delighted. At last it seemed the hard slog was going to pay off.

Charlie Sinclair: "It was a fairly good contract. We were rehearsing in the basement of St Matthew's church hall in Brixton, and on the day we got the deal we went up there by tube and came back in a stretch limo."

Gordon: "With the money from Raft, we bought a big van and completely new gear for everybody. We were doing two or three gigs a week and were out on the road a lot. Then, the 'three-day-week' came in and there was no power or petrol. I was a dentist at the time and we were gigging like crazy and I would come home at three or four in the morning and the band would bed down. I would go to work at eight the next morning and when I came home at 1pm they would still be asleep and they had to get up to get the petrol because there were long queues and it ran out by midday. I had to wake them up and say, 'For God's sake, get out there and buy the petrol, because we've got to do the gig,' and it was a worry that repeated itself over and over."

Following Humphrey's exit in December, Jerome Lucas had stepped into the breach. No relation to either Chris or Keith, the long-haired, bearded bass player was born in Kandy, Ceylon [now Sri Lanka], on May 31, 1952, and was educated, appropriately enough, at Cardinal Hinsley Secondary Modern School in Kilburn. He had come to the group via David Newton-Rohoman, with whom he played in the Sixties in Kripple Vision, and he had been involved with Orpheus and Clear Blue Sky before joining the Kilburns. But the only band member to actually reside in Kilburn High Road was gone before the new year. He was in the group just long enough, however, to feature in a 'Kilburns File' published in *Melody Maker*. By New Year's Day 1974, Ian had decided he was unsuitable and was looking for his fifth bass player.

Charlie Sinclair was at home in his native Shetland Islands resting after the Christmas season when the phone rang. It was Charlie Gillett. He told him that Kilburn & The High Roads were looking for a talented and physically striking bass player to take over from the gangly white-suited painter and invited him to audition. Sinclair had been playing the bass guitar since he was at school, most recently with the pub rock band Phoenix, and in stark contrast to Humphrey, came in at just over four feet. At the audition, the tiny Scot was clearly the best player, but although Ian was initially perturbed about the increasingly unsettling visual image of the Kilburns he was hired. The effect of the unnerving physical presence of the Kilburns and its schizophrenic songbook, was not lost on Charlie.

"Dave Rohoman used to come on stage with two sticks and I have never been an athlete myself," says Charlie. "It was pretty weird – people would just stand and stare. They would just crowd around the stage and gawp most of the time. It was probably quite a frightening thing for some people. At the time it was all glam rock, but there was none of that with us. It was just a bunch of guys you would see on a park bench with a can of Super Lager or something. It really did look like 'care in the community' some days. It was disturbing visually. Some of the music was excellent and some of it was pretty bad, but even the bad stuff had its good points because of the context of what was going on. The music we were playing had no bearing on how we looked, because there were soft waltzes in there."

Asked by Geoff Brown of *Melody Maker* what was needed to be a Kilburn, Ian could not explain other than to say that "nobody's ever been a puppet or subservient to a cause or a concert.

"Acceptin' the fact that it is a bit strange, a bit weird. I mean, Charlie said we wouldn't have had him if he hadn't been a midget. But that's a reason not to have him. But at the same time there is a certain outcast thing that he has got, that he knows about Davey Payne's got it too. It's not so much a physical thing. It's a mental thing. He knows what it's like to be outside the mainstream of society without being a hippie or a philosopher or a tramp. It's … oh, I can't explain."

In January 1974, almost immediately after Charlie joined, Kilburn & The High Roads descended on Apple Studios in distinguished Savile Row, near Regent Street, to start recording their first album. Tony Ashton, formerly of Ashton, Gardner & Dyke, who had reached number three in January 1971 with 'The Resurrection Shuffle' was invited by Warner to produce the album. After seeing a Kilburns' live gig, he agreed.

"I went to see them and just fell in love with the whole thing," said Tony.[8] "I had never heard a worse band – in one sense – in my life. It was so bizarre, the whole thing. But it was great and Ian Dury's lyrics were mind blowing."

The album sessions took place over a few months and were interspersed with drinking bouts in The Thistle and other local pubs, usually involving the producer. But as he sought to bring to vinyl what he had witnessed live, familiar frustrations emerged. In common with earlier studio sessions arranged by Charlie and Gordon, the riotous image and sound of the band which had been setting Dingwalls and other venues alight, did not lend itself to the strictures of recording. Changes in drumming personnel had become part and parcel of the Kilburns and it was a dilemma which remained unresolved when the band got to Apple. Terry Day's initial free-form jazz playing had been replaced by the rock'n'roll style of Chris Lucas. But when the forthright personalities of Ian and Chris clashed, Terry had been brought back, only then to be ousted by the ultra laid-back percussionist David Newton-Rohoman. Certainly he was an experienced drummer, but the fact that he walked on crutches had undoubtedly caught Ian's eye when he first saw him playing at Canterbury. His inability to use his feet at the drum kit and his extravagant style of playing meant that he did not bring a solid rock'n'roll tempo to the sound. On stage, band members would turn around during the last few bars of a song to see Rohoman crashing around the cymbals in a flamboyant finale. But whatever Ian's motivation had been for getting him into the group, he was to have an abrupt change of mind when the recording deal finally came.

Charlie Gillett: "At the last minute, Ian, who had defended Rohoman all the way through, suddenly decided he wasn't right and Louis Larose came in as the only musician being paid by the day. He had that kind of professional approach to the drums, but that wasn't what was required – it was a paradox."

So under Tony Ashton's production, the Kilburns' cast of Dury, Hardy, Lucas, Sinclair, Payne and Larose completed the recording sessions. The tracks recorded for the Raft album naturally featured the songs on which they had built their live reputation in the pubs of London and further afield. They included 'The Call Up', 'Crippled With Nerves', 'Patience (So What?)', 'You're More Than Fair', 'Upminster Kid', 'Billy Bentley', 'Huffety Puff', 'Rough Kids', 'The Roadette Song', 'The Badger And The Rabbit', 'The Mumble Rumble And The Cocktail Rock' and 'Pam's Moods'.

Despite the obvious frustrations of trying to bottle the live sound of the band, Ian savoured the recording experience. But he was dismayed at the outcome.

"I really enjoyed the whole process of making the album, although it turned out to be a bit of a drag, because it cost me a lot of money," Ian reflected.[8] "The lads were all broke, although I actually had a few bob at that time. I didn't pay for the studio time, but there were quite a few expenses. Then I went away for a week's holiday and when I came back, they had taken it out of my hands completely. They re-mixed the album and put strings on the tracks. I don't know if it was the manager or the record company's idea, but I was a bit pissed off about it at the time. I have the original tapes and the music just storms along."

Nothing, however, could have prepared the band for what was to follow. "The day that we finished mixing everything, we went into Raft Records and the A&R man was grim in the face and he said, 'I've just been closed down, the whole of Raft no longer exists, take this tape away and if you can find another record label, then go ahead,' " says Charlie Gillett.

A press release issued at the time stated that "all the artists on Raft have been invited to join one of the other WA [Warner Atlantic] labels", but while Family, previously on its Reprise label, were welcomed back from Raft, the Kilburns were a gamble that Warner was not prepared to take.

Of the immediate events leading up to the shock announcement, Ian told Peter Erskine of *NME* in August 1975: "You know what 'appened? They 'ad a big team of execs come down to see us at Dingwalls. Bleedin' 'undreds of 'em. A bit later, one of 'em takes me aside and asks me fings like 'Are you gonna be a superstar?' They was checkin' us out to see if we was worf 'angin' on to. And then a couple of days later . . . Bang! It all folded. Then, it was all excitement from Warner Bruvvers. Joe Smiff came over to see us at the 'Undred Club, but he didn't like us."

Joe Smith, then the all-powerful head of Warner Brothers in the US, had indeed flown to London and had caught the Kilburns playing in Oxford Street's famous 100 Club. But according to Charlie Gillett, he left after half an hour commenting: "What is this? I just don't get it at all. You're never gonna sell a record in America with this."

Charlie Sinclair is at pains to stress that while the episode resulted in disappointment, the Kilburns didn't emerge from the wreckage empty-handed. "There was some kind of rationing going on at Raft's pressing plant. It was more economical for Warner Brothers to cancel the entire output from Raft and they wanted stuff which would guarantee sales over Christmas," he explains. "Raft was all new stuff and I guess Family was the main band which would guarantee sales. I think we had to have an album out in a certain amount of time and they defaulted on that, so we just walked away with all the stuff we had already, including all the advance, and they called it a day. The gear was part of the advance. I think it was £50,000 cash, plus recording time, plus guaranteed subsidising of tours at various times."

Armed with a tape of the rejected album, Charlie Gillett and Gordon began banging on doors in search of a new home for the Kilburns. Glam and progressive rock bands were still dominating the charts, and the response of the major record companies was downbeat. But they were welcomed with open arms at Richard Branson's Virgin Records, which was reaping dividends with its first release, Mike Oldfield's *Tubular Bells*.

Charlie Gillett: "We played it to them and they knew a bit about

Kilburn & The High Roads and they just loved the whole thing. So we went back to Ian and said, 'Virgin are really interested.' But Ian's response was: 'Bunch of hippies. I don't want to be on the same label as Hatfield & The North. What's it going to look like, Kilburn & The High Roads and Hatfield & The North? No, I want to be on a label with Max Bygraves.' So Gordon and I went back to Virgin with our tails between our legs and said, 'Sorry, they don't want to be with you, but we would like to,' and they said, 'We would like you to be with us, what else have you got?' We retrieved the Louisiana material we had collected together two years earlier and they said, 'Wonderful, let's put this out.' So finally, in 1974, Oval Records got off the ground. And that was the end of our professional involvement with Ian."

In the wake of the Raft debacle, the Kilburns continued to gig in London and further afield, where they often received a much warmer response. Session drummer Louis Larose was replaced by long-serving pub rocker George Butler, whose CV included Eggs Over Easy, Uncle Dog and Clancy. But as they ploughed on in their more natural live environment, the group suffered another setback. Russell Hardy had been closer to Ian than most of those who had come and gone through the chameleon-like Kilburns line up and had been immensely loyal to him.

Throughout the Sixties and into the early days of the band at Wingrave, Russell had been the friend whom Ian had come to rely on in more ways than he might have wanted to admit. Musically, however, he was becoming more and more frustrated and he felt constrained by the kind of songs the band were playing. Minutes before a gig in Halifax, Ian's compliant right-hand man finally cracked.

Russell describes the events which led to his sudden departure. "We were in the Apple Studios one day and Tony Ashton came up to me and said, 'Look Russ, there's something I've got to say to you. Whatever you do, stay with Ian, stick together because as a writing team you're brilliant.' I just said, 'Oh yeah Tony, fine,' but unfortunately I have this really stubborn streak and when somebody rubs me up the wrong way, I just won't do it. And that, unfortunately, is what happened with Ian. I was doing a lot of work. I wrote all the songs and did what arrangements there were. I was doing quite a lot of the driving because nobody else could drive. I was drinking a lot and I was taking uppers and downers to calm me down and boost me up for playing. I had stage fright. All this was stacked against me and eventually I got to the point where I would be coming back from gigs and I had peculiar sensations in my skin, I was getting itchy, I couldn't keep still and I was really cracking up. I think that is really one of the reasons I had this fall out with Ian.

"We were playing the same sort of thing night after night and as a musician I just needed a change. I just wanted to go and play with some other people and do a different thing. But Ian never wanted you to do that, because he thought you were going to bugger off, which I had no intention of doing. I felt I needed to do some other things with other people, that's all it was. I was doing a couple of things with Charlie Hart and somebody else. One night, before a gig, Ian said, 'Look Russ, I think we ought to have a talk about this,' because we were all having a bit of a beef about things, and I said, 'No, I don't want to talk about it.' Then he started getting a bit heavy saying, 'We ought to talk about it,' and he can be very forceful and verbal when he wants. When someone confronts a situation, some people can sort it out. But I can't cope with it and I said, 'Fuck you,' and I just walked off and never did the gig. That was the last thing I ever did with Ian. It was quite dramatic. Ian went absolutely stark staring mad. After the gig, I saw him somewhere to sort it out and he was fucking and blinding and stomping along behind me and cursing and shouting, 'You fucking useless cunt, I don't need you.' But once I got over my initial thing, I didn't really care. Nobody else said anything – we were all very much under his thumb."

Back in London, Charlie and Gordon were launching Oval Records and getting ready to release their collection of Louisiana songs on a compilation album called *Another Saturday Night*. Meanwhile, Ian – reeling from the loss of a record deal, his management and co-song writer – was searching for a new manager. Eventually, he found someone to take on the task.

Tommy Roberts was short and overweight, but what he lacked in physical appearance he made up for ten-fold in attitude. A bubbly entrepreneur with an eye for the main chance, his lively personality was a dramatic contrast to the calm understated ways of Charlie and Gordon. In the Sixties, Tommy was 'Mr Freedom' with his own chain of trendy London clothes shops. It was at Tommy's former premises at 430 King's Road, Chelsea that Malcolm McLaren and his girlfriend, the avant-garde fashion designer Vivienne Westwood, opened Let It Rock (later renamed Sex) – an Aladdin's cave of clothes and fashion accessories, specialising in rubber. But he later lost most of his money and after meeting Ian through Malcolm McLaren, Tommy agreed in July 1974 to take charge of the group's affairs. Assisted by his business partner Willy, he injected a fresh impetus into the Kilburns and his eye for style gave them a new look. Ian began appearing in a yellow satin boxer's robe with 'Billy Bentley' – Ian's fictional character – sewn on the back, while Charlie Sinclair appeared on stage in a grey Harrods' schoolboy suit and fringed haircut. Vivienne Westwood also helped redesign the Kilburns' wardrobe.

Davey Payne: "Vivienne measured us up and said to me that I should wear black satin, but she didn't make the clothes. She designed them, sketched the ideas, and then sent them to some tailor in East London or something. I've still got my jacket. It was great, we all went to Smiley's for haircuts and had a backdrop made. A theatre down the King's Road was doing *The Rocky Horror Show* and we played there for a weekend with this big backdrop of Tower Bridge."

Denise remembers: "When Tommy Roberts took over, there was still some money in the bank – about £1,200 – and the first thing he did was to take us all down the King's Road to Malcolm and Vivienne's shop and buy suits for everybody. Ian got a de-mob suit. Their shop was stocked with de-mob suits and rubber and I remember having slight reservations about Tommy coming in and spending all this money because I thought they had the look before. Tommy was a risk taker. He had made a fortune and then lost it and that was his nature. He didn't know much about music, but he had an eye for things. Tommy was great fun on the road and a relief for me to have around because he could drive. Once we pulled into a petrol station and he got out of the car and tripped and fell over. He was a large chap and very short and he just flailed around like a beached whale for about a minute. I remember, there had been a big argument in the van beforehand and everybody was in fits of laughter for hours afterwards."

By this time Denise Roudette had also become a key member of the Kilburns' road crew. With Russell no longer on hand to ferry the band around, Denise took over at the wheel and lent a hand to the group's then roadies Joe King, an American folk guitarist, and Rob Pegg. She also helped Ian keep track of gig bookings and payments back at the flat. In a Kilburn & The High Roads family tree, handwritten by Ian, it says simply of Denise: "Personal manager. Promoters quaked. Sole driver of a bus full of nutters." Charlie Sinclair recalls: "She had a white lab coat and when she was driving us, it looked like 'care in the community'. It used to freak out hitch-hikers."

Denise also danced on stage and provided backing vocals, sometimes accompanied by another female singer. "None of them could drive, so I did all the driving and I got entertained along the way with all the songs and the stories," she says. "It was great, it was a living picture. Ian attracted all kinds of people into his life, but they had one thread in common – that they were all true to themselves. Ian knew his craft. He always said it's not about talent necessarily, it's about learning the craft. I was 19 when I met Ian and the Kilburns and for the next six years I had a life education."

Almost immediately after Tommy took charge, he secured a record deal with Dawn, a division of Pye – then the home of Max Bygraves. The label saw the band as "an art version of Showaddywaddy", Ian told Q magazine in 1991, and although the deal was deemed highly unsatisfactory when shown to solicitors, the group reluctantly signed it. The Kilburns were now back where they had been six months earlier, albeit with the obligatory personnel changes. In Russell's place, Ian introduced Roderick Melvin, a former Reading Art School student who had founded The Moodies, and the spurned drummer David Newton-Rohoman got a surprise recall.

At the Pye Studios in Marble Arch, under the production of Hugh Murphy, the Kilburns re-recorded most of the same songs they had produced for Raft. This time, Ian's weird and wonderful songs would see the light of day under the title *Handsome* (the band wanted to call it *No Hand Signals*). According to some of those involved, however, the Pye sessions were fraught and often ill-tempered, as the frustrations of the previous months rose to the surface.

"There were people fighting on the floor of the studio and other people being restrained," recalls Charlie. "A lot of that might have been the tension of recording and the adrenaline and trying to get some kind of deal. Other niggles would come to the fore, because the other guys had been hanging out together for far longer than I had been around. Ian is not the greatest singer in the world, in a melodic sense, and they were ignoring the spirit of what he was doing and trying to get more melody into it. But he was more interested in the spacing of the words and the poetry of it."

In November, 'Rough Kids' was released as a single, the very first record to feature Ian Dury. A rousing, sax-drenched song, on which Ian virtually screeched himself hoarse, it was set in the kind of bleak urban landscape which would serve as a backdrop for later creations, and opened with the sound of someone booting a crumpled tin can. It was coupled on the single with 'Billy Bentley (Promenades Himself In London)', a song written with Charlie Hart, in which a kid who heads for the big smoke gets more than he bargained for. This unusual song also went down well live, so much so that students at a college in Wrexham, south Wales, formed a Billy Bentley Fan Club.

It was also an early indication of how much Ian had been influenced by music hall artists: the lyrics were spoken, rather than sung, and relied heavily on London place names, which were arranged in a list. This, in time, would become another of Ian Dury's stylistic traits. But music journalists who had raved about the Kilburns' gigs in London were disappointed with the sanitised studio treatment of Dury's graffiti-sprayed urban anthem.

NME did include 'Rough Kids' in its Singles Of The Week, but noted that both songs had suffered in the production process: "Compared to the original recorded versions [Raft], both have been considerably dressed up. Singer Ian Dury performs with his customary grit, the saxist pulls out his best 'Rocking Goose' tones, and Russell Hardy, the recently departed piano player, stabs the ivories to good effect."

Chris Thomas, who later produced The Sex Pistols' début 'Anarchy In The UK', recalled his disappointment at the group's vinyl début in the sleeve-notes for a 1999 CD reissue of *Handsome*.[10] "I was originally approached by Charlie Gillett and I went to see them a couple of times at Dingwalls. They were fantastic and I wanted to try and capture some of that madness. We did the two tracks, 'Rough Kids' and 'Billy Bentley', and all the band played on these, we didn't use session men. On 'Rough Kids', Ian bashed or kicked a dustbin lid, and on 'Billy Bentley' he played skulls. But then they got a new manager in, Tommy Roberts, and it all went pear shaped . . . they got someone else to do the album. The funny thing was, a couple of years later, when I was approached by Malcolm McLaren about possibly doing The Sex Pistols, he set up a meeting with Steve Jones, Paul Cook and Glen Matlock, and they wanted me to produce them because they'd liked 'Rough Kids'. I didn't think anyone had ever heard it."

In February 1975 Pye released a second single, the soulful 'Crippled With Nerves', with the energetic bedroom romp 'Huffety Puff' on the flip-side. Reviewers gave this a warmer reception, but still mourned the absence of the group's live sound. *Sounds* magazine weighed in with the withering observation – "sounds as though the band aspire to be Britain's Dr Hook". Those who had seen the Kilburns on their extensive travels around Britain must have thought the reviewer had confused them with another act. The Kilburns they knew were menacing, aggressive and decidedly distasteful. At universities, boat clubs, and private clubs in small towns such as Cheltenham and Burton-on-Trent, punters stared up from their pints in amazement as Dury sinisterly slipped a gleaming knife from the inside of his jacket during the psychopathic 'I Made Mary Cry'. The Kilburns were not for the faint-hearted.

"If I look nasty tonight, it's all show-biz," Ian told an audience at Dingwalls, before taking up the microphone and singing: "Girl of fifteen is a little bit young in general for a boy to get excited thinkin." This was the opening line of 'I'll Have You', a disturbing tale of sex with a teenage girl. The chorus left little to whatever imagination the listener had left ("I'll have you, get us all in stitches/I'll have you, despite your tender years/I'll have you, I'm taking off my britches/I'll have you, I'll fuck away your tears").

Charlie: "We did this song called 'I Made Mary Cry' which was about a psychopath cutting a girl up in a bus shelter and it was a really quiet waltz which got really loud and ended up with a Dury scream. We did a gig in Windsor barracks for some regiment which was going overseas to Hong Kong and this very well-spoken officer comes up and says, 'Your songs are disgusting, but they're rather amusing.' "

But the Kilburns had a loyal following, as Charlie says: "There was always a hard core of people who would come and see us, no matter where we were in London. The Kingston boys would always turn up and in other places, certain people would turn up. There was a famous girl who always came to Dingwalls who wouldn't talk and sat in the dressing room until somebody talked to her and then she would get up and go out. She gave Ian a gold-plated razor-blade to put in his ear and that was the first time I ever saw someone wearing a razor-blade."

Even though rock'n'roll covers still cropped up on set lists, the Kilburns now had plenty of original material. Dury songs in the band's eclectic songbook included 'Okay Roland', 'Who's To Know?', 'The Old Bang', 'Back To Blighty', 'The Funky/Flunkey Jive', 'Beauty', 'A Band Called The Tights' and 'Bag Of The Islands', although these were never properly recorded and exist today only on the dusty cassettes of band members.

While Rod Melvin composed much of the music for the group at this time, Charlie Hart co-wrote 'Okay Roland' and Keith Lucas collaborated with Ian on 'Back To Blighty' and 'I'll Have You'. Whatever audiences made of this rag-bag of songs, on one thing everyone was agreed – they were unlike anything else that was happening in 1975, or indeed at any time before or since.

Although they did not realise it at this time, Ian Dury's cult band was providing the stimulus for a welter of future acts. As he limped across the beer-splattered stages of pubs, clubs and college halls in London, Ian was being closely studied by the next generation of would-be rockers. In the next few years his influence would become apparent as various strands of his image, music and stage manner were reflected by other performers. Wiry, spiky-haired adolescent John Lydon turned up for gigs with Malcolm McLaren and Vivienne Westwood, including some of the Kilburns' regular slots at that time at The Rainbow Room, situated above Biba's department store in Kensington High Street. When, as Johnny Rotten, he would later invade the nation's television sets screaming 'Anarchy In The UK', the grubby white scarf and the contorted way he dangled from the microphone were unmistakably Dury.

Saxophonist and singer Lene Lovich was fronting a soul band called The Diversions when she first stumbled on the Kilburns in London. Three years later, her own off-beat stage image would thrust her into the limelight alongside both Eric and Ian. She was struck by Ian's natural ability to communicate with his audience and the Kilburns' ability to add to the spectacle of a live show. "It was good clean anarchy," says Lene, who now lives in Norfolk with her long-time partner and musical collaborator Les Chappell. "It must have been way ahead of punk, but they were playing soulful things and Ian was hitting a lot of things – percussion. They were saying, 'We can do what we like and have a great time and be entertaining.' They were not alienating the audience, but they were not conforming to the usual accepted way of people performing."

Another Kilburns admirer, who would later find fame alongside Ian as Wreckless Eric, was art student Eric Goulden. When his eponymous début album was released in March 1978, it included a cover of 'Rough Kids'. "I had a band in Hull, where I was at art school, and we had all seen Kilburn & The High Roads and we were just inspired by them, because they were such a mess really," says Eric. "In a way, they couldn't play that well, they could play nearly well enough to do what they were doing, but it worked. I thought they must have all met in a home or something. You looked at them and thought, 'They're not normal these people.' "

Kilburn & The High Roads made their deepest and most significant impression on a group of young musicians from north London. Ian's stage theatrics, his indomitable Englishness and the bizarre-looking Kilburns, would inspire them to start their own band – Madness. Teenage friends Lee Thompson and Chris Foreman, who both lived in Highgate Road, Kentish Town, had seen a poster advertising the Kilburns at Tally Ho and, on the basis of the group's "stupid name", reckoned on an entertaining night.

"We went along to see them and I saw this fella limping along and he looked quite smart and I thought that maybe he worked in the pub. I said 'What time's the band on?' and he said 'I dunno mate,' and that was Ian Dury," says Chris. The impressionable lads were captivated by what they saw on the venue's tiny stage and within weeks were back with keyboard player Mike Barson, who they'd known since their primary school days in Gospel Oak. Soon they were regular faces in the crowd at Kilburns' gigs.

Chris: "Me and Lee went to Dingwalls one night. We were really young and it was the first time we had been there and they had this policy where drinks were half price before 11pm and they had peanuts in trays on the tables, which I thought was extremely sophisticated, and I remember sitting there with about 10 pints of beer on the table and eating these peanuts. Before the Kilburns came on, the pianist Rod Melvin was sitting at another table and he had cotton wool in his ears and he was knitting something and we were going, 'Oh look at him, he's so nutty.' "

Towards the end of 1976, the three began meeting at Mike's house and plotting their very own group, The Invaders. Gradually, more and more mates got roped in, including Graham 'Suggs' McPherson and Mark Bedford, and among the first songs they played live were 'The Roadette Song', 'Rough Kids' and an accelerated rendition of 'Crippled With Nerves'. But it wasn't until April 1979 that they assumed the moniker under which they would become one of the biggest success stories of the Eighties. Their début single 'The Prince' on the 2-Tone label – a tribute to early ska music protagonist Prince Buster – bore all the hallmarks of Kilburn & The High Roads, with its heavy reggae pulse and emphasis on Lee's saxophone. After signing to Stiff, the London lads then released 'One Step Beyond', the sleeve of which bore more than a passing resemblance to the Kilburns' early bus-stop-style publicity picture. Mick Hill's photograph was not directly responsible for the picture cover of the Madness single and the subsequent album of the same name, but the group was conscious of the Kilburns' visual ingenuity when it embarked on a career which would spawn more than 20 hit singles to date.

"We started doing posters like that when we first started doing photo sessions," explains Chris. "We had this thing called a 'Nutty Train' which was something I came up with which was based on a sketch by The Two Ronnies. There was a row of working-class houses and a bloke knocks on the door and another bloke comes out and gets right up behind him and walks exactly in his footsteps and it goes on and on until there's loads of them and they walk into a sardine factory which is where they work. I remember thinking that's really funny and we did some photos for the *NME* and I said, 'Let's walk close behind each other,' and we got closer and closer and then Mike Barson turned it into a train by pumping his arms. That is sort of where it came from. But the back of the album has got Chas Smash dancing around and that's because on the back of *Handsome* there's this nutty bloke and it says, 'Paul Hangs Loose.' To us, this geezer was so cool, we just thought he looked totally wacky with a big beard and creepers on and so we put Chas on the back like 'Paul Hangs Loose'."

Of the Kilburns' musical influence on 'The Nutty Boys', Chris says: "We liked them because they did reggae and they did this music hall type stuff, very English, and the lyrics were very good. Obviously that is the same line-up musically as Madness had. We had a sax player, a piano player, exactly the same line-up, and we used to do some of their songs. Ian Dury has a very distinctive voice and I think he is a great singer and Suggs isn't a fantastic singer in the true sense, but I really like the way he sings."

In the true spirit of the Kilburns, Madness earned a reputation as a good-time band, combining tales of everyday life with rhythms both frantic ('Nightboat To Cairo' and 'Baggy Trousers') and more laid-back

('My Girl' and 'Los Palmas 7'). Their Eighties videos were memorable and the level of consideration given to costumes and props mirrored Ian's own attention to detail, even though the 'Madness seven' tended to dress uniformly, something of which the Kilburns could never be accused.

Suggs paid tribute to his hero in the Radio 2 documentary about Ian broadcast in 1999 and confirmed his influence on his own quintessentially English vocal delivery. "It was great because Ian didn't seem anything like rock'n'roll or music biz. It just seemed like a lot of nutty characters on stage with instruments and he seemed more like a poet than a rock'n'roll artist. That inspired Madness to go down that route without actually having to know anything about the music business. We didn't understand the process of making records or PR or interviews because we had seen Ian Dury do it – somebody with polio – and you just saw all the possibilities for people who didn't necessarily look like rock stars. He was such a great performer as well. In between the songs he would pull a handkerchief out of his pocket or these gross pornographic magazines with people with clothes pegs on their nipples. It was amazing and it was how I imagined music hall must have been like in its heyday, a real theatrical performance; he's been a huge influence. I can tell you, there was a lot more Cockney on the early albums than there actually was in real life as a consequence of listening to Ian Dury."

In June of 1975, *Handsome* was released on the Dawn label. The sleeve – a beautiful painting by Betty – captured the band in contemplative mood sitting in front of a wire fence with Tower Bridge looming behind. The band's roadie Paul Tonkin, resplendent with brillo-pad hair, beard and thick rimmed glasses, was captured performing a strange dance in a black and white photograph on the back of the sleeve. The image, 'Paul Hangs Loose', was credited to 'Poundcake' – Ian's photographic pseudonym. "Ian set that up in the vicarage and he liked to see the shadow in the light," reveals Paul. "I had this jacket which I'd bought from a shop in the King's Road, which later turned into the place run by Malcolm McLaren. Anyway, Ian played this Chuck Berry record which I danced to and every so often he would say 'Freeze' and take a photo of me in these bizarre poses."

The track listing included many old favourites, but also some newer material: 'The Roadette Song', 'Pam's Moods', 'Crippled With Nerves', 'Broken Skin', 'Upminster Kid', 'Patience (So What?)', 'Father', 'Thank You Mum', 'Rough Kids', 'The Badger And The Rabbit', 'The Mumble Rumble And The Cocktail Rock' and 'The Call Up'. But like the two singles, the album failed to seize the anarchic Kilburns' live sound and was more clinical than the material recorded for Raft. Whereas the band members received little extra backing for the Raft sessions, a string of session musicians contributed this time.

The pedal steel guitars of Rod King and Pete Wilsher featured throughout and their liberal use on songs such as the soulful ballad 'Broken Skin', which was sung by Rod Melvin, gave this album a more mellow feel. He also sang the quirky 'Thank You Mum', the other song on the album which he co-wrote with Ian. Rod's cabaret keyboards, meanwhile, seemed to take the edge off songs like 'The Roadette Song' and 'Crippled With Nerves'. Backing singers had been used during the Raft recordings and two female vocalists were drafted in for *Handsome*. Clare Torry had famously sung on Pink Floyd's *Dark Side Of The Moon*, while Tina Charles would enjoy a number one hit the following year with 'I Love To Love (But My Baby Loves To Dance)' and subsequent chart successes. Other musicians who played on the album included guitarist Les Thatcher and all-rounder Jon Field.

Ian's singing was more restrained on the finished product. The grating voice which gave a serrated edge to songs like 'The Mumble Rumble' and 'Upminster Kid' and the finale of 'Crippled With Nerves' was gone. The absence of 'Billy Bentley' and the risqué reggae number 'You're More Than Fair' had arguably weakened its impact. It was as if someone had decided to smooth out the wrinkles and bring some discipline to the band's playing. In doing so, they had removed the blemishes to which the Kilburns owed so much of its appeal. *Handsome* sold less than 3,000 copies.

Charlie Sinclair comments: "We had played the songs a lot longer and we were probably more proficient at the arrangements, but when we got to the studios it was all changed to try and make it more acceptable. Everything then was 'glam rock' and big stereo sounds and I always thought we were the first punk band and we didn't really know how to market it. It was like taking something and trying to jam it ninety degrees sideways into a different sized slot. One of the problems was that we never really had a proper drummer. There was always someone filling in or somebody who wasn't quite right. Rohoman was there for ages, but he was crippled and had to walk on two sticks. That was typical of the thing that made us great live and all the spirit was drained out of it by what they tried to do in the studio, trying to make it 'proper' music."

Davey Payne told Q magazine in 1991: "The Kilburns were a rough band and the guitars were hard and heavy, but Ian wanted a record that sounded cleaner, where people sounded like they knew what they were doing. So he went along with a wishy-washy production."

An interview given by Hugh Murphy to Fred Dellar for *Sound International* some years later, indicated that the internal goings on at Pye had done no favours to the recording process. Murphy, who has since died, had also been disappointed by the finished product and admitted it had been a rushed job.

"The Kilburns were signed to Pye by a man who left after we'd been working on the album for a week," said Hugh. "I'd been told, 'I know it's a difficult band, so spend what you need and take as much time as you want.' Then the geezer we did the deal with left and then I got the phone call saying, 'What's going on down there? Finish that album, now!' So, I'd started one way, then all of a sudden I had to scurry around, get overdubs by anyone who could do them – Dave Mattacks did much of the drumming – slap on things, and mix it quick. And because the carpet had been pulled, I was only allowed one mix on the album. I think you need to get the feel of a track and mix it twice at least. But this one took just one mix and then it was shoved out.

"No one could understand what they were doing with this funny band, anyway. They were all weird people . . . a tiny, short bass player; a geezer whose legs didn't work; and little Ian Dury . . . cor! 'Oh dear,' they thought, 'What's all this? We've spent three thousand on this album, so go and spend another two, but finish it for those two thousand pounds.' The album eventually came out to terrible reviews, merely because there wasn't enough thought put into it. Maybe, in retrospect, I should have done it live . . . I wanted to get it as tight as possible and get that idiosyncratic Dury frame of mind over."

The *Handsome* sessions at Pye also led to the souring of another of Ian's long-standing friendships. Keith Lucas had taken part in the recording and appeared on the album cover. But his guitar parts were augmented on the finished record by one of the session players, leaving Keith – who had survived four versions of the group – furious. But there had long been a friction between Ian and Keith, whose manic and edgy guitar style on stage was later copied by Dr Feelgood maestro Wilko Johnson. If anything, it was a surprise that Keith had stayed so loyal to Ian, who was so often the root of any trouble in the Kilburns.

"Keith and Ian did hate each other in an odd kind of way," says Gordon. "Keith would go a bit mad. He was normally extremely polite, almost obsequious, but every now and then he would go crazy. Keith was a nice guy and the only one who tried and Humphrey was genuinely nice. But Ian just disrupted everything. He was always undermining situations and I don't know how Denise Roudette put up with it. He was very charming and articulate, but extremely disruptive."

The events which followed Keith's departure from the band were deeply unpleasant and he remains bitter and angry about them to this day. So much so that when Ian turned up at a party Keith and his wife were attending some years ago, the couple immediately left. Keith refuses to talk about Ian or his time with Kilburn & The High Roads.

Davey explains the background: "Ian wanted Keith out. I don't know why, but he wanted Keith out. Keith said, 'Look, I'm fed up with this, I want out anyway,' so we stole the PA which we had got through the Warner Brothers deal and sold it to Lene Lovich. Keith took over my flat in Streatham and some time after that 'Spider' [Ian's minder Fred Rowe] went round to duff him up and take his guitars. Keith was going to call the police but didn't. It wasn't a very nice thing to do really. We felt we were justified because they had two vans and we were the original people to sign this deal. Also, we needed some bread and Ian was turning down gigs, as always." Although Keith and others felt Ian had been behind this incident, Ian denied having anything to do with it.

Two years later, Keith embraced the burgeoning punk scene and re-invented himself under the alias Nick Cash. This time he would be the front man. His archetypal punk outfit started life as The Dials and then The Frantics, before 999 made its first live appearance in London on April 5, 1977, opening for The Jam at The Nashville. An independently released single 'I'm Alive' convinced United Artists to sign his band and two singles 'Nasty Nasty' and 'Emergency' quickly followed. But although 999 earned a solid live reputation, these singles failed to attain the kind of success which other punk exponents were enjoying. 'Homicide', the band's sixth single did enter the charts, but got no higher than number 40 in November 1978. Two albums were also released by United Artists, but 999 were dropped in 1979 and success continued to elude them after they were picked up by Polydor. A last throw of the dice with the Albion label produced three singles which scraped into the lower reaches of the Top 75 during 1981. But against the odds, 999 survived through it all and continue to play live in the UK, central Europe and the US.

David Newton-Rohoman had also displayed great loyalty to Ian, even after being sacked on the eve of the Raft recordings. But much of the drumming on *Handsome* was that of Dave Mattacks, ex of Fairport Convention and then with the Etchingham Steam Band, who was called in when Rohoman failed to measure up. When the album was released, the most laid-back member of the Kilburns, with his black broad-rimmed hat, left and never made contact again.

An extract from Pete Erskine's article in *NME* appears to shed some light on the studio shenanigans which pre-empted his departure. "David Rohoman, the drummer, quit because he no longer had the strength in his right leg to work the bass drum pedal. So they replaced him with

Malcolm Mortimer (sic) who used to be with Gentle Giant until a serious road accident incapacitated him and the doctors told him he'd never play again. 'He 'ad an amazing voice, but his legs didn't work too well,' Ian Dury says of Rohoman, ' 'Is drumming wasn't exactly metronomic because 'is 'ands were never in the right place.' Dury, however, has plans to introduce Rohoman as a singer. 'We would have 'ad him up front singing but it'd be such a performance with the crutches an' everything.' Dury opines that Rohoman could be 'big' as a singer because he always gets the words wrong. Like on 'Rainy Night In Georgia' he sings 'hoovering around the railway station' instead of 'hovering around the railway station'."

By the time *Handsome* was released, Charlie Sinclair had also quit. "We were working like bastards, touring all over the place, gigging here, gigging there, and Tommy Roberts said, 'There's no more money left, you'll have to go on the dole all of you and get paid that way.' I thought 'sod that' and upped sticks."

One of the last Kilburns' gigs in which Charlie and Keith played was at the Hammersmith Odeon, as support to Dr Hook & The Medicine Show. By this time, David Newton-Rohoman had already left and newcomer Malcolm Mortimore was ensconced behind the kit. He had played with GT Moore & The Reggae Guitars, as well as Gentle Giant, before receiving the Kilburns' call. This line-up made several public appearances, but the Kilburns were running out of steam. A tour of Belgium, Holland and France proposed for late July, and gigs in Yugoslavia and Poland booked for the first two weeks in August, were scrapped. In May 1975, after five separate manifestations and more reshuffles than a government front bench, Kilburn & The High Roads disbanded – dejected and broke.

During the lull that followed, Ian seized the opportunity to concentrate on his songwriting and adjourned into private session with Rod Melvin. Theirs was a new partnership, as Ian's productive relationship with Russell had only recently come off the rails. But this alliance was to prove highly productive and highlighted, not for the last time, the rewards to be gained from giving time to the writing process. One song in particular stood out when they emerged from these sessions.

'What A Waste' was a cleverly crafted song, peppered with funny rhymes and with a memorable hook. In the verses, Ian pondered the merits of a variety of professions. "I could be a lawyer with stratagems and muses/ I could be a doctor of poultices and bruises/ I could be a writer with a growing reputation/ I could be the ticket man at Fulham Broadway station". But in the chorus, he urged the listener to follow their instincts as he celebrated becoming "the leader in a six-piece band". For the moment, 'What A Waste' would remain a well-kept secret.

"I nicked that because it wasn't my phrase. Everyone used to say it all the time," said Ian.[8] "When I wrote that I was thinking 'Come on God, give me a break.' A friend of mine used to work in a factory, but he said he could be a playwright. Then one day he heard my record on the radio and thought it was about him. So he downed tools that day and went out to be a playwright. The song just says – put your money where your mouth is. Try it. Just do it." The Dury/Melvin co-operative also spawned 'England's Glory', a wonderfully eccentric and uplifting song, set firmly in the tradition of the music hall acts such as Max Miller whom Ian adored. Delivering a kind of Cockney alternative to 'These Are A Few Of My Favourite Things', the Pearly King of Upminster rampaged through the "jewels in the crown of England's glory", rhyming relentlessly as he went. "Frankie Howerd and Noel Coward and garden gnomes/ Frankie Vaughan and Kenneth Horne and Sherlock Holmes" he sang, before paying tribute to other quintessentially British characters real and fictional, ranging from George Formby and Enid Blyton to Mr Pastry and Muffin the Mule. It was a Dury classic.

In November 1975, Ian was reunited with his former manager Dave Robinson and he set about rebuilding the band, this time as Ian Dury & The Kilburns. Within weeks, they were back on the pub trail. Russian bassist Giorgi Dionisiev – quickly nicknamed 'George Dinner Suit' by Ian – was now on bass, Irishman John Earle, a stalwart of showbands such as Tripoli, Germany and Gnrndrilog, replaced Davey who had retreated to Clacton and started playing gigs with The Fabulous Poodles, and Ed Speight, who had played on Mike Oldfield's highly acclaimed début album *Tubular Bells*, returned on a permanent basis to play lead guitar.

Ian Dury & The Kilburns were still a strange sight, for all the personnel changes. Malcolm Mortimore walked with a limp as a result of an accident, Ian continued to dangle perilously from his microphone wearing a razor-blade earring and his knotted white scarf, and the extremely camp pianist, with savage crew cut, would sashay on to the stage wearing high-heeled shoes and a dress. Publicans who booked the band frequently did a double-take when the Kilburns arrived to set up their gear, but few would have dared to poke fun. "Fred!" Ian would roar in the loudest and most aggressive voice he could muster, and instantly his newly acquired roadie and personal bodyguard would arrive, towering menacingly over the offender.

Ian Dury was physically vulnerable and as a result was in awe of anyone whose stature alone could imply the threat of violence. His new minder was the ultimate form of protection for Ian and would cement his own hard-man image. Fred Rowe had spent much of his life in prison and his ability to creep up drainpipes and disarm alarm systems during break-ins had earned him the nickname 'Spider'. An Eastender who spoke in the Cockney rhyming slang which so fascinated Ian, he had served in the Korean War during his National Service. Now, he was living with his girl-friend and two children in Oval Mansions, glazing windows for the local council and trying to go straight. He had only been living there for a few weeks when he encountered Ian on the stairs and helped him carry an old mattress and some of his other possessions up to his flat. Over a mug of tea, his neighbour told him that his band was back playing the London pubs and some weeks later, when Ian needed a van, Fred agreed to lend a hand. Ian was delighted with his hew handyman and impressed by his genuinely villainous and working-class credentials. Not long afterwards, Ian handed him another assignment.

"Ian come down one Saturday and said, 'We've got a TV slot with Janet Street-Porter for London Weekend Television,' and I said, 'Blimey, that's great,' " recalls Fred. "He said, 'Will you come?' and I said, 'Well I don't feel very confident in doing it for a TV show, haven't they people there to do that sort of thing?' and Ian said, 'No, you're great, you can do it.' At the studio, Dave Robinson arrived and said to me, 'Are you their roadie?' I said, 'Yeah, I suppose I am really,' and he started giving me a hand getting all the extra stuff they needed for this show. I had never been in a TV studio before, this was all new to me, and Ian was just great. He did the interview with Janet Street-Porter and they did a couple of songs. It was really excel-lent and we were there all day Sunday."

'Spider' was still working for the council during the day, but at night he became a fixture at Kilburns' gigs, carrying amplifiers, setting up and checking sound equipment, and making lightning dashes onto the stage whenever Ian fell over. In return, he got "petrol money". Fred was simply a world away from the painting students and other arty types who had been at Ian's beck and call previously, and he instilled some discipline, both on and off stage.

Ed Speight remembers: " 'I Made Mary Cry' was a kind of lilting country Jim Reeves song about death, madness and murder, about someone who made Mary cry and as a result finished up all alone in a white dormitory. It was obviously humorous, but the thing was that as a band it was very difficult to play without cracking up laughing and Ian said, 'If you do this behind me I shall know, because my minder Fred Rowe will be in the front row taking notes and anybody who rolls their eyes or does anything he will be taking notes and immediate action will be taken'.

"We used to do Sunday afternoon prison concerts and one of these was in the chapel at Brixton Prison where Fred Rowe had himself been a 'guest'. Fred ran in the prison gate carrying amps on his shoulders trying to hide from the warders. The warder did a double take and then said, 'Spider Rowe,' and, of course, he wouldn't leave him alone. We played this song 'I Made Mary Cry In A Lonely Bus Shelter' to a chapel full of hardened prisoners and they loved it."

To Ian, Fred was much more than a stage hand. Back at Oval Mansions, he was a father figure, refereeing the frequent bust-ups between Ian and Denise who would often batter each other around their third-floor flat. Personal belongings flew from their window on to the street below and in the wake of one domestic dispute, Denise is said to have put his cherished typewriter up for sale in *Melody Maker*, advertising it as 'Ian Dury's old typewriter'.

Fred – in true army style – would sometimes order Ian to get his hat and coat and pack his bags before driving him to John Earle's home in Enfield, Middlesex, where he would stay while things with Denise were ironed out. At other times, Denise was sent into involuntary exile at her parents' home outside Blackpool.

Fred: "Denise and Ian used to have these amazing rows and she used to fight like a man. He used to come down to my place virtually in tears and I would have to go up and straighten it out with Denise. I used to put things to her and she used to say, 'Yeah, but the thing with you Fred is that Ian can't do a thing wrong in your eyes.' Well, you speak as you find and if people are good to you, you put that back, and when she said, 'Well he did this and he did that.' I said, 'Well, you know that is not him, that's not the real Ian.' I'm one of the old school and I don't like people slagging people off when they're not there to defend themselves and I said to Denise, 'You shouldn't say that when he's not here. I'm not saying that what you're saying is not true, but he should have a chance to say what caused that.' Anyway, she used to calm down and I'd say, 'Go on Ian, go up and give her a big cuddle and the old treatment,' so I was guiding him through this shark-infested sea of love. She used to say to me, 'I like to get him on his good leg so I can give him a whack and I know he can't support himself on the other leg. So she'd give him a whack on the shin and because he couldn't put his arm out to save himself, he would go straight down and he loved it. He loved every minute of it because he likes a bit of spirit in a girl."

Whatever fireworks went off between Ian and Denise, both he and his young girlfriend enjoyed a good relationship with Betty. Denise says that she baby-sat Jemima and Baxter while Betty painted the sleeve for *Hand-some* and, although it was a long time before Denise would meet Ian's mother, she was accepted by his wife. Ian meanwhile provided Betty with financial support, buying her a house. They remained close and enjoyed a relationship which was admired by those who knew them well.

"Betty liked me and we got on really well," says Denise. "It was extremely hard for her to bring up the kids, but we were good friends and we talked about Ian. I don't think it was a personal thing between them, I think they carried on having the same relationship they had before. They were obviously not still together, but they were always friends. There wasn't any animosity and she understood what Ian was doing."

After returning to the road, the Kilburns had landed a residency at the Hope & Anchor in Islington, north London, where Dave Robinson had a small studio. They also picked up badly needed earnings from some of their old haunts such as The Nashville in North End Road, West Kensington, and Dingwalls in Camden Lock, and they continued to draw a loyal following. But Ian was not receiving the kind of attention that his songs deserved. One talent-spotter/A&R man, Chas de Whalley, reportedly said of him: "Dury isn't the guy for a slick back-up band which means, ultimately, that he can't be groomed for stardom."

Dave Robinson had been instrumental in returning Ian to the pub scene, but now he was to play a much more significant role. In February 1976, he decided he could do no more for Ian and took him to meet Andrew King and Pete Jenner. On the surface of it, they couldn't have fitted in less with Ian's down-at-heel, working-class image, but their influence on his career would be telling. The pair were middle-class former Oxbridge graduates who ran Blackhill Enterprises from the top-floor of 32 Alexander Street, in Bayswater, west London, previously the home of Pink Floyd's Roger Waters.

Both Andrew and Peter had attended the same grammar school, won impressive university scholarships and remained close friends. So when they became tired of their respective jobs as an employee of British European Airways and a university lecturer, they packed them in and went into business. Blackhill began life in the mid-Sixties as the management firm which handled Pink Floyd, but when resident Floyd genius/acid casualty Syd Barrett was elbowed out in favour of guitarist Dave Gilmour, Jenner and King opted to manage Barrett while the Floyd became managed by their booking agent Steve O'Rourke. Assuming the group would flounder without Barrett seems in hindsight to be akin to Decca turning down The Beatles, but it reflected their integrity insofar as they realised Syd needed them more. In the event Syd went his own way and Blackhill ended up promoting free concerts in Hyde Park and managing, amongst others, The Edgar Broughton Band and Kevin Ayers.

Andrew had originally moved into Alexander Street after his marriage in 1968. To begin with, he and his wife Wendy lived upstairs, Wendy running a textile designing business from the ground floor room which had a large shop window overlooking the street. The basement housed her printing machinery. When they decided to live elsewhere, Blackhill set up an office upstairs and the ground floor was occupied by a variety of tenants including music promoter John Curd, and the Wasted Talent promotion agency, run by Ian Flukes. Ian Dury had initially been sceptical of Blackhill. He feared that Robinson – the highly persuasive Dubliner – was leading him into the company of hippies who wouldn't be able to understand what he was trying to do. His concerns proved unfounded.

"When Ian came to us, we became his publishers and the first thing I remember is reading the lyrics of 'Nervous Piss'," says Andrew King. "He brought a bunch of lyrics typed up and quite honestly, as soon as I read them I was absolutely determined to sign him as a songwriter. I remember sitting at this table in a great big room at Alexander Street and reading those lyrics. I have always warmed to writers who have really good lyrics, Syd Barrett of the Floyd wrote very good lyrics and so did Ian, so I instantly wanted to do it."

Andrew had once seen Kilburn & The High Roads when he had managed Alberto Y Los Trios Paranois and remembered thinking they were "the most scary bloody outfit" he had ever seen in his life. It was Ian's imaginative and carefully crafted lyrics, however, which he desperately wanted for Blackhill, and which he believed would eventually propel the singer to fame. Ian and Blackhill struck a deal in which Blackhill gained the copyright of some of Ian's most promising songs and Ian and the band got some badly needed cash for new equipment.

In January 1976, Ian's songwriting partner Rod Melvin had left the band to join the Scientologists. His announcement was a blow so soon after the Kilburns had reformed, especially as a clutch of fresh material, including 'Nervous Piss', 'I've Left The Rag Trade To Join The Drag Trade', 'Vidiot', 'Fits And Starts' and 'Back To Blighty', was ready to be rehearsed. Ian Dury & The Kilburns were also now making regular appearances at Dingwalls and a speedy replacement was needed. Ed Speight contacted his friend Mike King at Maurice Plaquat's music shop in the Uxbridge Road in Shepherd's Bush and asked him if he knew of a keyboard player/arranger who was available at that time. Days later, a young, out-of-work musician called Chaz Jankel walked through the doors of the shop wanting to buy a keyboard. The events that followed would not only solve Ian's immediate dilemma, but alter the course of his career and his life.

Chaz recalls the events which led to his first encounter with Ian at The

Nashville: "I went into Maurice Plaquat's in Shepherd's Bush to buy a keyboard and I bought a Wurlitzer electric piano from them. While I was in there, I happened to mention to the manager that if anybody was looking for a keyboard player to give them my telephone number, because I didn't have a gig at the time. I was about 24 or 25 and wasn't doing a whole lot, I was still living at home. I was doing the odd gig, but nothing really that was very stimulating. He said, 'Well that's funny, because Ed Speight was saying that their keyboard player was leaving Kilburn & The High Roads and they're playing tomorrow night. Why don't you go down and see them?' I said, 'Okay,' and the next night I went down to this pub. The band came on pretty soon after I arrived. I had no idea what to expect and my memory is of it being very energised and very bizarre. Ian was wearing a Tommy Cooper fez and 'Irish', John Earle, looked the spitting image of Frank Zappa with a big moustache and a saxophone. It was captivating, that's the only way I can describe it. It wasn't even like music that I thought that I liked, but the spirit was very moving.

"At the end of the gig, in a practically hypnotised state, I walked up onto the stage. The band had disappeared down the side of the stage behind a curtain and I just followed them down this route and about half way down their road manager Fred Rowe spotted me and said, ' 'Ere mate, where are you going? If you want to see the band go round the other way.' So I hopped off the stage, went around the front of the stage and then into the front door of the dressing room. I went in and it was all steamy and everyone had their back turned to me, but Ian was sitting right in the middle of the room. He sees me and says, ' 'Ere mate, do I know you? . . . Well fuck off then.'

"I stood rooted to the spot like a rabbit caught in the head-lamps, not knowing quite what to do. I stood there and a bit of mumbling went on and then I retired to the further end of the dressing room considering what I was going to do, whether I was actually going to follow his advice or not. Then Ed Speight informed Ian that I was the musician that had been invited down and Ian was really embarrassed about what he'd said and very upset. I got invited down to a rehearsal the next day and I got the gig. And from then on I started getting gigs."

Chaz, originally from Pinner, had played music from a young age. At junior school he appeared in a little combo called Charlie and The Muck-It-Ups, playing songs such as 'Let's Twist Again', and at secondary school he formed Call Of The Wild with his friend Peter Van Hooke, who played drums. The group spent about five years doing house concerts and college dances. In 1971 he had joined Byzantium, which featured Robin Lamble on bass, Steve Corduner on drums and Nicko Ramsden on guitar and vocals. He contributed keyboards and vocals to the group which cut two albums for A&M – *Byzantium* and *Seasons Changing* – before disbanding in the summer of 1973. After that, Chaz took up with Jonathan Kelly's Outside before getting session work with former Small Faces frontman Steve Marriott and Tim Hardin. Punk rock was making its mark on the London scene when Chaz met Ian. The dives in which the Kilburns had played many of their early gigs were beginning to accommodate more aggressive groups like The 101'ers (later to become The Clash), The Stranglers and Eddie & The Hot Rods.

The Kilburns were still very much a feature of London's sweaty and overcrowded live scene, but rehearsals had gone decidedly up-market. Not for the Kilburns a cold church crypt or a tatty studio room, now that Blackhill had taken over the reins. They were destined for something much more glamorous. Headley Grange was a grand house on a large country estate in Dorking, Surrey. where Led Zeppelin had been known to rehearse. It was a galaxy away from the band's usual surroundings and they eyed its rooms with glee as they and their wives and girlfriends moved in to its palatial splendour. The opulent surroundings didn't always make for a relaxing atmosphere, however.

"One day after quite a hot rehearsal, Ed Speight went up to the drum kit in a fit of temper and pushed some cymbals over on the ground making an almighty clatter. John Earle took him by the scruff of the neck and said in his strong Irish accent, 'You do not touch the fucking kit, all right, you do not fuck with someone's instruments.' Ed went off in a huff up to his bedroom and then didn't come down again until later. Ian, who had been a bit frisky that day, got an egg, put it on top of Ed's head and cracks it. Ed, who was not exactly in the mood for a joke having been through this incident with Irish, was sitting there with egg dripping down his head. Then Ian, in an act of remorse, got an egg and did the same on his own head. It was that eccentric and bizarre at times."

But even at this early stage, it was becoming clear that the fusion of Ian and Chaz was potentially explosive. Chaz enjoyed jazz and rock, but he was more influenced by the sounds of Afro-American funk groups like Sly & The Family Stone, Ohio Players and War. Ian was growing weary of much of the Kilburns' repertoire and was keen to give his songs a keener edge. Here was a musician with an entirely fresh musical agenda who could put Ian's songs to an infectious dance setting.

Ian said:[14] "One morning I got up and I was playing the drums on Malcolm's drum kit and behind me I heard a bit of funky music. My ears pricked up and I turned round and it was Chaz. At that very moment I heard what I wanted to hear. I felt a shared rhythmical inspiration, I just got a buzz, an adrenaline rush right up my body. It's hard to describe. I'm

English. I don't want to be American or sing in American, but I'm well influenced by Afro-American music and reggae and it is still dancing, there is still a place where you drop, where your spirit and your arse land at the same time. As soon as I heard Chaz playing very simple clarinet like piano behind me I knew there was a shared thing. I packed in the Kilburns in the end at the end of that week and we started writing together."

Ian Dury & The Kilburns played their last gig in front of a small crowd on June 17, 1976, at Walthamstow Assembly Hall, north east London, at the Midsummer Music Festival Benefit. The Kilburns were the headline act, but they were supported by two up-and-coming bands, The Stranglers, and a group of scrawny urchins calling themselves The Sex Pistols. The Stranglers had been formed by Hugh Cornwell, Jean Jacques Burnell and Jet Black, after they met at college in 1974, and had previously been known as Johnny Sox & The Guildford Stranglers. The following year they were joined by Dave Greenfield, whose brooding keyboards would give them a distinctive and powerful sound. The 'men in black' had caused a furore in London three months before their appearance in Walthamstow with a promotional poster which showed a victim of the Boston Strangler in a pool of blood, but they would not land their record deal with United Artists until December 1976 and their début single '(Get A) Grip (On Yourself)' would not be released until January 1977.

The Sex Pistols, under the Fagin-like stewardship of spindly street guru Malcolm McLaren, had only played a handful of gigs since making their first live appearance at St Martin's Art College in London on November 6, 1975, playing support to Bazooka Joe, led by one Stuart Goddard, later Adam Ant. But the band – Johnny Rotten (John Lydon), Glen Matlock, Steve Jones and Paul Cook – were already earning a reputation. The Pistols had demolished sound gear belonging to pub rockers Eddie & The Hot Rods during their first big London gig at the Marquee Club in Wardour Street in February and the music press was starting to take an interest, especially in the leery, green-teethed Rotten. In December 1976, they would begin their ascent to becoming Britain's most infamous band of all time, beginning with the release of the punk anthem, 'Anarchy in the UK'.

Tony Wilson, the presenter of the Granada TV show *So It Goes*, recalled in *Mojo* in March 2000: "My producer told me I had to see the Pistols again before we could book them, so I went to Walthamstow. It was a brilliantly hot summer, so it was still glorious sunshine outside, but dark and gloomy inside, and all you could see was a semi-circle of people standing in front of the stage. Mystifying until I went closer and realised that the arc of the circle was the distance Johnny Rotten could spit."

Rotten had frequently attended Kilburns' shows with his ginger-haired boss and had clearly been watching carefully. When The Sex Pistols took to the stage for their bottom-of-the-bill slot at Walthamstow Assembly Hall, Rotten's mimicry of Ian's stage act led to an uneasy moment for Malcolm McLaren.

Ian recalled: "He had the safety-pin, which was the sartorial elegance that I had inspired myself with, and was leaning forwards and growling and holding the microphone just like I did. And Malcolm had me on one side and Fred, our handler and social secretary, on the other, going, 'What's all that about then Malcolm? He's copying me isn't he?' and Malcolm was there just squeaking."

Renowned Irish rock PR and scenester BP Fallon, who had established a company called The Department of Corrective Truth, was by now representing the Kilburns and for some time had been urging Dury to wind up the group. Fallon was hugely impressed with Dury as a front-man and lyricist, but felt his talents had lain undiscovered for too long. By the end of that same evening, the one-time art school project was no more. Accompanying Fallon's own nagging voice had been warnings from Dury's doctors that his remorseless performing was endangering his fragile health; finances were also a growing concern.

"I had been saying to Ian for a long time that he should be rockin', because he would talk about Billy Fury, bless him, and he would talk about Gene Vincent, bless him, and I thought the Kilburns were a bit too cerebral really," recalls BP. "I had seen this geezer hanging around at a lot of Kilburn gigs and down the front watching Ian, who turned out to be Johnny Rotten. At the Walthamstow gig, the Kilburns were topping the bill and then there was The Stranglers and The Sex Pistols were stuck on at the bottom as a sort of apology. After the gig, I took Ian into a classroom and said: 'Now do you know what I'm on about?' and that was the end of the Kilburns. It was the turning point. The whole punk thing was happening with The Damned and The Clash and that kind of stuff. The Sex Pistols weren't brilliant musically, but their vibe was fantastic. Rock'n'roll had got so flatulent then, the roll had gone and it was rock music, which was so boring. People like Yes playing at the end of some stadium? Give me a break.

"The Kilburns were very good and Ian was a great front man, but the fronting had to be focused on, no disrespect to the other musos. Ian had to be brought out and that was the reason to bring his name out. Ian was recognised vaguely, but nothing more than that. I always thought he had it in him to be a rock star. He was intelligent and a great frontman, a good singer, brilliant lyricist and dynamite visually. It was no good as far as I was concerned for him to be in this well respected, art school band for the rest of his life. He had to reach out there and make girls horny."

6

IF IT AIN'T STIFF

"I remember being in Stiff's offices and saying to them that Ian was fantastic and asking what he was doing and they said, 'He's got a solo career, he's writing songs — there he is now.' And there was this bloke shambling along the street with a shopping bag and wearing a mac and a pair of kickers."

— Wreckless Eric

Out of the searing summer heat of 1976, Stiff Records emerged to launch an assault on what had become a complacent and yawningly predictable record industry. Impeccably timed, coinciding as it did with the detonation of the incendiary device which punk placed under the British popular music scene, it defied all the rules and would change the face of the singles market through imaginative sales devices and gimmicks. Stiff would also become a launch pad for dozens of artists and bands who might otherwise have remained on the margins or simply never cashed in their 15 minutes of fame. Executives at the major record companies looked on openmouthed as Stiff launched itself amid a barrage of self-deprecating slogans such as 'If They're Dead We'll Sign 'Em' and 'If It Ain't Stiff, It Ain't Worth a Fuck'. A 'stiff' in the music industry was a flop, a dud, a turkey, yet here was a label promoting itself as the very antithesis of established practice in the record industry.

But while the majors sniggered at such impudent enterprise, Stiff was to pull off a coup that few could have forecast. Young bands were plugging in their practice amps in bedrooms, garages and rehearsal rooms in every corner of Britain and punk was fast taking hold. Venues in the capital were packed to the rafters every night, often with three or four bands on the bill. While the pub rock acts that had provided a badly needed alternative to the glam bands were, in the main, disenchanted musos of the old school, the bands and artists now emerging were younger and far more shameful in their contempt of professional musos. And in Stiff and labels like it, they had resourceful champions with identical attitudes.

Stiff was not the UK's first independent label. Strictly speaking, older labels like Track, Charisma and Virgin were independent, as were more recent labels like Oval (established by Charlie Gillett and Gordon Nelki) and Chiswick. But its founders Dave Robinson and Andrew Jakeman, alias Jake Riviera, were resolute in one regard – they were going to take on the major labels at their own game.

"I was aware that something would have to happen because the record business was in a middle-of-the-road kind of trough and I think that it had been like that for about two or three years," said Dave Robinson in the Radio 1 documentary *From Punk To Present*.[10] "It was like a real kind of 'business music' era and it was a bit boring; it was certainly boring to be young. It was a time your mother actually did like, with all the Elton Johns and such like."

The seeds of Stiff Records were sown in the United States in 1974 while Jake was on tour with Dr Feelgood, the Canvey Island pub rock band he was then managing. He had discovered a number of small indigenous labels featuring local bands – Flat Out and Berserkly Records in San Francisco being prime examples – as he travelled around the country. This enterprising climate meant that aspiring groups were being played on local radio stations and then being picked up for nationwide distribution by larger record labels. By the time Jake and Dr Feelgood returned to England, he was buzzing with ideas for his own label and had even started dreaming up logos.

A former advertising executive from Pinner, west London, with a sharp line in cowboy boots and a vicious temper, Jake was an arrogant operator with aspirations to become an A&R man. Prior to his stewardship of the Feelgoods, he had managed pub rock stalwarts Chilli Willi & The Red Hot Peppers, whose début album was released on the obscure Revelation label. When this label folded, the larger-than-life salesman got the band signed to Mooncrest Records (an offshoot of Charisma) and they released the more successful *Bongos Over Balham*. In July 1976, Jake began plotting his own label in collusion with Dave Robinson, the then manager of both Ian Dury and Graham Parker and who had built up an extensive archive of live concerts recorded at the Hope & Anchor in Islington. Their game plan was simple: to create an outlet for the groups on the pub scene who had long been overlooked and to give some of the industry's misfits a chance.

"I was very frustrated being a manager in those days," Dave Robinson told the author in an interview for *Hot Press* magazine in 1996.[11] "The major labels were very pedantic, like they are now, and convinced that they were running the record business. So if you wanted any special marketing deal, or to do something off the beaten track, they didn't want to do it and it was going to cost money. Graham Parker was at Phonogram and we were having enormous live acceptance of him and his band. The records were good and we were doing okay, but we couldn't get onto first base in America, and nobody wanted to know Ian Dury. The major record companies just thought it was pub music – old R&B."

He continued: "The idea of Stiff was to be a conduit for people who could not find the music business any other way. My theory was that there's an Elvis Presley out there, but he's working in a factory in Coventry and he doesn't know how to get in touch with me. The best artists are out there, but they don't know how to connect with the music business, because it doesn't tell you that. If you go to a couple of majors, they'll put you off for life. You will sit in reception, nobody will see you, eventually some junior will come down and take a tape off you and you'll never hear from them again. How does anybody know what's going to be the next anything that's great simply by the clothing you wear?"

Even before this juncture, Dr Feelgood had been central to a plan which had highlighted the need for independent labels. Musicians from the popular R&B band, had joined with Nick Lowe of Brinsley Schwarz and Martin Stone of The Pink Fairies to form a band which gloried under the name Spick Ace & The Blue Sharks. This ad hoc ensemble had planned to record an EP for Skydog in Holland, but contractual difficulties meant it never happened. Numerous attempts by Jake to interest record companies in Nick Lowe – who had secured his release from United Artists – had also come to nothing.

"I spent years shouting at people over desks in record company offices. They turned down virtually every idea I had," Jake later told *Melody Maker*'s Allan Jones. The only route left was to set up his own label and in the summer of 1976 Jake borrowed £400 from Dr Feelgood and he and Dave Robinson formed Stiff. In a coincidence which was to prove highly fortuitous for Ian, Stiff rented the ground floor of 32 Alexander Street from his management company, Blackhill Enterprises.

Undeterred by repeated failed attempts to get Nick Lowe a record deal, Jake and Dave despatched Nick to a recording studio with only £45 to spend. The shoestring budget didn't affect the quality. Nick, accompanied only by drummer Steve Goulding of The Rumour, recorded 'So It Goes' and 'Heart of The City' – two devastating songs of less than two and a half minutes each. Excited by the raw quality and immediacy of these songs, Jake and Dave rushed to a pressing plant and on August 14, 1976, a single was released as Stiff Buy 1. The record, produced jointly by Nick and Dave, was sold mainly via mail-order from Alexander Street. But in contrast to the tatty decor at base camp, the record's packaging was slick and featured the kind of sharp-witted one-liners that would become Stiff's hallmark. Curious messages, 'Earthlings Awake' and 'Three Chord Trick, Yeh', were scratched into the matrix (the smooth bit between the groove and the centre). A distinctive black record bag carried the phrases 'If It Means Everything To Everyone . . . It Must Be A Stiff' and 'Today's Sound Today'. The record itself carried the messages 'Mono-enhanced STEREO, play loud' and 'The world's most flexible record label'. This was a whole new approach.

Nick told *Melody Maker*'s Caroline Coon: "It's a sound that's happening now. Clever words over a simple rhythm. Basically, I'll do anything. I can write in any style, but all my friends have become punks overnight and I'm a great bandwagon climber."

'So It Goes' didn't get near the Top 40, but the music press gave it and its flip-side a warm reception and Jake and Dave found it impossible to keep it in pressings as demand grew. Suddenly, they had found a hole in the market and Stiff's cramped office was alive with activity as they drew up a list of exciting artists to fill it. As word of the maverick label got around, there was no shortage of hopefuls calling at its door and Stiff had an open-house policy.

Nick Lowe set up shop at Pathway Studios in London and sat and waited to see who Dave and Jake would send along. Drummer Steve Goulding was on stand-by to accompany those who showed up and Nick recorded their rough and ready songs using an eight-track.

"Almost any nut-case who had a bit of front would get a try out at one time from Stiff, pretty much, until it got completely out of hand," said Nick.[10] "But for a while they were the best people around, those people that none of the other record labels would touch. They had genuine front, which used to scare proper sensible record companies. It wasn't musically on the case, but I think I had the attitude of the artist on the record."

Singles started coming thick and fast from Alexander Street and Stiff's inventive marketing ruses made sure they were eye-catching. The Pink Fairies, fronted by long-haired rocker Larry Wallis, provided the label's second 45 'Between The Lines' before being signed by Polydor. It was followed by the more laid-back 'All Aboard' by US group Roogalator, which was delivered in Sixties-style 33-and-a-third rpm. 'Styrofoam' by Tyla Gang, led by the growling pub rocker Sean Tyla, and 'Boogie On The Street' by Lew Lewis & His Band followed as Stiff gathered momentum. 'Artistic breakthrough! Double B-side' was stamped on the plain white sleeve of 'Styrofoam' with a guarantee that 'This record certified gold on leaving the studio'. The cover for Roogalator's début was a blatant parody of *With The Beatles* and when EMI complained about the use of the Emitex advert and trademark, the record was withdrawn and deleted. Stiff continued to use mail order and peddled some copies through a handful of independent outlets.

Stiff's sixth single was The Damned's 'New Rose' – the first British punk record. Dave Vanian, Captain Sensible, Brian James and Rat Scabies had recorded their raucous anthem in a drunken state at Pathway along with a shambolic rendition of The Beatles' 1965 hit 'Help!' as a B-side. 'New Rose' didn't make the Top 40, but it was an underground success and Stiff had to get United Artists to help out with the distribution. Not only was Stiff shaking the singles market into life with their picture covers, coloured vinyl and other novelties. It was also at the forefront of the biggest revolution in popular music for years.

Adding to the label's anti-establishment credibility, Jake verbally abused journalists, once famously yelling down the phone, "I'm not interested that you're interested" and Stiff's equally arrogant approach to distribution left some radio presenters aghast.

"I remember reading this massive article in *New Musical Express* about Stiff Records and I thought where are these records, I'm getting 60 records a week through the mail, why haven't I got these?" DJ Johnnie Walker recalled.[10] "So I rang up *NME* and asked how I could get hold of Jake Riviera and they gave me the number. So I rang him up and he said: 'Oh, you want the records, can you come down for 'em, this is where we are.' I was on Radio One at that time and I thought this is great, this is a really different way of doing things, because most of the record companies beat a path to your door and here was somebody saying, 'Well, if you want these you're gonna have to come and get 'em.' Jake's idea was right – 'I'll make these records for £30 each, I won't sign these blokes up, we'll just make the records, stick them in the back of the car, drive round a few record shops and sell them out the back of the car.' "

At 40 Oval Mansions, meanwhile, the Dury-Jankel partnership was flourishing. Although the fruits of their labour would not be presented to the public for almost a year, they would go on to have a profound effect on everyone who heard them. Chaz Jankel arrived each morning at Ian's Vauxhall flat with his Wurlitzer electric piano and acoustic guitar. Ian would disappear into the kitchen to make some coffee and then present Chaz with sheets of lyrics which he had copied out on his old typewriter. With a cardboard cut-out of Gene Vincent in Ian's sitting room for inspiration and Taj Mahal records playing in the background, the two chatted and experimented with this untested material.

In some aspects, the two men were very different. Ian was 34, had worked as a teacher and had two children from a failed marriage to support. He spoke in a harsh Cockney accent and had an abrasive manner. Chaz was still in his early twenties, single, and was softly spoken by comparison. But both were perfectionists and took a methodical, almost scientific, approach to songwriting. Ian laboured for hours on his lyrics, honing them and searching for a better rhyme or hook. Chaz, meanwhile, had the patience to work with the demanding songwriter and search for a suitable tune and rhythm, even when he had reservations as to the potential of some of Ian's eccentric lyrics.

"Ian would put some type-written lyrics in front of me and I would start going through them," says Chaz. "As soon as I got to one I liked I would say, 'Yeah' and I would start trying something out. There was this one which always used to crop up called 'Sex & Drugs & Rock'n'Roll' and any time I got to it I said, 'Naah, we all know about that, why write about it? It's obvious isn't it?' The next day I would arrive and it would be there at the top of the pile and he would keep trying to sell it to me. I couldn't think of anything for it and one day Ian came in and started singing this riff and singing 'Sex and Drugs and Rock'n'Roll'. I said, 'Bloody hell, that's good', because Ian didn't often initiate musical ideas. He was a lyricist and needed a melody and I was a musician who needed a lyricist. I was astounded at the fact that he could come up with this song and so then I wrote a lead section for it and we knocked it together.

"Later on, I was at his flat and he put on an Ornette Coleman record called 'Change Of The Century' with Charlie Haden and Don Cherry on it, and went into the kitchen to make some coffee. I was listening and probably looking at another lyric and suddenly, about a minute into the record, I heard this bass riff and I thought 'hang on a moment'. As I looked up, Ian was standing in the doorway grinning from ear to ear and I said, 'You sod'. Then Ian had this fit of conscience and thought he had to do something about it, so he wrote to Don Cherry and he sent back a card saying, 'This is not my music, you're fine', meaning that music comes around and goes around and is there to share."

A few years later, Ian made a further confession to the bass player himself, according to Terry Day. Ian and Terry went to see Charlie Haden, drummer Eddie Blackwell, Don Cherry, and an alto sax player, at the Hammersmith Odeon and, afterwards, they ventured back stage. Ian was just about to approach Charlie as he came out of his dressing room carrying his double bass when he spotted Ian and told him: " 'My daughter really digs you and your music.' Ian thanked him and then tells him about nicking two bars or so from his bass line and it being part of the music of 'Sex & Drugs'. But Charlie replied, 'Well, that's the name of the game – what's new?' " recalls Terry.

Chaz's fondness for funk brought a dimension to the songwriting process which had not been present in Ian's collaborations with either Russell or Rod. Compared to the rock'n'roll or blues rhythms that had carried many of the Kilburns' songs, the young musician's funk and jazz influences created a very different environment for Ian's words. Charlie Hart had also been a fan of funk groups and 'Billy Bentley', which he co-wrote with Ian, gives a brief glimpse of his influences. But, to Charlie's disappointment, his input was rarely welcome and the tunes written by Russell and Rod had mostly relied on more standard rock rhythms. Now, there was a very distinct change of direction.

Chaz: "There was a lot more syncopation in the sort of music I liked; you could say it was more southern hemisphere and less urban. But to say that was my only influence would be wrong. I was into bands like Free, Jeff Beck and Deep Purple, but when The Beatles made *Sergeant Pepper* and most of the world was bowing down and kissing their feet, I didn't like it, because it was nothing to do with a small group any more and the lovely little songs they could knock together. I was looking further afield for more bluesy, gutsy raw material and in a way, that is where Ian and I are very similar. He loves it raw and real and he loves good country music and jazz. I have spent many an hour listening to music with him.

"I think I can safely say that Ian introduced me to Bill Evans who is possibly the finest pianist this century. I think he felt a bit concerned about having a jazz group, because he didn't feel it was good enough and that he didn't feel he had the ability to sing jazz."

Chaz recalls one moment during these sessions at Ian's when a different set of ground rules regarding the rhythms they would use first emerged. "White music was based more on melody and chord changes and I was coming from a slightly different angle. In 'Wake Up And Make Love To Me', I was a bit concerned as I had been through 16 bars on the same chord and I hadn't changed and usually by this point Ian would be saying, 'When does it change?' One of Ian's friends, Smart Mart (Martin Cole), had a girlfriend from South America and one day she was round at Ian's. She was listening to the song and she said to us, 'Why does it have to change?' and we said, 'Oh yeah.' and that was the first real experiment of letting the rhythm build itself and building layers of melody on top of that. Lyrically, it was a very sensual song and lead singers have to be very careful about doing that in front of a male band when they go out live, otherwise you fall into the Barry White camp. But Ian always pulled it off. Since then, every gig we have ever played together as The Blockheads has opened with 'Wake Up'."

Chaz was not the only musician with whom Ian was collaborating at this time and this, too, would help develop the multi-faceted songbook which was taking shape. Ian was also presenting sheets of lyrics to American journalist and guitar player Steve Nugent and they would work on material into the evening together at Steve's flat in Parliament Hill Fields, Hampstead, north London. Ironically, his American friend would compose the music for some of Ian's most 'English' and best-loved songs. Steve was born in Newhaven, Connecticut, in 1950, moved to England in 1972 to take up a PhD at the London School of Economics and had written articles for the small music magazine *Let It Rock*. Lapping up the London pub rock scene he found on arrival, he had been captivated by a Kilburn & The High Roads show at the Tally Ho and had spoken with Ian at a couple of subsequent gigs. Steve had also interviewed Ian for the magazine one afternoon in Wingrave.

Steve recalls of this early encounter: "He is a power freak, so he checks people out very carefully and tries to get them in a place and keep them there. He was naive as a rock performer. He had finally dumped painting and illustrating and he was going to be a public person and I really had no experience of being a music journalist, so it was a meeting of the naive. He was in the course of developing his public persona and he was much less convinced of his central position in the universe than he was a few years later."

Steve left England for Brazil in 1974, but returned two years later and rejoined Ian at Catshit Mansions. Ian, who at one stage had considered taking a job as a lift attendant at Harrods, told him of the Kilburns' demise and of his new publishing deal with Blackhill and invited him to help write a few songs. He agreed, Blackhill gave him an advance of £25, and out of their writing sessions came six songs. One of these was 'Billericay Dickie'. A boastful account of sordid sexual conquests on the back seats of cars, it was narrated by an unreconstructed Essex plasterer in full Cockney colour and was set to a jaunty fairground tune. It was a prime example of Ian's clever use of rhyme and the portrayal of the seedy side of life through fictional characters.

Steve, who is now a Doctor of Anthropology at Goldsmith College, London, says of the now famous song: " 'Billericay Dickie' has big chords and is carried by the words more than the music. The lyrics were very funny to me and they seemed to be describing a kind of Englishness that I knew very little about. But it had a ring of authenticity in the way it was presented by him. That was in the text, as it were, and it was really more a matter of writing a simple vehicle to allow the words to get across. It was not very complicated."

The lyrics for 'Plaistow Patricia' – a no-holds-barred tale of heroin-addiction – was also in the batch of song ideas shown to the quietly spoken

American student. Ian had once again coupled a fictional character and an Essex address to devastating effect and Steve completed the picture with a jarring guitar intro and a fast-paced, aggressive rhythm. "It's a sort of travel tune. It's about the nether regions of inner London, that bit out there which is always geographically unspecified," says Steve.

Of the uncompromisingly stark images Ian was creating, he adds: "There was a much more literary take on the album compared with punk. To me, it was coming out of beat culture and noir culture and hard world thrillers, it had nothing to do with punk at all."

In the spring of 1977, Ian and Chaz decided to record some demos of the songs and were advised to try Alvic, a small studio in Wimbledon run by two men known as Al and Vic. Chaz played the bass, piano and guitar parts, while Ian sang and knocked out a basic drum beat. In spite of the paralysis of the left side of his body, Ian was extremely rhythmic and could keep a solid beat by using his right arm to hit the snare and his right foot to play the bass drum. The recordings which resulted sounded spartan, but they confirmed the potential of the material that had been building since the break-up of the Kilburns. Steve also went to Alvic to help work on the songs which they had originally recorded on a small cassette recorder: 'Billericay Dickie', 'Plaistow Patricia', 'My Old Man', 'Blackmail Man', 'Wifey' and another song, the title of which Steve cannot now recall.

During a session one day, the studio engineer told Ian of a great rhythm section who were also doing session work there and suggested that he check them out. It was a red hot tip.

Drummer Charley Charles and bass player Norman Watt-Roy were members of a band called Loving Awareness, but this 'concept' group had begun to lose its way and they were hiring themselves out for session work. Both were seasoned musicians and although they were unknown to Ian, they were top drawer.

Norman was born in February 1951 in Bombay, where his Anglo-Indian parents were stationed with the RAF. In November 1954, seven years after India gained independence, the Watt-Roys moved to England, with three-year-old Norman and his older brother and sister. He went to St Joan of Arc Primary School in Blackstock Road, Highbury, north London, where the family initially lived, before attending secondary school in Harlow, Essex. He studied art briefly at Harlow Technical College when he left school at 15. But it was in music, his first love, that he would build his life.

When he was about 10 years old, Norman had been shown some guitar chords by his father and from this early tuition he had learned to play by ear, playing in school bands alongside his brother Garth, who played lead guitar. When he was 15, he developed a passion for bass guitar and never looked back. A teenage friend who had a job was so keen to join the boys' band that he offered to buy a Top Twenty bass and a bass amp and Norman agreed to teach him the rudiments. When his pupil's blistering fingers caused him to throw in the towel, he donated his bass and equipment and Norman took over. At 16, Norman went off with Garth to tour Germany with show-bands and started to make a living. In the mid to late Sixties, he made his first recordings in a four-piece group called The Living Daylights, again playing alongside his brother. A single and an EP were released before the project fizzled out and in 1968 the Watt-Roys joined The Greatest Show On Earth, a nine-piece soul band with a black New Orleans singer, Ozzie Lane. When Ozzie later returned to the US and was replaced by Colin Horton-Jennings, the band signed with the Harvest label and made two albums, *Horizons* and *The Going's Easy*. The other members of The Greatest Show On Earth were Ron Prudence (drums), Dick Hanson (trumpet) – later with Graham Parker – Tex Philpotts (sax), Mick Deacon (keyboards), who later joined fifties retro band Darts, and Ian Aitcheson (sax).

The group folded in 1971 and Norman joined Mick Travis, Stewart Francis and Graham Maitland to form Glencoe. A solid rock band, Glencoe recorded an eponymous album and another called *The Spirit Of Glencoe* although they made only a minimal impact during the two years they were together. In early 1972, young guitarist John Turnbull had joined from singer Graham Bell's band Bell & Arc and when Glencoe split two years later, John and Norman remained together.

Since leaving school in his native Newcastle, Johnny had earned a living as a musician and he struck up a close friendship with keyboard player and fellow Geordie Mickey Gallagher. "Since I was a kid, music was all I could think of and I used to watch my uncle playing this huge Gretch guitar that I could hardly get my hand around," says Johnny. "I just wanted to play. I was banging on biscuit tins with knitting needles and during *Friday Night Is Music Night* I would be dancing on the lino. When my parents got me a toy guitar, I went outside and learned 'Peggy Sue' straight away and then I came back in and played it and they said, 'Oh we'd better get him a proper one.' Later on, I had my own little band in the clubs and I was working in a tailor's and then my old school friend Colin Gibson got together with Mickey in The Chosen Few and told Mickey about me. When Alan Hull left that band to do a solo album, I became a member of The Chosen Few with Mickey, Graham Bell, Colin Gibson and Tommy Jackman. We got a trial for colour television through Brian Epstein down here and Jimmy Savile and it was a disaster because we wore the wrong suits, but out of that we got gigs at The Marquee through Alan Isenberg and Don Arden. When we got a residency, we had to move down to London."

Mickey had worked for the Ministry of Pensions and National Insurance for a year after leaving school, but quickly abandoned the civil service and began playing the CIU working men's clubs in Newcastle with local group The Wayfarers. A versatile keyboard player, he was always in demand and had appeared in a string of groups by the time he joined The Chosen Few. At one stage in the mid-Sixties, he deputised for Newcastle band The Animals in between Alan Price's premature exit and the arrival of Dave Rowberry. Mickey played dates in Scandinavia and the UK with the group – the first hit act produced by Mickie Most and the first British band to top the US chart after The Beatles.

In the spring of 1966, Mickey, Johnny Graham, Tommy and Colin, formed a new group, Skip Bifferty, and released one album on RCA in September 1968. Subsequently, they became Heavy Jelly and recorded a single for Island before parting company towards the end of 1969. Following the collapse of this project, Bell joined Every Which Way, led by Brian Davison, the former drummer with The Nice, and Johnny and Mickey were recruited by Robbins Music as songwriters. To provide an outlet for their material, they briefly established Arc with Tommy Duffy on bass and Rob Tait on drums (later replaced by Dave Trudex), before reuniting with Bell in Bell & Arc.

Johnny and Mickey went their separate ways for the first time when Johnny joined Glencoe and Mickey became a member of Parrish & Gurvitz and subsequently Frampton's Camel, led by Peter Frampton. But following the break-up of Glencoe in early 1974, they were reunited, this time with Norman Watt-Roy, in a group which would have more influence on Ian's career than any other.

Loving Awareness was the brainchild of Radio Caroline pioneer Ronan O'Rahilly, but the group was slow to get off the ground and had taken some time to settle on a permanent drummer. Simon Phillips was initially involved, but he was committed to sessions for a Frank Zappa album and when he left, a string of other drummers were tried, including Lynyrd Skynyrd's Artimus Pyle. But it was while watching television one night that Norman stumbled on Charley Charles, the man who would complete the rhythm section and later become such a powerful and solid force behind Ian.

Norman remembers: "I was sitting at home watching *The Old Grey Whistle Test* with my dad and Link Wray was on and he had this guy playing drums who was wicked. My dad said, 'That's the kind of drummer you want' and I said, 'Yeah, yeah.' I rang up our manager and he'd seen *The Old Grey Whistle Test* and I said, 'They're in England touring, let's ring him up, he's probably American.' They were in Manchester or some-where that night and we rang Charley up and he was living in Tooting and he was only doing session work for Link Wray. After the tour, Link Wray was going back to America, but Charley wasn't doing anything, so he was up for it. We got him down and Simon was there that night and for that night we had Simon and Charley on drums. But even Simon said to us afterwards, 'That's your drummer, isn't it.' Charley was so solid, and what a lovely bloke. He was just lovely, completely off the wall and his ideas were so mad."

Curiously, Link Wray, whose real name was Ray Vernon, hailed from Norfolk, Virginia – the birthplace of Gene Vincent – and had played on some of the same country shows as Ian's hero in the mid-fifties before changing his name to Link Wray and recording a series of atmospheric instrumentals, notably 'Rumble'. Whether it was fate or simply good fortune, it was through the musician from Vincent's home town that anon-ymous session man Charley Charles had come to the attention of Norman, Mickey and Johnny.

Charley was born in Georgetown, Guyana, where his father Tom was a big band leader. He moved to London with his family at the age of 13 and later attended Wandsworth Technical College. After working for a couple of years at the Woolworth store in Whitechapel, he joined the Army and was posted to Germany and later Singapore where he drummed with various groups. When disillusionment with the military set in, he bought himself out in 1969 and toured the Far East with eight-piece band No Sweat. On his return to London in 1972, Charley was in great demand and backed artists including Kala, Arthur Brown, Arthur Conley, Casablanca and Link Wray, before he was invited to join Loving Awareness.

The group rehearsed intensely before flying out to Palm Springs, Cali-fornia, where they spent six weeks recording an album. The self-titled record was distributed by Phonogram in Holland, but after only 17 gigs back in the UK, Johnny broke a bone in his hand. Loving Awareness lost its momentum and the four musicians began doing session work.

Mickey: "It was called Loving Awareness and was all about love power and all that sort of stuff. Ronan's theory was that everybody lives from a position of defensive awareness and the only way to change it was getting people to live a loving awareness type of life. That was all great, fair enough, and then punk happened!"

Johnny: "Loving Awareness wasn't that successful and monetarily we had to do sessions, so we did all sorts of things. Me, Charley, Mickey and

Norman did sessions with Lulu and this guy called Adrian Gurvitz. We did work for various people in studios and sometimes people heard about you. It was great if we could get sessions as a band, but then sometimes people just wanted a rhythm section. So Charley and Norman started getting bits of work with people and one of them was Ian."

Norman and Charley immediately gelled with Ian and Chaz at Alvic Studios and completed the demos within about a week. The following week, they began recording the album itself at The Workhouse Studio in the Old Kent Road. Blackhill owned a 50 per cent share in the studio and Manfred Mann held the remaining 50 per cent, and it was agreed that Ian, Chaz, Norman and Charley would record songs in "dead time", when the studio was empty. Blackhill stumped up about £4,000 to pay for the projected album which was produced by Pete Jenner, Laurie Latham and Rick Walton. Pete had previously produced records for Kevin Ayres, Roy Harper and Mike Oldfield among others, but Laurie and Rick were younger and had little or no previous experience of production at this point.

A chance remark made during one of these sessions at The Workhouse would have great significance for Ian. Chaz remembers: "We were listening to the playback of a song Ian and I had written called 'Blockheads' and Charley was looking at the lyric and he got to the line which says, "You must have seen parties of blockheads . . . with shoes like dead pigs' noses". He glanced down at his footwear and he had boots that resembled dead pigs' noses and he said, "Ere Ian, that's me' and Ian changed one word in the lyric from 'You're all blockheads too' to 'We're all blockheads too'. To say that we're all stupid was better than saying you're all stupid." Charley's off-the-cuff remark was not forgotten.

Ex-Kilburns Davey Payne and Ed Speight were invited to help fill out the sound with sax and 'ballad guitar', while jazz pianist Geoff Castle, a friend of Ed's, played Moog synthesiser on 'Wake Up And Make Love With Me'. As these recording sessions progressed, it was obvious that the songs which Ian had been working on with Chaz and Steve respectively – a heady mixture of funk rhythms, Cockney language and urban stories – made for a unique package. Ian's coarse and untrained vocals clearly provided the perfect narration for these stories but even more crucial to the feel of the music was Ian's conscious decision to sing with a pronounced English accent.

"Ian wasn't afraid to speak the truth," says Chaz. "If he was angry about something he'd find a way of venting that spleen through his lyrics. That is what attracted me to Ian, because I had worked with a few different lyricists, but nobody who was as broad as Ian and tapping into his native England like he did. A lot of singers, including myself, were still putting 'baby' an awful lot in the songs and singing in an American accent. When we finally got to record 'Wake Up And Make Love With Me', Ian sang it in an American accent and somebody [Charlie Gillett] said, 'Hey, you sound like Barry White' and that really nailed it for him. He thought, 'Why try and do that?' You can slur it a little bit, you can give some of those nasty vowels a little bit of assistance, but it wasn't like we came from Liverpool. It was what Ian found colourful and it was what Ian chose to identify with. I think a lot of people do it subconsciously, we all did it in our teens, but Ian somehow allied himself with Cockneys – people who had drawn the short straw."

Of the completed album, Ian said:[8] "Some of the songs had been five years in the making, while some had come out real quick. There was a sort of pres-sure because lots of people without any talent were getting extremely famous and I was getting the hump. I was ultra jealous. But in many ways it was easy writing like that because nobody had heard of me. I was getting quite angry. I'd been working hard and not succeeding for six years."

Stiff had by now launched a plethora of new acts and was the power house behind an energised singles market. Punk band The Damned, Television bassist and vocalist Richard Hell and heavy metal band Motorhead were among those it had given a leg-up. But it wasn't just interested in selling records to the growing punk market. The label's 12th single release, Max Wall's interpretation of Ian's whimsical 'England's Glory' (produced by Dave Edmunds) was a typical Stiff single, insofar as it was the kind of record that major record companies would have dismissed out of hand. Commer-cially, the ageing comedian's outing on Stiff was a flop and most copies had to be given away with *Hits Greatest Stiffs*, a compilation album containing songs from its earliest 45s released towards the end of 1977. But Dave and Jake's willingness to give idiosyncratic, but nevertheless talented, song-writers, a start was best exemplified by the issue of 'Less Than Zero', the record which first introduced Britain to Elvis Costello.

Born Declan Patrick McManus, the gangly, bespectacled singer had first played his own songs live in 1972 as a long-haired teenager in Rusty, a folk rock group based in his native Merseyside. The following year, he was playing solo and had adopted his mother's Irish maiden name, Costello, and after moving to London, he established his own bluegrass group Flip City. At 19, he was married, living in Whitton, Middlesex, and working by day as a computer operator at the Elizabeth Arden cosmetics company in Acton (the 'vanity factory' in his song 'I'm Not Angry'). Skinny, spotty and with thick rimmed glasses, Costello looked every bit the nerd, but all the time he was bombarding record companies with tapes and when he got no response, he camped in their lobbies with a guitar and started playing. His persistence was eventually rewarded when, on August 15, 1976, his demos were played on Charlie Gillett's Sunday night radio show *Honky Tonk*. But it was a tape he sent to Stiff on the foot of an advertisement for new artists (the tape later emerged as a bootleg album entitled, in a parody of an Elvis Presley LP, *5,000,000 Elvis Fans Can't Be Wrong*) which finally broke the deadlock for the precocious singer-songwriter.

"The tape was actually the very first tape we received at Stiff," Jake told *NME*'s Nick Kent in August 1977. "I immediately put it on and thought, 'God, this is fuckin' good, but at the same time I was hesitating because, after all, it was the first tape and I wanted to get a better perspective." Jake subsequently wrote to D.P. Costello, asking him to be patient while he listened his way through the other demos which were arriving, but after receiving what he described as "a load of real dross in the mail", he agreed to sign him. In a west London bar, Jake christened him 'Elvis Costello', a move which caused some offence when, on August 16, 1977, Elvis Presley died at his Graceland mansion aged 42. This was just weeks after the release of the English Elvis's début *My Aim Is True* on which the words 'Elvis Is King' were written into the chequered sleeve pattern. The timing of Costello's début simply exacerbated the controversy, but the storm passed and the record went on to be a hit. Although his first three singles 'Less Than Zero', 'Red Shoes' and 'Alison' did not chart, much of the energies of those at Stiff were being devoted to their rising star during that summer.

Meanwhile, Stiff's cramped headquarters had become a giant sitting room for artists on the label and assorted unsigned musicians who, like Costello, had turned up looking for a break. One such hopeful was Eric Goulden. The baby-faced singer had arrived in London with empty pockets after leaving Hull College of Art where he had sung with Addis & The Flip-Tops and Rudy & The Takeaways. Taken with Nick Lowe's début 'So It Goes' and the raw sound of other Stiff artists, Eric had scrambled a tape of his songs together and headed for Alexander Street in search of his own bit of glory. Short, with an impish grin and scruffy blond hair, Eric had stopped off at a pub en route to calm his nerves. When he arrived, he stumbled drunkenly into the Stiff office.

Eric recalls: "I went in with my tape I had made in the morning and Nick Lowe was in there and I gave my tape to Huey Lewis. I just wanted to go and they said, 'Can't you give us your phone number or something?' and I was terrified and gave them my phone number. I left and I thought, 'What have I done, how stupid I am.' Three days later Jake Riviera rang me up personally and said, 'It's about this tape you brought in,' and I started saying, 'Oh, it's all right, you could just record something else over it. It's just an old cassette, you don't have to send it back, I'm really sorry.' But he said, 'No, we were wondering if you would like to come and talk to us and maybe talk about making a record. What are you doing, are you busy?' "

Such episodes were not uncommon. Having reeled in off the street with little more than a home-made tape and a lot of Dutch courage, the 22-year-old art student from Newhaven in Sussex had got himself a record deal and an appropriate new name – 'Wreckless Eric'. From there, Eric went to Pathway Studios where Nick Lowe produced and played bass on Eric's song 'Whole Wide World'. Disbelievingly, Eric went home to await the release of his very first record.

On a subsequent visit to 32 Alexander Street, Eric discovered that Blackhill Enterprises was located in an office above Stiff. Ian Dury had made a lasting impression on Eric when he had seen Kilburn & The High Roads on the pub circuit two years before. Now Eric was moving in illustrious circles.

Says Eric: "I remember being in Stiff's offices saying to them that Ian was fantastic and asking what he was doing and they said, 'He's got a solo career, he's writing songs – there he is now.' And there was this bloke shambling along the street with a shopping bag and wearing a mac and a pair of kickers – I just couldn't believe it. Shortly after that Stiff put on a big gig at Victoria Palace Theatre, with Graham Parker and the Rumour topping the bill, followed by Tyla Gang and The Damned. I had recorded 'Whole Wide World' and we hadn't got a B-side and I didn't know what we were doing. I was talking to Nick Lowe and he said, 'There's someone you ought to meet over there' and it was Ian. Denise Roudette was with him looking fantastic. It was astonishing – there he was. I had seen him in the distance, I had seen him on stage and I had a copy of *Handsome*, which was autographed, and 'Crippled With Nerves' and I just said, 'You're fantastic, you're the best' and I think he thought I was taking the piss. His minder Fred Rowe was standing nearby and Ian started shouting, 'Fred, Fred' and I thought he would have me thrown out. But Denise said to Ian, 'No, he means it.' So we got talking about lyrics and then Ian told me to go round and see him in his gaff."

It was the kind of offer that Eric could only have dreamed of six months before, but Stiff was now doing exactly what Jake and Dave had hoped. It was offering a voice to singers and musicians who, until this point, had been left to watch wistfully from the sidelines. It was also developing its own distinctive feel.

On the evening of December 1st, 1976, Eric took Ian up on his invitation. Not wishing to arrive early at Oval Mansions, he went into a pub

Ian circa 1978 *(Rex Features)*

One of the last performances of Kilburn & The High Roads in 1975. Left to right: Keith Lucas, Ian, an unknown singer, Denise Roudette, Malcolm Mortimore, Charlie Sinclair. *(Gordon & Andra Nelki)*

Sweet Gene Vincent.

Ian pictured backstage during the 1977 Live Stiffs tour. *(LFI)*

The Live Stiffs tour, 1977. left to right: Wreckless Eric, Nick Lowe, Elvis Costello, Larry Wallis and Ian. *(Stiff Records)*

Ian in 1978 with his Union Jack teeth. *(David Como/S.I.N.)*

and as he sat in the bar he remembers catching one of punk's most famous moments take place on the TV. The Sex Pistols, who had unleashed their début single 'Anarchy In The UK', were appearing live on Bill Grundy's early evening *Today* show. Queen had pulled out and the headline-making punk band had been called in at the last minute to replace them. But the decision was to prove disastrous. Grundy's line of questioning was designed to goad the band into saying something controversial and when he heard Johnny Rotten muttering the word "shit" under his breath, he saw his chance. Demanding that the snarling singer repeat his "rude word" he provoked a torrent of abuse from Rotten and Steve Jones. The incident led to Grundy being suspended by Thames and Sex Pistols' gigs cancelled around the country. It was compulsive television for the few minutes it had lasted. Eric finished his drink and walked round to Oval Mansions where he found Ian and Chaz writing together. They were putting the finishing touches to a new song as he walked nervously into the room. "What song is that?" asked Eric. " 'Sweet Gene Vincent' ", came the reply.

By the time he got home that night, Eric was in seventh heaven: "I wanted to play my songs, but I didn't know anybody and he listened to stuff I'd done. They were awfully nice and they gave me a lift home to Wandsworth in their Commer van. Even if I had gone on to work in a toothpaste factory, I would have had my moment."

By the spring of 1977, Eric was still in limbo. He had recorded 'Whole Wide World' with Nick Lowe, but no B-side had been prepared and he was without a band. Since moving to London, his CV had grown to include quality control inspector at a Corona lemonade factory in Wandsworth, cleaning toilets at a tarmac company in Greenwich and clearing plates off tables at Swan & Edgars' department store in Piccadilly Circus, where he had been hired on the basis that he could "fill in the application form". Waiting patiently for his big break, Eric spent his mornings cutting hedges and mowing lawns in nearby gardens, but in the afternoons, he practised his quirky songs in his rented lodgings in Wandsworth, in south London. Denise had started calling around to Eric with her bass guitar and the two giggled nervously like school kids as he taught her to play 'Hang On Sloopy' (The McCoys' 1965 hit). Gradually, they started to try some of Eric's own songs and, as the sessions progressed, Denise started camping out in the living room. Only a few months before, Eric had been a stranger in London, with few contacts in the music industry, but meeting Ian and Denise had opened the door to a welcoming and creative circle of artists where he could develop his songs. Ian was also to play a very direct role in the developments taking place at Eric's – as his drummer.

"When Denise moved back in with Ian, he wanted to come round and hear what we were doing," says Eric. "I don't know if he thought me and Denise were conducting some sort of torrid affair or something. He started coming round and he sort of tapped along with us and said, 'I need to come round again with some drums,' and suddenly we got a fire damaged Olympic drum kit that had been removed from the back of a second-hand shop by Fred Rowe. I would be clipping hedges in the morning and they would come around in the afternoon and we would just play. We were this little bohemian combo and life was very charming."

Over at Stiff, Eric's recording of 'Whole Wide World' had gone down a storm and Dave Robinson wanted to know what else the scruffy singer had to offer. Without hesitating, Eric replied 'Semaphore Signals' and Dave suggested that as Ian was already playing with Eric that he should produce it as a B-side for his single. The song was recorded with Eric playing electric guitar, Denise on bass and Ian on drums.

Eric: "Ian wanted to be a drummer, he was very percussive. I remember some interview Ian did and he said he wanted to be a drummer, which is stupid when half your body don't work. The thing is, it was only his right hand and his right foot that were really doing the work and he had the high hat clamped shut. He used to play the bass drum and the high hat and that was the basis of keeping it together. Then with the snare drum he would almost have the stick, not exactly taped to his hand, but giving that impression, and he would lift his hand up and drop it onto the snare drum. I mean, there wasn't much going on there and nothing going on with his left foot, of course. It was all with the high hat and the bass drum and then round the cymbals a little bit."

'Whole Wide World' featured on *A Bunch Of Stiffs*, a cash-in album of tracks by Stiff artists and mates of Dave and Jake, issued in March 1977. Elvis's 'Less Than Zero' and Motorhead's 'White Line Fever' were the only singles, while Nick Lowe weighed in with 'I Love My Label', a tribute to Stiff which he wrote with Jake ("Well, I'm so proud of them up here/We're one big happy family/I guess you could say I'm the poor relation of the parent company"). Other featured artists were Dave Edmunds (who also appeared under the pseudonym Jill Read), Stones Masonry, Magic Michael, Tyla Gang and Graham Parker & The Takeaways – a studio band comprising Nick Lowe, Dave Edmunds, Sean Tyla and Larry Wallis.

On August 25, 1977, 'Whole Wide World' was released as a single (Buy 16), hot on the heels of Elvis Costello's second 45 'Red Shoes'. On Side A, the matrix read: "Stiff Records – Wreckless Eric: We're not the same, he's not the same' and on the flip-side, the label's cutter George 'Porky' Peckham scratched 'Semaphorly yours'.

By this time, Eric's informal backing group had a new recruit. Humphrey Ocean had called around with Davey Payne and Davey asked if he could start bringing his saxophone along. His musical credentials were never in doubt and the former Kilburn immediately added a new dimension to Eric's unusual sound. The quartet rehearsed at Eric's over the summer months and a set gradually emerged including such songs as 'Reconnez Cherie', 'Personal Hygiene', 'Excuse Me', 'Rags And Tatters' and 'Telephoning Home'.

Meanwhile, attempts to find a home for Ian's by now completed album *New Boots And Panties* had initially been frustrated and the project looked doomed. Armed with the 10 breathtaking tracks recorded at The Workhouse, Andrew King and Pete Jenner tramped around the offices of all the major record labels, only to be shown the door on every occasion. Ian's unnerving physical appearance and the explicit nature of his lyrics made him a virtual outcast in the eyes of record company big shots.

"They all said, 'Oh, we really love his stuff, but it's not quite what we're looking for,' " says Andrew. " 'It doesn't really have any commercial potential and it's a shame he's not better looking'. I used to have a file with all the notes of all the people who passed on Ian who are now the biggest moguls of the lot, all of whom would happily deny that they passed on Ian, but they did."

But the solution was right under their feet. Downstairs they went to Dave and Jake and played them the songs which had been spurned by the major labels. Astonished by what they heard, they agreed to sign him straight away.

Andrew, who now works at Mute Records, explains: "We licensed the album to Stiff which was a very good thing, because we owned the tapes and there was never any trouble about ownership of the masters later on. If Stiff went under, all the rights automatically reverted to us. Down the line, Ian didn't get into half as much grief as some of the other bands on Stiff."

Of Stiff's strategy, Andrew observes: "Stiff wasn't the first independent label, but it was the first independent which had the bottle to take on the majors at their own game. It was something which Daniel Miller did at Mute Records a few years later, although fortunately he had his head screwed on rather better than Jake and Dave because he is still here. The other independents were quite willing to put out groovy records, but they weren't really going to break acts and be a major player. Stiff never had any shyness about what their position in the industry should be. As far as they were concerned, they were just as much a major player as CBS, Polygram, EMI or Island."

Commenting on the label's unorthodox policy and on the record industry in the late seventies, Ian said,[11] "Stiff was aimed at people whose arses were hanging out in the industry and couldn't get a look in. We were the unemployables really. We didn't fit into any of their stupid categories, since the record industry is run by shoe salesmen and drug dealers. We took *New Boots And Panties* to every single label, but they were just fucking stupid – they still are."

7

THE CAKE OF LIBERTY

"It's a riddle, but within that riddle, there's a truth – an eternal positiveness. What he is saying in 'Sex & Drugs & Rock'n'Roll' is that if you're going to choose an alternative lifestyle, just do it and enjoy it, don't keep having a fit of conscience about it. And, in a way, Ian has led his life like that – he has lived by the sword."

– Chaz Jankel

Ian's deal with Stiff could not have been better timed. In the summer of 1977, as Britain marked the Queen's silver jubilee with street parties and an outpouring of national pride, Dave and Jake plotted a nationwide tour and publicity offensive that would promote a number of their acts on the same bill. The concept was largely inspired by 'The Naughty Rhythms Tour' of 1975, which saw pub favourites Kokomo, Chilli Willi & The Red Hot Peppers and Dr Feelgood hit the road en masse. The Stiff tour was designed to both flag up the artists who had records out at the time and to feed the insatiable Stiff publicity machine. A private coach was hired and five artists were hauled on board – Ian Dury, Nick Lowe, Larry Wallis, Wreckless Eric and Elvis Costello.

Ian recalled:[10] "I saw Jake and Dave plotting and saying, 'We'll have Wreckless, we'll have Nick Lowe, we'll have Larry Wallis, and Dave Edmunds will be there, and we'll have Costello,' and I said, 'I'll have some of that, what is it?' That was the Stiff tour."

On August 26, 1977, – just five weeks before the tour bus rolled away from Alexander Street – 'Sex & Drugs & Rock'n'Roll' became Ian's first solo single (BUY 17). The black and white photograph of Ian on the sleeve was evocative of the American silent movie star Harold Lloyd, his closed eyes, blackened with make-up, standing out clown-like against his ashen skin. Wearing a safety-pin in one ear, the singer mournfully rested his fevered-looking brow in his right hand, in which he was clutching a dark handkerchief. The picture sleeve was as striking as any Stiff release to date. The B-side, 'Razzle In My Pocket', had been recorded during the very first demo sessions at Alvic and featured Ian on drums and Chaz on guitars and bass. It was a spoken account of an afternoon's shoplifting in Romford's South Street Shopping Arcade, narrated by a yellow jerseyed thief, and was described on the back cover as a "true story". The young shoplifter is caught red-handed, but is eventually freed with "the Razzle in my pocket as the second prize". In customary Stiff style, the record carried messages in the matrix which read: 'Watch Out For Hand Signals' on the A-side and 'Crime Doesn't Pay' on the flip. A 12-inch version was later released in France after the UK single was controversially deleted, with 'Razzle In My Pocket' replaced by 'Sweet Gene Vincent' and the old Kilburns' number 'You're More Than Fair'. A limited pressing of the single in orange vinyl was also issued in the UK as the label continued to push back marketing boundaries.

'Sex & Drugs & Rock'n'Roll' – coming as it did at the height of punk – was instantly interpreted as an anthem of excess and banned by the BBC. "Sex and drugs and rock'n'roll/Is all my brain and body need/Sex and drugs and rock'n'roll/Is very good indeed," snarled the cigarette-ravaged voice over a gritty guitar riff. In contrast to the limited shelf-life policy adopted by Stiff, the universal appeal of the song's title would prove timeless and become a generic.

"It is not really seen as an Ian Dury song title. It's like Durex or something," says Andrew King. "Ian has more entries in the Oxford Dictionary of Quotations than any contemporary English writer and also in Jonathan Green's new Dictionary of Slang where the *New Boots And Panties* songbook is listed as one of the sources. Every newspaper sub-editor in the world, if in doubt, will reach for 'Sex & Drugs & Rock'n'Roll' or 'Reasons To Be Cheerful'."

While audiences would rebelliously scream out the chorus, the song's more thoughtful verses contained a very different message. Ian explained:[8] "With this song, I was trying to suggest there was more to life than either of those three; sex, drugs and rock'n'roll, or pulling a lever all day in a factory. Of course, when I go out and perform the song, everyone sings along and you can't stop 'em! People say to me: 'Now there's AIDS about, don't you think that song was awful?' and I explain that the song was always a question mark over those activities. And I wrote it before these dreadful sexual diseases like herpes and AIDS appeared. I was saying, if all you think about is sex and drugs and rock'n'roll, there is something wrong. I wished I got a quid for every time that title has been used."

The song has become a standard feature of any punk compilation album. Chaz: "There is a moral in 'Sex & Drugs & Rock'n'Roll', but Ian never said 'Do this or do that'. 'Keep your silly ways, or throw them out the window/The wisdom of your ways, I've been there and I know/Lots of other ways, what a jolly bad show/If all you ever do is business you don't like'. It's a riddle, but within that riddle, there's a truth – an eternal positiveness. What he is saying is that if you're going to choose an alternative lifestyle just do it and enjoy it, don't keep having a fit of conscience about it. And, in a way, Ian has led his life like that – he has lived by the sword."

The single was an instant hit with the music press. *NME* (Oct 1, 1977) declared: 'In A Class Of Its Own And Single Of The Week For Sure' under the heading 'Seminal Punk Makes A Score'. "He and no other was the instigator of safety pin chic, wearing the objects in his lug holes when Richard Hell was still wearing them in his Mothercare diapers," observed the reviewer. Of his first solo record, the critic added: "Ian Dury has created a juke box classic around youth culture's holy trinity that would be a universal number one if Eddie Cochran hadn't died in vain and if our national media wasn't controlled by joyless reactionary loonies." 'Razzle In My Pocket', meanwhile, had "proved conclusively that Ian Dury is writing the soundtrack for this generation". Another music press reviewer described 'Sex & Drugs' as "a juddering, grease-soaked riff of insidious simplicity underlies Ian's throaty drawl. Wreckless last week, Ian this . . . what next?"

A 'New Wave Chart' supplied by the Rough Trade label showed 'Sex & Drugs' at number two shortly after its release, but its title alone destined it to remain an underground hit. After selling about 19,000 copies, Stiff deleted the single two months later, triggering outrage from the press and the record-buying public. But Stiff was unrepentant, insisting: "We're a record company – not a museum".

Alan Cowderoy, who joined Stiff in mid-1977 and was responsible for international distribution, says that while this marketing ploy had short-term spin-offs, the deletion of 'Sex & Drugs & Rock'n'Roll' may, in hindsight, have done no favours for either Ian or the label. "The whole policy at Stiff was to put out a single and then delete the single, whether or not it was a success. It would only have a limited life span," he says. "On the one hand that's great because it got people buying early and perhaps gave the record an earlier chart position. People were concerned that the shops might run out of copies or that the picture sleeve might not be available after the first run, so the shops themselves were much more animated and were keen to take the stock from us and the public were out there trying to buy it early on. But if we hadn't adopted that policy of deleting records and had put 'Sex & Drugs & Rock'n'Roll' on *New Boots And Panties*, it would have helped our cause a lot. I organised our releases in Europe and we pressed up 'Sex & Drugs & Rock'n'Roll' as a 12 inch. There were floods of imports coming into this country, where it was no longer available, everybody wanted 'Sex & Drugs & Rock'n'Roll', and I think we could have put it on the album at that time."

Commercial success eluded Ian's début single, but it served as a tantalising taster of what was to follow. On September 30, 1977, *New Boots And Panties* was finally unveiled by Stiff (Seez 4). The now famous black and white photograph on the sleeve taken by Chris Gabrin showed Ian dressed in turned-up denims, laced-up Dr Marten boots, a white jacket and dark neckerchief, and standing against a shop window displaying ladies undies and men's clothes. The impish-looking boy beside him with his hands stuffed into the pockets of a pair of flared trousers held up with braces, was his son Baxter. On the back of the album's memorable cover, Ian wore his own braces over a florescent green tee-shirt promoting a gymnastic club, his skinny frame silhouetted against a garish orange backdrop. The inner sleeve was a collage of pictures from his days in Kilburn & The High Roads, and one of them, showing Ian and Humphrey side by side, was used in a Stiff advertisement under the heading 'Me And My Best Friend Have Got New Boots And Panties'. The poster warned: "The first album from Ian Dury is larger than life and more fun than people. It's bound to be more popular than a Chinese pig in a synagogue, so get your *New Boots And Panties* now."

Baxter explains how the famous photograph on the sleeve came about. "I was about six and wearing football boots and flares. I think I just sort of did what six-year-olds do and walked up and stood next to him when they were taking that photograph in some place in Victoria or Vauxhall. It was a mad sort of lingerie shop and I don't think it exists any more. We had been driving about looking at places and they spotted that place. They whipped out and gave the geezer in the shop a fiver and I think he was all right about it. I just wandered into the frame, more randomly rather than in any orchestrated way. I don't think it was contrived."

He adds: "When you're that age you don't realise about fame and all that sort of stuff, so I never really thought about it twice, but I probably used to love it. I used to get old ladies coming up and asking me to sign record covers."

New Boots And Panties, a reference to the only items of clothing Ian would buy as new, was dynamite. And if the public thought they'd seen and heard everything imaginable thanks to punk, they hadn't bargained for this. The ten tracks which had been recorded so cheaply at The Workhouse were: 'Wake Up And Make Love With Me', 'Sweet Gene Vincent', 'I'm Partial To Your Abracadabra', 'My Old Man', 'Billericay Dickie', 'Clevor Trevor', 'If I Was With A Woman', 'Blockheads', 'Plaistow Patricia' and 'Blackmail Man'. Scrawled beneath the track list were the words 'There's

Nothing Wrong With It!!!' – the reaction of Ian and the rest of the group on hearing the finished product at Stiff Records.

Ian had expressed a strong wish for his singles not to be included on the album and as a result 'Sex & Drugs & Rock'n'Roll' was omitted. "I had this bee in my bonnet about doing an LP's worth of singles and not cheating anybody, which came to dust in the end, but I did try," Ian explained in the BBC Radio 2 documentary.[14] But as time would tell, *New Boots* wouldn't need singles or chart hits in order to sell. After all the frustrations and disappointments Ian had suffered during the Kilburns era, everything had come together at the right moment. The level of musicianship in his band was higher than ever, his lyrics were the sharpest he had written and the American funk rhythms imported by Chaz Jankel gave an immediate accessibility to his peculiar riddles. The music press would hail Ian as a new punk icon, but *New Boots* was way beyond anything else that was happening on Britain's volatile popular music scene in the autumn of 1977.

In the week that *New Boots* was released, sweat-sodden audiences around London and other major cities were gobbing and pogo-ing to The Adverts, Generation X, Sham 69, The Radiators From Space, The Buzzcocks, 999 and Bazooka Joe (fronted by Adam Ant). In common with The Sex Pistols – now joined by bassist Sid Vicious – and The Clash, these bands rammed their two-minute songs home with a minimum of guitar chords, a standard 4/4 rhythm, and a fistful of attitude. Those who ventured into The Vortex, The Roundhouse, The Roxy, or any other cavernous venue in the capital, could do so in the knowledge that amid whatever chaos and anarchy lurked within, a kind of uniformity would ultimately prevail. The first song on a punk set list was generally a good indicator as to what was coming next and the dress code – black leather jackets, jeans, tee-shirts and assorted ear-rings and safety-pins – would rarely be breached by the groups on the bill. Groups on the horizon such as Squeeze and The Undertones, who along with some of Stiff's artists were soon to be lumped into the category of New Wave, relied on choppy guitar chords and catchy melodies. Ian Dury's *New Boots And Panties*, however, was a different cup of tea entirely, albeit quintessentially English. He was a one-off.

Steve Nugent says: "*New Boots And Panties* came between the ice age of seventies rock and the hurricane of punk. If someone else had tried to do that, it would have been regarded as artifice, whereas, if it is done by a crippled Cockney wise-guy, it is the real thing. It would have been pretty hard to turn it down as a bad acting job. Ian was not a stupid person and he had a big network of people in various art worlds who were interested in supporting that sort of thing, so he was not regarded as a charlatan. Also, it didn't rely on radio play, in fact they went out of their way to make sure singles weren't taken off the album."

Steve quickly found himself shut out of the picture, however. He had occasionally visited The Workhouse during the recording of *New Boots And Panties* but Ian's tendency to put down his contribution led to Steve feeling a certain degree of hurt. As regards The Blockheads, he was an outsider.

Steve: "Ian and Chaz split the remaining royalties on those songs – I still had my third – because Ian felt that Chaz did something with the bass part which actually brought it together, which may or may not be true, but that was up to them. Ian was a real put-down artiste, you know. He said that Chaz was the one that actually wrote that song, but he did that on almost every song. I wrote the intro for 'Plaistow Patricia', but when Ian came back from playing the demo to Chaz, he said Chaz had told him where I'd nicked that from. Needling people doesn't even come into it, but that's what Ian was like."

'Wake Up And Make Love With Me', the record's opening track, announced itself with the sweeping piano playing of Chaz, before Norman and Charley laid in simultaneously with a pulsating rhythm. Then came the lyrics. "I come awake, with the gift for woman-kind/You're still asleep, but the gift don't seem to mind/Rise on this occasion, half way up your back/Sliding down your body, touching your behind." Funky, sexually explicit, but ultimately inoffensive, this opening gambit had all the characteristics which had drawn people to Ian for years. Thousands of singers wrote about love and women, but few, if any, had ever referred to love-making in such graphic and unflinching terms. 'Wake Up And Make Love With Me' would be used as the opening number for all the group's live performances and remained at the top of The Blockheads' set list.

'I'm Partial To Your Abracadabra' was also strictly bedroom. In it, Ian investigated "unforeseen erogenous zones" ("Stop it, insists, slap it with your wrist, it likes it when you leave it alone") and sexual climaxes ("There's been a manifestation/Nature made it answer the call"). The song had a steady beat and a melodic hook, but Ian had reservations about it and it had not been performed live for many years. In an interview with Vivien Goldman of *Sounds* during the Stiff tour, Ian said of the song: "I fucked that one up, didn't I? I wanted to make that hermaphrodite. No, hermaphrodite implies something sexy or some duality. It just seems to me that inevitably the human race will evolve eventually into one sex. Women will have their babies in a nice box, and we'll all fancy each other for what we are instead of what we're supposed to be or tits or all of that old bollocks."

'My Old Man' was one of the defining moments of *New Boots And Panties*. And it was this deftness of touch which elevated him above many of those coming to prominence around him. Aggression and anger was present in other songs, and with his razor-blaze earring, hard-geezer image and controversial material, he was inevitably perceived as a punk. But his touching tribute to his dad, told with such disarming matter-of-factness, personified Ian's talent for using prosaic language to devastating effect. What lyricist could sit down to write an affectionate song about one of their parents and have the courage to tell their story in such pragmatic terms? "My old man was fairly handsome/He smoked too many cigs/ Lived in one room in Victoria/He was tidy in his digs/Had to have an operation/When his ulcer got too big/When his ulcer got too big/My old man", went his unsentimental memorial.

New Boots And Panties had a dark side, and contained within 'If I Was With A Woman' was an unpleasant, seemingly misogynist theme ("If I was with a woman, I'd threaten to unload her/Every time she asked me to explain/If I was with a woman she'd have to learn to cherish/The purity and depth of my disdain"). Ian explained:[8] "It was written on the rebound from an argument with a woman, so it says horrendous things. The first impression you might get is of a very bitter person. It's a song of hate." However, its brutal directness and the quality of the playing on the track kept it in perfect sync with the provocative, and sometimes discomforting, aural experience which was *New Boots And Panties*. Certainly, Ian was not averse to male chauvinism and his treatment of girlfriends was far from exemplary – but he was no misogynist. Ian loved women and throughout the course of writing this book, female acquaintances spoke extremely highly of him.

Jenny Cotton, then an employee of Blackhill and who was closely involved in Ian's management for many years afterwards, says Ian was extremely "understanding of women". "He had some girlfriends over the years, he really had," she says. "One day Ian rang me up and one of his girl-friends was actually in the river near his flat in Hammersmith just trying to attract attention and I went round and found all these wet footprints from the door leading towards the street. Women really liked Ian and I think it's because he gives them a lot of attention and can be very sympathetic to feminine things."

It was, however, Ian's larger-than-life, characters 'Clevor Trever', 'Billericay Dickie' and 'Plaistow Patricia', immortalised forever on *New Boots And Panties*, who would especially capture the imagination of Ian's new-found audience. To this day, they remain firm favourites with his loyal fans.

'Clevor Trever' was a Dury gem. Ian had once again broken with songwriting norms, using the speech of his working-class hero to construct one of his most imaginative and cleverly drawn songs. It was a tongue-twister, sung at great speed and requiring a great deal of concentration from anyone trying to sing along. The stuttering guitar which punctuated the song throughout perfectly complemented its awkward language, while a strange keyboard sound swirled beneath. "Just 'cause I ain't never said no nothing worth saying/Never ever never never ever/Things 'ave got read into what I never said/'Til me mouth becomes me 'ead which ain't not all that clever," the song went. Naturally, however, it was the song's simple hook line ("Knock me down wiv a feaver/Clevor Trever") which would make the song a winner.

'Billericay Dickie' was a foul-mouthed, sexist brickie who bragged about his sexual encounters with a string of Essex girls, while at the same time cementing his image as a local boy made good. It was here that Ian's music hall influences were most prominent. The lyrics were liberally laced with funny rhymes and slang ("She took me to the cleaners and other mis-demeanours/But I got right up between her rum and her Ribena") and an oompah organ and banjo-style guitar gave the comical urban tale a fair-ground feel. Billericay's "favourite brickie" had sex with Nina in the back of his Ford Cortina, made Sandy "go bandy" with the odd barbiturate and bruised Janet's "pomegranate". But if the activities of 'Billericay Dickie' were an eye-opener, then a bigger shock was in store.

The tirade which announced the arrival of 'Plaistow Patricia' was a shock to even the most hardened listener. "Arseholes, bastards, fucking cunts and pricks/Aerosol, the bricks," yelled the Cockney narrator, in an elocution lesson from hell. "A lawless brat from a council flat, oh oh/A little bit of this and a little bit of that, oh oh/Dirty tricks." Then came her teenage journey from the Mile End Road to the West End and her descent into heroin-addiction ("Keep your eyeballs white and keep your needles clean") and a violent world of exploitation. But Plaistow Patricia, like Ian, was a winner and she emerged scarred but in one piece with her own showroom on the Mile End Road. If punk was the music of the streets, none of its anarchic ambassadors were depicting the vagaries of life there with the kind of brutal honesty employed by Ian Dury.

Rat Scabies, real name Chris Miller, was the drummer with The Damned, the notorious punk band renowned for smashing up sound gear and instruments and whose live shows were often violent. He recalls listening to 'Plaistow Patricia' on a rough demo of *New Boots* being played in Blackhill's office above Stiff. "I remember sitting there thinking, 'My God, what the fucking hell does this geezer think he's going to do?'" he recalls. "I mean Ian Dury had been around for a long time, he wasn't written off, but he wasn't really regarded in high esteem. He had a good band, but nobody really bothered. I thought, 'Blimey, he's going for shock value, he's really going for the throat.' I remember thinking 'Is he doing this to try and impress us or was he seriously saying, 'This is what I'm doing mate?' As things progressed and I listened to it a bit more, it became more obvious we were in the same boat, but it was a shock at first. I was surprised that I was shocked, especially as we were doing all the shocking and Ian was this pub rock bloke saying, 'Come up and have a listen to my demos.' "

Ian explained the origins of his infamous song:[8] " 'Plaistow Patricia' was based on a number of people I knew in the Sixties. I was always quite partial to a puff, which was well illegal and it was quite hard to find. One day I went to a house in Soho which has been knocked down now. In the front room were all these Picadilly boys asleep, and various dudes and smack heads with burnt hands coming in. This place was pretty squalid, and this bloke came back with my bag of grass and it was the closest I'd been to the reality of hard drugs. I still haven't seen any heroin and I don't want to either. I'm too worried about myself already to go that way. This place was like Hades. I really hated that day and never wanted to go back there. The song was about looking for hope. A girl on heroin meets a bloke who has enough money to send her to Switzerland to have her blood changed. The song had a happy ending, so good luck Plaistow Patricia."

In his interview with *Sounds*,[12] Ian admitted that in his original version of the song, Plaistow Patricia ended up walking into the Thames, largely because he "wasn't very positive then". Instead, it finished up as a modern fairytale and it was not the first or the last time he would display a humanity for his characters.

'Blockheads', the song from which the group would take their name, was a stream-of-consciousness rant about "pissed-up" gangs of lads who Ian watched from his flat overlooking The Oval and The Cricketers pub. It began with a blistering assault on the ear-drums, courtesy of a thunderous guitar and bass riff, before Ian launched his attack on the passing hordes ("You must have seen parties of blockheads with blotched and lagered skin/Blockheads with food particles in their teeth/What a horrible state they're in"). The lyrics were some of his most entertaining on the album, as he painted a vivid and compelling picture of passing yobs ("They've got womanly breasts under pale mauve vests/Shoes like dead pigs noses") and bemoaned "premature ejaculation drivers" with black and orange cars. But by the end of the song, he was also directing his sneers towards those who looked down on life's 'blockheads'. In the last line, he concluded, "Why bother to talk about blockheads/Why should you care what they do/ 'Cause after all is said and done, you're all blockheads too". As the song came to a frenzied finish, Ian yelled hysterically over a fizzing keyboard solo and rock'n'roll undercurrent and to accompanying cries of 'Oi Oi' from his own Blockheads.

At the time of the album's release, Ian gave the following explanation: "It's just describing blockheads quite accurately, and attacking people in a certain area beautifully accurately," he said.[12] " 'Imagine finding one in your laundry basket' [mimicking the snide voice he uses on the record]. I could measure you with sugar to that. I know exactly who'd shiver to that, and I hope it gets right up their pinafores."

Nearly 20 years later, Ian said he had come to find some compassion for his subject:[3] "I'd see them on a Sunday afternoon with orange hair over their shoulders and purple tank tops with patched flared trousers. I just described these people coming out of the pub all yelling drunk and fighting and going berserk. I kind of hated them, I must say. I wrote a song about them, but then thought, 'Who am I to criticise them?' So at the end I put 'We're all block-heads too' to try to absolve myself from my venom. It was easier to hate them, knowing we're all part of the same hideous pageant."

The album's finale 'Blackmail Man' contained some of the most astonishing lyrics of all. In a violent outpouring of rhyming slang, he lashed out at racists on behalf of almost every minority group. Barely coming up for air, he spat out a vengeful diatribe over a screeching guitar which made 'Anarchy In The UK' sound restrained by comparison ("I'm an Irish cripple, a Scottish Jew, I'm the blackmail man/A raspberry ripple, a buckle-my-shoe, I'm the blackmail man/I'm a dead fish coon, a pikey Greek, I'm the blackmail man/A silvery spoon, a bubble-and-squeak, I'm the blackmail man"). He worked himself into a frenzied state, almost choking as the song came to a clattering and feedback-drenched end ("Blackmail man and I think you stink/You pen-and-ink, I'm the black-mail man/I 'ate your guts, Newington Butts/I'll put the black on you, I'm the blackmail man . . . wooooaaahh").

From the raunchy opening bars of 'Wake Up And Make Love With Me' to the cacophony of 'Blackmail Man', Ian Dury had produced a record which would leave the listener reeling. The success of other bands and other artists had made Ian bitter, but the recognition which had been so slow in coming was now close at hand. *New Boots And Panties* earned lavish praise from journalists and in the days immediately following its release, Ian Dury's name was written large in the pages of the daily papers and music press.

Roy Carr of *New Musical Express*, in one of the very first reviews, described Ian as one of the country's "most unique and uncompromising talents", who had "vindicated himself with a vengeance" after the disappointing Kilburns' effort *Handsome*. "It's impossible to bag Ian Dury, except to say that he has taken the essence of the Cockney music hall and utilised rock as a contemporary means of expression," wrote Carr. "On occasions, Ray Davies has dallied with a similar approach, but Dury has none of the self-conscious pretensions that Davies exposed in his flawed Flash Harry caricature. Ian Dury feels no need to adopt a transatlantic voice to comply with his subject matter, preferring to deliver ribald and bittersweet monologues in the tone of voice he was born with. Max Wall with a back-beat. Max Miller on mandies." The no-holds-barred 'Block-heads' 'Plaistow Patricia' and 'Blackmail Man', were "prime-cut Brit-rock, each one faster and more psychotic than its predecessor. Not since George Harrison's 'Piggies' has any one song numbered an unpleasant sector of society with as much venom as Dury's 'Blockheads'." Carr concluded: "I really don't know if the public is ready for the eccentricities of Ian Dury. Perhaps they never will be. Whether or not you buy *New Boots And Panties* at least make hearing the album a priority. It's your loss if you pass."

Vivien Goldman of *Sounds* awarded the album five stars and quoting enthusiastically from the album's astonishing lyrics, observed: "Lawless brats from council flats have finally found a voice that speaks from, of and about the people. A voice that combines passion with the vernacular 'she got into a mess with the NHS' – sage street advice, plus cinematic observation, plus humour."

Under the heading 'Dury's War and Peace', Allan Jones of *Melody Maker* also praised Ian's warts-and-all examination of "the violence of working-class existence", which he described as "superior" to Steven Berkoff's musical production *East*, then running in the West End. "It's a tense, harrowing account of urban degradation, that conveys with more vocal, musical and lyrical vehemence than any so-called 'new wave/punk' combo has yet been able to muster, the desperation and squalor of the social conditions (and the effects of those conditions upon individual personalities) it so provocatively illustrates."

New Boots And Panties was not only applauded in the music papers, but in the arts columns of broad-sheet newspapers and other highbrow publications. Much weight was attached to Ian's lyrics and it was clear that he was being hailed more as a heavy-weight writer and social commentator than a passing pop singer.

Writing in the *Guardian* on October 11, 1977, Robin Denselow warned that *New Boots* could not be recommended to all readers of the paper, even those who had "braved The Sex Pistols" and said the honesty of Ian's songwriting would "send self-consciously daring punks scurrying back to the safety of their dole queue clichés. I admire him for the way he throws himself full tilt into his emotions, using a backdrop as squalid as the worst of the East End for songs of unashamed sexuality, admiration, or hate. The tribute songs – straight and never mawkish – are to Gene Vincent and to Dury's father, and equally honest are the demented, stream of conscious-ness tirades."

The review concluded: "The nearest transatlantic equivalent, as poet and chronicler of the seedy back streets, is Randy Newman. But his excellent new album *Little Criminals* is a far more subtle, understated and melodic affair. Newman writes few songs, but when he does eventually release an album he has pared them down to the simple, dry and ironic basics."

The verdict was unanimous – Ian Dury had produced a masterpiece.

The Stiff tour of Britain kicked off just four days after the release of *New Boots And Panties* and called for reinforcements to Ian's still unnamed group. Charley and Norman had played on the album and they suggested that Mickey Gallagher and John Turnbull, the other half of Loving Aware-ness, be invited along. They agreed and at 4pm on October 3 they were among the motley collection of musicians boarding the Stiff bus from 32 Alexander Street, heading out west to High Wycombe Town Hall, in Buckinghamshire. From Ian's point of view, the publicity surrounding the tour could not have been better timed.

There were 18 musicians on board, some of whom would provide backing for more than one of the artists being promoted. Each act had rehearsed in Fulham in the weeks leading up to the tour and were now primed and ready to go. Wreckless Eric's backing combo The New Rockets reunited the Melody Road trio of Ian on drums, Denise (still his girlfriend) on bass and Davey Payne on sax. Contributors to Nick Lowe's Last Chicken In The Shop were rocker Dave Edmunds, former Pink Fairies' singer Larry Wallis, drummers Terry Williams and Pete Thomas, and keyboard player Penny Tobin. This same cast doubled up as Larry Wallis's Psychedelic Rowdies.

Elvis Costello had also pulled together a backing band to accompany him on the 25 dates – The Attractions. They were pianist Steve Nieve, bass player Bruce Thomas and drummer Pete Thomas (no relation), previously with Chilli Willi & The Red Hot Peppers. US band Clover, later Huey Lewis's backing band The News, had provided the accompaniment on Elvis's début *My Aim Is True*, which had been released in July with the usual Stiff fanfare. The first pressing of the record contained a 'Help Us Hype Elvis' flyer asking fans to send their reasons for liking the 'English' Elvis and the cost of postage. The first 1,000 customers to respond had a free copy of the album sent to a friend. By the time the Stiff entourage took to the road, 'Less Than Zero', 'Alison' and 'Red Shoes', had all been released as singles, and 'Watching The Detectives' was still to come.

While The Attractions had only recently been introduced, Mickey, Johnny, Norman and Charley had already played together in Loving Awareness, effectively providing Ian with a ready-made band. And while Elvis's hostile demeanour succeeded in alienating some audiences, Ian's idiosyncratic stage persona won people over in droves as he lurched behind the microphone stand in a range of assumed guises. Sometimes he was Bill Sykes from *Oliver Twist*, dressed in a tatty jacket, brown bowler hat, and with black eye make-up. On other nights he was the Pearly King, glittering under the lights in a black sequinned jacket, or a Cockney cabbie with chequered flat-cap and patched-up overcoat. One picture from the tour shows him wearing a striped night-cap, ski goggles and a tee-shirt advertising Deliverance Removals, a firm operated by his Irish neighbour from Oval mansions, John Carroll. During guitar solos or other instrumental breaks in the songs, Ian turned Tommy Cooper, stuffing handkerchiefs into his mouth and waving feather dusters, rattles, plastic toys and other strange props he had despatched the fresh-faced Stiff publicist Kozmo Vinyl to buy from nearby shops. A stool was often placed beside him on which he could place his theatrical props, plastic beer glass or take a brief rest.

"We used to go out and buy the most outrageous toys and things, water pistols and a plastic fried egg what he used to hang on his coat, dodgy old plastic fruit an' that," says Fred. "He used to squirt water at the audience and they loved it, they used to fight to get to the front to cool down."

Ian knew he was no Mick Jagger and never wanted to be, and introduced these gimmicks because he simply didn't know what to do when he wasn't singing. In doing so, he deepened the audience's sense of intrigue. And, according to Fred, his preparations for these shows and his attention to detail went even further. "He used to send me out to find the name of the local nut house, the chief of police, a famous man there and a famous criminal and he'd bring all this up in the gig and say, 'Hang on, hang on, don't go nutty or you'll wind up in Park View' and they'd all go, 'Cor, he knows about Park View' and the people used to like him because he went to the trouble of finding out about their little town. Or he'd say, 'I'll have police chief so and so after you' and they'd all laugh and joke. He used to stop 'em dead.

"He'd say to me, 'Who's in the bar Spider? Get 'em out of the bar', so I'd go in the bar and say, 'Hang on everybody, stop drinking for a minute and listen to me. That bloke's travelled 200 miles to play here and you're drinking beer when you can do that every night, let's have you out of here and give him what he deserves.' "

Spider was at Ian's side at all times, ushering him up and down steps, on and off stage, adjusting his microphone and keeping unwanted visitors at bay. If Ian began to fall during his set or his calliper became unhinged, Spider leapt into action, picking him back up or lending a strong arm, often to deafening cheers from the crowd. But there was another member of Ian's back-room staff who Ian described chillingly on his scribbled history of Kilburn & The High Roads as 'The Sulphate Strangler. 4 men'. Peter Rush was a native of Uxbridge, Middlesex, and was six foot six inches tall and muscular. But while Spider was into physical fitness, Rush, aka The Strangler, was a hopeless drug addict. He had been working as a roadie for Yes in 1976 when he turned up to see Ian Dury & The Kilburns playing at The Hope & Anchor. He spotted Spider, got chatting and offered to help him move a heavy piano from the venue's basement. Spider instantly identified him as a potential asset and recommended that Ian add him to his security team. Fascinated by the power of the two as a team, Ian found their presence both reassuring and thrilling in equal measure.

The critics were more than impressed with Ian and his new group and mesmerised by his stage act. Reviewing the opening night at High Wycombe Town Hall, Vivien Goldman of *Sounds* took Costello to task for his "totally self-absorbed way of lecturing the audience like a parrot in NHS specs, holding a warning finger in the air while cocking his head pensively to one side. He sang 'Less Than Zero' well, but I preferred Wreckless Eric." As for Ian, Goldman had only praise: "Although Ian had lost his voice, he still managed to grip the onlookers by the appropriate areas. He was great when he barked out the staccato litany of "white face, black tie, etc" from 'Sweet Gene Vincent' like a demented fairground barker on STP and his rendition of 'Billericay Dickie' got three stars. The band's musicianship was showcased in touches like the neat guitar solo in 'Clevor Trever' and by the time Ian had finished 'Blockheads' and was going into 'Plaistow Patricia', there was untrammelled ecstasy all around me. Even if people don't know Ian's songs they can enjoy them, 'cos they've got music hall/fairground/end-of-the-pier roots that elicit a Pavlovian instant fun response. See him if you can."

Fellow Tynesiders Johnny and Mickey had at first been bemused by their southern counterparts in the group and Ian's Cockney patter. Ian was the first southern lyricist Johnny had worked with and due to Johnny and Mickey's Catholic backgrounds and Ian's Protestant upbringing, their approach to things was different. But musically and socially the group that had barely played together prior to the Stiff adventure, had a natural affinity. After playing for years in groups which had never made it, Johnny, Mickey, Norman and Charley's enormous musical abilities were now fused together with one of the most unusual performers ever to stand on a rock stage. Even during this honeymoon period, there was a sense that this was a perfect musical marriage.

"We had a tailor-made band and we knew how to play because we had just done gigs with Loving Awareness and we really wanted to play Ian's songs, we wanted to be his band," says Johnny. "That first album was just a bunch of fantastic songs that he had taken his time over and it was riding on that punk thing. In my book it wasn't punk at all. It was very musical. Chaz is a fantastic musician and great arranger and Ian is a one-off, there is nobody writes like him in the world. He was the first white rapper.

"On the Stiff tour, it did seem to click, even though I hadn't played with Chaz or Davey before. It seemed as if it was tailor-made for us all. Ian was well on form, he was young, fit and healthy and brimming with confidence and after a while we all were. I don't think The Blockheads ever really had any nerves on stage. The people who came off the best were Wreckless Eric and The Blockheads. Wreckless didn't have that big a sound. He had powerful songs, but it wasn't a huge heavy metal guitar type sound, and sometimes with Elvis Costello, you could hear the songs were good, but the hall didn't do them justice at all. The songs were quite involved and complicated and had a story to them and it would have been better to hear those songs in a much better venue. Whereas with The Blockheads, we did have some tender moments and some good, listenable songs, but we also had the anthems. With the raw stuff like 'Plaistow Patricia' and 'Blockheads', you could just churn it up and the energy was going up in the room, waiting for 'Sex & Drugs & Rock'n'Roll' at the end. And there was me, a good recovering Catholic, singing 'Sex & Drugs & Rock'n'Roll'."

Ian and his band continued to steal the limelight as the tour went on and were joined on stage by the other artists as the final chorus of 'Sex & Drugs & Rock'n'Roll' was screamed out. For all his fire and fury, Elvis Costello found himself increasingly overshadowed. Ian's Vaudevillian act, crude songs and red hot band made him the surprise package.

"No one really knew how big Dury was going to be," says Glen Colson, who had been brought in by Stiff to do some publicity work for *New Boots And Panties*. "The first night of the Stiffs tour, Ian blew everybody off and everybody knew from that night onwards that he was going to be enormous. I had taken all the press down there to see Elvis Costello and give all the other guys a little bit of press just to keep them happy, but it turned out that Ian totally stole the show and nobody I had taken down there was remotely interested in Elvis Costello, because he had had his bit of fame and they all chased after Dury.

"Ian was put on the cover of *NME* and he shot from absolutely nowhere to being on the cover of papers overnight. I hadn't got the journalists down to do that, because I was in the pay of Elvis Costello who I had worked with from the off. Elvis deliberately cut his own throat by doing a set of songs nobody had ever heard before. They were all waiting to hear the tracks from the first album and he did covers and songs from the second album which completely went over people's heads. He was just a perverse sort of guy and he did that sort of thing."

Along with Kozmo Vinyl, who was masterminding the publicity drive for *New Boots And Panties*, BP Fallon was involved in stoking the promotional fire for Britain's hottest new band. He watched from the sidelines in sheer delight as the crowds screamed for Ian, a year and a half after the Kilburns had broken up.

"I remember that when The Rolling Stones' 'It's Only Rock'n'Roll' had come out these students paid by the Stones had written 'It's only rock'n'roll' on bridges all over England and so I got hold of them and said, 'Would you write 'Sex & Drugs & Rock'n'Roll?' in separate words, but they chickened out at the last minute. So I had these badges made in different colours which together made up the title Sex & Drugs & Rock'n'Roll and I used to throw them out at gigs. Elvis Costello and his band had a bigger profile at the time and Jake used to freak out, because I would do this during Elvis's set. People would say, 'Oh, I've got two Ands' or 'I've got two Sex's.' With The Blockheads it was happening straight away, steaming at 100 miles an hour. It was the tour that established them as a happening band, which was very significant."

Many of those who climbed aboard the Stiffs Live Stiffs coach retain happy memories of the hectic four-week tour. A diary of the tour that is now held by Denise details the inebriated off-stage antics of the '24 Hour Club', whose membership included publicity man Kozmo Vinyl, Larry Wallis, Pete Thomas, Terry Williams, Dave Edmunds, Nick Lowe and Penny Tobin. It also records some of Jake Riviera's foul-mouthed assaults on students and anyone else who crossed his path. Of the behind-the-scenes shenanigans at the Glasgow Apollo, the unknown author wrote: "There was a bit of aggravation in the dressing room which led Elvis to threaten a bouncer with the jagged edge of an orange juice tin, while Bruce [Thomas] was frantically jumping about gritting his teeth. Congratulations to Davey [Payne] for the brilliant way he got the message over that you don't like cold tea – communication is such an art. And was that really Larry Wallis under that police helmet shining a torch in a copper's face? Pete Thomas has gotten quite serious about the art of dropping his trousers for everyone's enjoyment. It wasn't enough that he shocked 200 students while they were calmly watching TV – he was next seen with bare bum pressed against the coach window while driving down the M1. Wreckless Eric was refused service in a nice Scottish pub. Seems they thought he'd already had enough to drink (at 7.30pm). But I think it was because he wasn't wearing tartan."

Amid the camaraderie, however, there were some unpleasant exchanges and Davey Payne was never far away from the hostilities. His hot head and reputation for being quick with his fists was no secret to Ian. But to others on the Stiff tour, it came as a painful surprise. Eric: "We were backstage after the gig had finished and Davey Payne came around the corner and I said, 'Oh hello, what's happening?' and the next thing, he hit me full in the face and carried on. It was totally unexpected. I was on the floor and he was kicking the shit out of me, but then a roadie came around the corner and pulled him. They were picking me up and I was covered in blood – it was horrific. Then Ian heard about it and he came around the corner, and everyone had had a few drinks by this time, and he said to me, 'You've been asking for that, you've been winding him up for days.' But he didn't know what had been going on, because there was so much weirdness happening . . . like Davey trying to undress middle-aged women in hotel lifts; Davey waking up in the morning, sitting up in bed and going 'Fuck it all' and then throwing a glass ashtray which would shatter all over the room; Davey throwing the breakfast table across the dining room; heavies coming up and asking you to leave when you were half-dressed because Davey had wound them up. I was horrified and because of all that, when Ian came out on his side, I felt very unprotected."

The idea of alternating the headline act each night caused further tension, most notably between Ian and Elvis. Surprisingly, Elvis's set featured very few songs from *My Aim Is True*, his début album on Stiff. Instead, he concentrated on songs from his follow-up album and a series of covers such as Richard Hell's 'Love Comes In Spurts', Bacharach & David's 'I Just Don't Know What To Do With Myself', The Damned's 'Neat Neat Neat' and Lovin' Spoonful's 'Six O'Clock'. He also churned out a rendition of the one-time Kilburns favourite 'The Roadette Song'. Virtually from the outset of the tour, however, there had been little love lost between Elvis and Ian.

Denise: "There was an animosity between Elvis and Ian. Elvis had a habit of snoring loudly and one night on the coach, people saw that he was fast asleep. They tied his shoe laces together and emptied an ash tray into his mouth and he woke up absolutely furious and went spread-eagled all the way up the coach. Elvis had a hard time after that."

Mickey Gallagher: "Ian was as cool as cucumber on the Stiff tour because we knew we were fucking good and he had that confidence of knowing no matter what anybody said to him, he could blow them off the stage that night. There was this Elvis and Ian thing going on all the time. I never saw it overtly, but if they passed each other on the bus they wouldn't talk."

In an article by Will Birch entitled 'Stiff's Greatest Stiffs Live' published in *Mojo* in October 1997, Costello aired his own version of events: "It was anti-boring stab-you-in-the-back stuff," he said of the tour in general. "But it's impossible to look into the mind of someone who was out of his mind on vodka and amphetamines."

In an interview with Nick Kent for *Creem* in May 1979, Elvis said: "The Stiff tour was a failure as far as I was concerned. Like every night the encore would be 'Sex & Drugs & Rock'n'Roll', right, and . . . it quickly reaches a point where the tour started to take on the manifestations of the song. And, like, it was getting so ugly I was compelled to write 'Pump It Up' . . . Well, just how much can you fuck, how many drugs can you do before you get so numb."

Alan Cowderoy says that the real winners from the rivalry between Elvis and Ian, were those who paid to see it. "Elvis and Ian were clearly the strong two acts and of course it made everybody work that much harder, particularly at The Lyceum, when Ian was closing the London show and Elvis was on immediately before him," he says. "I mean, Elvis pulled out every stop to make it difficult for anybody to follow him on to the stage. So his show was fantastic and Ian's band was so hot and it was such a good groove, the audience was absolutely over the moon.

"During the tour Ian would perform, a bit like a magician, and at the end, when you'd seen this fantastic show with everybody rocking away, you would see Ian being helped off the stage. You didn't have any idea that he might have any disabilities and then at the end there was this person limping off stage, being helped off stage, and you just thought, 'That's fantastic, I've just been entertained by someone like that.' It kind of doubled your appreciation, although he never laboured it or even talked about it really."

By the time the tour came to a close at Lancaster University on November 5, 1977, journalists had confirmed Ian as the star of the show. Radio 1 disc jockey Anne Nightingale wrote in the *Daily Express*, beneath a headline 'Tiny Ian – the big new rock hero': "Rock's latest hero is the very antithesis of the stereotype, flamboyant, aggressive sex symbol. Dury is 35 and still semi-crippled by polio which struck him at the age of seven. The walking stick he uses on stage is no theatrical prop, though along with the bowler that he wears, Dury can't help but cut a Chaplinesque figure."

She continued: "An elderly woman once arrived backstage to see Dury, gave him a bunch of flowers and compared him to Judy Garland. To liken a gruff-voiced singer with a strong punk image to Judy Garland may sound far-fetched, but I don't think so. They share many similarities. One is that intangible thing called stage presence. The other, infinite star quality." The other connection she could have made was their apparent vulnerability.

A review of the Stiff tour which appeared in the *Guardian* six days later hailed Ian as "a massive success". "I can't possibly justify his horrifying songs about the mating habits of Billericay Dickie or his triumphant anthem 'Sex & Drugs & Rock'n'Roll' but merely note that he is the most scandalous and hilarious anti-hero to have emerged in the year of punk, and is such a professional that he left even the excellent Elvis Costello looking like a beginner," it read.

On October 28, Charles Catchpole of London's *Evening Standard* raved about Ian, but he was not optimistic for the future of Stiff Records. "It's almost too good to be true and of course it can't last," he observed. "Already, Elvis, Lowe and Riviera have quit. Stiff are confident they can be replaced, but it is hard to imagine the intense bond that this unique tour has engendered surviving in the same form. Tonight at the Lyceum Ballroom in The Strand will not be the end, but it will be the end of a modern rock'n'roll beginning."

Things had indeed turned sour at Stiff and had reached a head shortly before the tour had begun. Dave and Jake's relationship had become increasingly fractious and after a series of rows, Jake had decided to join Radar Records, formed by ex-United Artists staff Martin Davis and Andrew Lauder. Critically for Stiff, he was taking Elvis Costello, Nick Lowe and Liverpool band The Yachts with him. Even given Dave Robinson's canny way of dealing with difficult situations – "I see no problem" – and idiosyncratic manner – "just make sure the record's got a hole in the middle, otherwise nobody will play it" – the situation looked grim. Two of its most promising artists had gone, rumours of the fall-out had reached the press and creditors were in hot pursuit. Despite the tour, the publicity and the good will, Stiff had in reality enjoyed little serious commercial success. Elvis Costello's 'Watching The Detectives', made it to number 15, becoming the only one of 22 singles to breach the Top 40. But now Radar was to reap the rewards of Elvis's songwriting genius and the catchy pop songs of Nick Lowe. By December, rising punk band The Damned had also cut its ties with Stiff.

Although the Stiff tour had launched Ian and Elvis, it didn't catapult them into the spotlight in Europe or America. International manager Alan Cowderoy was disappointed. He, like others working in Alexander Street, was astonished at the sudden break-up. "Stiff was very much a press-driven thing, and radio was being somewhat supportive, and all the press had focused on Elvis Costello and Nick Lowe and I suppose on the flamboyant style of Jake and Dave," says Alan. "The marketing for Elvis had been very aggressive and he was very much the high-profile, very visible artist on Stiff, but at the same time, we all recognised that Ian had a fantastic band and had made a great record. I think we all thought. 'Christ.' Certainly I was in shock, thinking that Elvis had gone, because certainly overseas Elvis was one of the big things that got everybody excited about. Dave and Jake worked together in an office sitting next to each other and I never detected any bitterness or acrimony between them and in my view it was a fantastically good team. It was a complete and utter shock to everybody when it happened. I can only think the office wasn't big enough for their two egos, but I thought they complimented each other very well."

Back in July that year, Stiff had struck a crucial distribution deal with Island Records (in turn distributed by EMI), which also gave them access to the cash-rich company's press office, film-making equipment and other facilities. As a result, Stiff had moved to 28 Alexander Street and taken over the whole building. Fortunately, Island took an understanding view of the domestic rift and Dave Robinson managed to placate those to whom the label owed money. With none of its remaining artists having yet scored a hit, Stiff carried on regardless, pinning its hopes on Ian Dury.

Said Dave:[11] "When Jake left, I was very unhappy. It was the worst possible time and it was really stupid. I had worked hard and Jake had worked very hard, but it seemed to me there was some other agenda and I didn't know what it was. I said, 'You have Elvis.' I liked Elvis, I thought he was great, but I thought Jake needed something. He was giving me a very sad story, whether it was right or wrong.

"It was a key time, because we were just on the cuffs of making a very large deal in America, and when I say 'on the cuffs', they had agreed our terms. It was a licence deal and the finance we had always yearned. We had always been hassling from one cheque to the next, just like any independent. I spent a few days around the office panicking and I found drawers full of receipts and I couldn't make head nor tail of the accounts. I found out anyway that we owed about £150,000. The Americans didn't want to do the deal for a while and eventually we convinced them that the label would survive in a cut-down version. So instead of getting the large sum of money, I think they were going to pay us $350,000. Also,

Elvis was leaving, who was one of the things they liked, and so we got something less.

"We hadn't spent a lot of money on Ian Dury, although the record [*New Boots And Panties*] had sold about 40,000, and I thought there was a real vibe for Ian, but we were going to have to promote him properly. We had cash in the bank and we booked a series of provocative ads. 'Give up smoking and give us your money', was one of them, and it worked. Suddenly the record started to move by itself."

By the time the tour bus arrived back in London, Ian's previously anonymous backing band had been officially christened. The name was one which would live on years after the Stiff posters had worn off the hoardings, bus shelters and student union walls. Ian said on the sleeve-notes for the 1991 live album *Warts And Audience*: "We had meetings and discussions and wrote lists, but nothing seemed hilarious. It was Norman who twigged it; just before a gig in somewhere like Derby, we became The Blockheads and carved her name with pride on all our hearts."

Ian, in a typically blunt interview with *NME* during the Stiff tour [published December 24, 1977], said: "I'm fed up with being called Ian Dury all the time. It's impossible to pronounce for starters. Everyone says 'Drury'. My mum can't say it properly, but she never got on well with me old man. She says 'Doo-ery'. Names are funny. Thought about Plus Support, Preferred Closed – Thursday at The Marquee, Closed. No one would have the bottle to do that. Was gonna call this outfit Cripple, Nigger, Yid, Chink & Dead Fish. Easier to say than Dozy, Beaky, Mick & Wotsit, innit? But Blockheads just happened of its own volition."

The level of musicianship in Ian's group was in no doubt. Within a matter of weeks, chance had fused together one of England's greatest undiscovered songwriters and some of its hottest session musicians. Now, Ian Dury & The Blockheads were being touted as the most exciting band in Britain.

"We had worked for so long and I think that is why we were so impressive on that tour," says Mickey. "Everybody had put bands together to go on the tour, but Ian slotted in with a ready-made rhythm section and we turned out to be the band of the tour. That was a great springboard and as Ian said, 'I'm one lucky bloke to have fallen into this,' and we were lucky too."

8

IT'S NICE TO BE A LUNATIC

"When we finished recording 'Hit Me', I phoned up my mum from The Workhouse and said, 'Mum, I've just recorded my first number one'. I knew it – I just knew it in my blood."

– Chas Jankel

"Blue Jean baby". Tenderly sung and with a haunting echo, these were the opening words of 'Sweet Gene Vincent', Ian's carefully crafted tribute to the tragic singer from Norfolk, Virginia – one of rock'n'roll's earliest casualties. Ian's celebration of the crippled rocker who gave us 'Be-Bop-A-Lula' cleverly managed to encapsulate biographical details, song titles and lyrics, in a foot-stomping rock'n'roll anthem. He began in contemplative mood, mourning the premature demise of the "skinny white sailor" and "the voice that called my heart" over a gentle background provided by piano, guitar and percussion. When his tearful opening lament came to a close, there was an elongated pause which was suddenly interrupted with four notes, the words 'Who slapped John?' (a Vincent song title) and a spiky rock'n'roll guitar riff which played tribute to the kind of frenetic sound which had put Vincent's name in lights. As the song burst into life, he chanted: "White face, black shirt, white socks, black shoes, black hair, white Strat, bled white, dyed black, Sweet Gene Vincent, let the Blue Caps roll tonight."

Vincent Eugene Craddock, born on February 11, 1935, was the singer Ian had cherished most in his teenage years and his place in the rock'n'roll hall of fame was guaranteed from the moment his unforgettably raw and energising début 'Be-Bop-A-Lula' hit the airwaves in the summer of 1956. But the fresh-faced and vulnerable-looking singer's life was to be marred by tragedy.

When he was 17, he dropped out of school and enlisted with the US Navy, but he never saw military action. On a July weekend in 1955, he was knocked off his new Triumph motorcycle when a woman driving a Chrysler ran a red light and his left leg was smashed to pieces. The doctors

187

in the naval hospital considered amputation, but he begged his mother not to allow the operation. When he was finally released from hospital, he walked with a limp and his leg was encased in a steel brace. However, a year later he burst onto the rock'n'roll scene, standing at the microphone in the kind of precarious stance that would be mirrored by Ian Dury more than 15 years later, and rock'n'roll music was never the same again. In September 1955, with his leg still in plaster, Gene attended Hank Snow's All Star Jamboree in Norfolk which had been brought to the town by the country music radio station WCMS, and by early the next year he had taken to hanging around the station looking for a break. As a result, he sang with its in-house band, The Virginians, and started to appear on its *Country Showtime* programme. It was on a slot for this show that the words "Well, Be-Bop-A-Lula, she's my baby" were heard for the first time. Sheriff Tex Davis, a local DJ, was enthralled by the song and steered Gene and his band into the WCMS studios on April 9, 1956, where they recorded 'Be-Bop-A-Lula', 'Race With The Devil' and a country ballad 'I Sure Miss You'.

The demos were despatched to Capitol and when the record company suggested a recording session in Nashville, Tennessee, the enhancement of Gene's resonant vocals and the playing of his group, now renamed The Blue Caps, gave the songs an astonishing and unique sound. 'Be-Bop-A-Lula', his first single, was coupled with an equally unusual number 'Woman Love', on which the singer's jumpy, breathless vocal style made the words unintelligible and which seemed so suggestive that it was banned from the radio. 'Be-Bop-A-Lula' became a massive international hit and was helped on its way by its inclusion in the film *The Girl Can't Help It*, a cinematic vehicle for screen idol Jayne Mansfield with an electrifying rock'n'roll soundtrack.

Ian selected the enigmatic 'Woman Love' – the lyrics of which he has never been able to decipher – as one of his eight all-time favourite songs when he was a guest on Radio 4's *Desert Island Discs* 40 years later. Describing his reaction to hearing Gene Vincent singing 'Be-Bop-A-Lula' for the first time in the film, Ian said: "It's in the film for about 18 seconds and you can hear him in the background. I couldn't believe it. I thought, 'What's that?' The voice, the song and the visuals together, my brain exploded, my heart exploded."

In the UK, the song which so moved the 14-year-old Ian Dury, charted three times and Capitol's latest star followed it up with two more hits, 'Race With The Devil' and 'Blue Jean Bop'. By the close of the fifties, Gene Vincent and The Blue Caps had faded from the limelight, although as a solo artist Gene scored minor chart entries in the UK with

'Wild Cat' and 'My Heart' in the spring of 1960.

Tragically for the talented young singer, and for rock'n'roll generally, more trouble lay ahead. On April 17, 1960, Gene left a gig in Bristol in a taxi with Eddie Cochran and Eddie's girlfriend Sharon Sheeley, and in the rural town of Chippenham, Wiltshire, the cab rounded a bend and smashed into a cement post. Eddie Cochran died from his injuries two days later and although Gene survived, he sustained more injuries to his already damaged leg. Just two months after the accident, however, he had his biggest British hit when 'Pistol Packin' Mama' went to number 15 and the next year he had lesser successes with 'She She Little Sheila' and 'I'm Going Home'. But behind the scenes, he was heading for disaster. By the mid-Sixties, heavy drinking, a dependency on pain-killing drugs and a self-destructive lifestyle were taking their toll on his marriage and his health and drove him back to America. Several comebacks were attempted and in 1971 he recorded a number of songs in England and played a couple of gigs before his health gave out and he retreated again to the US. Gene Vincent died from a bleeding ulcer in Newhall, California, on October 12, 1971. He was just 36.

Ian's heartfelt tribute to his hero brilliantly displayed the author's attention to detail and it became his second single (Buy 23) on November 25, 1977, with the old Kilburns' crowd-pleaser 'You're More Than Fair' on the B-side. There was no picture sleeve, as with a number of the earliest Stiff singles, but simply a black bag revealing an image of Dury on the record label. The record also stated the A-side was 'produced by Nobody' but that the flip was produced by Pete Jenner; the obligatory scratched messages in the matrix read 'Porkey Not Por Kee' (a reference to cutter George Peckham) and 'Hello Kilburn fans'. Ian Dury was still an unknown quantity at this stage and the name Gene Vincent would have meant little to younger record buyers at the time. Only those who were close to Ian knew of the huge influence which the song's subject had made on its author.

"Ian loved Gene Vincent. He was a tragedy of Macbeth proportions," says BP Fallon. "When he died, he was in his mother's arms and his stomach exploded. 'You can call the ambulance now mum' – they were his last words. He was the first rock'n'roller I ever met. I was a kid at school and I went to York Rialto where he was rehearsing with The Outlaws, which was Ritchie Blackmore and Chas Hodges from Chas & Dave who had talked him into doing 'Rocky Road Blues'. There was this dancer on called Peter Gordino and he said Gene had drunk half a bottle of whisky on the train on the way up and Gene was swaying along, supporting himself on his microphone, looking up into the ceiling as he did. I said, 'Can I try on your jacket please?' – it was a leather jacket with a medallion on it – and I put it on. The next thing they were letting in all these blue-haired old ladies for bingo and I thought, 'Jesus Christ, this thing is being stopped because they are putting on bingo, this is sacrilege.' So he said, 'Hey, you'd better give me back the jacket, because the faces are coming in.' It was the first time I had heard slang, 'the faces' meaning the people.

"Gene Vincent was a tragedy waiting to happen, but maybe that's why he was great. He was a beautiful singer, but there was a sense of danger off him, which was attractive. I remember talking to Paul McCartney about him, because they were all in Hamburg together, and he described how they were all so impressed by him, but yet they were frightened by him at the same time. He used to pull out guns and wave them around. But then again, they copied the visual of the black leather. For Ian, it would have been the idea of people like Gene Vincent and Billy Fury as much as the sound, the imagery of them."

Commenting about the song, Ian said:[8] "Sweet Gene Vincent, because his voice is sweet. I don't think Gene Vincent was a particularly sweet guy, although I think he was very polite. I've heard stories that before lunch he could down a bottle of whisky. When he was very young there was something like a ferret about him, a wizened creature of the night, before he became more bloated. He was really a country singer but there was something mystical about his voice that got to me."

Like its predecessor, 'Sweet Gene Vincent' was a hit with the music press, but failed to chart. This was particularly frustrating for Ian after Elvis Costello's raw and menacing single 'Watching The Detectives' had climbed to number 15 in the UK Top 40 just weeks before his own release.

But by the end of 1977, *New Boots And Panties* had sold 50,000 copies. Ian and Denise had flown off to Barbados for a rest after the Stiff tour, but there was to be no let-up on their return. In December, Ian Dury & The Blockheads embarked on their first headline gigs in the UK on 'The Dirty Dozen Tour'. By this time, Davey Payne, who had played with The Blockheads on the Stiff tour, had defected from Wreckless Eric's combo to join the group on a full-time basis. Ian Dury was the name on everyone's lips – despite the two non-charting singles – and he was the darling of the press. One thousand copies of a limited edition disc pressed by Stiff were handed out to revellers at the *NME* Christmas party at Dingwalls in Camden Lock. The novelty single featured the deleted 'Sex & Drugs & Rock'n'Roll' on the A-side and two unreleased live Kilburn & The High Roads numbers 'Two Steep Hills' and 'England's Glory'. The party was a star-studded event with members of The Clash, Generation X, The Ramones, The Heart-breakers, Thin Lizzy, The Damned, The Fabulous Poodles and Squeeze among the guests, Dave Edmunds and The Flaming Groovies providing the entertainment.

Another 500 copies were pressed up for an *NME* competition to find the biggest blockhead in the country. Contestants posted off pictures of themselves which were judged by Ian himself and the cross-eyed, double-chinned 'Slim' (Clive Pain from Alton, Hampshire) took the title. The honorary 'top blockhead' was presented with a copy of the rare single, a signed copy of *New Boots*, a pair of new boots and panties, and enjoyed a night out in Hemel Hempstead with the band.

Of the meteoric rise of Ian's début album, Andrew King says: "When *New Boots* came out I remember Pete and I listening to the finished tape in the top room at Alexander Street which had a bright yellow carpet and big old speakers which we had bought second hand from Abbey Road, and saying to ourselves, 'That's really good. If things go well we could sell 25,000 copies.' Then a few months later we were saying, 'We could sell 50,000 copies,' and the next thing we were running up towards the million mark. Whenever you went into someone's house it was playing on the turntable."

As 1978 dawned, Ian was still living in his Spartan rented quarters in Oval Mansions, where he was paying £3 per week because it had no bathroom or mains water. "I've been here for four years and I like it. But I only get paid £65 a week – it takes a long time to break even in this business," he told the London *Evening News*. From interviews given by Ian at this time, it is clear that he thrived on his roguish working-class image and was only too happy to play the 'rough diamond'. He willingly regaled journalists with tales of his shoplifting exploits when he was still "a young sprat", his part in a roving gang in Walthamstow, and his intimate knowledge of rhyming slang. He also waxed lyrical about the frustrations suffered by kids incarcerated in grim tower blocks and council estates. Ian Dury was simply a gift to journalists, who found him highly entertaining and returned to their offices laden down with colourful quotations from the master of repartee. He occasionally threw in a reference to his 'muvver' and her 'BBC' way of speaking, but generally he preferred to put the emphasis on his 'farver'. A veil was drawn over his days as a pupil at a private boarding school in Buckinghamshire and he continued to play up his Essex origins. Photographs which accompanied interviews in *Melody Marker*, *Sounds*, *NME* and *Record Mirror* only reinforced his image as a street-wise geezer, capturing him lurking outside run-down shops in the streets near Oval Mansions, his own high-rise home.

"I'm a wordsmith, ain't I?" Ian asked rhetorically in an article in *Melody*

Maker on November 19, 1977. "Slang is an alternative language. Slang is creative. There are so many restrictions put on your muvver tongue, right? It can be repressive, 'cos you associate it wiv your environment and if that environment is a bit gruesome you need an alternative language to be free of it. Free to wander and think." Describing some of his own childhood ducking and diving, he said: "I've got this thing called the Grisly Book, full of cuttings from when we all went to see Disc Jockey Jamboree at the Romford Ritz. The night all the seats got done, shocking stuff. At school, I remember, we used to get out at night and do the Cadet Force Armoury. Break in and walk about wiv guns pretending we were terrorists. Bit like commando raids, they was. Planned jobs. Nothing amateur. Everybody does things like that. I can understand the excitement of being a bit naughty and causing a bit of damage. Putting bricks across a road. Shooting out the street lights with an air rifle."

Mickey comments: "Ian's background is posh. I said to Ian once, 'You are making money pretending to be what I am. You're pretending to be working class, but you're not working class, not at all. It was the same with Joe Strummer. During the punk time, to be working class was credible and everybody who was famous then thought it was better to come from the working class or at least to be seen to be sticking up for the working classes."

In February 1978, a live compilation of songs recorded on the Stiff tour was released entitled *Stiffs Live Stiffs*. Like the majority of the shows themselves, the album concluded with Ian's songs and the raucous finale 'Sex & Drugs & Rock'n'Roll'. The track listing on the album was: Nick Lowe's Last Chicken In the Shop: 'I Knew The Bride When She Used To Rock 'n' Roll' and 'Let's Eat'; Wreckless Eric & The New Rockets: 'Semaphore Signals' and 'Reconnez Cherie'; Larry Wallis's Psychedelic Rowdies: 'Police Car'; Elvis Costello & The Attractions: 'I Just Don't Know What To Do With Myself' and 'Miracle Man'; Ian Dury & The Blockheads: 'Billericay Dickie', 'Wake Up And Make Love With Me' and 'Sex & Drugs & Rock'n'Roll'. The same month as this stark testament to the live power of the band came out, they were delivering their intoxicating blend of music hall and funk to an American audience for the very first time. They had been invited to take part in a six-week tour supporting the former Velvet Underground legend Lou Reed and had jumped at it. The Blockheads played 30 cities, travelling in a 12-bed coach, which was an excellent opportunity for Ian and the band; the chance to play large venues and test the unpredictable American market. The headlining artist was sure to attract plenty of publicity for The Blockheads, who were still unknown in North America.

Stiff had succeeded in arranging a licensing deal for the album in North

America with the major label Arista. Andrew King describes the less than cordial atmosphere in which the Anglo-American deal was struck: "In America, big deals come out of the barrel of a smoking gun. It is no good having great records, you have to have great records and a gun. Deals get done out of fear. People like Arista don't do deals because they think your stuff is wonderful, they do deals because they are frightened that someone else is going to do the deal. It is all done on terror. Jake knew that and they were up there slinging bottles through windows.

"We had this meeting with Clive Davis, the boss of Arista, and he told us all these lies about radio play. He told us we were getting all these add-ons, and we said, 'No we haven't. We knew you were going to say this and we spoke to the programming director half an hour before we came to this meeting and he confirmed that we had not been added there'. It was all like this and Clive Davis didn't like us at all. Anyway, we did a gig at the Bottom Line [New York] and Clive Davis is one of these people who can't bear to be touched. When Kozmo Vinyl finally got Clive Davis to come to the gig at the Bottom Line, which was a major operation because he didn't want to come to see a show at all because he was going to the Lincoln Center to see Metropolitan Opera or one of his great soul singers. He came in and Kozmo got up and said: 'Look, it's Clive Davis. Oh, he's got a Pringle sweater,' and got hold of him by the top of his jumper."

But although The Blockheads went down a storm with some of their American audiences, two shows a night and gruelling coach trips left the band exhausted and by the end of the tour, Ian and Lou were trading insults. In one withering put down, Reed snarled: "That guy sounds like he's got tongue disease".

Andrew King: "The main thing about the Lou Reed tour was that it required tour support of about $100,000. If Ian wanted something or said something should be done this way, we said, 'Fine Ian' and did it that way. He didn't expect to fly first class to America, I'm sure we all went economy class, although he did stay in the most expensive hotels and there was no let-up on the size of the crew we took. There was about 12 of us on the road. Lou Reed would sack his tour manager every day. Practically every day we got to a gig, and sometimes there would be days in between, there would be another tour manager. Lou Reed never came to the sound-checks, he spent the whole time in his hotel room watching old videos of himself. You would see this white-faced geezer running around with a briefcase and that was today's tour manager. There were all these rumours going down that the other members of his band were not allowed to fraternise with The Blockheads, especially the girl backing singers. Lou Reed said in one interview: 'Ian Dury and The Blockheads . . . I sure know why he called them The Blockheads'. The Blockheads would do their set first and then go off, then they would set up Lou Reed and he would start playing, by which time they were ready to go. On at least one occasion, when The Blockheads left, they walked right across the stage waving to the audience from behind Lou Reed while he was playing."

Of the egocentric former Velvet Underground star, Ian said:[8] "Arista thought we'd get an open-minded audience supporting this famous American lounge lizard Lou Reed. But he had a pot belly and trainers and was about as subversive as a packet of crisps."

Johnny says of the Blockheads' first American visit. "We had done one gig where we had stolen the show in a way. Our gig had been held up at the border in Buffalo and the gig was in Toronto and the people in customs impounded our gear. We got there with no gear and so we hired absolutely everything and went on with no sound-check and we just rocked, we just didn't care, we just went for it. We got the front page of the paper the next day 'Cockney singer blows away Lou Reed' or something and so the daggers were out after that with Ian and Lou. There were dates with Lou where Ian had these temporary crowns with a Union Jack on his bottom teeth and in some of the Irish towns it didn't go down too well with the Republicans. In one place, I think it was Detroit, they couldn't get their heads around us at all and we were escorted off stage by this massive policewoman who said to me, 'Come on buddy, you're history'. We swore and they weren't used to that at all."

In an interview with the *Sunday Times*[13] on his return from the US, Ian said the "redneck" audiences had been appreciative. But the underlying impression was that Ian Dury had not achieved what he had always been best at – connecting with people. The writer commented: "Ian Dury was unknown in the States before the tour (now his record is a modest 180 in the Top 200) and once there, with 'verbals' heavily spiced with rhyming slang, he felt he wasn't likely to be understood. So the Union Jack was less a display of patriotism than a means of indicating country of origin. Likewise, the label. At each of the 200 interviews when the question was posed 'Are you the new wave?' up would come the boot and the label and, 'Wot's me label say today then darlin'?' "

Fred Rowe, who accompanied the band on the American tour, paints a very different picture. He says The Blockheads made a lasting impression on audiences there and recalls people travelling from city to city to see them on shows which they headlined on the western side of the country after the Lou Reed dates. Lou Reed was simply envious of the publicity Ian was attracting and the musical power of what he saw as a jumped-up British pub band, says Fred.

"We were in this university doing the last gig and we had had this shit off Lou Reed for quite some time now and Ian was on stage and he announced to the crowd, 'Well, this is our last show with Lou Reed, good old Lou, he has looked after us and we are very pleased to have been on the tour with him and I'm sure this tour would not have been successful without him' – which was bollocks anyway – 'so I would like to dedicate this song to Lou and all the people who have helped us and loved us throughout this tour, so here we go . . . 'Arseholes, bastards, fucking cunts and pricks'. I was laughing and Lou Reed was standing behind me with his tour manager, so he said to me, 'Well, you've just done yourselves out of a case of champagne,' and I said, 'Poke it up your bollocks, we don't want your champagne, we just want rid of you.' When Ian came off stage, he said to the crew, 'Don't take offence, it's only a song.' He'd done him up like a kipper and it was really excellent the way he did it.

"We did seven nights at a nightclub in San Francisco and on the first night there was about two or three hundred people, the second night there was about a thousand, and on the third or fourth night it was pissing down with rain and we got there about three in the afternoon for another check and later I looked out the window and there was a queue three deep. I said, 'Ian, look out the window', he goes, 'Yeah, a queue for fucking Lou Reed,' and I said, 'Lou Reed ain't on until ten, that's your queue out there. They don't start queuing at seven o'clock to see Lou Reed at ten, they are here to see you at half past eight.' From that night, the place was packed with 4,000 people every night and the promoter said to me, 'You've got the man's ear, will he do another night?' I said, 'Well, we're controlled by the Lou Reed promoters,' and he said, 'Just one night, will you come back and do one night, they fucking love you man.' "

When Ian returned to Britain, the demand for Blockheads shows was growing and they went straight back on the road. On the front page of *Melody Maker*, under the headline 'Ian Dury's May Days', Ian was pictured sitting against a railing outside Oval Mansions wearing a flat cap, black jacket, turned up denims and his obligatory Dr Marten's boots. A side column reeled off the venues he would visit on a 26-date tour of Britain, accompanied by rockabilly band Whirlwind and the legendary Jamaican trombonist, Rico.

Ian's tour kicked off at the Birmingham Odeon on May 11, 1978, and included various halls, civic buildings and Odeons. At the Hammersmith Odeon – a venue that Ian had always dreamed of playing – the audience were told to prepare for "one of the jewels in England's crown" but they were less than hospitable when veteran music hall star Max Wall appeared. Ian came on to quieten the crowd and ended up leading Wall off. "They only want the walk," he is reported to have said resignedly to Ian as they retreated to the wings.

Before the tour started, Stiff released his third single 'What A Waste', a song which he had written with Rod Melvin in the dying days of the Kilburns. 'Wake Up And Make Love With Me', the opening song on *New Boots And Panties* served as the B-side on the record, which was the first to be issued by Ian Dury & The Blockheads (Buy 27). As Ian Dury mania gathered pace in response to his electric live shows, 'What A Waste' was playing on transistor radios everywhere and became Ian's first British hit. On April 29 it entered the Top 75 and as the tour progressed it began to climb. By June it was number nine. His first hit, it would spend 12 weeks in the charts. Belated as it was, Ian Dury's phenomenal songwriting ability was no longer a secret, and with *New Boots And Panties* continuing to perform in the album chart, he was now enjoying the commercial recognition which Elvis Costello, Nick Lowe and other 'new wave' luminaries had already found. And while Ian was now "a writer with a growing reputation", The Blockheads were widely recognised as one of the tightest and most talented bands of the day.

Jona Lewie, who was also signed to Stiff at the time, was in the audience for one of their earliest headlining shows. "There was a certain curiosity value because of his polio and on stage he did look larger than life and very attractive and interesting, because of his unusualness," he says. "Ian held himself with such authority and such a proud demeanour that he turned his disablement into a strength. I remember thinking to myself, wow this is great – this figure who moved in a strange way and people coming in off the street as they might do to see an act which is causing a lot of excitement and who might not necessarily know that he had polio and it just made his whole act even more remarkable."

Ian's ascent into the Top 40 inspired a cynical move by WEA whose cloth-eared A&R department had hitherto deemed Ian Dury's music of insufficient commercial potential. Now that he was no longer an anonymous pub rocker and had a successful album and single in his own right, WEA dug deep into its vaults and dusted down the Kilburn & The High Roads tracks recorded for its ill-fated Raft label. An album entitled *Wotabunch* was released as 'Kilburn & The High Roads featuring Ian Dury' – an obvious ploy to increase its commercial appeal. The musicians who had played on the songs were not mentioned at all. The cover featured cardboard cut-outs of Ian and assorted Kilburns surrounded by stuffed animals. In another blatant attempt to cash in on Ian's new found success, WEA also issued 'Billy Bentley' as a single with 'Pam's Moods' on the reverse side. According to a story which appeared in *NME* at the time, Ian had heard about the planned release of this album and approached Warner, suggesting that the tracks be re-cut using The Blockheads. But Warner was said to have refused as it expected to sell no more than 25,000 copies and re-recording the songs would be too costly.

More old Kilburns' material was also unearthed. A five-track EP, *The Best Of Kilburn & The High Roads Featuring Ian Dury*, came out on Bonaparte Records containing 'Father', 'Thank You Mum', 'Upminster Kid', 'Rough Kids' and 'Mumble Rumble And The Cocktail Rock'. The cover was the same painting of the band by Betty which had adorned *Handsome*, while the back of the sleeve contained a number of scribbled messages. "Bonaparte bring you hits others like to bury" it bragged, adding "PS: 'Buy some *New Boots And Panties* today'." *Handsome* had also been re-released on the Pye label (as opposed to Dawn) with a sticker saying 'Featuring Ian Dury', and a 10-inch record entitled *Upminster Kids* was released which featured a photo of Ian, Davey, Keith, Charlie and David outside a pub.

Soon after 'What A Waste' became Stiff's biggest hit to date, the label issued a record with a strong Ian Dury influence and which continued its tradition of promoting musical oddities. 'Whoops-a-Daisy' by Humphrey Ocean & The Hardy Annuals was a song written by Humphrey, Ian, Chaz and Russell and was recorded and produced at The Workhouse. To add to the Kilburn & The High Roads nostalgia, the B-side was 'Davy Crockett', the song Ed Speight had first taught Ian to play at secondary school. Five hundred singles each in red, blue, green, clear and white vinyl were pressed by Stiff. At the time of its release, the small Kilburns reunion even went on the road with The Blockheads, playing support during a 12-date tour of Odeons, beginning in Edinburgh and winding up in Ilford, Essex.

Denise Roudette recalls: "I sang for the first time on that tour with The Hardy Annuals. It was Russell on piano, Humphrey on bass, and me. I sang a couple of songs with Ian, but it was difficult for us because we weren't actually together and just after that he gave me the Oval flat and moved out."

Fame brought sweeping changes to Ian's lifestyle. He swapped his £3 a week tower block flat for expensive hotel suites in the centre of London. He took up residence at the plush Montcalm Hotel in Great Cumberland Place near Marble Arch and stayed for about six months. At this grand address he held court, despatching his aides to bring back whatever substances he required to maintain his gruelling lifestyle. Spending money like water, he then adjourned to the Kentish countryside to a stereotypical rock'n'roll star's paradise, complete with swimming pool and landscaped gardens. Ian was undeterred by the extortionate rent commanded by the property in the quiet village of Rolvendon, near Tenterdon, and insisted on relocating there. He also issued an open invitation for members of The Blockheads to stay there and his young son Baxter also visited.

"We were the managers and here was the goose who was laying the golden egg and the only way to cope with it was to give him anything he wanted," says Andrew King. "All right, he wanted to go and stay in some absurdly luxurious house. It was like the rectory at Wingrave, but this was the Claridge's Hotel version. It was an incredibly flash place with a swimming pool and a gardener and all that sort of thing. He did untold damage to the place and there were enormous bills – it was a vast waste of money."

Mickey Gallagher says of this time: "We were from the hippie generation, whereas Ian was from an institutionalised background. He had been to college and had been a teacher himself. It was totally different, it was all regimented, what I call a Protestant work ethic, whereas we were Catholic and more cavalier. We all went down to Rolvendon and Ian had this way he wanted to work. He would have all these lyrics that he had come up with and he would give us all a lyric and put us all in separate rooms. It wasn't comfortable really, but it was very early in our relationship."

Johnny: "Ian and Chaz were writing and everybody else would go down to rehearse and sometimes Ian would give you a lyric to work with. We had a couple of tunes which I had started in Loving Awareness, which we hadn't finished any lyrics for, which were 'Quiet' and 'Mischief'. There were various other tunes that we ended up doing which were riffs from Loving Awareness instrumentals. When we play 'Clevor Trever' live, the end is the end of one of my songs from Loving Awareness which was never published. We all had these little rooms with our practice amps, guitars and keyboards and it must have sounded like a right cacophony walking down that hallway and hearing all the different things that were going on."

The atmosphere at the rural retreat was far from relaxed. Despite the communal setting and Ian's requested input from all band members, it was clear that Ian and Chaz were in control of the songwriting process and their more exacting attitude to songwriting and rehearsing was markedly different from that of the others. As the weeks went by in Ian's unlikely songwriting laboratory, a batch of new songs emerged which owed more to Chaz's Afro-American funk influences than those on *New Boots And Panties*. These new dance-driven tracks seemed to form a natural collection and were noticeably less aggressive than their predecessors. But one song in particular stood out.

Chaz: "In the living room, Ian had set up a drum kit, a little Roland drum machine and a keyboard and a few of the lads would come down and play. One particular day, I went down there, Ian and I just jammed. Ian was playing the drums and the drum machine was going and I was playing the keyboard. We had this Latin/funky vibe going, because that is the way we naturally tend to play when we get together, and I started playing this riff. I remember that when I went home that was the part of the whole jam that appealed to me. Then I was listening to the end of 'Wake Up' and I thought, 'Why is it I really like the piano solo on the end of it?' The reason was that there was a blip just before it and I thought, 'Hang on a moment, why don't I take that blip and put that before this new rhythm pattern I had got going.' And it was that little note which was so quiet that you would really have to listen out to hear, which actually gave me the idea. I went back to Ian and said, 'Listen, you know that jam we had the other day, I've got a great idea for it.' Ian said, 'Great, hang on a moment.' By this time he had moved the drum kit and piano into the garage outside and so he went out into the house and came back into the garage and said, ' 'Ere you are,' and gives me a typewritten sheet with the words for 'Hit Me With Your Rhythm Stick'. He said, 'I'll see you in a little while,' and went back into the house and literally within half an hour, I wrote the intro and incorporated his verses and choruses into it. I went back into the house and said, 'I've got it,' and then he came in and played drums and he loved it. The next day, we got the band down, they rehearsed it and loved it. Three days later we were in the studio recording it. When we finished recording it I phoned up my mum from The Workhouse and said, 'Mum, I've just recorded my first number one.' I knew it – I just knew it in my blood."

The lyrics which Ian casually handed Chaz that afternoon in the autumn of 1978 were unforgettable. 'Hit Me With Your Rhythm Stick' seemed to brilliantly encapsulate all the aspects of his Empire State-sized personality and its stream of rhyming couplets typified his distinctive style. "In the deserts of Sudan, and the gardens of Japan/From Milan to Yucatan, every woman, every man," he sang, as he set out on a geographical journey which inspired such irresistible twinnings as Borneo and Bordeaux, Eskimo and Arapahoe, and Tiger Bay and Mandalay. But it was the song's suggestive title and chorus which would capture the public imagination and ensure the song a lasting place in the national consciousness. "Hit me with your rhythm stick, two fat persons click click click, hit me, hit me," he implored.

What made the rhythm particularly memorable was Norman's quick-fingered bass line, Chaz's catchy piano riff, and Charley's solid drumming. Unlike other songs of the era, 'Hit Me With Your Rhythm Stick' didn't have a soaring guitar solo, but rather a saxophone break which was in keeping with the personality of its player. Davey Payne, with just Charley accompanying him, achieved his now famous saxophone burst by playing two saxophones simultaneously. This quirk undoubtedly added to the record's party feel.

Davey says of his memorable solo: "I was quite influenced by Roland Kirk who played two or three saxophones at once, but I hadn't played that sort of stuff for years and so it was all out of tune. But it kind of worked. Ian said, 'Can you do your two saxophones at once thing?' and I said, 'I'll just put them in my mouth and blow and see what happens', so it was very spontaneous and quick and that is what came out. I could have said, 'I want to spend more time on it', because you get keyboard players sitting there for hours and hours doing overdubs and working out a sound on the synth, but instead I just left it and that is how it came out. When we did *Top Of The Pops*, it was Christmas time and after I did the solo I was spraying everybody with a can of fake snow."

Norman had also given a great deal of thought to the accompanying bass line, which bubbled away constantly underneath the vocals and gave the song the kind of beat usually associated with black funk groups or the kind of jazz players whom Ian had adored in his youth. Like Davey, his playing on the record was inspired by one of his own heroes.

"If I was totally honest, where it all came from is Jaco Pastorius because at the time he was one of the world's greatest bass players, a very jazz influenced player, and he doubled up a lot of his stuff. I went and saw him at the Hammersmith Odeon and he was absolutely fantastic and then I went down to Rolvendon and Chaz and Ian were playing this song they had. Chaz was playing the chords and Ian was singing 'In the deserts of Sudan' and because I was still buzzing from this gig I had seen, I wanted to play like that and I started doubling up everything. So with the little melody that I had, I thought I'll make it 16ths and funk it up a bit and that's what I did. It is a great bass line, but things like that come from being inspired by something or someone. With loads of my playing, I'm just trying to play like jazz players like Charlie Mingus, a phenomenal double bass player, and Charlie Parker. I love his sax playing and I try to transpose what he played on a saxophone on to my bass. It's great exercise, it opens your mind up totally to what you can do on the bass."

Ian said of the lyrics to 'Hit Me':[8] "I had that lyric for about three years before I suddenly realised it was a single. It has a natural rhythm that marches along. Plus it had some German phrases, so I thought it would get the Common Market vote. I'd written it before I even met Chaz. It was about rhythm and dancing and it was also saying, 'Dance, don't hit me.' Chaz accuses me of nicking it off a George Clinton record, but I disagree. The 'hit me' phrase is really James Brown, but who cares?"

According to Johhny Turnbull, the origins of 'Hit Me' were in the band's American tour. "I remember walking around in America singing various things. We had this habit where Ian would start a chant and one chant he started was 'Hit Me With Your Rhythm Stick' and everybody else joined in, singing a different thing. When we would get up to leave breakfast and walk through the swing doors of the hotel to get to the van, Ian would be banging his stick saying, 'Hit me, hit me, hit me with your rhythm stick,' and Charley, who was behind him, started going, 'I want a beef burger, I want a beef burger.' Then someone else went, 'Chips and beans and a beef burger, chips and beans, hit me, hit me.' There was this whole trail of people chanting, 'Hit me with your rhythm stick,' before it ever had any verses."

'Hit Me With Your Rhythm Stick' was released on November 23, 1978, (Buy 38) coupled with the deliciously comic 'There Ain't Half Been Some Clever Bastards', co-written with Russell Hardy. In this, he doffed his cap to Noel Coward, Einstein, Vincent Van Gogh and other legends, concluding that they "probably got help from their mum". It was an instant radio hit. Boney M's Christmas release 'Mary's Boy Child' was at number one when 'Hit Me' entered the UK Top 75 on December 9 and began its glorious ascent. Ian Dury fever was spreading around Britain and at a gig at the Ilford Odeon in east London on December 23, such was the exuberance of the audience that the floor caved in. A sagging carpet was the only thing which saved the pogo-ing fans from falling into the basement. By the new year, the record had its sights firmly on the top spot which was now occupied by Village People's gay disco anthem 'YMCA'. On January 27, 1979, Ian Dury & The Blockheads celebrated their first number one.

Fred Rowe recalls the moment when Ian heard the news: "We were on the beach in Cannes when 'Hit Me' went to number one. The hotel staff brought us a bottle of champagne on a tray and said to Ian, 'Your record "Hit Me" has gone to number one.' I remember when we first kicked off with Kilburn & The High Roads, Ian said, 'I can't sing,' and I said, 'Yeah but great lyrics Ian, I could listen to them all day.' He said, 'It might be a number one,'and I said, 'I tell you what Ian. If you ever get a number one with this sort of work, I'll eat a piece of shit.' So that day on the beach, Ian said to me, ''Ere, I'm going to find you a bit of shit around here to eat.'"

Denise collected them when they returned to England to sample the record's success first hand: "I remember I had to go and meet them off the ferry after they had done some gigs and TV shows in Europe," she says. "Fred had driven them from Paris in about an hour and a half to catch the ferry and their knees were like jelly and they were ashen faced. I thought, 'My goodness, what drugs have you been doing?', but in fact Fred had been driving on the wrong side of the road, clocking 130mph to make it. As they stepped off the ferry I said, 'Yep, you're number one.' "

On *Top Of The Pops*, it was Dave Lee Travis – Radio 1's 'Hairy Cornflake' – who announced the news. "Right now, it's number one time and, yes, he's made it. Ian Dury and the Blockheads," he gushed, before the whole group came into view, dressed in tuxedos, frilled white shirts and black bow ties. Ian, with a ring in each ear, pointed sideburns, tinted hair, and a white scarf over a tuxedo, clutched the microphone with a silver gloved hand and waved a wooden stick with the other. It was their moment and they enjoyed one week of glory before Blondie broke up the party with their disco classic 'Heart Of Glass'. 'Hit Me' sold one million copies before disappearing from the charts, 15 weeks after it had arrived. As it reached the one million mark, Stiff deleted it and then re-issued it, reportedly selling another 100,000 in the process.

Charlie Gillett said of the song's wider importance:[14] "That was the record that made Ian a national institution all in one go. Up until then he had been a quirky eccentric and the danger with the kind of approach that Ian has is that you become dismissed as a novelty artist, you are just thrown away again, like Benny Hill or something. 'Hit Me With Your Rhythm Stick' was so great musically. The famous British jazz funk thing is supposed to have started in 1981 or 1982, but it didn't, it started with 'Hit Me With Your Rhythm Stick'. That was the first British jazz funk record, this really brilliant record."

Johnny remembers: "We had a feeling it was great and that was corroborated when we were sat outside the Kilburn State Theatre waiting to go in to do the sound-check. We pulled up and Capitol Radio was on and it was number one and we all sat in the car going, 'We're number one, we've made it.' My local pub then was The George Robey in Camden and it was always on the jukebox and people would come up and pat me on the back and say, 'Well done, you're number one.' It sounded fantastic on the jukebox. Now, when I think about it, I don't know how people danced to it, because I can't dance to 'Hit Me'. You can move your leg, but you can't actually dance to it like you can to a Funkadelic song, or James Brown or Prince or other funky tracks."

Pop videos were beginning to play an important role in the promotion of singles by 1979 and for 'Hit Me', Ian's old friend from Walthamstow art college Laurie Lewis was called in. Laurie had studied film at the Royal College of Art and had made a name as a photographer and he directed the video at Shepperton Studios, west London. Unlike many of the pretentious videos of the Eighties – all costumes, theatrical sets and computerised effects – this was a low-budget affair in which The Blockheads were filmed performing on stage. But image was crucial and it was during the shoot that Ian, now in the full glare of the public, took a courageous decision.

Laurie: "Ian came up to me at some point early in the day and said, 'Laur', I wanna do it without the jacket.' Ian used to wear this pink jacket which hid the fact that he had a skinny arm. Up to that point, every gig he had ever done was all about hiding his disability and he decided for whatever reason of his own, at that point, he was going to come out about his disability. So he sung it without the jacket, which meant you saw his skinny arm, and that was his decision. Well, somebody must have ratted on us, because suddenly a limo comes screeching up outside the studios and all the Stiff people and other bigwigs came flying in saying, 'What the hell's going on? We've heard that Ian's doing it without the jacket,' and I said, 'Well, it's his decision.' There was a real row about that, but we went ahead with it anyway and in that film he's still playing with the scarves. He had this wonderful routine where he takes silk scarves, he throws them up in the air and they take a second or two to fall down and during that time he does all kinds of numbers and turns around and catches them. It's magician's sleight of hand stuff which, for a person who doesn't have good balance or mobility, was nothing short of breathtaking and mesmerising to watch. He looked fantastic – really dangerous."

Ian's new found fame had effectively signalled the end of his partnership with Denise. She had been "coming and going" from his rented quarters in Kent in the weeks and months preceding his rise to number one and the increasing demands of the media were putting a further strain on a liaison which had always been tempestuous. Six years after they had first met, it was all over.

"*New Boots And Panties* was released and that started selling and his following started from there," says Denise. "It was a huge turning point and Ian started doing a lot more interviews and having to be around the press. We split up shortly after that. Ian was getting a lot more attention, there were a lot more girls and men find that wonderful. I had been very supportive for a long time and there comes a point when you have got to get your own life. It wasn't that sort of relationship where you know you will be together for always and walk off into the sunset. It wasn't always amicable between Ian and me, because we were strong characters and he is not the easiest person to live with and get on with. He has got a big life and he is a challenge.

"I did get very hurt and I decided that as things were happening for him, I was very sure that I didn't want to be dragged into any media thing and it was important for me to break away and re-establish. That meant I didn't see most of the people I knew in London, because most of the people I knew, he knew. But at the same time I was adamant that we would be friends. It is very easy in those situations to walk away and obviously it is harder for guys to keep ladies as friends after they split, but I knew that it was important. That six years was quite intense. Ian had a lot of respect for me and the one thing he did say to me was, 'Look Denise, you've got to do it on your own,' and I don't think I understood that at the time, but I did eventually."

Ian's day-to-day life had been turned inside out. His anonymity had been snatched suddenly from him and his distinctive disability made him doubly recognisable around London. He enjoyed the attention from women in bars and restaurants and at parties, which his new found fame bestowed on him, and he continued to oblige demanding journalists queuing up to interview him. *New Boots And Panties* had by now gone platinum (half a million copies in the UK) and was still in the album charts; 'Hit Me' had enjoyed phenomenal success, selling 900,000 copies during the Christmas period alone; and in the eyes of the press, he could do no wrong. The album had even had some success in the US where some distribution was provided by Arista and it reached number 168 on the *Billboard* chart. The Blockheads were widely regarded as the hottest live band in the country and tickets for their gigs were like gold dust. Everybody wanted a piece of Ian Dury.

Among them was composer Andrew Lloyd Webber who approached Ian to write the lyrics for his latest musical *Cats*. Not wishing to compromise his integrity and never bothered about material wealth, Ian turned him down, telling people simply, "I can't stand his music." Richard Stilgoe subsequently wrote the libretto based on T. S. Eliot's *Old Possum's Book Of Practical Cats* and reportedly earned millions as a result.

The national recognition of his abilities which he had so craved, made him distinctly uncomfortable. All his life, Ian had loved being the centre of attention. At parties, he was happy while the guests were hanging on his every word and those who ignored him did so at their peril. Ian sometimes claimed that he liked the intimidating figures of Fred 'Spider' Rowe and Peter Rush – 'The Strangler' – around him as they siphoned attention away from him, but the likelihood was that they merely drew more attention to the contorted figure hobbling alongside. At the beginning of 1979, Ian's fame was total and he was beginning to feel claustrophobic. Everything was going into overdrive, including his drinking and partying, and he was becoming ominously stressed. Rather than boosting him up, it had the reverse effect; he couldn't sleep and started taking Mogadon tablets. He became addicted and for the first time in his life felt out of control.

"We were gigging night after night and I had a kind of manic energy.

But your reserves of energy do get depleted, especially when you have to act out some of the songs. Then it all gets a bit freaky," said Ian.[8] "From being a 36-year-old struggling, angry, but quite happy and well balanced lunatic, to being a successful lunatic, meant that the safety net had gone. The safety net is the struggle, it's a kind of reassurance. Those emotions like hatred, jealousy and despair are tangible."

Denise says of Ian's adverse reaction to fame: "I believe he lost himself for a while, but that's only my perception of it. I think his feet left the ground a bit as they do when you are whisked off on that whole star trip and in a sense it is undermining. Okay, you get lots of acclaim and attention, but your creative energy is cut off at the base. My own view is that after people make it, a malaise sets in."

In interviews Ian gave over the years, he consistently denied seeking out such status and downplayed the importance of celebrity. But some of those who knew him best reject these claims. In his teenage years he was part of the Upminster gang, but never the leader. From this he went on to be an attention seeker at Walthamstow who strove to be the star in every situation – from wild house parties to a tea-break in the canteen. When he finally got to head up his very own 'gang' in Kilburn & The High Roads, he lapped up the publicity it brought, especially the attention lavished on him by women. And when punk exploded in 1976 and brought instant fame to young groups and singers, Ian watched enviously from the wings, resenting the injustice that he wasn't one of them.

He was nasty and derogatory about other artists and bands and was possessive of those who were close to him, including his band and management. Steve Nugent recalls that "when Blackhill had The Blockheads and they tried to do anything else, Ian regarded that as a serious subversion of their focal interest. There was some poor fella, a singer songwriter, who would come into Blackhill's office, and Ian would just lay into him. The guy was just coming in to talk to his management, but Ian was very unpleasant to all the other people who were managed by Blackhill Enterprises."

Fame, when it did come, simply didn't agree with Ian Dury. According to members of the group, his personality changed for the worse and he became more and more arrogant. Andrew King described the transformation as "a very bad attack of number one-itis".

"Ian is one of those people who was a full square," said Andrew. "He will dominate any situation you put him in, which is why you never wanted to invite Ian to someone else's party. It would become his party and if it didn't become his party, he would ruin it for everyone else. We all had some tremendous run-ins with Ian. He is fine when it is his gig and it is his territory, but if it is someone else's gig and someone else's territory he is not quite sure if he likes that. He likes to establish his territory. If he had been a dog he would have been lifting his leg absolutely everywhere."

Ian admitted that he found the trappings of fame disturbing and invasive and spoke openly about the discomfort he felt at this time. In this regard, his disability only exacerbated his feelings of vulnerability and lost privacy.

"If you walk down the street and you've got a disabled leg, people look at you, they can't help it," he said in a Radio 2 documentary broadcast in May 1999.[14] "I would be down the street, before I was a well-known person and I would be noisy, shouting at my mates, giving it whistling, singing, the lot, enjoying myself. Then, I got well known and I got looked at and then I got recognised immediately and that really upset me. It made me feel disabled because I only got recognised because of the way I walked, I didn't get recognised because of my face or anything like that. Paul McCartney said once that if he gets recognised in Soho, he walks brusquely away. But if I walk brusquely away I fall over. I felt trapped, I really did."

9

DO IT YOURSELF

"I always felt that 'Inbetweenies' should have been a single and that would have turned Do It Yourself *into a real hit. But it was on the album and therefore it couldn't be a single. Once Ian had said it, it was a point of pride, and I have nothing against pride, but it was being proud of being completely bonkers as far as I was concerned."*
– Andrew King

The importance of Ian Dury to Stiff Records cannot be overstated. 'Hit Me With Your Rhythm Stick' was only its third Top 40 entry out of 38 singles and its first number one hit. Not only that, it had sold more than one million copies in the UK, while *New Boots* had gone platinum and remained in the UK album charts for a staggering 90 weeks, peaking at number five. With Elvis Costello and Nick Lowe gone, the 30-something pub rocker whom Stiff had brought in from the cold was now its beacon of hope. Those who had forecast gloom when Dave and Jake had parted company had been proved wrong as Stiff celebrated one of the then 100 best-selling singles of all time. And there was more good news to come as a clutch of new artists were about to find their niche as the New Wave.

Stiff was at the vanguard of this movement and included in its publicity slogans 'Surfing On The New Wave'. Artists like Ian Dury, Elvis Costello and Nick Lowe had loads of front and a powerful battery of songs, but they didn't fit the punk stereotype. Soon these and other artists on independent labels like Chiswick were being herded together under a new banner, along with singers and bands like Joe Jackson, Squeeze, The Pretenders and The Boomtown Rats. The overblown guitar solos and pretentious antics of Progressive Rock groups like Pink Floyd, Genesis, Yes and Emerson, Lake & Palmer, which had been in vogue in the early to mid-Seventies had proved too much. The British music scene was being shaken up whether it liked it or not. Stiff, having played a major role in pop music's very own gunpowder plot, was determined to champion yet more unsung heroes.

In October 1978, in a sequel to the previous year's Stiff Live Stiffs Tour, five singers boarded a train and set off on a meandering journey around

Britain, taking in colleges, town halls and other venues near rail stations. Wreckless Eric was the only survivor from the original coach party; the 'Be Stiff' tour introduced audiences to four other artists; Lene Lovich, Jona Lewie, Mickey Jupp and Rachel Sweet. Each was as different from the other as could be imagined, but all bore the Stiff hallmark of originality.

Lene Lovich, a deeply intriguing figure with long plaited pig-tails, had first surfaced in the mid-Seventies, singing and playing sax in a group called The Diversions, along with her partner Les Chappell. They had a minor hit in 1975 with the novelty reggae song 'Fattie Bum Bum' but were destined to be a one hit wonder and they disbanded shortly afterwards. Lene's first solo venture was a Shirley Temple-style version of the cheesy Christmas song 'I Saw Mommy Kissing Santa Claus', released by Polydor in December 1976. It took Oval (run by former Kilburns' managers Charlie Gillett and Gordon Nelki), however, to spot her real potential and direct her towards Alexander Street.

Stiff pressed only 5,000 copies of her début single, a haunting cover of the Tommy James Sixties hit 'I Think We're Alone Now', with an original composition on the B-side, 'Lucky Number'. This weird and wonderful song was also featured on her first album *Stateless*, the release of which was timed to coincide with the beginning of the train tour. When Stiff decided to issue the song as a single in its own right the following spring, they hit pay dirt. She fascinated *Top Of The Pops* viewers with her outlandish make-up, head bands, scarves and eerie voice, and 'Lucky Number' soared to number three, becoming the label's second biggest hit. In May 1979, she followed up her success with a second hit 'Say When', which reached number 19.

Jona Lewie, in direct contrast, looked like a department store floor-walker. Although he had only just emerged on Stiff, he was a seasoned performer, having served his time in blues bands in the late Sixties, and had scored a number two hit in 1972 with 'Seaside Shuffle', glorying under the name of Terry Dactyl & The Dinosaurs. He re-emerged with The Jive Bombers in 1976 and the following year he was picked up by Stiff. His début album, *On The Other Hand There's A Fist*, came out in time for the tour. The accompanying single 'The Baby She's On The Street' flopped, but Jona would more than repay Stiff in 1980. 'You'll Always Find Me In The Kitchen At Parties' made number 16 and his Salvation Army tinged anti-war song 'Stop The Cavalry' went to number three that Christmas, a seasonal classic which continues to earn him a healthy income.

On the back of the tour, teenage American prodigy Rachel Sweet would bask fleetingly in the glow of the Top 40 with her upbeat single 'B-A-B-Y'. In one of its more outrageous stunts, Stiff marketed the youngster as a "jailbait" country singer. The Akron-born star's career had begun at the age of six and encompassed everything from commercial jingles to touring with Mickey Rooney and opening for Bill Cosby's Las Vegas act. She had done a few failed country tunes for her local Derrick label before coming to the attention of Stiff through songwriter Liam Sternberg, who had passed the label some of her demos. Backing for her début album *Fool Around* was provided by Stiff stable-mates The Rumour. But 'B-A-B-Y' was her first and last hit, peaking at number 35 in the UK.

Wreckless Eric's self-titled début album had been released about six months before the tour and had strong associations with Ian Dury. It included a clattering rendition of 'Rough Kids', Kilburn & The High Roads' first single, and Davey Payne and Charlie Hart were among the musicians who played on the record. Amid the excitement that had followed the first Stiff tour, Dave Robinson is believed to have thought about sending Wreckless and Davey out as a double-act in the vein of John Otway and Wild Willy Barrett, although this alliance was never forged. As Wreckless boarded the train for the second Stiff outing, his cover of Buddy Holly's 'Crying, Waiting, Hoping' was about to be released, but it slipped away virtually unnoticed. His follow-up album *The Wonderful World Of Wreckless Eric* failed to make an impact. Seasoned rocker and songwriter Mickey Jupp also benefited little from the tour and because of his fear of flying had left the cast by the time it went on to the US.

Ian was now too established to join this outing, but he nevertheless remained central to Dave Robinson's game plan. He was contracted to record another two albums for Stiff and all concerned were determined to sustain the powerful momentum that had been built up by *New Boots* and 'Hit Me'. In the spring of 1979, Ian Dury & The Blockheads began recording some of the songs which had evolved during the sessions at Rolvendon and which sounded so different from the material on *New Boots And Panties* and his four singles. The result was *Do It Yourself* – a strictly Ian and Chaz affair, both in terms of compositions and musical style. Few Blockheads' fans could have predicted the more laid-back, jazzy feel of the album's ten tracks, a sound more akin to Steely Dan's massively successful *Aja*, one of Ian's favourite albums. What had made *New Boots* so distinctive – the tapestry of colourful characters, the unbridled swearing and the sheer ferocity of 'Blockheads' and 'Blackmail Man' – were noticeably absent here. Ian's vocals were more restrained, clean-sounding keyboards and saxophone dominated and although the funky rhythms which had driven 'Wake Up And Make Love With Me' and 'Hit Me' were present, the overall sound of *Do It Yourself* was more clinical and polished. Ian's use of the vernacular and Cockney slang was used to great effect on a number of songs, however, and he was as sexually suggestive as ever. "Shake your booty, when your back is bent/Put your feelings where my mouth just went", he sang on 'Inbetweenies'.

Success, meanwhile, had done nothing for Ian's temperament and members of The Blockheads found him cantankerous and difficult in the studio. Recollections of the making of *Do It Yourself* at The Workhouse – the studios where *New Boots* had been recorded – reveal a growing impatience with Ian's moods and desire to control the entire recording process.

Chaz: "We had got to make a second album and because of the intensity in the group and the intensity of touring, we pieced together what we had left, the songs which hadn't been used for *New Boots*. I also came up with a few relatively new ideas and so we put together *Do It Yourself*. But it was very different because when we were doing it, Ian was being very oppressive. He would just come into the control room and go into his Laurence Olivier monologue and would just want to hold the fort. Once Ian has grabbed the attention, he doesn't want to lose it.

"At one point I called him up on the phone and said, 'Look Ian, I think it would be a good idea if you stayed away from the session.' There was the longest gap ever and then he said, 'I don't fucking believe it, I have just been asked to stay away from my own session.' He put the phone down on me and I carried on and more or less finished the album without him, although he came back in to finish his vocals. He had been using up so much time and it was frustrating. In his eyes, it was not a very good album and he wished he had stopped after *New Boots And Panties*, although I don't think that was necessarily the case."

Behind the sound desk at The Workhouse was Londoner Ian Horne, who had first worked as a sound engineer for Ian during the closing days of the Kilburns in 1976 after having previously been employed by Paul McCartney's Wings. He had an enormous respect for Ian and continued to work with the band right up to Ian's death, but he too found Ian a hard taskmaster.

"When Ian got behind the sound desk he turned into a different character," he says. "In the studios, when I engineered him, he used to insist I looked at him and say, 'I'm the road and you're the driver.' Sometimes I'd have to look at him for eight hours and if I looked away he'd have a go at me. So I had to suffer with his suffering. He didn't want 100 per cent from someone he wanted 110."

Do It Yourself was released on May 18, 1979, and Stiff spared no expense in the publicity drive for its biggest star. It issued the album sleeve in 12 different Crown wallpaper designs, ranging from garish green and brown stripes to purple and pink floral patterns. Newspapers, magazines and shops were deluged with promotional badges, paint brushes, wallpaper ties and wallpaper, and in a publicity tie-in with *Do It Yourself* magazine, Stiff despatched representatives to home improvement stores to organise window displays. Paper-hangers also converged unannounced on the offices of the music weeklies and decorated their foyers.

The eye-catching sleeve design of this and many other Stiff products was down to the creative genius of Barney Bubbles (real name Colin Fulcher), Stiff's long-haired, in-house artist and former lighting engineer with heavy rock band Hawkwind. Barney was also the brains behind the Blockhead logo, which first appeared on the record label of 'What A Waste' and has appeared on Blockheads merchandise ever since. Tragically, he would later take his own life.

"The whole artistic vibe of the place was from this mad designer in the basement," explained Ian.[11] "I phoned him up once and said, 'I want a Blockheads logo and it's got to be black and white and square' and somebody in his office went, 'Wow' and he'd said, 'I've done it.' He did it while I was talking to him. He just made this little face with Blockheads and we still use that. We had these watches and when it was three o'clock it said Blockhead. It was all part and parcel of his incredible off-the-wall fun.

"Barney had designed the man in the Norman helmet used on the Bulmers Cider bottle and he got £15 for that and Jake phoned up Bulmers and said, 'We want a tanker of cider round here as back-payment, royalties for our designer who designed your little man with the helmet,' but they never sent one. It was worth a try though."

Alan Cowderoy recalls: "Barney Bubbles was a hugely innovative artist, very talented. He worked in a little room underneath the loo and either Dave or Jake was in there one morning having a wee and they missed and it was all coming through the floorboards and going all across his artwork. Barney came out screaming at them to stop."

On the back of the *Do It Yourself* sleeve, the band stood in a queue in a photograph reminiscent of the Kilburns' publicity poster. Each wearing sailors hats, they posed outside the window of a wig shop displaying photographs of their customers with their hair-pieces. Ian's balding handler Fred Rowe stood alone on the other side of the shop, grinning at the camera. "Any resemblance to characters living or dead is not meant to be unkind to men in syrups. Plus love to TRB [Tom Robinson Band], TAJ [Taj Mahal], Clash and everyone else," read an attached label. Unfortunately, the owner of the shop hadn't been approached about the picture and didn't see the funny side. He is understood to have sued Stiff for £15,000.

The ten tracks, all previously unreleased, were: 'Inbetweenies', 'Quiet', 'Don't Ask Me', 'Sink My Boats', 'Waiting For Your Taxi', 'This Is What

We Find', 'Uneasy Sunny Day Hotsy Totsy', 'Mischief', 'Dance Of The Screamers' and 'Lullaby For Francis'. As with *New Boots And Panties*, Ian was determined not to include singles on the record and 'Hit Me' was omitted. He wanted his albums to offer his fans new songs, but however laudable this may have been his stubborn philosophy would hit the band financially in the months after its release. But hits or no hits, Ian's second album was highly awaited and advance orders ensured its immediate entry into the charts.

The opening bars of 'Inbetweenies', the ultra smooth opening track, set the tone for the album's overall sound and feel. In it, delicate piano and jazzy saxophone breaks were laid over a steady and deep-funk rhythm, and combined with some of Ian's most curious lyrics, 'Inbetweenies' had all the sophistication and light touch of vintage Steely Dan. 'Inbetweenies' was without doubt one of the album's strongest songs and, although it eventually disappeared from the group's set list, it remained a favourite with Ian and band members. "In the mirror, when I'm debonair/My reactions are my own affair/A body likes to be near the bone/Oh Nancy, Lesley, Jack and Joan/I die when I'm alone," he sang in the first verse. Commenting on the idiosyncratic words, Ian said:[8] "What's it about? I haven't a fucking clue. I think it's about friendship."

The following songs, 'Quiet' and 'Don't Ask Me', also bore testament to the jazz influences of its two composers and benefited from Chaz's imaginative arrangements and frequent contributions from Davey. 'Sink My Boats' was one of the first songs that Chaz and Ian had ever written together and was built on a more orthodox rock rhythm. It was also one of the most melodic songs on *Do It Yourself*. 'Waiting For Your Taxi' was a very different affair and contained just one Dury 'verbal' – "Waiting for your taxi/Which taxi never comes". Ian and Chaz had dreamt up the song at 11.30pm on December 31, 1978, in Barbados and put the finishing touches to it at 1am on January 1, 1979, according to Ian.[8]

In 'This Is What We Find', Ian introduced a string of unforgettable characters and told their suburban tales like a gossip talking over a garden fence. It was vintage Dury and one of the album's standout tracks. "Forty-year-old housewife Mrs Elizabeth Wark of Lambeth Walk/ Had a husband who was jubblified with only half a stalk/So she had a Milk of Magnesia and curry powder sandwich, half a pound of uncut pork/ Took an overdose of Omo, this made the neighbours talk," went the first verse. In the second, he introduced "single bachelor with little dog" Tony Green or Turnham Green, followed by a music hall style interlude. Then, he told the funniest story of all: "Home improvement expert Harold Hill of Harold Hill/Of do it yourself dexterity and double glazing skill/Came home to find another gentleman's kippers in the grill/So he sanded off his winkle with his Black & Decker drill."

His cheeky use of London's A-Z failed to amuse the BBC which deemed the song unsuitable for airplay, although the language in the uproarious 'Uneasy Sunny Day Hotsy Totsy' would no doubt have caused even more offence. ("Bank rob the banks, withhold the rent/Shitters are a wank and the landlord's bent/It's time that the babies kept quiet/No it ain't". 'Mischief' relied more heavily on Johnny's lead guitar and Mickey's keyboards than other songs and wound up with Ian yelling, "I'm sorry I done it".

Do It Yourself had its more serious moments, however. 'Dance Of The Screamers' pointed to a darker side, focusing as it did on people with mental illness. "Some of our self-pity, lover, comes from facing up to facts/It's hard to be a hero, handsome, when you've had your helmet cracked", he mused over a highly infectious beat. Tortured screams punctuated the song which, at six minutes 41 seconds, was the longest on the album, due largely to a lengthy instrumental. It was a powerful example of Ian's ability to confront aspects of life which make us feel uncomfortable while keeping his audience on board with Chaz's dance rhythms.

Do It Yourself signed off with 'Lullaby For Francis', a slow reggae track which epitomised the high standard of playing and musical arrangements maintained throughout and served as a fitting finale.

In June 1979, the group set out on a British tour entitled Slam And Segue And Break A Leg, opening at the Colston Hall, Bristol, supported by American oddity Root Boy Slim & The Sex Change Band. When this tour wound up some weeks later at the New Theatre in Oxford, The Blockheads travelled to Europe to play yet more dates. Despite the Englishness of his act, Ian had made an impact in Germany. 'Hit Me' had gone to number 24 in March 1979 and, in turn, it generated interest in *New Boots And Panties*, propelling it to number 29 in the German charts. A series of German dates during this foray into central Europe paid off with steady sales of *Do It Yourself* and a highest chart position of 23 there. Back in England, the news was better still. Within weeks of its release, *Do It Yourself* shot to number two in the album chart, behind Abba's *Voulez-Vous*. It stayed in the chart for 18 weeks and earned Ian his second platinum album. But the 200,000 album sales were neatly cancelled out by the European tour which lost in excess of £40,000. Those involved in the episode cite an extravagant tour budget as the root cause.

Andrew King: "It was weakness on our part, but also, if Ian could find something wrong with the hotel he was in he would and he would make a fuss about it. In order to shut him up, we just went in the five-star deluxe ones all the way, which was a complete waste of money. He wouldn't even have the crew stay somewhere cheaper around the corner. 'No. I look after my crew,' he said. If we had released 'Inbetweenies' as a single and it had all gone on, it would have been all right because we could have used this month's income to pay last month's bills. But there came a point when there was no next month's income to pay it off. That was the beginning of the end. It was a huge tour and they did wonderful gigs, but in retrospect, we were hard at work constructing our own coffin."

Ian's determination to keep singles off albums meant that he could not countenance the release of 'Inbetweenies' once it was on *Do It Yourself*. Andrew blames this school of thought on the group's energetic publicity supremo Kozmo Vinyl, later the manager of The Clash. Andrew believes it was a stance which severely hampered the commercial impact of *Do It Yourself*.

"It wasn't quite as essential in marketing terms then as it is now to have a single on an album because there was a much more genuine singles market then," says Andrew. "There was also a sort of religious reason why it didn't become a single, for which I have always blamed Kozmo – that The Small Faces never had their singles on the album, therefore we shouldn't either. I said to Ian: 'It doesn't reflect on you how people couple your recordings. You make an album and you can see this is an album and that is fine. But there is nothing in principle against making your hit single part of that album and working out a way for that to fit.' I always felt that 'Inbetweenies' should have been a single and that would have turned *Do It Yourself* into a real hit. But it was on the album and therefore it couldn't be a single. Once Ian had said it, it was a point of pride and I have nothing against pride, but it was being proud of being completely bonkers as far as I was concerned. We all knew it was bonkers, but it was going to be done because we had pride and because we thought we could get away with anything. And for a while we did."

Laurie Lewis: "I got a phone call from Dave Robinson and he said, 'Have you heard the album?' and I said, 'No, I haven't,' so he said, 'Right, I'm sending it round.' At the time they were in Camden Town so it came through the door about five minutes later and what he had sent me was a white label. Dave had basically said to me, 'Listen to it and tell me which is the single,' so I played it through and I honestly felt there wasn't anything on it that could be a single. I loved some of the tracks very much and the track I particularly loved on it was 'Inbetweenies'. If I'd had to choose a song to be the single, that would have been it. At the time, Pink Floyd and Led Zeppelin didn't even do singles and from a marketing point of view it was suicide, but they were so big they could transcend all that."

A single was on its way, however, that would more than compensate for the absence of a 45 on the album. 'Reasons To Be Cheerful (Part 3)' was not recorded at The Workhouse during the making of *Do It Yourself*, but was cut in a spontaneous session at RCA studios in Rome during the European tour to promote the album. Like a discofied rendition of 'England's Glory', it demonstrated yet again that when it came to lyric writing Ian Dury was in a class of his own.

Mickey: "We were on a long tour in Europe and we got to a town somewhere in Italy and the further south you go, the more ill-equipped they are to do rock'n'roll. So we got to this lovely venue but the electricity is not earthed and when you've got a singer with a metal leg you can't take chances, apart from the guitars and anything else. So we said, 'We can't work this venue, the electricity isn't up to scratch, there's bare wires sticking out of the walls', so we pulled the gig without too much fuss. The crew there had obviously had this happen before and what happens in Italy in that situation is that the house crew and the PA crew start beating each other up and involving the English and then call the police. So they're all beaten up with cuts and bruises and the police impound the equipment and you are stuck in this country – that's the ploy. So we all got on the coach and we were all going to go off, but they blocked us in with cars in the car park, so we went over the grass verges and out and away and they were all chanting 'Bologna, Bologna' which was where our next gig was. So we thought 'Fuck Bologna' and we went straight to Rome. We had a few free days so we went to Eretcia Studios which belonged to RCA Victor, who we were with in Italy, and recorded 'Reasons To Be Cheerful' and the B-side 'Common As Muck'."

Ian said of the origins of the song's title:[8] "We nearly lost Charlie, one of our lighting roadies, somewhere in Italy. He was leaning over a mixing desk and touched the microphone stand. He got the electricity up his arm and another roadie saw him shuddering, leapt across the stage and kicked him off the gear. If you touch someone you get joined to them. It could have killed him. Then we tried to unload the gear and a group of Italian youths tried to stop us and we nearly had a major fight. We cancelled the Italian gigs and went to our hotel, where we quickly wrote 'Reasons To Be Cheerful' and recorded it in RCA's studios in Rome. The phrase came because Charlie was still alive – that was the reason for being cheerful. It's a bit like saying 'Count your blessings'."

'Reasons To Be Cheerful (Part 3)' (Buy 50), issued on July 20, 1979, was a rap song with lyrics that read like a Cockney version of 'These Are A Few Of My Favourite Things' from *The Sound Of Music*. But its disco beat meant it would find its way onto the turntables of nightclubs where black

US groups such as Chic, Earth Wind & Fire, Rose Royce, The Jacksons and Sister Sledge, were filling the dance floors. 'Reasons To Be Cheerful' began with a deep sounding African type drum-beat which was then bolstered by assorted percussion. "Why don't you get back into bed?" The Blockheads chanted as the rhythm got into full swing and Ian stepped forward to deliver a white-rap classic. "Summer Buddy Holly, the working folly/Good golly Miss Molly and boats/Hammersmith Palais, the Bolshoi Ballet/Jump back in the alley and nanny goats." The verses moved at speed and the tongue-twisting rhymes made the song difficult to perform live. Later, Ian would draw up "cheat sheets" to help him remember the sequence.

According to Johnny, the circumstances in which the song was recorded influenced aspects of the sound which was achieved, in particular his guitar solo.

"We were recording at RCA in Rome and I was playing this hired Strat with really heavy strings on and no pedals, because all the gear had gone on to a gig and we had half a day to record. Ian said, 'Go on, play that,' and I plugged straight into the amp and it was such a hard thing to play this guitar with heavy strings on. But he persevered and he kept saying 'Go on, you can do it, you can do it' and he made me play. I couldn't bend them like Eric Clapton because they were so hard and that's the solo on 'Reasons To Be Cheerful' which was really a bit painful. You can tell I'm not getting the whole tone bend."

In August, 1979, the single climbed to number three, two places beneath The Boomtown Rats' second number one single 'I Don't Like Mondays'. Frustratingly, however, fate conspired to prevent it making that final ascent to the top spot which was instead claimed on August 25 by Cliff Richard's 'We Don't Talk Anymore' – his first number one hit since 'Congratulations' in 1968.

" 'Reasons To Be Cheerful' went to number three and the next week we were due to go on *Top Of The Pops*," recalls Mickey. "But *Top Of The Pops* was cancelled that week for some reason and the next week it had dropped, and if you go down, you don't get on *Top Of The Pops*. Timing is everything and that was a major blow to the flow of the thing."

Laurie Lewis, who had filmed the video for 'Reasons To Be Cheerful', found himself being blamed for the missed opportunity. Due to the band's exhausting tour schedule, the video was shot in the middle of the day at the Birmingham Odeon and Laurie used footage of the audience taken at gigs to simulate the impression of a live gig. Meanwhile, he had the whole rig and stage at his disposal and, unlike a live concert situation, the camera had a free rein. The hand-clapping was dubbed and doubled up with echo to achieve the effect of the audience clapping in sync with the song, a live-recorded introduction by Kozmo Vinyl was cut into the video, and Ian and the band were sprayed with water to make them look like they were drenched in sweat. But there was a last-minute hitch in getting the video completed.

Laurie: "I was under tremendous pressure to get the film out fast and for the last minute with the guitar solo I just ran a long shot of the band playing because it wasn't going to be ready in time for *Top Of The Pops*, but then there was great drama. It went down to the Beeb, but there was a strike and *Top Of The Pops* didn't go out that night. Dave Robinson went bananas and blamed me, but it was nothing to do with me. That meant I had another week to edit that last section, which I did, and so when it was finished properly it went back to the Beeb. However, a friend of mine rang me up from the States and said, 'Listen, I've seen your film, it's great' and I said, 'Where did you see this, it's not even finished?' What had happened was that someone from the Beeb had stolen it, pirated it over to the States and it was already in the shops when I was still working on it. But if it had gone on the telly that week it would have gone to number one, no question."

Nonetheless, by the end of 1979, Ian Dury was a household name in Britain. *New Boots And Panties* had achieved platinum sales and remained in the album chart for a marathon 90 weeks; 'Hit Me' had made it to number one, selling in excess of one million copies along the way; *Do It Yourself* had occupied the number two spot in the album charts; and 'Reasons To Be Cheerful' had breached the top three and been one of the most memorable singles of the year. He was one of the biggest names in British pop music – the outsider had been truly accepted.

While Ian ascended to this level of celebrity a musical sea-change had occurred in the UK. Not surprisingly, punk had burned itself out and many of the bands who rode to glory on the tidal wave of phlegm had crashed and split up. For some of those who survived intact, like The Buzzcocks, Generation X and Sham 69, the Eighties would bring no further commercial success. The all encompassing term New Wave became blurred at the edges, eventually incorporating so many different styles as to become quite meaningless. In Britain, ska was the new craze. This native West Indian style of music experienced an unexpected revival thanks to the birth of the 2-Tone label and a brief re-flowering of Mod styles made fashionable in the mid-Sixties by The Who and The Small Faces. Green parka jackets, bowling shoes and Lambretta mopeds were the look on the streets and the movie *Quadrophenia*, based on The Who's original album, was a smash hit.

Madness, who had been galvanised into action after witnessing Kilburn & The High Roads gigs, released their first single 'The Prince' on 2-Tone Records in August 1979 and scored an instant hit. Their tribute to ska legend Prince Buster reached the Top Twenty, following in the footsteps of stable-mates The Specials and The Selecter, who had made their mark with 'Gangsters' and 'On My Radio' respectively. For their follow-up, Madness deserted 2-Tone and joined Stiff and stormed the Top Ten with 'One Step Beyond'. The band's string of consecutive hits (13 up to 1982) ensured an unrivalled financial return for the label and put Ian's successes into the shade.

The Beat, a Midlands group which also united black and white musicians, also entered the fray with a double A-side single combining a cover of Smokey Robinson's 'Tears Of A Clown' and a breathless dance song 'Ranking Full Stop'. They fused the Jamaican dance rhythms with punk's aggression producing an unexpectedly angry finale to the Seventies. Traditional ska songs were resurrected to stunning effect, including Prince Buster's 'One Step Beyond', covered by Madness, and Jamaican singer Dandy Livingstone's 1967 song 'A Message To You, Rudy', to which The Specials paid tribute. But the ska movement – which aimed to unite different races through music – attracted skinheads with laced-up boots and National Front sympathies. Multi-racial bands like The Selecter walked a tight-rope on stage – running a gauntlet of Nazi salutes and chants of 'Zeig Heil'. Fights frequently broke out on the dance floors at such gigs as the new dance craze gripped British teenagers.

1979 had indeed been an eventful year and, in its last days, a benefit concert staged at the Hammersmith Odeon in London brought together under one roof many of the musical successes of the decade, regardless of their age or musical style. Ian Dury & The Blockheads took their place on a star-studded bill. The concerts were in aid of an emergency relief fund for the people of Kampuchea (formerly Cambodia) and had been organised as a result of talks between Paul McCartney and the then UN Secretary-General Kurt Waldheim. Promoter Harvey Goldsmith was involved in staging the ambitious four-day event and the International Red Cross and UNICEF co-ordinated the distribution of monies raised. Queen opened the event on Boxing Day, while Ian Dury & The Blockheads shared the bill with The Clash the following night. The Who, The Pretenders and The Specials donated their services on December 28, and the last night brought together Elvis Costello & The Attractions, Rockpile (fronted by Nick Lowe and Dave Edmunds) and Paul McCartney's Wings. Just before the curtain fell on what amounted to a preview of Live Aid, the audience was treated to an extended jam session led by McCartney which featured eleven guest musicians, including Billy Bremner and Dave Edmunds (from Rockpile), James Honeyman-Scott (The Pretenders), Robert Plant, John Paul Jones and John Bonham (Led Zeppelin), Ronnie Lane (ex-Small Faces and The Faces), Bruce Thomas (The Attractions), Gary Brooker (Procol Harum), and Kenny Jones and Pete Townshend (The Who). An album entitled *Concert For The People Of Kampuchea* was later released and featured a live version of 'Hit Me With Your Rhythm Stick'.

Behind the scenes, however, all was not well with The Blockheads. The relationship between Ian and some members of his band had come under strain and rows were developing, predictably about money. While 'Hit Me' had sold a million copies, band members were continuing to draw only £100 a week from Blackhill and the exhausting *Do It Yourself* tour schedule seems to have brought the resentment to a head. Ian, meanwhile, was staying in extravagant hotel suites and living the archetypal rock star lifestyle. Drinking heavily and receiving more female attention than ever, time spent with Ian was becoming increasingly unpleasant. His domineering presence left little allowance for band members' personal lives. While they remained on a set wage, he demanded their undivided attention and he resented girlfriends or spouses who distracted them from what he saw as their number one priority – him.

Mickey Gallagher describes one incident from this alcohol-soaked era: "We would go out for a meal after the gigs and Ian would always like to be the last chicken in the shop. So, everyone had eaten and had a good time and gone back to the hotel just over the courtyard from the restaurant and I was left there looking after Ian. I don't drink, but Ian's there saying, 'Another Guinness' and there's only three people left – the two of us and the waiter. He doesn't talk any English, so Ian starts talking this pigeon French and then starts insulting him – really insulting him. He doesn't understand, but they can tell by the body language it is not good. I am thinking, 'We'd better get out', but by now Ian's too pissed and he can't stand up. It took about half an hour to get from the table over to the hotel and he's stopping all the time. I had him by the arm and we would just get a flow going and he would fall back against the wind. Then he started insulting me saying, 'Without me, you're fucking nothing' and then he fell over and so I said, 'Fuck you mate, I'm going' and left him. So Ian's flat on his back outside the hotel and as I'm going in up the stairs I can hear him shouting for the sound man and so Ian Horne came down and picked him up."

But however much Ian pushed his band and entourage by behaving like a spoilt rock star, he seemed to retain their esteem. Mickey stressed: "I have an ultimate respect for his art – he is a one-off. There is no one else who writes a lyric like Ian or delivers a lyric like Ian and there is no one that I have found who is as enjoyable to write music with as Ian.''

Ian had always got a buzz from the female attention which accompanied his fame and, in hackneyed rock'n'roll tradition, attractive women would be welcomed into his dressing room after gigs. Amid the bottles of champagne and brandy, stacks of canned beer, and the fug of cigarette smoke, Ian held court, lapping up the adoration. If boyfriends were in attendance he humiliated them, his battalion of heavies keeping them at bay.

"I was quite a muscular bloke then, I kept myself fit and there was no one that would come near," says Fred. "There were these boyfriends I used to sling out and Ian used to say, 'I don't need a security team, I've got Spider.' Sometimes in the audience there would be girls that would adore him and want to come back and they would make their way backstage and their boyfriends would be there seething with jealousy. This French bloke came in and said, 'I'd like to hit him over the head with an axe,' and I said, 'Well, you've gotta hit me first.' He said, 'Do you think you're going to stop me,' and I said, 'No I don't think it, I'll stop you all right. Anyway, why are you talking like that, what's he done?' and he said, 'He talks to my girlfriend,' and I said, 'It's just that he is a public figure.' So he took a swing at me and I grabbed hold of his arm and I said, 'Don't do that because I eat people like you for breakfast, get out of it, I don't want you in this area now.' Ray, this big black geezer, came up and said, 'Shall I get him out?' and I said, 'No, he'll get out of the way on his own.' I said to the bloke, 'I know you don't understand what I'm saying because you're a Frenchman but I want you to go,' so he stood back and tried to kick me, so I grabbed his leg and kicked him up the bollocks and said, 'Now take him out Ray.' He was screaming all about the police.''

Ian's minders were also called upon to stand in the way of those whom Ian had drunkenly abused. Staff in restaurants and bars would regularly bear the brunt of his heavy drinking, but customers would also find themselves in the firing line. Several times, members of Ian's entourage had to agree to meet dry cleaning bills, after the inebriated star threw soup and other dishes over waiters. But Ian never curbed his behaviour; he knew that if his mouth got him into trouble, Spider or The Strangler would bail him out. Fred describes one such fracas which took place in a hotel in Berlin.

"The receptionist bloke was wearing a wig and Ian's come in and said, 'What's that fucking thing you've got on your head? A dead rat?' He was really pissed and so I said, 'You'll have to excuse my friend, he's a bit drunk,' but I was smiling because of the way he'd said it and Ian has a very infectious way of laughing. I said, 'I'm not laughing at you, I'm just laughing at what he said,' and as I'm saying that, Ian was doing things to make me laugh even more and I was struggling to stay serious. Of course, this bloke was absolutely furious and in no time at all, he leapt over the counter and grabbed Ian's scarf. Now you must never grab Ian's scarf while Spider's about, so then it was serious. I grabbed hold of his wrist to ease the pressure on Ian, so Ian got all brave again, and I pushed the receptionist to the back of the reception where the keys were, and he came at me and so I just hit him – bang – and put him on the floor. I leaned over the counter, and Ian's laughing his dick off, and I said, 'I'm ever so sorry mate, but you mustn't touch the man.' He gets to his feet and says, 'I'm going to call the police,' and I said, 'By all means call the police, but I'm apologising to you.' So another hotel employee comes out and sees the blood on the other bloke's lip and I said, 'I've had to restrain him from attacking my man. Do you know, this is Ian Dury, he's a cripple and you mustn't touch him,' but Ian was going, 'Ah fuck him, he's only a cunt anyway,' which wasn't doing much good. Anyway, the police came and got hold of me and took me down the station and Peter Jenner paid them some money and got me off the hook. The next morning Ian says to me, 'Why did you give that geezer a whack? You shouldn't have whacked him.' As we went back and forth, Ian always said, 'You won't touch me because Spider will kill ya. He'll pull your fucking head off.' But every time he had a go at someone, I had to rescue him.'"

Ian had a curious attitude towards violence. He opposed the use of force and regularly lectured Spider about the value of 'verbals' over the fist. To Ian's credit, he played no small part in keeping his roadie/minder on the straight and narrow after years spent behind bars, and even though Ian liked to portray himself as a 'hard case' who could handle himself, his most vicious assaults were of the oral kind. But the implication of physical force and an air of menace intrigued him and his inner aggression tended to manifest itself when he was on stage and drunk. During one period when Ian was being particularly obstreperous, one of Ian's aides remarked, "Whatever is wrong with Ian happened 45 years ago and we aren't going to solve it now." Many of those who worked with him believe there's more than a grain of truth in his observation.

"Ian had been institutionalised and had dealt with that as a young person and as an adult he was severely disabled," says his former musical collaborator Steve Nugent. "He feels physically precarious and has to depend on other people for physical and mental support and I think a lot of his discussion of violence dates back to his being institutionalised. In terms of his background, he was an early recipient of some of the major accomplishments of the welfare state, in the sense that he wasn't quite thrown on the scrap heap when he contracted polio. He has certainly got very mixed views about the relationship between his parents; his father was of the servant class, he drove cars for other people and drove buses; his mother came from a more domesticated background and by virtue of that marriage and his subsequent illness, she was a gentle lady fallen on hard times. That's enough to make you violent."

Davey Payne's violent confrontations, meanwhile, did little for industrial relations. Even in the early days of the Kilburns, the dishevelled sax man was infamous for his knife-edge personality and his tendency to go for people, sometimes in the middle of a gig. When Chaz counted the band in for a final encore in Madrid, during the European tour to promote *Do It Yourself*, Davey lost control. He grabbed Chaz by the scalp and nutted him so hard on the forehead that it burst open – all in full view of the audience. Chaz staggered back to his hotel room, took some pain killers and woke up the next morning to find the band had checked out. He flew to Barcelona only to find that there had been a room mix-up and the others thought he had left in disgust over Davey's assault.

Generally, those who knew Davey had learned to avoid winding him up as they knew what the consequences would be. Ian was wary of the band's 'loose cannon' and had turned a blind eye to his outbursts, relieved that he had not been on the receiving end. But Davey's building anger at Ian was ready to boil over.

Mickey: "If the band went to a restaurant, Ian would be obsessed that Davey was looked after. I think it deflected attention away from Ian and Ian quite enjoyed it. He could still be in the limelight, but, 'Hey, look at that crazy person over there.' There were times that were totally alien to me where, because Davey was a violent person, fights broke out on stage between various members of the band. I would be shocked, although in terms of the show it looked great. Ian didn't condone it or defend it, but it still went on and Ian just said, 'Ah . . . rock'n'roll man.' The next day Davey would be back on stage and everything was forgotten, but I'd still be traumatised."

"Davey's rage came on because Ian was getting all the dairy and he wasn't. He was on a drip feed and so that was the root cause of it. If Davey beat somebody up, the bottom of it was that he was enraged with Ian and Ian thought that was fine, because at least he wasn't getting it himself. He lived in fear of Davey turning on him and he did once at the Gresham Hotel in Dublin on the *Do It Yourself* tour. Ian had the big suite in the hotel and the rest of us had single rooms. We found out that Ian had a suite and he said, 'We'll have to have a party up here, everybody can come up and have a party.' So we do the gig and go back to the hotel and Ian gets ensconced up in his room with what is the perfect combination for Ian – a young girl who is obviously enamoured with 'Ian Dury' and her boyfriend, who he can sit in a room and put down in front of the girl. He's pulling the girl and insulting the geezer and she's thinking, 'Why am I with this plank?' I rang up to Ian and said, 'We've got all these people in the bar downstairs waiting to go to the party and they've all invited people' and Ian says, 'Oh no, party's off, have the party down there.' We couldn't have the party down there because it was only for residents, so we just barged into Ian's room and Davey is really enraged by this stage and he is talking about something that had gone down at the gig he wasn't happy about. I could see Davey getting more and more wound up and I was there telling him, 'It's par for the course Davey' and then he was gone. He rushed over, picked Ian up and rammed his head against the wall."

Davey Payne believes that Ian was overindulged as a child and that this caused him to abuse the loyalty of those around him in later life. Even though Ian was often obnoxious to those around him, his expectations of them were always high.

"Ian didn't have a dad at home to give him a smack now and again. He had these middle-class aunties with Burberry rain macs and sensible shoes," observes Davey. "That's how he was brought up and because he had had polio, he could throw his weight around and they'd be fussing over him. I don't think he has really ever done anything by himself. The things that went wrong in his early childhood were what went wrong and they have affected him like things have affected us all in one way or another."

At the beginning of 1980, as Ian subsumed himself in a draining rock'n'-roll lifestyle, the band was dealt a terrible blow. Chaz, disillusioned with Blackhill and the energy-sapping gigs, left to pursue a solo career. The announcement shook Ian, but Chaz was steadfast in his desire to achieve recognition for himself and to compose new material. Like Russell Hardy before him, Chaz too had become weary of Ian's difficult behaviour and found his possessive nature stifling. The partnership which produced 'Sweet Gene Vincent', 'Clevor Trever', 'Hit Me With Your Rhythm Stick', 'Reasons To Be Cheerful' and other classics had finally come apart.

Ian said later:[14] "You can't live in each others' pockets all the time. Chaz obviously had to go and breathe his own breath and sing his own songs. He's a much better singer than me. He may not have certain front man skills that I've got, but he's got loads of other skills he felt he had to explore. Anything that Chaz has ever done in his life has always been with my blessing and I guess vice versa too. There have been times we haven't seen eye to eye, but very, very rarely. There's never been a time when I have worked with Chaz when I haven't enjoyed it and I haven't seen him smiling. I have never seen him play an instrument without a smile on his face, ever. I've got nothing except love and admiration for Chaz and if I get angry with him it's only because he's left my bloody video on top of his car and driven off, that's all. It's never because I think he's out of order. Chaz is slightly a nutty professor and absent-minded about other things and other realities, but he exists beautifully within his own plane."

Chaz explains the reasons behind his decision to go it alone: "After 'Hit Me' we did a three-month tour of 80 gigs and I remember saying to Ian, 'Look, I've got to have a break.' One of the reasons I wanted to have a break was that the management [Blackhill] were creaming it and wanted to get as much mileage out of our success as they could. The problem was that we didn't have time to write any new material. We knew the tunes we were playing so well that we could have got a robot to play them and I knew I had a lot more to express. One of the last shows we did on that three-month tour in 1979 was an amazing gig at The Paradiso in Amsterdam. One of the features of the gig was that the floor started to collapse while we were playing and they had to get the fire brigade in. When we went to the dressing room, this beautiful Dutch model appeared and I started chatting to her. We were staying at the Hotel American just across the square and so the band wandered back across and she was with us and all of a sudden we were all separated and somehow or other I had this beautiful girl in my room. She said, 'Would you like some grass?' and I said 'Yeah, shall I get some wine?' and then other various things were offered to me and in the midst of this incredible best day of my life, a melody popped into my head for a song called 'Ai No Corrida'. I had my guitar and checked the key and I called Norman in his room and he came and jammed on it. Then I realised that the piece was not right for The Blockheads, it was too melodic, something didn't feel right. So when I had my time off, I went to a musician friend of mine Pete Van Hooke, who I went to school with, who knew a guy called Kenny Young, who was a lyricist. He invited me around and I took a few tunes and that was one of them on the tape and he wrote the lyrics to 'Ai No Corrida'. I had no idea what it was about, but it turned out it was all about Oshima's film *In The Realm Of The Senses*. I went into that area, which was good in retrospect because I got a record deal with A&M on the strength of that and made four albums and Ian co-wrote a lot of songs on those albums, in fact some great songs.

"I adopted a stance away from the group. I think I had said I didn't want to do any gigs and every now and again I would have to do that. I don't think Ian particularly liked it, but he respected it. Ian said that he always felt more secure when I was playing with the band, probably because we co-wrote a lot of the songs. Ian was a wonderful person and he was also very intense sometimes and that intensity would get too much for me. There was a time when he was drinking quite a lot and his humour could change. He could get a little bit spiteful, defensive about a lot of things and sometimes I used to feel that the intimacy that had been built up through writing songs together was actually being encroached upon in a way I didn't like. I was confused about how I related to him. As you get to know somebody, over the years you get to see the full picture and you start to see a pattern and I was aware of that. When it got out of order sometimes I used to tell him, 'I have had enough,' or just not be there, not call him. Ian knew at the end of the day I wouldn't let him down, but at the same time it was important that he could see I was an individual. Sometimes I felt he wanted a gang, he wanted the winning team, and he cherished the members of that gang so much that he was in danger of becoming claustrophobic. I think he did try to control things."

10

I QUIBBLE WHEN I SCRIBBLE

"I thought that it was disgusting, the Year of the Disabled. I didn't think anyone had the right to go around telling people like me, who is disabled, what is going on with their lives and how to do it. Nobody has got the right to give me a quality of life assessment. I wrote the record simply off the top of my head to tell 'em to stick it up their aris."

— Ian Dury on 'Spasticus Autisticus'

Laughter it was to be called, but mirth was a precious commodity during the ill-tempered recording of Ian's third album, in a basement studio in Fulham, west London. The Blockheads were still reeling from Chaz's untimely exit and the absence of his songwriting and musical arranging made for a more disjointed collection of songs. The decision to make the record was motivated more by Ian's legal obligation to Stiff than any creative flow and this, combined with his fluctuating moods, resulted in some extremely fraught sessions. The finished product — a schizophrenic songbook to which all the Blockheads made contributions — was to be a disappointment in the light of the group's huge chart success to date. Johnny says simply of this period: "There were months and months of sessions and a lot of pain."

The resumption of the recording process brought to an end a hiatus for the group. After the endless touring to promote *Do It Yourself*, The Blockheads party had broken up. Chaz had departed on a solo mission having been signed by A&M Records. Mickey Gallagher and his family had embarked on a US tour with The Clash, and Ian, assorted band members, road crew and their wives and girlfriends had flown to Barbados for a well-earned rest. Ian booked three villas on a beach and he and his entourage partied for about three weeks on the Caribbean island. In April 1980, after Mickey's return from the US, The Blockheads arrived at Milner Sound [later The Producers Workshop], in Fulham, south-west London, and began experimenting with songs of their own. Johnny, Davey, Norman, Mickey and Charley all had their own ideas for songs and had no record company deadlines or tour commitments looming. But as they jammed away in the basement studio, Ian was growing restless.

Mickey: "There was this situation where Ian was saying he wanted to do some recording. Chaz was away and The Blockheads were down in Fulham, so he came to have a listen to what we were doing and basically took over. He says, 'I'll do an album down here,' and we said, 'But, but, but . . .' Of course, he had the money and had another album to do, so we agreed and we used some of the ideas that we had been putting down against his lyrics and joined them up. Then, Ian says, 'Let's get a new member in – Wilko Johnson.' "

Wilko (real name John Wilkinson) had studied in Newcastle, worked as a teacher before returning to his native Southend-on-Sea in 1971. Together with singer Lee Brilleaux and bassist John B Sparks, he formed The Pigboy Charlie Band and after John Martin, alias The Big Figure, was recruited on drums, a fantastic R&B band was born – Dr Feelgood, the name taken from a song by Johnny Kidd's Pirates. Wilko's mad, staring eyes, manic guitar playing and acrobatic stage antics had given these Canvey Island rockers a strong visual dimension when they emerged on to the pub rock scene in 1973. They played their first ever London gig at the Tally Ho, where the Kilburns had cut their teeth, and released their début single 'Roxette' and album *Down By The Jetty* in 1975. At this time they toured the country with Chilli Willi & The Red Hot Peppers and Kokomo on the Naughty Rhythms Tour, a precursor to the Stiffs Live Stiffs package.

Before long Dr Feelgood earned a formidable reputation with their electrifying live sound, Lee Brilleaux's gargantuan stage presence and Wilko's crazed side-show in which he would machine-gun the audience with his guitar and career dementedly around the stage. Wilko had also shown himself to be a great songwriter through such heady concoctions as 'Roxette', 'She Does It Right' and 'Back In The Night' – all live Feelgood's favourites. In the mid to late Seventies, the band released a number of singles including 'She's A Wind Up' and 'Down At The Doctors', but 'Milk And Alcohol' was their biggest hit, climbing to number nine in January 1979. By this time, Wilko had left to front his own group, The Solid Senders (Alan Platt, drums, Steve Lewins, bass, John Potter, keyboards), and they released one album in 1978. But by mid-1980 he was at a loose end and it was while he was playing on stage with The Stranglers at The Rainbow Theatre in Finsbury Park, north London, that he received his Blockheads call-up. For the pub rocker, the invitation to join a group which commanded such massive respect on stage and which had enjoyed so much success, could not have been better timed.

Wilko describes the events which led him to join Ian Dury & The

Blockheads. "I was moping around back stage and Davey Payne came up to me and said, 'How are you going Wilko?' and I said, 'Oh I don't know, I'm thinking of knocking it on the head,' and he said, 'Oh really.' Then the next night, Ian came up and said, 'Me and The Blockheads are down the studio, do you want to come and make a single with us?' and I said, 'Yeah,' because I knew Ian and Davey from Kilburn & The High Roads days. I had never met The Blockheads, but I'd seen them on telly and I'd seen Norman and he was my favourite bass player. I didn't even know his name, I just knew that Ian's bass player was my favourite bass player. Ian said that when I was doing my numbers on stage with The Stranglers that night, I looked so lonely that he decided that I should record this Don Gibson number 'Oh Lonesome Me' which was a favourite song of mine from when I first started playing. I think everyone had been discussing me because a week or so later, Ian called me and said, 'Listen, do you want to join The Blockheads?' My own career was right in the doldrums, I was feeling pretty down and I joined them."

Ian felt sorry for Wilko, but he also saw a chance to import another real talent into the band. Ian hoped that with Chaz having left, the blues man would give the band a fresh impetus. Wilko headed straight for Fulham, where The Blockheads had already begun work on their new album, and on August 22 the first song featuring the new Blockhead was released by Stiff (Buy 90). 'I Want To Be Straight', written by Ian and Mickey, was firmly tongue-in-cheek and was played at a slower and more bluesy tempo than its most recent predecessors. The initial black sleeve displayed a yellow school prefect's badge while later copies had a pink-tinted photograph of the boys wearing smart suits and wide ties and Norman holding a briefcase. At Ian's suggestion, the song began with spoken introductions by each band member over bass and keyboards – an ingenious touch which made it stand out when it started receiving airplay. "I'm Charley, you know, I'm Norman, pleased to meet ya, I'm Mickey, 'allo, Wilko, I'm Johnny, how are ya doing Harry, my name is David, and I'm Ian and guess what . . . Oi, I wanna be straight, I wanna be straight/ I'm sick and tired of taking drugs and staying up late/ I wanna confirm, I wanna conform/ I wanna be safe and I wanna be snug and I wanna be warm". The song also had in its armoury a rasping sax solo from Davey over football terrace-style chants of 'straight' from the remaining Blockheads, whose vocal contribution was noticeably to the fore. On the B-side was a rare collaboration between Ian and Davey called 'That's Not All', a tribute to a friend. The record charted, climbing to number 22 before disappearing from the Top 75 after only seven weeks.

In the video, Ian had put on a clown's face and for one *Top Of The Pops* performance, the band dressed up as policemen and afterwards performed a mock 'raid' on Wessex Studios where The Clash were recording. It was to be the only bright moment in a long grind to put down the remainder of songs for *Laughter*. Those who were involved in the album found Ian's unpredictable moods and his desire to control every situation, difficult to bear.

Mickey: "It was never easy being in a studio with Ian, especially in the early days. He wants to be dominant in a studio, doesn't like giving anybody else power or proving themselves. If he had a drink in the studio it was fatal. He was probably at his horriblest during *Laughter*, really horrible. I remember sitting in the studio with the sound engineer Ian Horne and hearing the front door opening and hearing Ian's voice and both of us froze and thought, 'Oh fuck, he's here.' Then he came in and we said, 'Oh, you all right Ian?' and he says, 'What's happening?' He sacked my keyboard roadie at that time for doing something naughty with drugs in the studio. He was a bit of a dictator. We used to call him 'The Raspberry' [raspberry ripple – cripple in Cockney rhyming slang] and after gigs everyone used to wait until he had gone."

Sometimes Ian Horne would drive Ian home after the recording sessions, and one such incident, after Ian had had a few, sticks in his mind. "Once I was taking him back from Milner in my Golf GTI 16-valve car which I was very proud of because it was clean and nice. But Ian wanted a kebab and he kept insisting. So finally I got him a kebab and then I got to his house and I thought, 'Where's all the rubbish?' " He needn't have worried about getting chilli sauce over his new car seats, however. "He'd eaten it, the wrapping and everything. There was not a trace left of this kebab."

The unsettling atmosphere at Milner was not helped by a freak accident which happened during the recording of *Laughter* and had an immediate and serious impact on the health of Johnny Turnbull.

Johnny explains: "Ian had this flat near Baker Street, when we were recording songs for *Laughter* and I used to give him a lift home. One night he says, 'Can you kick me door in, 'cos I've left my keys behind and the cats are starving?' So I had me big DM boots on and it took me about five attempts. I kicked this door in and I don't know how I did it because I'm only five foot six and eight-and-a-half stone. What I didn't know was that it had jarred all the way up my spine and moved my skull. I went a bit do-lally and had a nervous breakdown, but all Ian said was, 'Go home to your mam.' I went to a cranial osteopath and he said, 'Your skull has moved and it's rubbing and producing this sugar very akin to lysergic acid.' I was flying."

Ian had collaborated almost exclusively with Chaz in the songwriting process to date, but with the pianist and guitarist now enjoying his own success in America, Ian began handing lyrics to other band members which meant the royalties were more evenly distributed. Mickey was especially productive, contributing to four of the 12 tracks which would later appear on the record, namely 'Hey, Hey, Take Me Away', 'Take Your Elbow Out Of The Soup, You're Sitting On The Chicken', 'Manic Depression (Jimi)' and 'Delusions Of Grandeur'. He had helped to shape some of the songs on *Do It Yourself*, such as 'This Is What We Find', although on this occasion he was given a much more influential role in the song-writing department. In 'Delusions Of Grandeur', which began with bar-room piano and Wilko's blues guitar, Ian narrated the tale of an ego-tistical rock star ("I've got megalomania, I've got megalomania/ To be a twinkle in the showbiz dream/ To which effect I do connive and scheme/ I dive into the dairy and I lap up all the cream/ I'm up to the armpits in self-esteem."). It was over in just under three minutes and its sound would have been more familiar to Dr Feelgood devotees than those of The Blockheads, but Wilko's string bending worked well on this track.

With the songwriting being shared around, and even drummer Charley Charles getting in on the act, the sleeve notes would suggest an all-round team effort for Ian's third Stiff album. Unknown to fans of The Blockheads, however, major cracks were continuing to emerge in Ian's relationship with the band with whom he had shot to fame.

According to those involved in the *Laughter* sessions, Ian's insistence on controlling things went into overdrive and anyone who dared question his judgement triggered off ugly displays of defensiveness and aggression. If Ian hated one thing, it was people believing they had worked out how he ticked. But band members felt he was simply choosing to ignore the damage being caused by his binge drinking and desire to control people.

Mickey: "It became much easier in the last few years to work with Ian because he cut down on drinking. Years ago, he would quite happily sit drinking alcohol until the pub closed and he liked to be the centre of attention and he couldn't not be. He walked into a room and you just couldn't ignore him. A strange anomaly about Ian is that there was a blinkeredness in his intellect which all of us have used to our advantage. I noticed it in some songs and I did even mentioned it to him. He did this song on *Laughter* called 'Delusions Of Grandeur' and when I got the lyric and read it, I said, 'Fucking hell Ian, that is a real own-up lyric that is – that is really good,' and he went, 'Wha'daya mean? It's not about me,' and I said, 'It fucking is.' In lots of songs, Ian was writing about himself, but he would never admit it. I think the guy was so intelligent that he must have seen it, but he chose not to see it and chose not to acknowledge certain problems. What I have found out over the years is that there are many ways to skin a cat. What you tended to do with Ian was that if you saw something glaring which he seemed to be missing or not acknowledging, if you made a point of it, it was always unpleasant, because you were making him face a certain thing and he would argue you down. The best thing was not to argue with him and say, 'I just thought I'd mention it, but sorry I'm wrong,' and then a couple of weeks later something would change and it would be his decision. He is very sensitive and very protective about certain things."

From this winter of discontent came another single in the shape of 'Sueperman's Big Sister' (spelled wrongly to avoid copyright problems), one of two songs which Ian had written with Wilko. Released on November 7, 1980, the record had special significance for Stiff as it was the 100th single released by the label. Allowing Ian to bring up the century said much about the affection in which he was held by his record company. To commemorate the occasion, the paper labels of Stiff's first release, Nick Lowe's 'So It Goes'/'Heart Of The City' were put on the records' centres showing the words crossed out and replaced by the correct band and song titles. Of the 100 oddball singles issued by Stiff at an average rate of one a fortnight, 18 entered the British Top 75. This second offering from the new-look Blockheads was one of them, but it stayed there for only three weeks, grinding to a halt at number 51. The opening bars of the song must have sent alarm bells ringing for die-hard fans, as they were greeted with sweeping orchestral strings followed by an incongruous rock beat. The Afro-American rhythms of Chaz which had so invigorated songs like 'Hit Me', 'Reasons To Be Cheerful' and songs on *Do It Yourself* like 'In-betweenies' were gone and the stilted rock beat seemed to limit the lyrical possibilities. The chorus gave the song some chance of lingering in the memory, but overall it fell short of Ian's usually impeccably high standards. Some believe the song was written about the actress Vanessa Redgrave, whom Ian met at this time. Ian, however, said of the song:[8] "It was inspired by a photograph of a Teddy Girl. The idea that Superman has a big sister has got to be pretty cool. We got Ivor Raymonde to do an arrangement for this and I love the strings."

The flip side of the 7-inch single was 'You'll See Glimpses', a truly wacky song by Ian and Norman in which the narrator outlines his utopian vision of the world's future. Ominously, the song closes with the line "This has been got out by a friend". This gem made it on to *Juke Box Dury*, a compilation album issued by Stiff a year later. But on the plain sleeved 12-inch single, 'You'll See Glimpses' was replaced by 'Fucking Ada', a full-on swear-box filler from Ian and Johnny, the very title of which would be enough to send shivers down the spine of radio station bosses everywhere.

Even Johnny had cause to cringe when it was released. "Of course, me mam bought it and me auntie saw it – two really raging Catholics – and she said to me mam, 'Eee Lily, how could you let him put his name to something like this?' And on the label it didn't even say Dury and Turnbull, it just said Turnbull!"

Laughter was released in the same month and did include 'Sueperman's Big Sister', only the second Ian Dury 45 ever to make it onto an album on its initial release. The track listing was: 'Sueperman's Big Sister', 'Pardon', 'Delusions Of Grandeur', 'Yes & No (Paula)', 'Dance Of The Crackpots', 'Over The Points', 'Take Your Elbow Out Of The Soup You're Sitting On The Chicken', 'Uncoolohol', 'Hey, Hey, Take Me Away', 'Manic Depression (Jimi)', 'Oh, Mr Peanut' and 'Fucking Ada'. The album featured a special guest appearance by veteran jazz trumpeter Don Cherry and string arrangements by Ivor Raymonde. The mixing and re-mixing, meanwhile, was done by Phil Chapman and veteran Blockheads sound engineer Ian Horne.

The bleak cover and the exhausted faces staring out from it said much about the atmosphere in which it had been recorded. The plain white sleeve showed black and white photographs of each group member. Most looked tired and gloomy and only Ian and Davey's faces held the faintest glimmer of a smile. The head and shoulders shots of the band members and sound engineer Ian Horne on the back sleeve didn't amount to a barrel of laughs. But although *Laughter* lacked the punch of *New Boots And Panties* and would not be received as warmly as *Do It Yourself*, it did contain some memorable moments.

From its sweeping orchestral overture to its shocking end, *Laughter* was a roller-coaster of a ride, full of unexpected twists and turns. Overall, it seemed disjointed as the band hopped from style to style and it was less accessible for a first-time listener than its predecessors. Ian's decision to add his lyrics to tunes that The Blockheads had written without him showed on some of the material. But its unpredictability and the eccentric and dark nature of its material gave it a different kind of appeal.

"New digs and prospects of a job. New digs and . . . prospects" announced the voice at the beginning of the second track 'Pardon', a more bass and keyboards-driven affair with quirky lyrics. The 4/4 rhythm of 'Delusions Of Grandeur' (the song Ian had denied was about himself) gave Wilko plenty of licence to provide the kind of choppy, rock'n'roll guitar playing that the band knew he could bring to The Blockheads' sound.

'Yes & No (Paula)', began with the pocket trumpet of Don Cherry, the veteran American jazzer who had played on the 1959 Ornette Coleman album *Change Of The Century* which had made such a lasting impression on Ian. The words formed a meandering lyrical maze ("You think I'm wrong, I think/I think you're right/I think, I think you're wrong/You think I think I think/And then again, again/And then and then"), while Cherry's trumpet soared majestically over a classic Blockheads beat. Disappointingly though, the dirge-like refrain of 'Yes and No' added nothing to what was an otherwise strong track, containing some of the most enjoyable playing on the record.

'Dance Of The Crackpots' was a rip-roaring hoe-down in which the hallmark Dury rhymes came thick and fast ("From Rosemary Clooney to Jerry Lee Lewie/From Debussy to Thelonious Monk/It's the modern art of the human heart/The shape of things to funk"). Some fancy footwork from a tap dancer rounded off one of the album's most uplifting songs.

Ian became "an actual train" in the surreal 'Over The Points', speaking matter-of-factly over assorted locomotive sound effects ("Sometimes the track is lined with decapitated schoolboys' heads, still wearing their caps/Upon me at any given moment/Ten or twelve people might be taking craps").

'Take Your Elbow Out Of The Soup' was based on an off-beat rhythm and was instrumentally impressive. 'Uncoolohol' (Charley Charles's only song credit) was more melodic and, bearing in mind Ian's tendency for drunken and obnoxious behaviour, members of The Blockheads would have had no trouble relating to the subject matter ("The war cry of the drinker of the drink/Can send your senses reeling to the brink"). Mickey's full-on keyboards and Cherry's improvisation gave the chorus a triumphant ring.

That Ian was depressed during this period was reflected on what was a more autobiographical and introspective album. His traumatic days on the wards and dormitories of Chailey were graphically represented in the tortured refrains of 'Hey, Hey, Take Me Away'. At the outset of the song, Ian shouts out to his pal 'Lawrence', begging him to escape with him and what follows is a disquieting account of the place in which he spent many miserable days and nights: the "nutters" who whistle and cheer at the one-legged race, the one-legged prefect who "makes me play with his dick" and the one-legged orderly "shouting the odds". Here, Ian's earliest anxieties about the implications of his disability and his treatment at the hands of the Chailey staff were laid bare. "When I get better, when I get strong, will I be all right in the head/They're making me well if they're caring for me/Why do they bully and punch me/Why do they bash me and punch me/Some of the counterpanes are pink and other ones are blue" wrote Ian. It remains one of his most personal songs.

'Manic Depression (Jimi)' was a more palatable affair than the title implied, with Ian warbling over a gentle Hawaiian type lilt created by the sublime guitar playing of Johnny Turnbull. The title appeared to be a reference to Jimi Hendrix, who recorded a song entitled 'Manic Depression' on his début UK album *Are You Experienced*, but this was not evident from either the lyrics or music. 'Oh Mr. Peanut' meanwhile rattled along with a rock'n'roll rhythm and Ian bawling over the top and the saxophone and bar room piano gave it a rousing finale.

The album had served to reflect Ian's own low spirits at the time and the finale to *Laughter* was gloom-laden and spectacular in equal measure. ("Failure enfolds me with clammy green arms/Damn the excursions and blast the alarms/For the rest of what's natural I'll lay on the ground/Tell me tomorrow if I'm still around," he sang.)

David Hepworth, reviewing the record in *The Face* in January 1981, found much to recommend it and concluded that the personnel changes had not substantially changed The Blockheads' sound. He singled out 'Dance Of The Crackpots' and 'Take Your Elbow Out Of The Soup' for particular praise, remarking that either would have made more rousing singles than 'I Want To Be Straight' and 'Sueperman's Big Sister'.

"Unlike most authors, Dury doesn't grasp one idea and belabour it for 40 minutes. Whether dealing with feminism ('Sueperman's Big Sister'), or booze ('Uncoolohol'), early life and hard times ('Hey Hey Take Me Away'), or simply trains, his words are chosen for their refractive qualities," he wrote. "Sentences come studded with tiny illuminations, his delivery slurs from triumphant to abject, from tender to bullying, in the space of a syllable. His music reproduces the complexity of experience rather than expecting it to conform to the banality of a viewpoint; there are 12 Wednesday Plays on this record, all of them good ones. Anyone who detects nothing more than a musical comedy version of *Minder* simply isn't listening hard enough."

Davey felt that *Laughter* contained some excellent tunes, but he was aggrieved at the way in which Ian had hijacked what had begun as a Blockheads venture. Looking back, he has mixed feelings about it. "I know that the album didn't sell, but it's got an edge to it," he says. "At the time, Ian was being depressed and there are a lot of reflections on his past and the hardships he had had. *Laughter* was the ideal title in a way, it was such an irony. It's difficult really. It's one thing to make records to make money and not enjoying it, but it's another stifling people's creativity, which happened a lot.

"When The Blockheads first went into Milner where they did *Laughter*, they were really buzzing and doing some really good stuff and Ian came in and I think the creativity got stifled. There are loads of great tracks that were made too clinical and were over-dubbed. I think the strings were Dave Robinson's idea and they worked on 'Fucking Ada', but not on 'Sueperman's Big Sister'. Ian always thought that if the lyrics were good enough, he'd get a hit and if they weren't he wouldn't, but I don't really think that matters. There weren't the good tunes really and I think arranging did a lot."

Norman: "Ian spent ages on *Do It Yourself*, because the money was around, and it was over-produced and a bit too sophisticated musically. When Wilko came along, it gave us an edge again, a rawness which had somehow got trapped up in the production, and getting back to the roots of it all was what he was injecting. We met Don Cherry half-way through touring and he toured with us for a while and he is on a couple of tracks. I still listen to some of the tracks on that album which I really like a lot. My favourites were 'Sueperman's Big Sister', 'Fucking Ada', 'Delusions Of Grandeur' and 'Uncoolohol'. Musically we were still creating, but there was an element of the roughness, although maybe it might have been too rough."

In spite of the mediocre chart performance of 'Sueperman's Big Sister', the Soft As A Baby's Bottom UK tour which accompanied the album's release quickly sold out. The long-running rows about money were meanwhile resolved, with the band guaranteed a healthy remuneration for their part in the tour. But privately, no one really believed in the album.

"At the time of the *Do It Yourself* tour we had no idea what was happening with the money," says Mickey. "Believe it or not, when 'Hit Me With Your Rhythm Stick' was out, the band were on £100 a week from Blackhill. Ian doesn't believe it, but that was our complaint. When it came to *Laughter*, we got £350 a week. It was the end of the line, everything was falling apart. The tour we did for *Laughter* was at places like Top Rank Ballrooms, whereas before we had always played Odeons and big student gigs. This was a 'make money' tour which they had sold out before we went out and to keep us happy they gave us £350 a week, which was great money."

Sales of the record didn't help the band's finances. *Laughter* reached only number 48 in the album chart, where it managed a paltry three weeks; in the US, the record peaked at number 159. Although The Blockheads continued to play gigs both at home and abroad to sell-out crowds during 1981, internally, things had gone from bad to worse and Ian's incessant drinking was a major problem. In March, the band appeared on French television and were flown to Cannes for Midem, the music industry bash, to receive an award from the country's big pop station Europe Numero Un. By the time the band left Paris to return home, however, Ian's name was mud in the French record industry.

Andrew: "We were on Barclay Records which was owned by Eddie Barclay, the king of rock music in France. He had Johnny Halliday, he had licensed Elvis, he was Mr Big and Ian & The Blockheads went to a reception at his flat in Paris. It was one of those scenes where there was a grand piano covered in photographs of him with John Kennedy and all the rest of it. We went to Midem to get this prize and then Eddie Barclay is giving this huge dinner for about 200 or 300 people, absolutely amazing food, probably the best food I have ever had. Ian was in the place of honour, sitting at Eddie's right hand, between Eddie and his girlfriend, who was some French film star about 30 years younger than Eddie. Ian and this girl were getting on really well, in fact they got on so well that after a bit Ian said, 'This is fucking boring, shall we go somewhere else,' and she said, 'Yes, let's.' So they got up to leave and Eddie said, 'Where are you going?' and Ian said, 'Well I'm fucking off with your bird.' So Eddie said, 'You stupid ignorant man, sit down at once, who do you think you are,' and Ian said, 'Eddie Barclay tu es merd [you are shit],' and Eddie Barclay said, 'Ian Dury, you will never sell another record in France,' and that was pretty much the case. I don't know if he sold any, but he certainly never accounted for any sales there. I should have enjoyed it, but I didn't. I was crawling with embarrassment."

In the summer of 1981, Ian finally parted company with Stiff. *Laughter* had not performed as well as had been hoped and there seems to have been a feeling at the label that he had lost his way. Relations between Stiff and Blackhill were also far from amicable by this time and Blackhill quickly got Ian signed to Polydor for an undisclosed, but considerable sum. But, as it was to transpire, it was Ian's songs and not the Blockheads input that Polydor wanted. Blackhill was also aware that if Ian went solo, it would dispense with the need for any future wrangles with The Blockheads over money.

In many ways, Ian Dury had been a saviour for Stiff. The phenomenal success of *New Boots And Panties* and 'Hit Me' had been a turning point for the company and *Do It Yourself* had been the subject of one of its biggest ever marketing campaigns. Now, after the lukewarm public response to *Laughter* and 'Sueperman's Big Sister', Ian Dury's popularity was on the wane and over at Stiff's new headquarters in Bayham Street, Camden, the attention had shifted to the band that had scored consecutive Top 10 hits with its first four singles for the company. After issuing their début single 'The Prince' via the 2-Tone label, Madness were snapped up by Dave

Robinson on October 1, 1979. They were the new stars and they would continue to be a cash–cow for the label for some years to come.

Alan Cowderoy of Stiff says of Ian's exit from the label: "I think we all felt that it had run its course and that we'd got as far as we could with Ian and by that time other things were in the wings and we were less reliant. I think it's fair to say that at Stiff, there was always one act at one time and we never quite managed to have two acts being hugely successful at the same time. I suppose, as long as there was another group to take up the slack and start to sell records, one was less concerned."

He added: "Blackhill's and Ian's philosophy was to save everything up and wait for the *Greatest Hits* and that would all be fantastic, little realising by then that having had three albums out, if your star was not still in the ascendancy, it was still going to be difficult to sell a *Greatest Hits*, and that was the case, unfortunately."

In an interview with *The Face* in September 1981, Ian denied rumours that his departure was down to Stiff's failure to promote *Laughter*: "The trouble with Stiff was the boss. Dave Robinson is one of my best friends. If we were liking each other we couldn't respect each other. And if we were respecting each other, we couldn't like each other. I mean I've still got an old coat of his in my wardrobe.

"My leaving Stiff was exactly the same as Elvis Costello's. He left to make way for me and I left to make way for Madness – who are a very good band indeed. I like being with a solid old name like Pye or Polydor. They talk to me one day and James Last the next. They tell me about 'units'. They say Philistine things about music and they read the *Daily Express*, very nice."

"I'm Spasticus, I'm Spasticus, I'm Spasticus Autisticus/I dribble when I nibble and I quibble when I scribble." 1981 was the International Year of the Disabled and Ian Dury was angry. "Hello to you out there in normal land/You may not comprehend my tale or understand/As I walk past your window give me lucky looks/You can beat my body but you'll never read my books," he sang in protest. Ian's first single for Polydor was anti-commercial, highly contentious, and incredibly brave. British radio stations flatly refused to play it and, in a twist of irony, 'Spasticus' was deemed offensive by many people who misinterpreted its lyrics ("54 appliances in leather and elastic/A hundred thousand thank yous from 27 . . . spastics") as distasteful. While the International Year of the Disabled was designed to bring attention to a section of society that many prefer to ignore, the achingly honest 'Spasticus' was brushed straight under the carpet.

Even Ian's mum disapproved of the words, but for Ian, it was one of the most important and honest songs he had ever written. He was dismayed that in Eighties Britain, the word 'spastic' had been hijacked to describe a kind of dancing and was also being used as an all-purpose derogatory term. In 'Spasticus Austisticus' he reclaimed it, but most people found the song as unnerving as being in the company of spastics and other disabled people. And hence, just as easy to ignore.

Ian explained.[14] "It was made against the Year of the Disabled. The Year of the Disabled in 1981 implied that everyone who was disabled was going to be okay in 1982 which was not true and patronising didn't come into it. I thought that it was disgusting, the Year of the Disabled, I didn't think anyone had the right to go around telling people like me, who is disabled, what is going on with their lives and how to do it. Nobody has got the right to give me a quality of life assessment. I wrote the record simply off the top of my head to tell 'em to stick it up their aris.

"It is a rock'n'roll song. Had it been on another subject matter it would have been a divine number one hit, but I knew that at the time. I also knew that it would not be played on the radio. To me, 'Spasticus Austisticus' was the second best song I've ever written; that begs the question what the first one is. Well, I can think of 15 first ones, but some people said that song was a nail in my career coffin, because they thought I'd deliberately blown it and made myself unpopular or made myself too far away from the mainstream, or some old bollo. But I don't think that at all."

Chaz says of the reaction it provoked: "It was totally nuts and it showed there was a complete hypocrisy taking place in certain areas. It was an important song lyrically for Ian and musically it seemed to be very much expressing his anger and frustration."

As the International Year of the Disabled got under way, Ian was inundated with requests to appear at events and help promote the campaign. As one of the most prominent disabled figures in the country, he got letters from people living in sheltered homes, telling him how lonely it was when the staff went home for weekends, and tapes with songs they had written about the Year of the Disabled. But Ian saw the entire project as a farce and instead came up with his own anthem for disabled people.

Ian explained:[3] "I said, 'I'm going to put a band down the road for the Year of the Disabled: I'll be Spastic and they can be The Autistics. I have The Blockheads and that means they're autistic anyway.' And my mate [Ed Speight] goes, 'No − Spasticus Autisticus, the freed slave.' Great, I'm Spartacus. So I wrote this tune. I put in the second verse, 'So place your hard-earned peanuts in my tin/and thank the creator you're not in the state I'm in/So long have I been languishing on the shelf/I must give all proceedings to myself.' When they said, 'Are you going to give it away to

charity?' I said, 'No, I'm not, the second verse explains that.' I thought it
would be a war-cry type of item. But it wasn't allowed to be played anywhere and people got offended by it – everybody except the spastics. All
the spastics went, 'Yeah man, what a tune, yeah right.' "

In fact, the song had been inspired by a spastic who had come to Ian's
dressing room at the Sobell Centre in Holloway, north London, in 1980.
He spoke with a croak out of the side of his mouth and this, coupled with
his thick Glaswegian accent, meant that he couldn't make himself understood. But, as Ian told *The Face* in September 1981, "He had two honours
degrees from Oxford, English and History, and I think, a very brainy
geezer, but he said, 'The most difficult thing for me is that nobody knows
what I'm on about.' So that's what the song is."

'Spasticus Autisticus' was released as a single in August 1981. Issued in
both 7 and 12-inch formats, it featured an alternative version of 'Spasticus'
on the B-side, credited to The Seven Seas Players, and came in a white
picture sleeve depicting a childishly drawn plate of fried food. A message
on the back sleeve read: "Spasticus says: My tribe knows no national
boundaries and pays no heed to race or creed. I come among you as an
example sent by my tribe to portray them as they are, as beautifully as I am.
In all my glory my tribe can generate warmth and fear in people from
other tribes: some people would stone my tribe and cast them out: others
foster and nurture we of my tribe. The extreme members of my tribe are
killed at birth. Without the aid of others my tribe can only crawl slowly.
Hallo to you out there in normal land. We too are determined to be free."

As expected, it sank like a stone and was deleted the following month. In
a defiant statement, Polydor said: "Just as nobody bans handicapped people
– just makes it difficult for them to function as normal people – so
'Spasticus Autisticus' was not banned, it was just made impossible to function." The United Nations rejected the song as a contribution to the International Year of the Disabled.

'Spasticus' had been written and recorded by Ian and Chaz in the searing
heat of the Bahamas in the Caribbean. At the suggestion of Island Records
supremo Chris Blackwell, they had flown out to Nassau and teamed up
with the legendary rhythm duo of Sly Dunbar and Robbie Shakespeare
(who were signed to Island) to record Ian's début album for Polydor – *Lord
Upminster*. Since leaving the Blockheads, Chaz had hit the jackpot with 'Ai
No Corrida', a song which featured on his 1980 début album *Chaz Jankel*,
was picked up by Quincy Jones and turned into a worldwide hit. A dance
song with a chorus which guaranteed radio play, it reached number 14 in
the UK in April 1981. Still on a high from his own successes, Chaz agreed
to rejoin Ian on his first solo project and in April 1981 they arrived at

Compass Point Studios. However, they had insufficient material for an album and they spent their time sitting on the beach and beside swimming pools putting the finishing touches to songs, including 'Spasticus', and writing others from scratch. They were forced to work quickly as the album had to be recorded and mixed in just two weeks and as a consequence the songwriting process suffered gravely. Upon its completion, 'Spasticus' would be the only song which Ian could bear to listen to ever again.

Ian said:[14] "We had fun with the musicians. Chaz walked in holding his guitar first day and Steven Stanley, the engineer who was a young Jamaican, went, 'Hello white boy, you play the guitar, ahahaha,' like that, and had Chaz not been able to play the guitar I think we would have been wiped out. But luckily Chaz just went, 'Yeah I do,' very cool. Had we been two soppy little prats from I don't know where, Hounslow, going over there thinking we was Jack the lad, I think we would have got roasted. No I didn't like it. I've never listened to it, to be honest with you. I'll listen to 'Spasticus', I like 'Spasticus'. We finished it too quick, we shouldn't have really even mixed it in . . . but we just whacked it off, it's okay. I don't really regret it, what's the point."

Lord Upminster was released in November 1981, his first album for his new record company Polydor. On the sleeve – framed like an old portrait – Ian was dressed in a ripped white cardigan, flowery shirt, corded trousers and a black and white Panama hat, resting his hand on a chair in a mock Victorian pose. On the other side, Ian, Chaz, Sly and Robbie were photographed in a car lot, with Ian wearing cheap sunglasses and a tee-shirt depicting a cannabis plant and the words 'Weed of Wisdom'. The record contained the following songs: 'Funky Disco Pops', 'Red Letter', 'Girls Watching', 'Wait For Me', 'The Body Song', 'Lonely Town', 'Trust Is A Must' and 'Spasticus Autisticus'. All nine songs were written by Ian and Chaz, with the exception of 'Girls Watching', written by Sly Dunbar.

Lord Upminster was based on the kind of mellow reggae rhythms more commonly associated with artists like Eddy Grant and the sound was relatively uncluttered. The songs lacked the driving momentum of The Blockheads and apart from the obvious exception of 'Spasticus', Ian's vocals were unusually understated. Whereas Norman's thumping bass rhythms, Mickey's keyboard playing and Davey's sax had injected a raw energy into many Blockheads' songs, here the musicians provided a slow measured background, where a more aggressive environment was needed to realise the full potential of the lyrics.

The opening track, 'Funky Disco Pops' arguably came the closest to the tried and tested Dury combination of canny lyrics and dance rhythms ("I want to take you courting/but bopping is the boss/hugging makes you angry/kissing makes you cross/Your only inspiration/is booty of the seat/in this position your disposition/is always very sweet"). Scribbled on a sheet of paper, they were unmistakably Dury, but the music was lacklustre.

In 'The Body Song', he took a simple theme and then wrapped entertaining couplets around a catchy hook line ("The foot which steps with measured tread/receives instructions from your head/It's the body song/It's the body song"). But these trademark lyrics and the sheer impact of 'Spasticus Austisticus' failed to rescue an album which was simply too clean cut and which seemed to have locked Ian in a vocal straitjacket. The album went to number 53 in the UK album chart, but then slid in the opposite direction and into oblivion.

Chaz was also disappointed with the finished album. "These songs did suffer because they were recorded very quickly and what I discovered with Ian, and with myself as well, is that songs need time to mature; you can't just write them and slam them down that quick, they need to be developed. It is only with time that you can see where songs should go, what the weak points are, where the strengths are, and you adjust them accordingly and then record them. 'Spasticus' was the strongest song and it was the only song that we included in our set afterwards. Every single gig I ever did with Ian we did 'Spasticus', it was always in the middle of the set, it was very charged and the audience loved it. It had a very strong rhythmic and vocal pulse to it, but with the other ones, there wasn't enough flesh on the bones and that is why that song has stood the test of time."

Chaz did, however, have one other favourite on *Lord Upminster* although it was destined to remain an obscurity. "There is something about the melancholy of 'Lonely Town'. Sometimes, a lot of people who live in cities are very cut off, desolate, and I thought it was a very honest portrayal. Ian sang it the first day and he was a bit inebriated at the time and something happened whereby we couldn't finish it as a master, but it was beautifully sung. He then re-recorded it and it never quite captured the way it was to start with. I think I was on a beach with him and we had just written the song and I thought, 'This is gorgeous.'"

The Caribbean adventure, although largely a flop, did produce one memorable episode that continued to amuse Ian and Chaz for years afterwards. "While we were there, the band Smokie were mastering their album," says Chaz. "In 'Reasons To Be Cheerful' Ian sang 'Sing-along-a Smokey', and he was actually referring to Smokey Robinson, but they thought he was talking about them. So they came in and said, 'Ian, that's really nice of you to give us a mention' and proceeded to give him a presidential chair in front of the two biggest speakers in Nassau probably, and played him their new album. I discreetly sidled out and made my way to the door. I think they felt really honoured to have Ian there!"

On their return to England, Ian rejoined The Blockheads for a series of gigs. In June, they played a special concert at Hammersmith Odeon to mark the wedding of Prince Charles and Lady Diana Spencer. During August and September, they wowed festival-goers in Castlebar, in the west of Ireland, Gateshead, Edinburgh, Barcelona and Lisbon. On November 17, 1981, the group jetted off for their first ever tour of Australia and New Zealand, where *New Boots And Panties* had been enthusiastically received. The itinerary included Melbourne, Sydney, Brisbane, Adelaide, Perth, Christchurch, Wellington and Auckland, but internal rows about money almost scuppered the entire trip before they got off the ground. In the weeks leading up to the Australian tour, frustration over the cash share out had reached new heights.

"We were offered a terribly small amount of money to go to Australia for three weeks," recalls Mickey. "I found out how much we were being offered and so I did a calculation. I took into account the air fares, a percentage for the agency, the amount left and the number of people there were in the band, and worked out we should be getting at least £7,000 each. I was the spokesman for The Blockheads and I had a meeting with Peter Jenner and Ian, who was pissed at the time. I had also found out that Ian had assumed we would go and had paid £20,000 in air fares, so if we turned it down he was going to be out of pocket by £20,000. So I said, 'Well, we want this' and they said, 'No, there's no way you can have that – £2,000 is what you're being offered. I said, 'No, there's enough money there for £7,000 each and I don't think The Blockheads should go for less than that' and he said, 'We're not giving it to you' and I said, 'Well The Blockheads aren't going, bye.' Ian started saying, 'Where's your song catalogue? and all that bollocks, and I just left the office and I heard Jenner saying, 'You fucking idiot Ian.' Ian had presumed we would go and he had been insulting and they knew somebody was going to have to apologise in order to get a band together and go and do it and it wasn't going to be Ian. It was Peter Jenner who rang up and apologised. So we did go and that was our first coup over Ian."

Wilko Johnson was with the band as they jetted off for the tour. He had to learn the remainder of The Blockheads' material, as well as songs from *Lord Upminster*, such as 'Spasticus' and 'Girls Watching', as he had played only on 'I Want To Be Straight' and *Laughter*. The behind-the-scenes antics of The Blockheads, who had a habit of 'kidnapping' people and bringing them to gigs, appealed to Wilko's own sense of humour. And he found the on-stage high jinks entertaining in equal measure.

"At that time over in Australia we met this character Spartacus, who was a bass player and he kind of hitched onto the tour for a few nights," says Wilko. "He used to stand next to me and we did this kind of running on the spot while we were playing. One night in Canberra we were doing this and there was a bit of a commotion and we looked over and Johnny and Davey are on the ground punching hell out of each other and having this really vicious fight. This has meant that Johnny's lead had pulled his amplifier over so there's equipment on the ground, and then suddenly Charley leapt over his drums to try and separate them and the roadies are coming on. I looked at Spartacus, and Spartacus looked at me, and we shrugged our shoulders and carried on running. It all got all sorted out, everyone was pulled apart, all the equipment got put back up and we continued the show. We were walking off stage and this guy from the Australian support band walked up to me and said, 'Do ya do that every night?' "

On their return from Australia in December 1981, The Blockheads played one London show at The Lyceum Ballroom in The Strand, but Ian was at a low ebb and the future of the group looked bleak. In the following weeks, Ian developed hepatitis and was laid up in bed at his Hammersmith flat. Just months after he signed a new record deal and released his first solo album, he decided to take a year off. Ian Dury & The Blockheads went their separate ways. It was finally over.

For Mickey, Charley, Davey, Johnny and Norman, the break-up left a nasty taste in the mouth. Each had a deep respect for Ian's songwriting, his stage presence and had grown close to him over the four years they had been together. But rows over money had brought discord and resentment. While Ian had negotiated himself a record deal and was investigating other projects, The Blockheads were out on their own.

"We all felt at the time that Chaz and Ian had used us as a runway," says Mickey. "When it all broke up, I remember going to EMI, who we were signed to through Stiff, and we said, 'We're The Blockheads and we'd like to do a few demos,' and they said, 'Who are you?' I said 'I'm Mickey Gallagher, I'm with The Blockheads,' and they said, 'What do you play?' I said, 'Keyboards,' and they said, 'But Chaz Jankel plays keyboards in The Blockheads.' I mean, this was our record company and they weren't interested, so it was very difficult."

Johnny: "After we had the split from Ian we carried on as The Blockheads with just me and Charley singing and we had great instrumentals. Some of them nearly made it to songs. Charley was writing very bizarre lyrics and so was I, and Mickey made a lot of sense out of our lyrics. Davey would also have a go at writing some lyrics and we had this great instrumental which was ever so funny which was called 'Rubber Annie' and was about a blow-up doll. That went out the window, but we resurrected it again and Davey wrote the lyrics and it was called 'Take Out The Lead' which was about pollution. We released one single in Australia, a cover version of 'Twist And Shout' with a huge bass riff and a Moog. We got Laurie Latham to mix it and he did a good job, but it was on a tiny little label and it disappeared. I've still got tapes from when we went to The Who's studios and did tracks there which were quite good. Having worked with Ian, I have this complex that my lyrics are crap, because compared to his they probably are. For my tunes they are probably fine."

At the beginning of 1982, while Ian was ill at home with hepatitis, Blackhill's finances were in equally poor health. By the time Ian had fully recovered later in the year, Ian's management company since 1976 was bankrupt. In the aftermath, Pete Jenner went off to work for Charisma Records and Andrew and fellow Blackhill employee Jenny Cotton continued to represent Ian under their newly formed company Cotton & Carruthers. They would manage Ian and other acts, including Mari Wilson and Doctor & The Medics, before it too would close in around 1992. Blackhill's demise effectively presented Ian with a windfall as it allowed him to buy all his master recordings. His publishing catalogue, which had been held by Blackhill Music, as opposed to Blackhill Enterprises, was sold to Warner which later became Warner/Chappell.

Andrew says of Blackhill's handling of Ian Dury & The Blockheads: "We had a royalty agreement with Ian and The Blockheads which was chaos and took years and years to work out and The Blockheads never really had a proper deal on royalties until about three or four years ago. When we finally got all the master tapes back and we were licensing them out here and there, there was an agreement made between The Blockheads and Ian as to how that income was going to be split. It is all very straightforward and easy now and everyone understands it. That is another reason why everyone finds it so much easier to get on with each other now because there is very little room for lurking feelings of business paranoia. We wanted to be like that in the old days, but partly incompetence and partly living hand to mouth, it was never as open as it should have been. Down the line, that was one of the things which unquestionably contributed to the thing breaking up."

He adds: "All credit to Blackhill, we did succeed by hook or by crook in taking Ian Dury & The Blockheads the distance. We did crack it. Up until the release of *Do It Yourself*, Blackhill hadn't put a foot wrong, I think we did a great job. I won't rewrite history, but I will say for Blackhill that we had avoided making any huge mistakes. We were inventive, but we weren't barmy."

11

THE MUSIC STUDENTS

"There was always a sense of urban London mystique associated with everything Ian did. I remember that during a gig Ian sidled up to me and said, 'Have you met The Strangler yet?' and I looked up at this towering minder. It was always slightly intimidating and of course it was intended to be."

– Merlin Rhys-Jones

Digby Mansions is an elegant mansion block that overlooks the north side of the River Thames at Hammersmith Bridge in west London. The river curves at this point and its upper floors command impressive views towards Fulham in the east and Chiswick in the west. On Sunday afternoons the residents of Hammersmith walk their dogs and children along Lower and Upper Mall, stopping perhaps for a beer in one of the many pubs that line the route. Motor launches and house boats, some as long as 50 foot, are moored along the stretch between the bridge and the famous Dove Inn, and for every pub there is a boat-club from which crews of strapping men and women emerge with their narrow and oddly delicate looking racing boats. On boat race day, when Oxford take on Cambridge, the area is thronged with people but on most weekdays it is a quiet backwater where house prices can today command seven figures.

It was here that Ian Dury chose to invest some of the proceeds of his chart successes. He entered a period of transition as he settled into the flat which would be his home for many years to come, rebuilding his health and working on new material. Now a household name, he found himself in a relative sanctuary and with time to genuinely relax for the first time since he shot to fame.

The Blockheads, meanwhile, had dispersed. Chaz was carving out his own solo career in the US having already been signed by A&M. Mickey was playing keyboards with Eurythmics, the pop sensation which rose from the embers of Seventies band The Tourists, and continued to do session work with The Clash. Davey had retained close links with Stiff Records since the release of *Laughter* and had released his own single 'Saxophone

Man'. The record – which had 'Sax and Drugs and Rock'n'roll' scratched into the matrix – was co-produced by Davey, former Kilburn Charlie Hart and Pete Jenner. Davey also played on Wilko Johnson's solo single on the 'Blockhead' label, 'Oh Lonesome Me', written by Don Gibson, which had the Kilburns' song 'Beauty' (Dury/Hart) on the B-side. Stiff executives had optimistically introduced the 'Blockhead' label as a vehicle for solo releases by musicians from the defunct group, but both these singles flopped and proved to be the only solo Blockheads' missions on Stiff. The label did give Davey Payne the funding for a solo album, however, and in 1983 he flew to New York City with young musicians Michael McEvoy and Adam Kidron and ex-Kilburns' drummer Terry Day to record material. Michael was an American bass player and keyboardist with a talent for arrangements, while Adam had been involved in record production for the Rough Trade label. The four spent time in a studio in New York, but the projected album never materialised, and it was at this time that Davey suggested that Michael get together with Ian. Michael went to see Ian and talked him into making an album with him, but instead of Ian calling on the services of The Blockheads to make another album, they were spurned in favour of aspiring young musicians – The Music Students. The Blockheads were deeply hurt.

"The Blockheads were waiting to work always," says Davey. "I had just got a house with a big mortgage and I needed to work and if we did solo things it was no different to Ian doing solo things, but we wanted him to come back to The Blockheads for The Blockheads stuff. But I think he was advised by Ronnie Harris that he would be better off just using these session guys and copping all the bread for yourself, even though we were there right at the beginning and had helped him get there and had proved to be an important band for him."

Ian and Michael started working on songs together and Ian also got back in touch with former Kilburns' collaborator Russell Hardy, who worked diligently at a keyboard in Ian's flat. But the finished product *4,000 Weeks' Holiday* (a reference to the average person's lifespan) was a disaster and remains an embarrassment for Ian.

Asked about the record, Ian said:[14] "Arrrgh . . . yeah. Wow-wee . . . oh my God. I have never ever actually played it. I can remember it, God. I knew at the time I shouldn't have been there. I don't know what you do when you know you shouldn't be there, but what do you do? I got waylaid into it. I should have said 'no', instead of which I said 'yes'. Projects come along and I sort of wobbled into it, I'm not a planner. It was just after my 40th birthday. Michael came round and I said, 'How old are you mate?' He said, 'I'm 20 man.' I said, 'I'm 40, I'm much too old to do this,' and he said,

'No Ian, you've got to work with the young guys.' So I said, 'Oh, all right,' and gave it a go. I think I'm to be commended for giving it a go but at the same time, I'm a silly prat for doing it. My contribution is fairly limited don't forget, I'm not a musician. I can say 'I don't like that bit,' or I can say 'Change that bit.' But I can't reinvent and I can't replace something I don't like because I'm not a musician. So, if I know something I don't like is happening there is very little I can do about it, except get extremely depressed. The only other thing to do is to bugger off. Now, I don't really think that's the proper thing to do, so I was trying to stick with it and show a little Essex spirit, but I just get depressed and feel like I'm ploughing a furrow with my head."

Rehearsals for *4000 Weeks* began in November 1982, at practice rooms in Hammersmith, just a stone's throw from Ian's flat, and involved all manner of acquaintances, old and new. The backbone of Ian's new backing band was made up of Merlin Rhys-Jones (rhythm guitar), Tag Lamche (drums), Michael McEvoy (bass/keyboards) and Jamie Talbot (sax). In cameo roles, recorded and mixed at Basing Street Studios, Notting Hill, and The Townhouse, were Ed Speight (guitar) and Geoff Castle (Moog), both of whom had played on *New Boots*, Chaz (lead guitar), Ray Cooper (percussion) and trombonist Rico Rodriguez, who had unexpectedly risen to prominence with The Specials during the ska revival. Charley Charles was even drafted in on backing vocals on one track, while former Amen Corner singer and Seventies hit-maker Andy Fairweather-Low was credited on another. Queen were at the recording studio in Notting Hill at the same time, causing Ian to mockingly inform his band one morning: " 'Ere, Queen are all outside calling each other 'My liege' an' that."

Ian lived up to his reputation as an unrelenting party animal and proved that despite having had a break, his insatiable appetite for alcohol and accommodating women had not diminished. During the recording sessions and everywhere he went, he was shadowed by his sinister side-kick The Strangler. Some years later, the drug-addict would die in a cell at Bournemouth Police Station. Merlin observes: "There was always a sense of urban London mystique associated with everything Ian did. I remember that during a gig Ian sidled up to me and said, 'Have you met The Strangler yet?' and I looked up at this towering minder. It was always slightly intimidating and of course it was intended to be. Ian exuded menace in a way that I found quite interesting and quite impressive."

The public unveiling of Ian Dury & The Music Students came in November 1983 when Polydor released a single 'Really Glad You Came' backed with 'You're My Inspiration', songs co-written by Michael McEvoy. The failure of the record to perform commercially did not auger well for the experimental project. It had been two years since *Lord Upminster*, his disastrous début album for the label. 'Spasticus' had been grossly misinterpreted and the release of his second Polydor single coincided with a major disagreement between Ian and label executives. *4000 Weeks' Holiday* had been scheduled for release in the autumn of 1983, but the label's refusal to include 'Fuck Off Noddy' and another song about holiday camp king Billy Butlin had delayed its issue date by several months. Ian had stubbornly insisted that 'Fuck Off Noddy' be kept on the record, but others outside Polydor had warned him of the potential fallout.

Laurie Lewis: "I talked him out of releasing 'Fuck Off Noddy'. It was very funny, but at that time there was a huge scandal about people interfering with children and I said, 'Ian, they will crucify you. It is one thing going out with 'Spasticus', because you have a right to do so, but with all this child pornography thing breaking, they will pillory you for this.' I lent on him harder than I had ever done. I had never really lent heavily on him, because I had never felt strongly enough about anything, but I felt a bit like his dad and I said, 'Don't do it.' To give him his due, he didn't do it."

While Ian's war of words with Polydor rumbled on, he entered a new relationship with a stunning young woman called Belinda who had walked into the dressing room after a Chaz Jankel concert at The Electric Ballroom, Camden, on December 29, 1983, and sat on Ian's lap. Hardly believing his good fortune, Ian was instantly taken with her and the couple embarked on a tumultuous relationship. Musicians who took part on the subsequent *4000 Weeks' Holiday* tour recall lively altercations, reminiscent of Ian's relationship with Denise Roudette. Often their rows ended in violence and on one occasion band members had to rescue her from his hotel room. Bust-ups between the couple in restaurants, bars and other public places were common. When a policewoman arrived at Digby Mansions one night during a particularly nasty fight between Ian and Belinda, Ian told her he was rehearsing a Shakespearean scene with Vanessa Redgrave. Later, he would write a song about the police officer entitled 'PC Honey', which would appear in a later musical project, 'Apples'.

While Ian and Belinda were warring behind the scenes, to the British public Ian became the face of CND, the Campaign for Nuclear Disarmament. On January 1, Ian Dury & The Music Students took part in a CND benefit with U2 at The Apollo Theatre in Victoria. In the same month, the internationally recognised logo of the anti-nuclear campaign appeared on his shaved head on the cover of *4000 Weeks' Holiday*. The picture was also used on the sleeve of his second Music Students single, 'Very Personal'/'Ban The Bomb' and on the 12-inch version, which included an additional track 'The Sky's The Limit'. The group played anonymously at the Hope & Anchor in Islington as 'Wanker & Son' as a warm-up for a national tour and followed it up with a slot on Channel 4's cult music show *The Tube*. The following month, Ian Dury & The Music Students flew to Tel Aviv in Israel for a week's residency at an old cinema called the Koalna Dan. Mickey Gallagher, who had not played on the album, was drafted in for the live shows and Ed Speight, who had played on only three of the recorded tracks, also joined the tour party. For seven consecutive nights (November 21–27) Ian Dury & The Music Students sent Israeli audiences wild, interspersing new songs with old Blockheads favourites.

Merlin recalls: "Those shows were quite an eye-opener because in Israel you get people showing up with machine guns and things to watch the gig, so in the dressing room afterwards there was The Strangler going, 'Give us a go on that mate.' The hosts were very obliging and we used to get these little tickets that entitled us to free cocktails at the end of the gigs called Crowbars, so we would spend all night drinking these Crowbars and getting completely off our faces and then driving around Tel Aviv in taxis."

The ten tracks which made the final cut after Ian's tussle with Polydor were 'You're My Inspiration', 'Friends', 'Tell Your Daddy', 'Peter The Painter', 'Ban The Bomb', 'Percy The Poet', 'Very Personal', 'Take Me To The Cleaners', 'The Man With No Face' and 'Really Glad You Came'. Of these, four resulted from collaborations with Russell Hardy, while Michael McEvoy composed the music for the remaining six.

Ian's former art tutor Peter Blake was delighted with 'Peter The Painter', a funk-driven song which he had asked Ian to write for an art exhibition ("Who's got the toughest brush with the sweetest strokes/At the Royal Academy of Jack-the-lademy/Mr Blake is the actual bloke/At the Royal College of useful knowledge").

Peter said:[14] "I was having an exhibition at The Tate and I wanted to play music in all the rooms and I suddenly thought, I can't ever remember an art exhibition that's had a theme song. Television programmes have a theme song, films have a theme song, so I thought it would be wonderful to have an art exhibition with a song about it."

Ian and the band toured in the UK from the end of February until the beginning of April, and then played at venues around Spain throughout May. When they returned, they embarked on a British summer tour, but although upbeat songs such as 'You're My Inspiration', 'Percy The Poet' and 'Take Me To The Cleaners' were well received by audiences and the album was heavily promoted, sales were poor. Tellingly, not one of these songs survived to feature in future live sets. The album scraped into the UK chart, but reached only number 54, while 'Very Personal' made no impression whatever on the singles chart. Following this second commercial disaster, Ian and Polydor parted company, and Ian was left with huge debts.

Merlin says that *4000 Weeks' Holiday* took Ian in a direction which did not always suit him. "I think Polydor had hoped they were going to get The Blockheads, but for some reason Ian thought it was time to move on to newer pastures and liked the idea of working with young guys," he observes. "He had always been into R&B anyway, so that album did go more in that direction and you can hear from the backing tracks, there was a lot of slap bass going on. In a way, it would have been nice if Mike had taken the time to investigate a bit more of the Gene Vincent angle where Ian was coming from, combined with the music hall element and given it a bit more continuity. I felt that was the weakness of the album, it didn't really have that continuity. I was interested in working with Mike, but then I felt that conflict when we were working together. It should have acknowledged Gene Vincent as an influence, contained a bit of rock'n'roll and a bit of punk, whereas it went a little bit clean and funk oriented.

"Ian seemed perfectly into it at the time, but he gave Mike his head in a way and let him carry on and create backing tracks without really interfering too much with the music. I suspect he probably got more involved musically with Blockheads' stuff and, on reflection, probably regrets that slightly. I think the whole success of The Blockheads had been quite a strain for him and at that time he might have been thinking, 'Well I've got a nice deal, I'm going to have fun with it now and not going to get too stressed out by it,' and consequently, perhaps he feels that the creative input suffered a little bit."

A rare glimpse into Ian's meticulous songwriting methods and his frame of mind during this period in his life was given in a revealing Channel 4 documentary, shot in 1982 during the making of *4000 Weeks' Holiday*. This film had an intimate feel and Ian spoke candidly about his childhood, his disability and his struggle with fame. The camera roamed freely inside the Hammersmith flat he had bought earlier that year, capturing him scribbling lyrics under an Anglepoise lamp, working himself into a sweat on his exercise bike and thrashing about on his drum kit. The one-hour film, directed by Franco Rosso and produced by Laurie Lewis, also included footage of Ian working with Russell Hardy and Michael McEvoy as the music and lyrics for *4000 Weeks' Holiday* came together. In it, Ian came over as a highly creative and conscientious artist, burning the midnight oil and lovingly thumbing dictionaries, thesauri and phrase books in search of the perfect rhyme or word. He was still known to the public for only a handful of songs, but revealed here was a prolific writer, knee-deep in handwritten songs, most of which would never meet his exacting standards. Also laid bare in this intimate film was Ian's long-held fear – that he would ever be mistaken as ordinary. The man for whom art school had represented the "glamour of not being normal", wanted to be seen as a nagging outside influence, an anti-celebrity. At 40 years of age, Ian Dury was happy to enjoy the money and lifestyle, but he was angry at the invasion of his privacy which fame had brought with it. He had been accepted in mainstream British society, but he didn't like it. He was angry.

"When I made *New Boots And Panties* I was a very happy geezer," he said.[15] "Until I was 36, I didn't have any psychological problems that I can think of. I didn't have any hang-ups, I didn't worry about who I was or what I was. I felt like I was a dirty little pig and I was quite happy to be that. Then I stopped being that. I started being required to be a household name – not Des O'Connor, but along those lines. People kept coming up and saying, 'You're a household name you know.' I felt like a piece of Tupperware, I felt like I was being ordinaried, like I'd become plastic."

Later in the documentary, he confided: "Everyone imagines that people like me really want to be popular and really want to be famous. But I don't. I don't like being popular and famous. I like being a lurker, I like being in the shade, I like being naughty. It's very difficult to go and put your fingers up to somebody. Johnny Rotten can do it. He can stick his fingers up when people say hello to him in the street, but I don't like doing that to people. I feel like doing that to people, but I had a hit record, or a couple of hit records, and that removed my right to be rude to people. In fact, it seemed like it was my duty. People come up to you and go, 'Give us an autograph,' and I go, 'Don't be silly,' and they go, 'Give us an autograph, I bought your record,' and you go, 'Oh.' They get very irate because they feel it is your duty to do that, which it is in a way. So I accept that it was my fault. It happens less now and I'm a far happier person because I'm more involved in my work."

Ian's relationships with his managers had always been strained. He invariably tried to dictate situations and his volatile temperament – especially when drunk – made him hard work to be around. In later years, Ian's feelings towards Peter Jenner, for example, would sour considerably, and unlike Andrew King – the other half of Blackhill – Ian had no further contact with him. But in the Channel 4 programme, Ian spoke in glowing terms of the man who had helped him through the most crucial years of his career, and was openly apologetic for some of his own actions.

In confessional mood, Ian said:[15] "You see, to be like me, you've got to be a bit of a selfish loony and not worry about things like night and day and not worry about right and wrong and so on and so forth and one's behaviour does make one ashamed quite often, so I try to keep away from those relationships where somebody's going to suffer because of my behaviour, and Peter is a very nice, very kind man, a very lovely man. I love him to death. We don't always get on too well, because his job is, in a way, to look after my weaknesses. He's managing me, he's managing the things I can't do for myself, that's what a manager is."

Peter Jenner, who went on to manage Billy Bragg and Eddi Reader, displayed a protective attitude towards Ian and said that if Ian had neglected anyone, it was himself. The intense financial and artistic pressures placed on Ian towards the end of his period with Stiff Records had distracted him from spending time writing new songs and taking a well-earned rest, he believed.

"As the records stopped selling as much, it was hard because of the way Ian works, because Ian is very personal," said Peter.[15] "He is not the sort of person who just hires you and fires you, people do see themselves as part of the family and when the family starts going broke it becomes very difficult. I think Ian has been under pressure to do things which have not necessarily been in his best interests, in order to provide the flow of money to keep things going. I think Ian has just gone along with that because he himself has enjoyed having the people in the office, the band, The Blockheads, all that thing going on, all around him and all revolving around him, and that was the thing which was obviously a lot of fun."

His former manager added: "Ian has wound down his operation. I think he found he had very little time to actually do any work because he spent all his time with industrial relations problems. He's very good at it, but the amount of energy and time he put into holding that thing together was time that he didn't have for either being a human being or writing or whatever."

But however much Ian neglected his songwriting during the manic, booze and drug-filled tours with The Blockheads which had drained so much of his energy, he had clearly returned to the drawing board. In the documentary's opening shot, the wispy smoke from a cigarette could be seen in the faint lamp light as Ian poured over a thesaurus, mulling over words out loud. Here, like a poet engrossed in his work, was a man with a scatological mind and a talent for giving language a rhythm all of its own.

Trawling the avenues of alliteration ("I'm sharper than splinter/I'm meaner than minter/I'm cooler than winter/I'm smarter than Pinter" – 'Percy The Poet') or experimenting with simple, but evocative themes ("When Freddy Frost was in my soul/And Tommy Tear was in my eye" – 'Friends'), Ian covered huge sheets of paper with his neat, childlike handwriting. At one point during an interview, he allowed the huge pile of lyrics to fall to the floor. Out of an entire year's worth of ideas, about seven or eight would be recorded, if he was lucky, he confided. Cackles of laughter could be heard from behind the camera, as he pulled out lyrics at random and read them out.

"Sometimes I can get really involved with just writing words. Somebody nicknamed them shopping lists and I think that's a really sweet way of describing them," commented Ian.[15] "I find that's enough, it's just words, each thing means something, it doesn't have to join up. It just goes, 'To be specific/We're terrific/To be precise/You're Awfully Nice/To be Quite Clear/I love you dear/And that's a fact/To be exact' . . . 'Winnie The Pooh/Is having a wank/Oh, what are you up to?/Said Tommy The Tank/Peter the Rabbit/Is at it as well/And all the young pixies/In Dingly Dell/Singing 'Fuck off Noddy/You stupid prat/Fuck off Noddy/In your rotten hat'.' Here's one . . . 'We snorted our cocaine/And we fucked with true disdain/and then we did both of those things again'.

"Here's one called 'The Reporter' [later to be entitled 'Byline Brown']. 'I'm here to find out what makes you tick/I'm here to discover the secret you/I want to reveal/That you're crooked and sick/In such a way that it makes you spew/Because I'm Byline Brown/From the national daily/And this is how I earn my wages/After 14 pints and a bottle of Baileys/I'll spread your guts across the centre pages'." Ian was no fan of the media and this song would later form the basis for one of the characters in his own musical.

He also spoke about Chailey and chose to recite from a book of poetry written by a former Chailey boy who also had polio. In one poem, the author described the hurt he had felt when his parents had left him at the 'special school' and the pain he had noticed in their eyes. The heart-rending poem went on to describe the violence he had experienced: being bullied and beaten up, being spat full in the face by a big crippled boy who jumped out at him, being held down with metal chairs while his legs were stung with stinging nettles. Unused to violence, the poet had found himself in a place where the 'law of the jungle' reigned, and where he had grown accustomed to 'dying'. Ian's narration of the harrowing poem was moving and it clearly stirred up bitter memories of his own, but here he concentrated on the positive, including the fact that the ethos of Chailey was a great social leveller.

"I'm really glad I went there. It sounds very heavy, but in fact it was really good," said Ian. "If you fell over, the law was that nobody was allowed to pick you up, you had to get yourself up, and you would get the occasional turtle, who would be there maybe an hour because nobody was allowed to pick him up. Things like that were very good, it was a very equal place. Disablement cuts across barriers of class and creed quite effectively, but I should think 80 per cent of the children at Chailey were what you would call working class. I think my dad was working class."

Ian's expression hardened when he talked about the grammar school at which he spent five miserable years. Just as he would state in a BBC documentary 17 years later, Ian said he loathed the school because his disability conspired to make him an outsider and where, initially, he was killed with kindness.

"I hated it there. I went to play a gig at Oxford once and someone came up to me and showed me an old school magazine and I opened it up and it said: 'We remember Ian when he was a happy little fellow falling about all over the place.' Well, I was never happy there. I came out of Chailey and went there and people were making my bed for me and things for about three weeks until they realised I could do it myself and I felt like a fish out of water."[15]

In keeping with the confidential feel of the documentary, viewers saw Ian swimming in a hydrotherapy pool. The camera was set up above the pool in order to film him swimming against the strong current – an allegory for his own struggle against attitudes towards disabled people and 'the establishment' he so despised. Ian had happened on the pool in south west London, and its owner, an elderly and forthright lady named Dr Kitt, about two years before. This facility was nothing short of a revolution for Ian, the current helping to build up the strength in his muscles and the private pool offering him a rare freedom. Dr Kitt meanwhile proved inspirational and became a close friend.

Speaking at the pool, Ian said:[15] "She would just stand with her arms folded and her back against the wall watching me swimming against the tide, she was just standing there with a big smile . . . I had been in love before with an old person, but there was a nice sparkle about her, she was really terrific. Such a cheerful person, such a positive, naughty, wicked, terrific person. She said, 'Yeah, I've been an atheist since I was four, I've been a Marxist since I was five' and I would be swimming away, just listening to all this.

"I think people like Dr Kitt don't get lauded and they don't get put up in headlines, but in fact they do more good than all the publicity-seeking under the sun will create. I think she's probably the most totally beautiful person I have ever met and I think it was for about four months that I used to come down here every day. The night before her birthday, she had given me loads of information and there was a party planned for her the next day. We made a record and the B-side ['That's Not All'] was for her and I played all the demos through these speakers. But I never played that song because I wanted to save it for her birthday. Then Horney, our sound

Ian at a Cancer BACUP charity event, January 1999.
(Stewart Mark/Camera Press)

Ian's second wife, Sophy Tilson, pictured with little Albert at Ian's funeral, April 2000.
(Evening Standard)

The horse-drawn carriage takes Ian on his final journey to Golders Green crematorium.
(Evening Standard)

Ian in the garden of his Hampstead home with Billy and Albert. (Rex)

engineer, came round here and he had found out that she had died that night. She died on the eve of her birthday party."

What the documentary succeeded in doing more than most interviews was to capture the sensitive side of Ian's personality and his talent for communicating with people on a very human level. The prickly outer shell which journalists had been presented with over the years was at times absent here and a more vulnerable figure came into view. He had been pilloried for his 'Spasticus Autisticus', but the documentary showed the singer, who helped promote organisations for the disabled, talking with disabled children at Brookfield House School, Woodford, in Essex. He held his young audience spellbound, adopting a humble tone and answering their questions with a bracing honesty. When one boy asked what had given him the idea to become a singer, Ian replied: "Well, I don't really think of myself as a singer, I think of myself as a sort of actor really. I was doing painting and I weren't really good at it and I just got fed up with it. I just wanted to go out and get up on a stage and be flash, so that's what I did. I don't know how I've got away with it for so long really."

But the highlight of this discourse was still to come. The camera suddenly homed in on a young disabled boy who enquired plaintively, 'Ian, do you believe in God?' Perhaps thinking of Dr Kitt as he spoke, Ian replied: 'Do I believe in God?' I believe in good and I think that is probably the same thing."

' But do you believe in God in heaven?" persisted the boy.

' Um . . . I used to. I don't any more, but I probably will again soon," countered Ian.

"Why not?" the boy continued more emphatically.

" 'Cause I think it's here on earth that you've got to get your nut together, basically," explained Ian.

On 'Spasticus' and disability, Ian took the opportunity to crush any illusions that might have existed that he was a crusader or spokesperson for the disabled. Ian had faced a barrage of questions about the record, his motivation for writing it and its message, ever since its release. He was at his most hostile and defensive when talking about the song and while he had been able to come to terms with his own disabilities, he was clearly struggling to rationalise his new found and somewhat burdensome responsibilities as 'a celebrity' and public figure.

Ian said:[15] "There is no way I can go up to a bloke who's got the same disabilities as me and offend him. I felt my job was to put the needle into the person who was disabled who was restricted. I'm half disabled and half not. I'm not severely disabled compared to somebody who can't speak or move, and my compensatory activity is maybe doing rock'n'roll, being

Flash Harry. For somebody who is much more disabled, for me, they need much more distraction, but from within themselves, not from organising or being told it, but from being able to tell, being able to display their own humanity. And I don't have a manifesto about it and I don't have a philosophy about it. I've no philosophy. It's almost as if it's necessary, because it's too much just to keep cracking."

He went on: "I've got a song, it's called 'The Brutal Hiawatha'. It goes, 'Naked, swearing, blind aggression/Learn that first when just a baby/ Teach that fuckin' noisy baby/Hit that kid'. Now, if I made that record, 'Go on whack your kid, go on, do it again, crash', I've done a little bit of research, friends of mine are social workers and the like, there are children in every town in this country put in spin dryers as a common occurrence. If I made a record along those lines, made it very sparkly, very nice to listen to, very easy on the ear, with a message in it saying 'Don't do it', but saying 'Don't do it' in such a way that everyone who heard that lyric felt sick, would that stop it, would that stop even one person doing it? I doubt it, because it's not done in logic, it's not done with thinking. You don't get whacked on the head for a reason, not ever. There is no reason to whack anyone, ever. There is no reason to have a gun in your hand and to threaten someone with it. So how can I be reasonable?"

12

THE COURT JESTER

'Roman Polanski was doing a film called Pirates *and they were looking for the part of a rather peculiar hunchback, odd-looking character. I was speaking to the casting director, and she was saying, 'Oh, I can't find this,' and I said, 'You know who is perfect for this, Ian Dury.'*"

– Pippa Markham

Occupation – Performer. So stated Ian Dury's passport, and throughout his career, that is how he referred to himself. From the moment he stepped onto the stage of High Wycombe Town Hall on the first night of the Stiff Tour, it was clear that he was more an entertainer than a singer. With his brown bowler hat and his plastic toys, his beguiling stage persona owed more to Max Miller or Tommy Cooper than to Gene Vincent or Elvis. It was no surprise then when pop's Vaudevillian figure added acting to his growing curriculum vitae, but few would have predicted the colossal list of credits which he would amass after first treading the boards in 1981. In total, Ian appeared in 16 feature films, four stage plays, numerous television dramas and his very own musical. He also worked alongside some of Britain's finest actors, among them Bob Hoskins, John Hurt, Michael Gambon, Helen Mirren and Hayley Mills. Few of the movies in which he appeared won the sort of critical acclaim which his early records enjoyed – in fact, many of them bombed. But from blink-and-you-missed-it cameos in big-budget films such as *Judge Dredd* to more weighty performances in television projects such as *Skallagrigg* and *King Of The Ghetto*, Ian threw himself wholeheartedly at every task he was handed. His versatility and have-a-go attitude made his a life fully lived.

Ian was in illustrious company indeed for his acting début in 1981 in a charity production of a high-speed *Hamlet*, written by Tom Stoppard. Ian co-starred with Vanessa Redgrave and Derek Jacobi in this 15-minute production and played no less than six parts, including Laertes, the son of The Principal Secretary of State, Polonius. He was keen to learn from the best and when Vanessa Redgrave offered him a lift home after the first read-through, he grabbed the chance with his usual finesse.

"She had a minicab radio in the car and I said, 'You doing a bit of mini-cabbing on the side love, when you're 'resting'?' he recalled in an interview with the *Observer* in 1989.[16] "As we were driving along I said, 'Tell me.' She went, 'What?' I went, 'Ow d'ya do it?' and she went, 'Ow d'ya do what?' I said, 'Ow d'ya do this acting then?' And she didn't answer me. That was my first lesson. I felt a bit of a dingbat. I don't know what I said that for. I think I might have been taking the mickey out of her, actually. I don't know if I was or not. I thought it was quite comical. She might have been laughing inside."

Ian performed in repertory theatre in 1984 in order to learn the ropes and obtain an Actors' Equity card. He appeared as The Devil in Mary O'Malley's play *Talk Of The Devil* at Watford Palace Theatre in what was a valuable learning exercise that would stand him in good stead for the film work that was about to come his way.

"When I was a kid, I wanted to be an actor, and then I met quite a lot of actors and I changed my mind," he said.[1] "So many rock'n'roll people go into the acting game, none of them can act and they get a part that's too big for 'em and they're terrible actors all of 'em. I dunno one, 'part from myself who's quite good, but that's because I learned by doing tiny things and working at Watford Palace Theatre for a month. I sort of enjoy it. A Saturday afternoon when there's 40 people in there and three old ladies eating crisps in the front row. They see Annette Crosby come out and go, 'Oh look, there's Queen Victoria there,' and the top actor goes, 'Tsssk, tsssk,' telling 'em to shut up.

"I remember that we came out into the green room, which is normally called the bar, after the matinee in Watford and Caroline Langrish says, 'Well I'm afraid I rather busked it this afternoon,' and TP McKenna says, 'I have never busked a performance in my life.' I went, 'Oh, you fibber.' Afterwards a bloke in a green velvet suit and a cravat comes up and says, 'My darling, I laughed 'til I cried,' and I went, 'On your bike, you never,' and he was all crestfallen. I like the congratulation aspect of acting. I like how they really do stroke each other's egos and massage the old neck muscles and there's all that old caper going on all the time. I love all that. It's all bollo, but I love it."

Italian director Fellini auditioned him for *The Ship Sails On*, and wasn't impressed, but Ian was to have more luck with British director Les Blair. He offered him his first film role in a production which was set in the same kind of environment in which he would more normally pitch one of his songs. *Number One* followed the fortunes of snooker hustler Harry 'Flash' Gordon – played by Bob Geldof – who is conned into competing in a national championship by his promoter Billy Evans (Mel Smith). When he reaches the grand final, Harry, who is dating a prostitute called Doreen (Alison Steadman), comes under heavy pressure from criminal types to throw the match. The dimly lit, bottom-rung London snooker halls and the story's underworld characters were right up Ian's street. And what better part for the consummate diamond geezer to play?

But the film, released in 1984, flopped and his performance as Teddy Bryant went largely unnoticed. The *Time Out Film Guide* concluded: "When it steers clear of snooker, there's much to enjoy, but any film which lurches from grainy realism to outrageous cartoon with such abandon simply can't be number one."

The previous year Ian had been busy recording and promoting *4000 Weeks' Holiday*, but as this unrewarding spell with Polydor ended acrimoniously, he found himself with more time and energy to devote to acting. A chance conversation between theatrical agent Pippa Markham and a casting director ensured that his flirtation with the world of stage and screen was not a fleeting one.

Pippa explains: "Roman Polanski was doing a film called *Pirates* and they were looking for the part of a rather peculiar hunchback, odd-looking character. I was speaking to the casting director, and she was saying: 'Oh, I can't find this,' and I said, 'You know who is perfect for this, Ian Dury.' She said, 'What a wonderful idea, but how on earth would I get hold of him,' and I said, 'I could probably track him down because I know his manager Andrew King.' I phoned Andrew, who is the most wonderful man in the world, and he said, 'I think he would love it.'"

Pirates was filmed in Tunisia and France and went on general release in 1986. The high seas romp starred Walter Matthau as Captain Thomas Bartholomew Red, a rogue who has his beady eyes on a Spanish galleon filled with Aztec gold. Ian played the part of Meat Hook, a gnarled old hunchback pirate, but sadly much of his contribution ended up on the cutting room floor and audiences would have to have been concentrating hard to glimpse him. In the US, *Pirates* took $1,642,000 at the box office, but it made little impact in Britain. In the same year, Ian played a jester in *Rocinante*, a drama filmed in England by Portuguese directors Eduardo and Ann Guedes. In this, Ian popped up on John Hurt's road journey, emerging in the middle of Dartmoor, spouting poetry and irony, but his jollification and Hurt's usually commanding presence couldn't save this project from sinking into cinematic obscurity.

Ian was also picking up some television work, including a part in the controversial drama *King Of The Ghetto*, acting alongside Tim Roth for the first time. But he was not happy with his own performance. "It should have been an hour and a half long movie, I think that's what's wrong with it," he told Q magazine in 1987.[17] "It just rambles bloody on. It did create quite a bit of aggravation among the Bengalis in the East End, too. Misrepresentation. And I just thought I was a pale imitation of myself which was really quite disappointing."

Ian returned to pop prominence fleetingly in 1985. He had given English producer Paul Hardcastle permission to record a remixed version of 'Hit Me With Your Rhythm Stick'. When the record entered the UK Top 75 in May, 'Nineteen' – Hardcastle's stuttering rap about the Vietnam War – was number one, a position it enjoyed for five weeks. But his treatment of 'Hit Me' (released on Stiff) never even entered the Top 40, stalling at number 55. (A second re-mix of 'Hit Me' released in July 1991 would reach only number 73 in the singles chart.) However, attempts by Mickey Gallagher to get him to record with The Blockheads at this time fell on deaf ears. In August 1986, Mickey started calling regularly to Ian's flat in Hammersmith, discussing ideas for new songs and walking with him in Richmond Park. The keyboard player was keen to bring back the glory days of *New Boots And Panties*, but Ian, embittered over his ill-fated spell with Polydor, did not share his enthusiasm.

"What is it that the record companies want from me?" asked Ian. "They want another 'Hit Me'," replied Mickey. "Exactly" said Ian "and I'm not gonna give it to them". But although he was earning good money from his various acting roles and lucrative television commercials, The Blockheads were not and they needed to keep working.

In September 1986, The Blockheads forged an unlikely alliance with Japanese singer Kiyoshiro Imawano, a fan of the band and of the British punk era who had wanted to record an album containing such influences. The singer, who had shot to fame as a child star, recorded an album in Japanese and then handed The Blockheads an unexpected financial bonus by inviting them to accompany him at shows in Japan which would pay far more money than they had ever earned with Ian. They agreed and went down so well in Japan that they came home and persuaded Ian into doing a one-off tour in June 1987. Reunited, Ian Dury & The Blockheads played gigs in Osaka, Kyoto, Nagoya and Tokyo, and the trip was a huge success, despite an unfortunate episode which took place at Kiyoshiro's home after they had returned from a restaurant.

"Ian was making some remarks to him about 'using my band . . . you wanker', and their English wasn't too good, but we all knew what Ian was saying," recalls Mickey. "I was sitting on the couch with Ian on one side and Davey on the other. Davey was very proud of the fact that he was playing parts with this trumpet player because he is a very free player and

Ian made some snide remark about it, I don't even know what it was. But the next thing I know, Davey has smashed a bottle on the table and lunged across me at Ian and I've caught his hand inches from Ian's face. There's glass all over the floor and because we are in Japan no one's got shoes on and all the women are all jumping around and stroking Davey and massaging him. I just thought, 'That's it . . . that is it.' "

But Mickey needn't have worried about Davey's behaviour offending their host. "Kiyoshiro just went, 'Ah . . . lock and loll man, lock and loll.' He thought it was fucking great." So entranced was the singer with the drama which unfolded that a cartoon depicting Davey's violent outburst was later featured in his fan magazine.

Unlike so many rock'n'rollers, Ian Dury had shown little interest in hard drugs. He had smoked dope since his college days and remained a heavy cannabis user, but those who knew him say Class A drugs were always out of bounds. Booze, however, was a different matter. One source said that Ian's "love affair with alcohol" had put them off drinking. His drunken behaviour often caused incidents as the more drink he consumed, the more cocky and confrontational he became. But the consequences were usually short-lived and his antics are remembered with great fondness by The Blockheads and other friends. One episode, which took place towards the end of the eighties, has gone down in Blockheads' history.

Norman had played bass on a solo album by Who singer Roger Daltrey and as a result, both he and Ian had been invited to appear in a video being filmed in a boxing club in Harrow, west London. Arriving at 9am, they had found the filming process long and boring and had spent their time emptying bottles of champagne down their necks. At about 7pm, during a break from filming, the pair went to an exhibition of Humphrey Ocean's work at the National Portrait Gallery where they bumped into Peter Blake and his wife Chrissie. Peter suggested they meet him later at the highly fashionable restaurant, Le Caprice, near The Ritz Hotel, and after returning to the video shoot in Harrow they went on to the restaurant. By now, they were extremely drunk and Ian was in typically ebullient form.

Norman describes what followed. "We sit at the table and we're having dinner with Peter Blake and his wife. There's all these stars all over the place, and in the corner is Omar Sharif with two minders and a girl. Ian suddenly looks round and he happens to know the girl with Omar, from art school or something, and he's going, 'I'm gonna go over and talk to her.' Peter is trying his hardest to talk him out of it, saying, 'I don't think that's a good idea,' because Peter knows Omar, and we're saying, 'No Ian, you're a bit too drunk.' But Ian goes, 'Naaah, I'm going . . .' and he hobbles over there and I'm watching what's going on.

"Peter's sitting at an angle and doesn't want to look up and watch, so he was asking me, 'What's going on? Is Ian getting angry? Is Omar angry?' and I said, 'No, it's all right at the moment, he's sitting down talking to the girl.' So, Ian sits down next to the girl and starts talking to her and I could see Omar wasn't too happy and then I saw Ian lean over and start talking to Omar. Ian said something, Omar said something, Ian said something back, and the next thing, Omar stands up and he's going bang, bang, bang, and he's really punching fuck out of Ian and there's blood and everything. So I jump up, run over and I grab hold of Omar Sharif from behind and throw him across this settee thing and his two minders jump up and I just go, 'Wow,' and I pick Ian up and carry him back and I say to them, 'Look, I'll just take him away, he's not going to hit you back or anything, that's enough.' Luckily, the minder didn't go for me. So I take Ian back and he's sitting there with blood everywhere and Peter Blake's really angry and Omar and his party start to leave and as they walk past, Peter says to Omar, 'There was no need for the violence at all,' and Omar is all flustered and they walk out. I said to Ian, 'What did you say to him?' and Ian says, 'I leaned over to Omar and said, 'I think the first film you made was your best one, everything else was shit,' and Omar turned round to him and said, 'I don't give a fuck what you think,' and Ian said, 'Well, then you're a cunt.'

"We were going home in the cab and Ian's covered in blood and his lip is all swollen and he says to the cab driver, ''Ere, I just got punched in the teeth by Omar Sharif,' and the cabbie goes, 'Well that's the most expensive fist you'll ever have in your mouth.' What a night!"

Ian was enticed to The Royal Court in London's Sloane Square in 1986 when director Simon Curtis, now a BBC television producer, head-hunted him for the lead role in a new play. Jim Cartwright's *Road*, an earthy tale of working-class life in a Lancashire town, had already enjoyed a successful run in the upstairs auditorium of The Royal Court, after opening on March 22, 1986. In that production, the role of the narrator Scullery had been filled by Edward Tudorpole, the lanky ex-singer with Tenpole Tudor, who had appeared in the movie *The Great Rock'n'Roll Swindle*, Malcolm McLaren's story of The Sex Pistols. His interpretation of the part, which involved lurching around the theatre and talking to members of the audience, had been well received and on June 9 *Road* was transferred to the theatre's main auditorium. When Ian was contacted by Simon Curtis about taking over the same role the following year, his experience of stage acting was still fairly limited.

Ian later claimed he hadn't the faintest idea what Jim Cartwright's play was about, but he agreed to sign up to a role which would have interesting spin-offs, both for his acting career and his personal life. Asked about the play by Q magazine in February 1987,[17] just after it opened with the new-look cast, Ian said: "It's about a road, innit? I dunno . . . When you read something and you see the writer is really in love with Otis Redding and Sam Cooke, well, that put the hat on it for me. I thought it was triffic."

The in-your-face narrator who roams the stage was purpose-made for the garrulous performer, according to the show's producer, Max Stafford-Clark. "*Road* was staged as a promenade production and the narrator, which Ian played, wandered round the stage at the Royal Court, contacting members of the audience en-route and talking to them. Basically, his role linked scenes, and it suited Ian's personality very well. *Road* is often compared to Dylan Thomas's *Under Milk Wood* in the sense that it begins at the beginning of an evening and traces these people as they go through the evening, getting ready to go out, getting drunk, getting home and ends at three or four in the morning. By which time the character that Ian played is the worse for wear, as are most of the characters in the play.

"I think there comes a point, particularly with music, when you have got to try your hand at something else. Music is not a sustaining medium, so Ian tried his hand at being an actor and he was very personable and his personality came through very well. I think he was required to be 'Ian Dury', but just a northern version of it, and he did that extremely well," says Max.

Two of the seven actors who first performed *Road*, Susan Brown and Mossie Smith, had survived into the new-look production, but this time the part of Louise was played by a talented young actress, who was herself from Lancashire. Jane Horrocks was just 22 years old and had attended technical college in Oldham before being accepted for RADA where her extraordinary abilities earned her a Bronze Award. In *Road*, she, like the other cast members, played three separate parts (Louise, Clare and Valerie), although Ian appeared only as the hard-drinking Scullery. Then inexperienced, she impressed reviewers as the play reopened. But it was a spontaneous display by the waif-like actress at a behind-scenes cast party which would truly ignite her career. Jane, to the amazement of company members, got up to do her party piece – impressions of legendary divas whom she had taught herself to mimic from the age of 10 as a way of drawing attention to herself. Moving seamlessly from Marilyn Monroe to Edith Piaf and Judy Garland, she held the party spellbound with her spookily accurate recreations of their singing and speaking voices. It was at this moment that Jim Cartwright, astonished at the ease with which she slipped from her frail Lancashire accent into the deeply seductive tones of Shirley Bassey and other femmes fatales, decided to create a vehicle for her special talent.

The result was *The Rise And Fall Of Little Voice* in which Jane would take the lead role. Seven years later the movie adaptation of his play (also starring Michael Caine and Brenda Blethyn) would make her an international star. However, when *Road* reached the end of its run in 1987, Jane Horrocks was still largely unknown to the public, and an even better kept secret was her newly forged relationship with Ian Dury, who was exactly twice her age. They remained a couple for more than a year and for a time Jane stayed at his Hammersmith flat. But the actress preferred to be discreet about the liaison and little is known about the circumstances surrounding their eventual split.

As far as Blockheads fans were concerned, Ian had packed in his music career and, with the exception of the odd gig and glimpses of the singer in television dramas and Toshiba commercials, he had disappeared from view. But away from the sweaty colleges, music halls and clubs which filled to bursting point whenever he performed, whether or not he was selling a record, he was putting his talents to use in very different mediums. When *Road* ended its run at The Royal Court, another show opened which featured a batch of new songs written by Ian and Mickey Gallagher.

Serious Money by Caryl Churchill opened on March 21, 1987, and was directed by Max Stafford-Clark. The musical poked fun at the greedy Thatcherite era which was then at its height, and was based around the kind of sharply observed, satirical songwriting at which Ian excelled. The cast boasted such names as Gary Oldman (*Sid And Nancy/True Romance*) and Alfred Molina (*Letter To Brezhnev*) and the show was hailed by *Observer* critic Michael Ratcliffe as "a vigorous, aggressive, funny, and much-needed attack on British values" and "an unruly piece, much of it written in a loose, springy, assonant, and semi-rhyming verse". Featuring songs by Ian and Mickey, such as 'Count It Out, Oh Fuck It', the show ran for about a year in the West End, and the music was released on an accompanying album.

Ian didn't perform in *Serious Money*, but the following year he starred in a project which was a creation all of his own. Max Stafford-Clark had suggested that he combine his writing and performance skills in a musical for The Royal Court and Ian, envisaging the proceeds which a long-running hit in London's West End would bring, agreed. His confidence in the theatrical world had grown through his involvement in *Road* and in the light of his contribution to *Serious Money*, it seemed a natural progression. Ian and Mickey had begun working on new songs during afternoons at Ian's Hammersmith flat and now Ian began to use them to shape a story line. Ian also dusted down a couple of songs he had written years earlier with Kilburns' pianist Rod Melvin, 'England's Glory' and 'Apples', and named his musical after the latter. By the time the show was due to go on, they had amassed more than 20 songs and it was around the following songs that Ian drew his plot: 'You Are Here', 'Byline Browne', 'Courtroom Song', 'Sinister Minister's Theme', 'Bus Driver's Prayer', 'Apples', 'Love Is All', 'Still Waters', 'Another Dark Day For Derek', 'Sally', 'Looking For Harry', 'Bit Of Kit', 'Game On', 'The Right People', 'On Top On Top On Top', 'England's Glory', 'All Those Who Say Okay', 'George and Reenie', 'On The Game', 'PC Honey', 'Its You' and 'Riding The Outskirts Of Fantasy'.

The central figure in *Apples*, played by Ian, was Byline Browne, a hard-bitten and heavy-drinking newspaper reporter who represented the worst excesses of the British tabloid press. Dressed in a camel-hair coat and with a large moustache, he was on the trail of the kind of scandal in high places which was regularly making headlines at the time. His quarry, Sir Hugo Sinister, although not inspired by one politician in particular, more than echoed the likes of MPs tainted by sex scandals like John Profumo and Cecil Parkinson. The topicality of the story was also very much in keeping with plays like *Road* and *Serious Money*.

In an interview with the *Guardian*[18] prior to the opening night, Ian stressed that any real life scandal in Margaret Thatcher's cabinet was purely coincidental. "First there was a woman who worked in Harrods who sold stories of her affairs to one of the Sundays, then Pamela Bordes appeared, and then the film *Scandal*. Then Princess Anne's secretary denied opening her briefcase and nicking the letters, and everything I had written seemed to turn up in the papers."

Ian said of his own journalistic monster Byline Browne:[18] "I've never been done over by the press like poor old Boy George or Elton John. I started writing the song called Byline Browne about 12 years ago, long before I'd ever thought of the musical. I wanted him to say out loud what a slimy bastard he was and it developed into my character in the play. He goes through some changes in the show, he's not the same person he was at the beginning. He wants to get a job on the *Independent*, no, it'll have to be the *Correspondent* now, it's got to be."

Ian also seized on *Apples* as an opportunity to release his first album for five years and struck a deal with WEA. A 12-track album was recorded at both Liquidator Studios and the Old Masters Studio in Caledonian Road in the summer of 1988, using Wreckless Eric and members of the former pub rock combo Kokomo on backing vocals. Peter Blake painted a colourful sleeve and his design was later used on posters advertising the musical. In October 1989, the album was issued to coincide with the opening of the show, and 'Apples' was released as a seven-inch single, with 'Byline Browne' on the flip side.

After recording the album, Ian and Mickey began putting a band together for the stage production and in the summer of 1989 rehearsals finally got under way with the other cast members, Bob Goody, Pam Ferris, Jesse Birdsall, Lee Whitlock, Frances Rufelle and Alan David. Meanwhile, a small 'orchestra' was formed which would play during the nightly shows at The Royal Court, consisting of Mickey Gallagher (keyboards), Dean Garcia (bass), Davey Payne (saxophone), Merlin Rhys-Jones (guitar), and Steve White (drums); with Frankie Collins, Dyan Birch and Paddie McHugh on backing vocals. The rehearsals in which the musicians and actors came together forced their alien cultures to unite with sometimes chaotic results.

Mickey recalls: "I had to rehearse the band with all the songs and then we had to get together with the actors. The great day came when we came together with the director and the choreographer flouncing about and we were just cracking up. I've got this rock'n'roll band in and the actors are all milling about and suddenly the director claps and everybody goes quiet. We go through the first number and the actors sing it and we get to the end and the director goes into a huddle with the choreographer and when they turn around the band has disappeared. The drummer has thought, 'Right, I'll ring the girlfriend,' the bass player has gone for a cup of tea. There's nothing's happening, so they're off. That's the rock'n'roll way, but that's not the actors way, so I was going 'Oh dear' and rushing to get everyone back again. It was just two cultures in the same room together colliding."

Apples opened for ten days of previews on October 6, 1989, and then to the public 12 days later. Director Simon Curtis, whom Ian had worked under in *Road*, had high hopes of a long run for Ian's play-writing début, but *Apples* lasted just ten weeks and was given a tough time by the critics. The album, which had broken a five-year silence by Ian, was also panned.

A savage review of the project in Q magazine read: "Unfocused, unfunny and not well sung either by the ageing Dury or his Elaine Paige-y leading lady Frances Rufelle. *Apples* is at best a very pale imitation of The Blockheads' cockney rhyming funk and at worst a gauche attempt to match the sentimental ballady gush out of which West End musicals are commonly made. Dury's loyal sideman Davey Payne tries hard on sax, but Mickey Gallagher's tunes and arrangements are as toothless and lame as the gorblimey lyrics. A hollow panto this, out of which nobody emerges with much credit."

Ian conceded that it was a mistake to construct the plot from a cobbled together collection of songs and was not proud of the outcome. "I think now, looking back, that I should have worked with a playwright, but I didn't, I thought I was a playwright," Ian confessed.[1] "Well, most playwrights have to write about 15 plays before they get one accepted, so what I did was to string a load of songs together and tried to write a story around it, and it was a bit dodgy, let's face it. Although, even though it was well dodgy, as Max said after we got slagged in every single paper, except the *Evening Standard*, 'It could have gone the other way, so don't worry about it. They could have all loved it, there's no telling.' However, I'll never do it again. I might try and write some songs with a playwright, strung around a proper plot."

Mickey comments: "Simon Curtis was a good director but he didn't have any control over Ian at all, whereas Max was quite an authoritative figure who Ian respected. So Ian stepped all over Simon and basically, Ian didn't know what he was talking about. What we did was write a load of songs and at the same time Ian was talking about doing this play at The Royal Court, a social comment on the Eighties, and intellectualising about what he could do. So he looked at the songs and he was trying to make a story up around the songs, instead of writing a story and letting the songs develop out of that. 'Apples' was a very old song and that is where he got the idea from. It is about a barrow boy and a prostitute, whatever . . . I don't even know what it's about, just telephone boxes and songs, and of course it didn't work because it just had no substance."

Max Stafford-Clark was disappointed at the show's brief run and also felt that although the music was good, a weak script had resulted in its downfall. Overall, *Apples* had been an over-ambitious project. "Ian is really a wonderful music hall artist and so he has wonderful scatological songs, lovely inventive rhyme, but also a certain amount of sentimentality and I think in *Apples* he went down that route a bit too much," he says. "It was a bit of a patchwork and the story was always the weakest point. All power to him, he was venturing into something that he wasn't necessarily an expert in. I've no idea what the story was at all, which was probably what the weakness of the whole enterprise was. What we were hoping for was a much longer run and a very big popular success, and we didn't get that. But what we did get was a lot of Ian Dury fans, couples in their forties, who were obviously not really theatre-goers, but were really loyal Dury fans."

Ian had been honest about his début as a playwright, but he had revelled in the experience and by the end of the Eighties, although he would forever be linked with The Blockheads by a significant chunk of the British population, his acting had brought him to the attention of a broader audience. His ego had been suitably flattered by his associations with celebrities and respected actors and directors.

In 1987, in between his various stage commitments, he took part in two movies. *Red Ants* was a children's movie filmed in Greece under the direction of Vassilis Bouduris, in which Ian was the only non-local actor. Set in 1950, Ian played a crippled acrobat who comes to the aid of two teenagers who seek refuge in an abandoned bus after being thrown out of the house by their prostitute mother. Later the same year, Ian appeared in Richard Marquand's rock'n'roll tale *Hearts Of Fire*, starring Bob Dylan as a retired and reclusive rocker and Rupert Everett as a jaded singer. Sadly, it proved to be the last film made by Marquand of *Jagged Edge* and *Return Of The Jedi* fame. He suffered a stroke and died, aged 49, before the film was released. *Hearts Of Fire* was panned by the critics and Ian's performance as a musician named Bones will be remembered by very few.

It did, however, leave Ian with a moment to savour. "When we were making *Hearts Of Fire*, I was in a caravan getting the make-up put on, five o'clock in the morning, thinking, 'Christ, I wish I was in bed for another seven hours'," he said in *Q* magazine in December 1992. "But then in the mirror I caught sight of this bloke who was looking even more haggard and wizened than me, and I thought, 'Christ, who the hell was that?' Then there was a flash of recognition. It was Bob Dylan. Then when I was walking out of the caravan, there he was, so as I passed him, I said, 'All right, geez?' And he looks at me and says, 'Sweet Gene Vincent!' I says, 'The very same,' and we shook hands."

The acting assignments found for Ian by his agent Pippa Markham were certainly varied and included several foreign films. These included *Brennende Betten* (Burning Beds), a German romantic comedy released in 1989, in which Ian played a kettle drummer and 'room mate from hell', called Harry. Gina, played by the director Pia Frankenberg, agrees to share a flat with Harry after splitting up with her boyfriend and makes it clear that she can bed down with whom she pleases but forbids Harry from bringing female company home. The fireworks start when he arrives home with a pretty violin player in tow and his penchant for pyromania causes mayhem and destruction. But scenes of chaos were not confined to the film set, and by the time Ian arrived in Hamburg the following year to take part in *The Voice*, directed by Gustavo Graef-Marine, word of Ian's anti-social behaviour had spread.

Pippa says: "I went over and saw him in Hamburg and he was obviously having a roaringly good time and a year later I suggested him for another film, also in Hamburg, and he said he would be absolutely delighted to do that. Just before he was due to go, I get this frantic phone call from the producers, German and very phlegmatic, and they said, 'Pippa, we have the problem' and I said, 'Oh do you, what?' thinking, 'Oh God, the film's gone down,' and they said, 'Well we can't find a hotel in Hamburg that will take Ian.' So I said, 'Ah, why would that be?' and they said, 'Well, we think it's his Himmler impersonation.' Apparently, the previous year, every time he got slightly the worse for wear, he'd get up on the table in the hotel and impersonate the entire Third Reich. In the end, the film-makers had to find him an apartment, because they couldn't find any hotel that would have him."

It was Ian's subsequent involvement in two movies of much finer quality, both filmed in the UK, which have stood the test of time. *The Raggedy Rawney* was Bob Hoskins' directional début on the big-screen, a warts-and-all tale about a group of Romanies in Eastern Europe during the Second World War. Dexter Fletcher plays a soldier who escapes the blood-letting by disguising himself as a woman and going to ground in the fields. He is found by the gypsies, mistaken for a 'rawney' – a Romany term for a vagabond female fortune-teller – and is taken in. Once in their company, he and the audience are opened up to the strange vagaries of life with the gypsies led by Darky (Hoskins). Here, in the role of Weasel, Ian enjoys a strong profile, although it was clear that the kind of characters film directors saw him playing were generally wily, rough around the edges and living on the margins of society: the same role he had been playing since his teens.

No surprise then when Ian turned up as a low-life gangster in *The Cook, The Thief, His Wife And Her Lover*, directed by his former Walthamstow art college friend Peter Greenaway. The art-house movie was a luscious visual spectacle, steeped in rich colours and stylised costumes and drenched with foul language and London low-life. At its rotting core was a tale of adultery, jealousy and revenge. In the opening scene, a man is stripped naked, force fed excrement and urinated on as Greenaway sets out his grotesque, but compelling stall, and the theme of debasement remains strong throughout as loud-mouthed hoodlum (Michael Gambon) runs amok in the gourmet restaurant he has bought. He ritually humiliates his wife Georgina (Helen Mirren) and terrorises his guests and customers. While she and her clandestine lover cavort in toilet cubicles, kitchens and cold storage rooms, her unlikely husband gorges himself on the finest foods in the company of other nasty pieces of work, such as gangster Terry Fitch (Ian Dury). With a dark beard, his hair worn long in wringlets and dressed in a shiny red boxing style robe, Ian sits at the foot of the table during a dinner hosted by the repulsive restaurant owner who is eager to impress him. The following extract is typical of Greenaway's sordid tale.

Fitch: "Cor, your restaurant's noisy, Speaker."
Speaker: "It's popular on a Sunday night."

Fitch: "I like a quiet restaurant with floor shows."

Speaker: "Cook is a culinary artist, not a fancy entertainer, but we're here to please you Terry, we'll get you a floor show. Cory, phone Santini, five girls, strippers."

Fitch: "Make it decent will ya, my daughter's present."

Speaker: "Five dancing girls with music, strictly no filth, only class."

Fitch: "And make it quiet will ya. I want to keep my ears 'til I'm 90."

Speaker: "God Terry, what sort of floor show do you like? Mute nuns?"

Fitch: "If they called me Mr Fitch I might. I'm only Terry to my wife Speaker."

Speaker: "Like me."

Fitch: "So, you're Terry an' all are ya?"

Speaker: "I'm only Albert to Georgina."

Patricia (a prostitute): "Even when she's in the loo?"

Speaker: "Shut your whore up Cory."

Fitch: "God, you're noisy Speaker. Makes for indigestion, don't ya find love. What's your name?"

Patricia: "Patricia, Mr Fitch."

Fitch: "Are you a good dancer, Patricia? You look as if you might be a good dancer. Now, we'd like to see you get up and dance Patricia, with Geoffrey."

When a guest makes a snide remark about food poisoning, the 'Speaker' invites them to inspect the kitchen and when the prostitute takes up his offer, Fitch opportunistically escorts her away from the table. Once outside the back of the kitchens, he enquires what her boyfriend pays her and offers her some money. In the scene which follows, a look of shock falls on her face as she gropes around in his trousers and the humiliated Fitch becomes abusive, clutching his genitals in pain.

Patricia: [Laughing] "Sorry Mr Fitch, I had a surprise."

Fitch: "What bloody surprises can there possibly be left for you? Cor, I give up, you bitch. I'm sick of jumpy whores. You only get the Fitch one star and that ain't for looks, it's for availability."

Bearskin, Ian's second venture with Eduardo and Ann Guedes, was released in the same year and was also populated by criminals and oddities, including Tom Waits as a Punch & Judy man and Damon Lowry who, on the run from hoodlums, dons a bear-suit. Filmed in both Britain and Portugal, this urban fairytale was just too peculiar to make any impression at the box-office.

While some of Ian's film and television work undoubtedly came to the attention of his fans during the late Eighties, his collusion with the Royal Shakespeare Company in the early Nineties has been less well documented. On the invitation of Max Stafford-Clark, Ian and Mickey put their songwriting talents to a difficult test, composing lyrics and music for some of England's oldest surviving plays. The lyricist who had created his very own bawdy characters from the 20th century was now required to apply his vivid and comic imagination to 17th century England. Mickey Gallagher, meanwhile, set to work studying music he had never heard before as he prepared to recreate the music of the era in which the romantic comedies were set. Put up in a charming, olde-worlde cottage in Stratford-On-Avon, the Seventies rockers turned Shakespearean wordsmith and minstrel and their stay in the bosom of the Royal Shakespeare Company was an immensely pleasurable one.

A Joviall Crew or The Merry Beggar is a romantic comedy written by Richard Brome and was first acted in 1641. Of the 15 plays by the author to survive, it is considered his masterpiece, although it has remained largely unknown compared to other works of the same era. In this tale, the daughters of a kindly and wealthy country squire called Oldrents, and their two lovers, frolic with a group of beggars in order to fulfil a gypsy's prediction, but their panhandling exposes them up to dangers they had not counted on. Meanwhile, the Justice Clack's niece has run off with the Justice's clerk and they also fall into the company of the beggars, giving rise to a humorous search for the party of vagabonds. Stephen Jeffreys' adaptation of the play opened on April 21, 1992, at the Swan Theatre, and was performed by a large cast of young actors, including Emily Watson.

Such was the success of *A Joviall Crew* Ian and Mickey were invited to compose words and music for a Stratford adaptation of William Wycherley's *The Country Wife*. This classic of English literature, first performed in 1672 or 1673, is a debauched affair which seeks to highlight the foolishness of both extreme jealousy and confidence in lovers. The fun begins when Mr Pinchwife comes to London for the wedding of his sister Alithea and brings with him his naive country wife. Unfortunately, his excessive suspicion starts to put ideas into her head. In contrast, the faith displayed by Alithea's husband-to-be results in her leaving him at the last minute for a new lover. The RSC production featuring Ian and Mickey's lyrics and music opened on August 10, 1993.

Max Stafford-Clark directed both productions and was immensely impressed with the dedication and attention to detail which both Ian and Mickey brought to their work for the RSC. "Ian is a wonderful music historian and he has a wonderful ear for other people's music," he says. "*A Joviall Crew* was a play which went on just before the theatres closed down in the English civil war and the guy who wrote it was writing a kind of huge metaphor in that there was this genial autocrat, who is a very benevolent but huge landowner, whose daughters rebel against him, and you can see really that this was as near as a playwright could get at the time to anything even vaguely commenting on Charles I's behaviour. She decides to become a beggar, so there is this Sloane ranger who has suddenly left her estate in Berkshire to hang out with these gypsies. Beggars were perceived a bit like refugees are to us – quite a threat to society – and there were always rumours of beggars running amok in a town. So, it was an Elizabethan obsession and Ian captured that world wonderfully. He used their language and beggars' counting talk and got into it absolutely."

Mickey: "Ian and I wrote the stuff on synthesiser and he did bongos and things. We did tapes of the parts, so I did a violin, keyboard and flute part, and then we got it all transposed by Stratford. Then the day came, just before the rehearsals, you would get the whole band. We wrote for specific instruments and for *A Joviall Crew* it was bongos, an accordion, a fiddle, a flute, all portable instruments, because they were supposed to be a gypsy band. I really got into the period and started listening to Corelli. I had never listened to that sort of music before, but I thought, 'This guy is absolutely amazing.'"

Back in 1985, Ian had written and recorded 'Profoundly In Love With Pandora', the theme for the Thames TV comedy *The Secret Diary Of Adrian Mole Aged 13¾*; the record made it to number 45 in the chart in November of that year. Nine years later, he found himself writing directly with its author, Sue Townsend. The in-demand Dury & Gallagher writing co-operative was invited to collaborate on *The Queen & I: A Play With Songs*, directed by Max Stafford-Clark and performed by his own touring theatre company Out Of Joint. The play opened at The Haymarket Theatre in Leicester.

Here, as in Stratford, Mickey and Ian shared a house as they wrote and recorded the music, but on this occasion they found themselves in a soulless housing estate, surrounded by cement mixers and the disruptive sound of drilling. Aside from being his collaborator, it was also Mickey's task to look after Ian, helping him negotiate stairs or assisting him with other things that his disability made difficult. Ian was a continual source of entertainment and could be relied upon to enliven any party. But while his capacity to communicate with people from all walks of life, from dodgy London underworld figures to Shakespearean directors, was admirable, his propensity for making an unholy show of himself in all kinds of company made for some embarrassing, if hilarious, moments.

One night during the rehearsals in Leicester, Ian became extremely drunk at a party held at Sue Townsend's home and he had to be escorted away under Mickey's supervision as he hurled abuse at her guests. The scenes which followed were a comedy all of their own.

Mickey: "Ian started getting pissed and completely obnoxious and to try and get him out of Sue's at four o'clock in the morning into the car and back to the hotel took an eternity. He stepped out of Sue's house and he was pissing on her garden. Then we got in the car, and by that time I'm really pissed off because he's just spent the night getting pissed and abusing everybody. Then he goes, 'I want a kebab,' and I said, 'I'm going straight back to bed, I'm knackered. There's no way I'm going searching for a kebab at four o'clock in the morning in Leicester for you.' Ian goes, 'You're fucking well sacked.' So I threw him the car keys – he was absolutely langered and leaning against the car – and I said, 'Fair enough, I'm going back to my hotel room.' So I went in and went straight to bed and ignored him. The next thing the porter is ringing me saying, 'There's someone banging on the door and he's screaming for you,' and I said, 'Well actually, he's staying at the hotel and you should let him in,' and he said, 'I'm not letting him in.' So I had to go down and he's banging on the door and pointing at the porter through the glass shouting, 'I'll get you, you . . .' The porter opens the door and I get hold of Ian and start pulling him into the hotel and said, 'Right, behave yourself Ian. Go straight to the lift, up to your room, you're going to bed,' and he goes, 'Urrgghhh.' We get to the lift and I just move slightly aside to press the lift button and he's off along the wall, going for the porter who's hiding behind the counter, and he's whacking the counter with his stick. So the porter rings the police. I get Ian up to his room and then I get into my room, shut the door and think 'Right.'

"Of course, the next thing, he's knocking on the door going, 'Let me in, let me in, the police are coming.' He comes into my room and he's sitting there and I'm in bed. The police come to the door and they can't step into your room otherwise it's trespass and so they're looking in and one of them is saying, 'I used to be a Blockhead fan, but now I've met you,' and Ian is spitting at the policeman going, 'Leave my boyfriend alone,' and I just thought, 'Oh God.' Eventually the police tell him to behave himself and leave and I get rid of Ian into his room. Then I hear the phone ring at seven or eight o'clock in the morning and I just ignore it and I wake up at eleven to find that he's left the hotel. I say 'What's happened to Ian?' and the receptionist says, 'Well, the police came back because he got really obnoxious and was threatening the porter, and they took him to the railway station and put him on a train for London.' So I had to finish the rehearsals for *The Queen & I* on my own, which was quite pleasant, because he'd gone."

13

THAT'S NOT ALL

'The doctor said, 'Is there anyone in this party here who you think might have polio?' and I could see another little person putting their arm up and pointing to Ian. The doctor said, 'Even the white man can be afflicted by polio and it's really important that you bring your children forward.' I turned to Ian and said, 'How do you feel about that?' and he said, 'The most humbling moment of my life,' and tears were just running down his face."

— Jo Bexley of UNICEF

Charley Charles appeared as if by magic in an alleyway beside The Royal Court Theatre just as Ian and Mickey were debating the suitability of the drummer playing in *Apples*. The two looked up in wonder as the former Blockheads drummer came into view and tears welled up in Ian's eyes. "Charley's come to the rescue," he sniffed, as he hugged the Guyana-born musician whom he had last played on stage with some eight years earlier and who was now driving taxis.

Charley accepted Ian's invitation to go inside and watch a performance of his début stage play, but never took up Ian's suggestion that he take over on drums for the show. He had been deeply unhappy about the circumstances surrounding the band's break-up and had instructed lawyers at various times to pursue the money he felt he had been due for his part in the band's success. Charley did not take part in any of Ian's musical projects following the release of *Laughter*, and after attempts by The Blockheads to carry on without Ian came to nothing, he was involved in only a smattering of musical projects. In 1981, he had played on Chaz's solo album *Questionnaire* and joined up with Chaz and Norman again in 1985 on another Chaz project *Looking At You*, playing dates with them in the US and Canada. But by 1989, Charley – still living in London with his Australian-born common-law wife Suzy – had put his rock'n'roll past behind him.

Norman Watt-Roy had also been asked by Ian to take part in *Apples*, but had declined the offer out of loyalty to Charley, with whom he remained in regular contact. "I was thinking, Well, if Charley felt that strongly about things and didn't want to work with Ian until things were sorted out, out of his respect I was saying, 'I'm part of his thing,' and I think it made Ian realise in a little way that he needed people like Charley and me to do things. I think everyone realised that after all these years that we needed each other," he says.

Charley had always hankered after being under the spotlight and was full of off-the-wall ideas for songs. When Ian and The Blockheads went their separate ways, both Charley and Davey had leapt at the chance to write lyrics and tunes of their own and Charley had shared vocals with Johnny.

Johnny: "He was the only drummer I played with who had the confidence to shout 1-2-3-4 at the beginning of a song – Charley was just brimming with confidence in any situation. We met Paul McCartney at Air Studios. We were there with a friend from Apple who was introducing us to Trevor Churchill, who was McCartney's engineer and who we wanted to use on The Blockheads. So we were invited up and there was George Martin and Paul and funnily enough I had just bought a McCartney album and I said, 'I like your album mate,' and he said, 'Oh thanks mate.' And then, when the conversation relaxed, Charley went steaming in straight away and said, 'Paul, do you want to listen to these demos I've got? I've got this idea, it's a bit long and complicated, but I think we can do something.' He really wanted to get his song on a McCartney album and he had no qualms or nerves – he was straight in there with Paul. It was really funny."

When 'Hit Me With Your Rhythm Stick' was climbing the Top 40, it was the filming of the video at Shepperton Studios that put the proudest smile on Charley's face, remembers the film-maker Laurie Lewis. For once, he was not hidden in the background, hunched over his kit, but was under the full glare of the camera. "He was just beside himself with pleasure when I got the band together to talk about the way we were going to shoot the video," says Laurie. "What we were effectively doing was recreating them playing live and Charley said, 'Why don't we just do it live?' and I said, 'Because, you can't put the camera where you want to put it when it really is live. You, for instance. I want to see your hands. How often do you see drummers' hands?' And he looked at me and said, 'You want to see my hands?' and I said 'Yeah.' He was knocked out by that."

Shortly after Charley had turned up unexpectedly at The Royal Court, the news came that he had stomach cancer. The announcement was a terrible shock to the band but did prompt a decision which most believed should have been taken years earlier. It was agreed that Ian Dury & The Blockheads would play three gigs at the Kentish Town & Country Club in north London to lift Charley's spirits and to raise money towards his treatment. The concerts were booked for September 25 to 27, 1990, but Charley did not live to see them. On September 5, just a day after coming out of the Park Royal Hospital in west London, he died from an embolism. He was 45.

In what was almost certainly his last public performance, Norman had played alongside Charley during an encore for Wilko Johnson at a pub in Harrow before he became ill. His friend's death was a terrible blow. "Me and Wilko saw him the night before he died. We had a gig that night and we went and saw him and he was sitting up in bed and we said, 'You're looking great Charley' and he said, 'I'm going to beat this thing.' Then the next morning Suzy rang me and said, 'He's died.' It was horrible."

Johnny recalls: "I was away in Spain when I got the news. Part of my world just went."

The live shows went ahead as benefits for Charley's family and the money had to be divided between his first wife Patsy, from whom he was divorced, his partner Suzy, his son Hughie, and other family members. Meanwhile, the ecstatic audiences which packed the venue for each of the shows to hear The Blockheads prompted the permanent reunion which for years had seemed a distant dream. On December 22, Ian Dury & The Blockheads played Brixton Academy, and the concert was recorded on The Rolling Stones' mobile recording equipment. In Charley's place behind the drum kit was Stephen Monti, a young musician who had first played with Ian during the staging of *Apples* at The Royal Court. He had also featured in the Apple Blossom Orchestra, an ensemble which toured in Japan in February 1990 after Ian's ill-fated musical ended its run after only 10 weeks. Coincidentally, as a child Steve had lived opposite Wilko Johnson's in-laws in Canvey Island at the time when Wilko was playing with The Blockheads. Now he was part of the same group.

"Doing *Apples* was an experience because I had never played in a theatre before and I had never learned 30 numbers without actually having played them with the band," says Steve. "On the first night I smashed the cymbal really loud in the wrong place, but it only happened once. Ian was fantastic because I was dead nervous and he made me feel totally brilliant about it, saying little things like, 'That sounds funky' and that was my introduction." The line-up at the Brixton Academy was completed by Will Parnell on percussion and Merlin Rhys-Jones on rhythm guitar.

The result was *Warts And Audience*, a live album released in August 1991 on Jake Riviera's Demon Records containing the following Blockheads numbers: 'Wake Up And Love With Me', 'Clevor Trever', 'Billericay Dickie', 'Quiet', 'My Old Man', 'Spasticus Autisticus', 'Plaistow Patricia',

'There Ain't Half Been Some Clever Bastards', 'Sweet Gene Vincent', 'What A Waste', 'Hit Me With Your Rhythm Stick' and 'Blockheads'. On the album's back cover, Ian reminisced about how Charley had inadvertently christened the band in one of the first recording demo sessions in the summer of 1977. "When it came to recording Blockheads, he read the words and said, 'Ian, this guy is dressed like me.' This made me realise that all of us are blockheads and I changed the last verse."

Since the dissolution of The Blockheads in 1982 and Ian's sojourn into acting, The Blockheads had found work with a variety of artists. Frankie Goes To Hollywood's 1983 sex anthem 'Relax' was one of the biggest success stories of the Eighties and sparked widespread controversy, but few people realised that Norman Watt-Roy had played the unforgettable bass lines and Mickey and Johnny had also played on the record. The notorious single sold an estimated 13 million copies worldwide and shot the Liverpool band to mega stardom. Effectively, what was packing out dancefloors across the world was in fact 'Holly Johnson & The Blockheads'. Norman also played on Chaz Jankel's early eighties albums *Questionnaire* and *Looking At You* and backed Roger Daltrey on some of his solo material. Even before the Blockheads had disbanded, Norman had played on The Clash's sprawling triple album *Sandinista!* and records by Nick Lowe, Jona Lewie, The Selecter and Rachel Sweet.

Johnny linked up with Paul Young on his mid-eighties album *Secrets Of Association* and toured with the former Q-Tips singer. He also lent his talents to Talk Talk and Londonbeat. Davey, who had also contributed to *Sandinista!*, had gone on to play with The Jets, Howard Jones and Feargal Sharkey before the surprise Blockheads' reunion. Mickey had collaborated extensively with Ian, but had also found time to work with a host of artists including Joe Ely, The Clash, Eurythmics and Roger Daltrey. He also contributed to Gail Ann Dorsey's 1989 album *Corporate World* and Aztec Camera's 1990 release *Stray*. Chaz had recorded a number of solo albums and composed the soundtrack for the 1986 movie *Making Mr Right*, but he had now settled back in London after living in the US.

Charley's sudden death had united them on record for the first time in a decade and Ian Dury & The Blockheads supported the album by going back on the road. Norman had been touring Spain extensively with Wilko Johnson and the promoter there suggested that he take The Blockheads over to do some shows. Chaz flew in from LA and they clambered on to a coach and travelled around Spain, playing all the old favourites. Late one night, when the band were sitting in a tatty back-stage dressing room, Chaz turned to Ian and said pointedly, "Former glories, Ian?" "Fuckin' hell, just a bit, Chaz!" replied Ian.

Buoyed up by the joyous response to their live shows, Ian went straight back to the recording studio to start work on a brand new album, *The Bus Driver's Prayer And Other Stories*. This would not be a Blockheads album, as Norman was not involved and the others did not play on every track. It did however, bring Ian together in a recording studio with Mickey, Davey, Chaz and Johnny, for the first time collectively since *Do It Yourself*, 13 years earlier. Former Music Students, Merlin Rhys-Jones and Michael McEvoy, Ray Cooper, who played percussion on *4000 Weeks' Holiday*, and drummer Steve White also contributed to the sessions which took place in the spring of 1991 at Joe's Garage and also Liquidator Studios.

Some of the material is understood to have been written for *After Midnight* a movie filmed in Dublin, starring Saeed Jaffrey and Hayley Mills, in which Ian played a disabled hotel porter. One of them, 'O Donegal', had been composed by Ian and Mickey before going out to join the filming at the Killiney Castle Hotel on the south Dublin coast.

"Ian and I discovered that both our families were from Donegal, mine from Killybegs and Ian's from Rathmullen," says Mickey. "Ian was Protestant Donegal and I was Catholic Donegal, so we wrote a song . . . "Fresh mist on the morning and tears in my eye" . . . two English blokes writing about Donegal."

Merlin Rhys-Jones had also worked on the song for the film and Ian had invited him to produce a couple of tracks. He agreed, got in touch with Jamestown Studios in Whitechapel, and arranged to do some demos with Ian. But his production début had to be abandoned amid chaotic scenes.

Merlin: "Ian got a bit pissed and also pissed off with the studio, partly because he had to get upstairs to go to the control room and he doesn't like stairs. I had been out to get a couple of beers and when I got back, Ian was threatening to burn the studio down. 'I'm gonna torch the gaff,' he was going and I was saying 'Relax Ian, it's not worked out, so we'll go home.' I was trying to keep the peace, but before I knew it the engineer had called the police. Ian goes into these things partly as a kind of boredom thing – he's into a bit of drama, a bit of excitement. So the police come and Ian's calling them all homosexuals, but they know who he is anyway. For a while they're finding it quite amusing, but they get a bit bored and say, 'Look, unless you leave, we're going to have to take you down the nick.' So, Ian carries on calling them homosexuals and they go and get the van, lift him up and plonk him on the pavement outside. He's sitting on the pavement trying to eat the rest of his stash because he doesn't want to get nicked for possession and they bung him in the back of a police van, bring him down to the nick, take his shoe-laces and go through all the usual procedure. Ian is off his face because he is pissed and he's eaten his stash as well and Baxter had to come down and bail him out."

The Bus Driver's Prayer And Other Stories, released on Demon Records in 1992, came closer to hitting the target than any of his post-Blockheads albums. As the song titles imply, it was filled with humour and had a keen eye for the absurd. The 14 songs were 'That's Enough Of That', 'Bill Haley's Last Words', 'Poor Joey', 'Quick Quick Slow', 'Fly In The Ointment', 'O Donegal', 'Poo-Poo In The Prawn', 'Have A Word', 'London Talking', 'D'Orine The Cow', 'Your Horoscope', 'No Such Thing As Love', 'Two Old Dogs Without A Name' and 'The Bus Driver's Prayer'.

The sleeve displayed the words of the title track which was spoken by Ian. "Our father, who art in Hendon, Harrow Road be thy name, thy Kingston come, they Wimbledon in Erith as it is in Hendon. Give us this day our Berkhampstead and forgive us our Westminsters, as we forgive those that Westminster against us. Lead us not into Temple Station and deliver us from Ealing, for thine is the Kingston, the Purley and the Crawley, for Irer and Iver, Crouch End."

Unlike his Eighties offerings, this record was bulging with clever ideas, uplifting jazz music and the kind of humour for which the public loved him. Music critics greeted him like a long lost friend and pointed to a return to form.

" 'I took a sudden notion/To go down to the ocean'," Ian Dury imparts in 'Poo-Poo In The Prawn'. When he gets there, however, the vista is of pollution from sand to sunset: 'Some turds were teeny-tiny/And some were big and shiny/But they all fucked up the briney/In which I dipped my toe'. "Such coarseness, such elegance, such rhyming crimes. Seems like old times. And so it proves," enthused Q magazine's Phil Sutcliffe in January 1993. "A dozen years on from his last good album, *Laughter*, and after a period of discouragement and off-hand execution, when only 'Hello Tosh, got a Toshiba?' stood between him and the workhouse, this is true Dury, untrammelled and unmitigated." Welcoming the range of musical influences, the crafty lyrics and the bizarre subject matter – a budgie in 'Poor Joey' and the abattoir-bound 'D'Orine The Cow', Sutcliffe saluted *The Bus Driver's Prayer* with four stars out of five: "A quip, a laugh, a kick in the bollocks: this is exactly the kind of hard entertainment he's always striven for," he concluded.

In *Vox* in March 1993, Patrick Humphries held up a score of six out of 10: " 'O Donegal' and 'Poo-Poo In The Prawn' are Dury by the yard, and while 'Bill Haley's Last Words' in no way stacks up against the triumph and tragedy of 'Sweet Gene Vincent' it at least tries. Good to see many Blockheads back behind Ian. More *4000 Weeks Holiday* than *Do It Yourself*, *The*

Bus Driver's Prayer suggests the '90s will be kinder to one of the great talents of the '70s."

On a personal level, this prediction was to prove tragically wrong. In October 1994, Ian's first wife Betty died of cancer aged 52. She had returned to her Welsh roots some years before with her second husband Clive Richards and had a share in a picture framing business and gallery with her close friend Janet Martin. She had remained close to Ian, regularly visiting him in London, and her death at such a young age was a devastating blow to all her family.

After their separation in the early Seventies, Betty and the children had moved from the vicarage at Wingrave to a house in nearby Aylesbury. But when Ian found success, he bought them a more comfortable cottage in the Buckinghamshire village of Tring, where Jemima attended a dancing school. They later moved to Chiswick when Ian again helped them to buy a new house, and in 1985 Betty and Ian divorced and she remarried.

Betty's paintings, like Ian's college creations, were precise and dominated by people. During her life, she had exhibited at the Royal Academy, The Royal College of Art, The West of England Academy and some of her paintings are still displayed in the Newport Museum. Betty was also very active as an artist in her native country and had been a member of the Watercolour Society of Wales, The Welsh Group and The Association of Visual Artists in Wales. During the latter years of her life, she became enchanted by Malta, especially attracted by the light which she exploited in 15 or so paintings of the islands. She had first been to Malta when she accompanied her artistic parents, Thomas and Lilian, on a vacation in Gozo and returned in 1989, at the suggestion of a local acquaintance Nicholas De Piro and stayed with Baxter in a flat in Sliema. In 1993, she went there for the last time with her husband and her mother, who painted the final picture of her there. In a Maltese newspaper article published soon after her death, Mr De Piro wrote of Betty: "Her style was meticulous, however, when speaking to her, and then examining her pictures, one soon realised that she was broad of mind and, at the same time, a rather relaxed and self-deprecating perfectionist." He went on: "In dealing with nature in a landscape, she was as able with the botanical side of things as she was with the human form and with architecture. There was no flattery. Her portraits were not 'popular', but they were great."

Acting roles continued to come Ian's way throughout the Nineties, albeit in low-profile movies and television dramas. The sheer number of appearances would probably amaze most people as his contribution to the majority of these projects was minimal. He tended to be killed off before most audiences would have realised who he was and only sharp-eyed film-goers would have spotted him in the big-budget US movies in which he was invited to appear. *Split Second*, an action film in which a detective, played by Rutger Hauer, is on the trail of a creature terrorising the streets of London, could have been named after Ian's appearance. The film, directed by Tony Maylam, was released in 1992 but was not well received. Ian cropped up again in an early scene in the Sylvester Stallone sci-fi adventure *Judge Dredd*, based on the comic strip character. He played Geiger, the owner of a small arms shop in the futuristic city policed by Judges – law-enforcers who act as judge, jury and executioner. He agrees to unlock his store when a villain named Rico (Armand Assante) comes calling, but within five minutes he is dead and his killer leaves, prising a cigar butt from between his victim's fingers on his way out.

Ian travelled to the US in the autumn of 1995 to film his scenes for *The Crow: City Of Angels*, a Gothic thriller starring Vincent Perez, Mia Hershner and the singer Iggy Pop. Ian was rather more prominent here as Noah, a tattooist working with a young psychic woman who is commandeered to help track down a marauding killer. But again his involvement was cut short in a violent scene in which he was tortured with his own tattooing needle.

Ian's television roles were more significant, however, and a 1994 BBC drama directed by Richard Spence dealt with a subject close to his heart. *Skallagrigg* took its name from the mythical protector of disabled people for whom a teenage girl suffering from cerebral palsy was searching. The 87-minute drama provided a glimpse of the abuse disabled people can suffer in residential homes, a subject which tragically remains topical. Ian appeared as Rendell, a residential home employee, acting alongside such established British performers as Richard Briers, Bernard Hill and Billie Whitelaw. As well as appearing in a number of television dramas, he was also chosen to present programmes during his career, including the BBC series *Talent Is No Handicap* and ITV's arts show *Metro*.

In 1995, Ian was awarded the lead role in a modern adaptation of Thomas Middleton's novel *The Changeling*, filmed largely on location in Spain. The budget for Marcus Thompson's period drama is understood to have been non-existent and those who agreed to take part did so without wages. Sadly, it sank without trace and few ever got to see Ian giving it his all as De Flores, a facially scarred opportunist who schemes his way into the heroine's bed. Ian's former art college friend Vivian Stanshall was also due to take part in the film and he did film some scenes. However, it was during filming that the fire broke out at his north London flat, in which he died. The scenes Vivian had already recorded were removed from the final cut.

"I was spiritually blackmailed into doing this film. If you like the director, you do it for nish, so Marcus Thompson got us all to do it for nothing. I kept saying, 'Get Bob Hoskins, then you'll get some funding,'" Ian told the *Independent* in an interview published in March 1998.

During the filming of the sequel to *The Crow*, Ian's digestive system started playing up, and at first he put it down to jet lag. But when he got back to London he read about Irritable Bowel Syndrome, recognised some of his symptoms and decided to have an exploratory colonoscopy. The result was not what he had hoped for, however, and it was then – at the age of 53 – that Ian was told he had cancer. An operation was immediately carried out to remove the tumour and after treatment he continued to have six-monthly hospital check-ups. For a time, Ian went into remission and the signs looked hopeful.

At the beginning of 1997, officials at UNICEF (The United Nations Children's Fund) were considering how to increase the profile of its campaign to eradicate polio around the world. Its mission to kill off polio by the millennium had been launched in 1977 in conjunction with the World Health Organisation and it had begun by staging National Immunisation Days in the worst affected countries. In the eighties, UNICEF negotiated one-day cease-fires in order to allow children in war-torn areas to receive the vaccine. The results were impressive.

Immunisation in El Salvador rose from three per cent in 1985 to 80 per cent in 1992, while in Sri Lanka, no cases of polio were recorded in the four years since the programme had been introduced there. But as the scheme neared its target date of 2000, senior figures at the charitable organisation needed to maximise publicity for the campaign. When press officer Jo Bexley was asked for famous 'polio people', one name sprang to mind. Without stopping to clear it with her bosses, Jo dashed off a letter to Ian Dury, telling him all about UNICEF's polio programme. Her expectations of a positive response were low. She was aware of Ian's stance on the International Year of the Disabled and had read about how he had filed away dozens of requests from charities and other organisations in his 'polio folio'. She was also unsure of what, precisely, she was actually asking him to do.

A week after posting her impromptu letter, Jo received a phone call from Ian's partner, Sophy, asking what role Ian would play in the programme. Jo, thinking on her feet, suggested that he travel to Africa to witness immunisation days first hand. Within days, Ian and his minder Derek Hussey were at UNICEF's London offices for a meeting with its then British executive director Robert Smith. It was emphasised to Ian that UNICEF was about looking after children and that it was determined to commit polio to the history books, but it was a far more personal connection with the charity that sealed it for Ian. During his time as a chauffeur, Ian's late father had once driven the actor Danny Kaye, of whom Ian was a big fan, and Kaye had also been UNICEF's first goodwill ambassador. Ian agreed to lend his weight to its campaign and in the summer of 1997 he boarded a plane to Zambia, where children lived in severe poverty and were particularly susceptible to disease.

UNICEF's now world famous National Immunisation Days – in which every child under the age of five is immunised in one or two days – prompted an incredible response in the countries in which they are held. Ian was treated like a king at the launch of the programme in a Zambian town, where loud speakers blared out the importance of parents bringing their little ones forward, and was feted by marching bands and clusters of local dignitaries. That night he was shown on Zambian national news delivering the first drop of the vaccine which had come too late to protect him when he was a child. During the expedition, two million children received the vaccine and Ian was overcome by what he saw. On occasions, he could not hold back tears.

Jo describes one poignant moment from the trip: "We were standing in a clearing in the bush at about 6 o'clock in the morning and there was literally just a nurse standing under a tree with a table and an ice-box on top of it with these polio vaccines inside. We gradually saw people emerging out through the bush, like a guy with a kid on a bath, strapped to the back of his bicycle, and women who had walked for three hours to get to this particular point. Ian was standing there, absolutely amazed at these people who had got up at dawn to bring forward their children, and before we knew it, there was a whole crowd of people lining up for their vaccine, all totally quiet, you could hear a pin drop. The doctor was asked to ask people why they had come along that day. Some of them gingerly put their hands up and said, 'Polio.' Then the doctor said, 'What does polio mean?' and one said, 'It's when your child goes lame.' Then the doctor said, 'Is there anyone in this party here who you think might have polio?' and I could see another little person putting their arm up and pointing to Ian. The doctor said, 'Even the white man can be afflicted by polio and it's really important that you bring your children forward.' I turned to Ian and said, 'How do you feel about that?' and he said, 'The most humbling moment of my life,' and tears were just running down his face. He was just really touched by it."

Jo was very impressed with Ian's work during this trip, adding: "It was a really momentous trip and to watch him and be with him. He learned very quickly and was a true ambassador for us. We were meeting dignitaries and

Ian looked unconventional, yet he was doing what he had to do, always asking the right questions, always very open, honest and humble, which is quite a rare commodity in a lot of celebrities."

The trip would revive unhappy memories for Ian. On one occasion, the party arrived at a school for severely disabled children run by nuns to be greeted by youngsters wearing pristine uniforms. The visiting group was shown around its sanitised facilities before being escorted into a large hall where about 100 children gave them a resounding round of applause. They were then treated to a performance by some of the disabled children that made Ian feel extremely uneasy.

Jo: "We were lined up on this sort of top table and I was sitting next to Ian and his knuckles were white and he was absolutely hating every minute of it. They were getting up and doing this sort of dance and it was like a freak show, there is no other way to describe it. Ian was saying, 'This is awful,' and hating the nuns because it brought back all those horrible memories, but I was saying to him, 'Just put on a brave face, we'll be out of here soon,' and he is a bloody intelligent man and completely understands that things are different in Africa. We gritted our teeth and bore it and we all had to say something and true to form, Ian just came out with the right words and we all thanked them for their little show.

"Afterwards, we had the chance to go around and meet these kids and they were all very bright, training to be doctors and lawyers and wanting to change the face of disability in Zambia. Seeing those kids as individuals afterwards really helped him get through some of that anger because he realised they were happy there. Academically, these children were doing really well and if you compared them with most disabled people in Zambia who were on the scrap heap, forgotten about and left to rot in the back of their small houses or whatever, these kids were being given a chance. That was lovely and Ian got mobbed again by the kids there, but that did bring up a lot of discussion about the best way of doing things and I think Ian does store a lot of anger about how he was treated."

In an article in *The Times* magazine in October 1998,[19] Ian spoke about the effect which his encounter with severe poverty and AIDS orphans had on him.

"One moment I was hugging as many children as possible, then I'd be rushing around the corner crying my eyes out. I returned extremely emotionally involved with UNICEF. I think it made me stronger and even more intelligent. And I'm extremely intelligent."

UNICEF was delighted with Ian's contribution to the trip and the following year he was invited to take part in a more dangerous expedition – two 'Days of Tranquillity' in war-ravaged Sri Lanka. The project was planned to take place in the Tamil-dominated northern peninsular of Jaffna, but just days before the party was due to leave London, a bomb exploded there killing several people, including the mayor. UN officials diverted them to the impoverished northerly region of Vavuniya. This time, however, Ian Dury was not the only celebrity on the trip. Ian had contacted former Take That pin-up Robbie Williams, whom he had met at a photo-call for Music For UNICEF, and unbeknown to the charity, he had agreed to come along. Robbie was a huge fan of Ian's and between them, the ageing rocker and teen idol packed a great publicity punch for the children's charity.

In September 1998, they set off to tour the refugee camps of poverty-stricken Sri Lanka and brought vaccination to hundreds of thousands of children. Incredibly, both the Tamil Tiger rebels – fighting for an independent homeland for minority Tamils – and government troops both agreed to lay down their weapons for two days, while the immunisation programme took place.

Robbie's involvement diverted some of the media attention away from Ian and he provoked squeals of delight from children as he played football with them and entertained them as the group toured schools, camps and clinics in the region. Ian, accompanied as ever by Derek The Draw, also threw himself into it, laughing and joking with the children they met.

The trip was emotionally draining and it was to leave an indelible impression on both Ian and Robbie. At a school where some girls were receiving a singing lesson, Robbie closed his eyes and started singing his hit 'Angels'. Afterwards, they went on to a camp housing refugees who had fled their homes in Jaffna for India only to return and find them demolished. Here, the excitement over their visiting celebrities reached new heights as the children mobbed Robbie. Later that night he said in an interview for *The Times* magazine: "What happened today has put my life into perspective. Here, I'm just some white bloke making funny faces. I'm not this Robbie Williams character who I have to be 24 hours a day in England. So much of my life in England has to do with money. I feel so much more serene and relaxed here. Being with those kids made me want to have my own so much. Oh, so much! I feel I've been and done some good and I've done some good for myself, too. Certainly, I'll never forget those children's smiling faces."

Ian's contribution to UNICEF's work earned him the title of Special Representative, the highest award the UK committee for the children's charity can bestow on its celebrity supporters. Ian proudly received the accolade, along with veteran war reporter Lord (Bill) Deedes at the UNICEF annual lecture at the Royal Society of Arts given by Vanessa Redgrave, herself a Special Representative, in November 1998. Marie

Staunton, deputy executive director of UNICEF, told those present: "Every parent, politician, journalist and celebrity in the UK will say that children are important. But Lord Deedes and Ian Dury have travelled to some of the most troubled regions of the globe to make the world listen to the needs of children. We are certain that Ian Dury and Lord Deedes will make children's voices loudly heard within these industries."

Since Ian Dury & The Blockheads got back from Australia at the beginning of 1982, Ian's failure to record another album with The Blockheads had caused friction within the band. Ian's acting commitments throughout the eighties had been a distraction and the income generated by his various projects had dispensed with his need to tour or record with his band. Members of The Blockheads maintain that they were always ready to reform the group, but with the exception of the odd appearance at rock festivals, benefits, and the tours of Japan and Spain, they had rarely played with him. Mickey and Davey had contributed to *4000 Weeks' Holiday* and only Norman had been absent from *The Bus Driver's Prayer* sessions, but the poor performance of these records had merely demonstrated that Ian only hit real form when complemented by The Blockheads as a whole. Similarly, The Blockheads as musicians had the biggest impact when they combined with Ian. Whether or not they cared to admit it, they needed him and he needed them.

The demand for tickets to see Ian Dury & The Blockheads even years after their split in 1981 confirmed a cult support, not just in the UK, but overseas as well. They often topped the bill over major groups and artists such as UB40 and Toots & The Maytals despite not having a record to promote and going for years without a hit. But in the mid to late Eighties and early Nineties, The Blockheads would have welcomed a lot more of these shows.

Davey Payne: "Acting got in the way and it went to Ian's head. He got easy money for acting and advertising Toshiba – £14,000 for a day's work – and The Blockheads never saw anything like that at all. I remember him saying that we couldn't do any gigs one Christmas because he was going to be in *Alien 3* – the alien I think, leaping out of someone's chest or something. Then he phoned me on New Year's Eve crying and lonely and saying, 'Ah Davey, we're the best fucking band in the world man, this year we're going to really do it.' He said to me, 'By the way, I've just been to Andrew King's and I've been sacked from *Alien 3*.' I would never have heard from him otherwise. He'd have been up there with the stars.

"Often we were offered stuff that he couldn't do, but that would have made loads of money for The Blockheads. We were offered two nights with Led Zeppelin at Knebworth for about £200,000 – about £15,000 each – and Madison Square Garden with Jethro Tull and he turned that down as well. They were chances for the band to all make a little bit of bread and he wouldn't do it."

In 1997, Ian Dury & The Blockheads began playing live together on a regular basis and they were invited to appear at the Roskilde Festival in Denmark. But they were growing tired of playing the same material and the old Blockheads' spark was fizzling out. Even Ian, who has given his all in just about every gig he has ever played, was off-form.

"When we were playing, Supergrass were in one 3,000-seater tent and Isaac Hayes was in another," says Davey. "All we had when we went on stage was about 5,000 people in front of us in a 50,000 area. I don't think that Ian knew about the liver cancer then, but he was probably feeling something was wrong with him, and he didn't make any effort. He just went on with his checked shirt and his walking stick and we were plough-ing away, doing the business, but it just wasn't happening for him. It was partly because of looking at the audience, although those who were there were into it, and I thought he was going to cry and walk off. He has never done that and that is the only time I have ever seen him like that. Like he didn't want to do it."

But just as things appeared to be going stale, new material began to emerge and these were songs that would comfortably sit alongside the clas-sics from *New Boots And Panties*. A year later they would form the basis for the record which Ian's fans had waited so long to hear – *Mr Love Pants*. What his fans didn't know, however, was that the album had in fact taken five years to complete.

Ian had sought seclusion and begun working on new songs at Straw-berry Acre Farm in Twyford, near Reading, Berkshire, in 1993. Chaz had returned to London having spent the latter part of the Eighties living in the United States, and he agreed to spend a few months with Ian at his new retreat. It was an idyllic spot. The house had its own grounds and swim-ming pool, and was situated near a nature reserve. In all, Ian would stay in the property for about a year, writing and jamming with Chaz. Ian was brimming over with ideas and he would hand Chaz his familiar A3 sheets of lyrics as he completed them. One of these songs was 'Itinerant Child', a pop shot at the police treatment of gypsies and other travelling families, and an affectionate tribute to their roving society symbolised by a run-down van, just like their own doomed maroon banger from 1973 ("It's a psychedelic nightmare with a million leaks/It's home sweet home to some sweet arse freaks"). But this agreeable state of affairs soon disinte-grated and an enraged Chaz stormed off to London.

"It was a memorable time really," says Chaz. "I remember one night, Ian got in a big argument with Ian Horne and there was a real air of discontent in the garden, so I walked inside and started playing the piano and that gave us the backbone for 'Bed 'O' Roses No 9'. He then wrote a lyric to that music. Every now and again it would happen like that."

Ian, finding himself deserted, called up Merlin Rhys-Jones and invited him down to the farm, suggesting he bring his four-track with him. Merlin initially helped to mix some of the songs which Ian and Chaz had already completed, but he then started composing music for other lyrics Ian had amassed. Two of the ten songs which Ian and Merlin wrote over a period of months, would survive to appear on the ten-track album. These songs, 'Jack Shit George' and 'Cacka Boom', would be two of the most critically acclaimed songs of all.

Merlin: "I was very struck by the lyrics. Ian had really got back into the idea of being a writer at that point. He had written a few lyrics already and had honed them down and chopped bits out, so there was a backlog of stuff which he had on these big sheets of paper he writes on. More time was spent on them, although with 'Cacka Boom' he came in and said, 'Here's a lyric, Merl. Get a groove together for that, I'll be back in half an hour, I've just got to go and finish it.' What I liked about that one was that it was more throwaway and sounded a bit more like 'Rhythm Stick' to me. Ian has two sides to him. When he is doing a throwaway thing, he injects a particular kind of humour which isn't always there on the more serious laboured lyrics, so I felt that had a particular lightness about it which I really liked."

Recording of the album finally got under way almost three years later and Air Studios in London was the venue for the long-awaited Blockheads reunion. The place of the late Charley Charles was taken by Steve Monti, a young drummer whose uneasy relationship with Ian resulted in some tension during the sessions that followed. Davey Payne, by now living in Falmouth, Cornwall, was involved throughout, although he would be excommunicated shortly after the album's release after lunging at one of Mickey Gallagher's sons during a concert with Paul Weller and Finlay Quaye at Victoria Park, east London. The band had spent about 10 days in Chaz's studio rehearsing the songs, before recording the album over a week at Air Studios, where veteran Blockheads engineer Laurie Latham completed the mixing in March 1997. Ian had meanwhile recorded some of the vocal parts on his home digital recording kit. *Mr Love Pants* was finally released on June 28, 1998, on Ian's own label, Ronnie Harris Records [the name of his accountant], and contained 10 classic new songs: 'Jack Shit George', 'The Passing Show', 'You're My Baby', 'Honeysuckle Highway',

'Itinerant Child', 'Geraldine', 'Cacka Boom', 'Bed 'O' Roses No. 9', 'Heavy Living' and 'Mash It Up Harry'. The sleeve, designed by Storm Thorgerson of Hipgnosis, best known for their work with Pink Floyd, showed a boxer dog wearing colourful boxer shorts on a beach. The band photos on the inner sleeve were taken by Ian and credited to Duncan Poundcake, the pseudonym he used as a photographer.

Among those featured in the photographs on the inner sleeve of *Mr Love Pants* was the one-time Irish crooner Ronnie Carroll, whose hits in the late Fifties and early Sixties included 'Roses Are Red' (No. 3 in 1962). Ian was a great admirer of Ronnie, believing his voice to most closely resemble that of his idol Gene Vincent. But his guest appearance on the album sleeve had simply been a bizarre coincidence, explains Ian's friend, Rainbow George. "Storm Thorgerson sent out a photographer with a remit to find some old boy somewhere who could wear a sailor's hat and they went down to the betting shop on Southend Green and spotted Ronnie [Carroll] and offered him a fiver to have his photo taken. It was so funny how that happened because Storm was round at Ian's and showing him the photos and Ian was playing a Ronnie Carroll record and talking about him and suddenly there he was."

Lyrically, Ian was on sparkling form and musically The Blockheads were as tight as they had ever been. Ian never lost his artist's eye for detail and the well-drawn characters which had so enlivened *New Boots And Panties* were back here in abundance; specifically sandwich shop girl Geraldine, school dunce Jack Shit George and the abnormally normal Harry. But *Mr Love Pants* was much more personal than any of his previous releases. It also indicated that Ian Dury had matured considerably.

"What did you learn in school today?" he entreated at the start of he record. "Jack shit," shouted The Blockheads in reply. The song was as funky as anything on his previous albums and contained some of his most eloquent lyrics to date ("I missed my chance when I was young/Now I live below the bottom rung/I was put on earth to discover my niche/Oh Lord, won't you make me Nouveau Riche"). This track owed its momentum to the technical brilliance of Norman Watt-Roy, one of Britain's most talented bass players, saxophonist Davey Payne and drummer Steve Monti, and the impact of the words, which were softly spoken but held utter conviction.

In the 'Passing Show', Ian vocalised his 'life's not a rehearsal' approach towards daily living that he had long advocated ("When life itself can chart the course/Then life's the product we endorse"). The theme was continued in 'Cacka Boom' another of the album's most uplifting moments which owed its biggest punch to Ian's use of rhyme. "Now you can put a name to it/You must lay claim to it/You'll have time to regret it/If you don't go and get it," he advised. As the aggressive funk beat slowed, causing a brief lull in the hell-for-leather tune, he observed in spoken-word, "No one said you must be good as gold/It's what you haven't done that matters when you're old/No one said these things are preor-dained/Nothing ventured . . ." before a victorious sounding saxophone solo returned the song to its energetic course.

Ian's contemplative mood was also evident in 'You're My Baby', an unusually sentimental song about Billy, the eldest of his two young children by his second marriage. In 'Heavy Living' he pondered the legacy of his hazardous lifestyle ("Heavy living's the condition I'm in/I wished I hadn't if I knew where I'd been"). 'Geraldine' was a typical treat that indulged his love of rhyme with such gems as "In beauty's eyes beholding my enamorata/As she works her wonders on a dried tomata" and sexual sug-gestiveness, as in "When she's buttering my baguette/I think I'm going to burst". In 'Mash It Up Harry', he started off poking fun at the suburban man with the boring nine-to-five routine and predictable life. "He's got his little mortgage, he's got his little lounge, he's got his bit of England to defend/He's got his little telly and he's got his little phone and he wants a bit of Wembley up his Ponders End", he sang. But he eventually softened his attitude to his grey-suited target and in a rousing finale, Harry is effect-ively lifted shoulder high to terrace-style chants of "We're On Our Way To Wembley".

Ian explained the respect he had eventually found for the Harrys of the world.[14] "I got a big laggety lawney one night. I was sitting in here listening to a rough version of it and I kept thinking, 'This is wrong, this song, I'm having a go at this geezer and I shouldn't be and I started singing at the fade out ending 'We're on our way to Wembley', because I'd had a few beers and it seemed like a really stupid thing. Then I Wemblied it through-out, I 'spun' it as they say, and instead of having a go at him, I saw that all he needs is a bit of Wembley up his 'arris. Instead of describing him as having a major kind of 'arris problem, I did it the other way around and said that the frisson of excitement when Alan Shearer puts one in the net at Wembley, that is what lifts a man's life up and that's what makes all the dif-ference, even though he will appear to be regimented. Actually, speaking as a bloke who isn't very regimented, I can feel towards persons who are routine in that I've got respect and I've also got a little jealousy. I'm not having a go at him. I was having a go at him and then I changed halfway through, I had a change of heart and I really like him now."

The vital ingredient appeared to have been time. Many of those close to Ian had consistently cited the amount of time spent on the songs on *New*

Boots And Panties for its massive success and pointed to the speed with which projects like *Laughter* and *Lord Upminster* had come to fruition as the reason for their failure. The five years over which the songs for *Mr Love Pants* evolved had now paid dividends. The perfectionist who was seen disappearing under a mound of his own song lyrics in the 1984 Channel 4 documentary had plucked 10 classics from his famous sheets of scrawl.

"Recording requires one thing – songs," said Ian.[14] "I've always said, I'm sitting here at this table and if I write a lyric that is okay it will get off the table, it will go out in the street, it will hail a cab and it will go down Denmark Street and make me a few quid, and there's nothing I need to do. It will look after me after that. So there is always that element that you are doing the pools, there's a little excitement there that you might strike a chord."

He added: "The songs on *Mr Love Pants* are worthy of The Blockheads and they're good songs and we play them live, most of them, and writing songs as good as that takes complete and absolute solid effort for a period of years."

Journalists declared *Mr Love Pants* a triumph. *Mojo* described it as Dury's best album since *New Boots And Panties*, while both *The Times* and the *Daily Telegraph* voted it "CD of the Week". Commercially, the record didn't grab any honours, but Ian had confounded those who believed he had long since run out of steam. Importantly, he and The Blockheads had again recorded an album of which they could be proud. At least half of these songs were immediately incorporated into his live shows. It had been 17 years coming, but *Mr Love Pants* had been worth the wait.

14

FRIENDS

"I don't worry about it, I don't think about it, I don't think it goes on afterwards. I don't care if I'm immediately forgotten, I don't care if my work floats down the tubes, I don't give a shit. I'm not here to be remembered, I'm here to be alive."

– Ian Dury

It was the cruellest blow of all. After a life-time coping with polio and having been treated for colon cancer more than two years earlier, Ian's doctors told him that the tumours had spread to his liver. They couldn't predict how long it would take to kill him, but they warned him that it could take as little as eight months. After two tabloid newspaper reporters knocked on his door and confronted him in May 1998, he went public in the *Observer* and his fans responded with shock and disbelief. Matters were not helped when, acting on a tip-off from a listener, Bob Geldof announced Ian's death during his XFM London radio show. Geldof was mortified over the error and made a public apology. Ian laughed it off saying, "Luckily, no one listens to XFM."

With characteristic bullishness, however, Ian refused to take on a mantle of self pity and in September went off on the gruelling UNICEF mission to Sri Lanka and, on his return to England, embarked on an eight-date tour to promote *Mr Love Pants*.

"I don't really spend a great deal of time thinking about it. I only get upset when I look at my kids, thinking that I might not be there to see them grow up. That does me right up," he said.[1]

Billy and Albert are the young children of Ian and his partner Sophy Tilson, whom he married at Camden Town Hall in April 1998, three months after he found out he had secondary cancer. The thirty-five-year-old sculptor is the youngest of Joe and Joss Tilson's three children. Like Ian, her father had studied at The Royal College of Art and was at the fore-front of the Pop Art movement in the early Sixties. She inherited his artistic talent and made sculpture her livelihood after studying at several art colleges, including the RCA. She and Ian had actually met at a gig in Chippenham in the Eighties, but it was not until the early-Nineties that they grew closer. Ian, having watched his first two children grow up, found himself experiencing fatherhood all over again in his mid-Fifties, with the arrival of Billy in January 1995 and then Albert in August 1997. Billy was one year old when he inspired his dad to write 'You're My Baby', a song included on *Mr Love Pants*, an untypically sentimental piece and one which prompted Ian to break his life-long moratorium on using the word 'baby' in his lyrics.

"Proudly at your beck and call, I'll make sure that love is all around you/Loving you is purity, blankets of security surround you – You're my baby," he wrote tenderly. But while Ian celebrated the new life of his son, this period of introspection also led him to write about the loved ones he'd lost over the years – 'The Passing Show'. "I wrote it before I was ill. It's about friends," he said.[9] "That would include Ronnie Lane, and my late wife, and Charley." The former Faces songwriter and bass player Ronnie Lane died from multiple sclerosis, while in August 1996 cancer killed his long-time friend from Dagenham, Alan Ritchie.

Ian's mum also died in 1995 and he registered her death and Billy's birth on the same day. She had lived for many years in a small hamlet near Barnstaple, in Devon, together with her sister Betty. For almost their entire lives they had been inseparable, living in Cranham and then Upminster before moving to the west country. It was only when Betty died that Peggy moved into the flat in Hampstead which Ian had bought for her. She had chosen the flat because it had a large dog-door into the garden, although Ian had indirectly influenced the location. The copy of the London A-Z which he had given her had a bookmark in the Hampstead page.

Denise: "It was hard for him to take all that really. His mum was with him, no matter what. She collected all the articles on him and all the photos. She sent him stuff that he'd never even seen and was very supportive. She would go and visit on a Sunday when he was living in Hammersmith and when his mum got sick, he would come up and visit her every day. When she had to go into a home, he would take her out for walks and they got on really well. The way he looked after her was a repayment, in a sense, for what she had done for him.

"After she died, he was clearing out her papers and found these wonderful photo albums of him as a baby: Ian with his first lollipop; Ian says his first word; Ian feeds himself for the first time. Here was this incredible story of his life in pictures. I think she suffered tremendous loss, but I never heard her talk about how difficult her life was. And I have never heard Ian say how traumatic or hard things were for him or 'Why did I ever get polio?' or talk about 'Poor me'. He is not that sort of person and he has always made the most of his situation."

She adds: "I once said to Ian, in a sense I felt he had had it easy. I didn't mean that in any real sense, obviously, but most of us have our disabilities on the inside and he had them on the outside and had to fight through it all. The rest of us look normal, feel normal, might be good looking, might have anything going for us, but actually we have our own shit to deal with on the inside. As a man, Ian has been able to push people further because of his disabilities. There has only ever been one person who fought him and that is Davey Payne, nobody else decided to fight somebody who couldn't fight back. So he has got away with murder with people. I'm sure he uses it as I'm sure anybody would. It is a way of teaching and being able to push peoples' buttons so they can think about something and knowing that they can't fight back, they have to go further than that."

Ian's positive approach to life was perfectly captured when he was asked about his illness during the 1999 BBC documentary. "I've had a major crack at life and more than most people get, so I wouldn't feel that I've been hard done-by," he said. "A very close friend of mine who lived in Dagenham [Alan Ritchie] died about two years ago, Charley our drummer died, my wife Betty died, and so I've known a lot of people who have passed away through cancer. Somehow their strength and their bravery, if it is bravery, their logic I call it, does help me deal with it, it really does. If I was feeling frustrated and unrecognised or unfulfilled or anything like that, I'm sure it would be much more difficult, but I don't. I feel very lucky, almost as if I'd had a blessed life really, because nobody has ever been horrible to me ever, and everyone's been very nice to me, very helpful, very encouraging and still are."

Ian added: "I don't worry about it, I don't think about it, I don't think it goes on afterwards. I don't care if I'm immediately forgotten, I don't care if my work floats down the tubes, I don't give a shit. I'm not here to be remembered, I'm here to be alive."

Chaz says of Ian's attitude towards his cancer: "He's got the spirit of a bulldog, he is a fighter, he's always had to fight, and to say that he doesn't have moments of grief would be untrue, because he does, I know he does, he has told me. But he has lived by the sword, he has always lived by the sword and his fortitude, I think, comes from his brazen attitude to life. I think he's an inspiration to a lot of people."

Ian began receiving an experimental form of chemotherapy, gene-therapy, which is largely self-administered. Attached to his hip was a holster-style pouch which concealed a bottle of a cytoxic drug and from this ran a Hickman Line direct to his chest. For several days a week, he plugged in to the device to receive the drug and occasionally travelled to Cairo to check in with his specialists. At his side at all times, at home and abroad, was the mysterious figure who has brought him on stage for every gig for the past eight or nine years – Derek Hussey.

Derek The Draw – an amateur guitar player and a loyal ally – cut a strange figure beside his friend and confidant. Standing tall, with white hair and a handlebar moustache, and usually dressed in a long overcoat, Derek met Ian through a mutual acquaintance in the early Nineties and soon became a regular visitor to Digby Mansions. When Ian's mother went into hospital and Ian moved permanently into her Hampstead flat, Derek would arrive on Sundays and take Ian to see her. Derek's close friendship with Ian took him almost everywhere with him; to Shepperton Studios for the filming of *Judge Dredd*, for which he helped to make props and costume accessories; Sri Lanka for Ian's UNICEF mission; the Irish Republic for the BBC documentary; and Egypt, where Ian went to see his specialists. An unflappable, comforting presence, Derek also became part and parcel of Blockheads gigs. When Derek appeared from the wings, it was his imposing presence that announced Ian's arrival on stage.

Derek, who took to wearing a fez-style hat adorned with stars, said of his cameo role: "It's a reassurance really because there are wires stuck down all over the stage and he doesn't want to take a tumble. He has always had somebody helping him and it has become a bit of a ritual. But in a hundred gigs, I have only lifted him off the floor once, so that's not much work."

Off stage, he saw a side of Ian's personality which was rarely seen by the public. He, like other close friends, knew Ian as an emotional person whose love for others ran deep.

"Ian's got a very hard exterior, which he has obviously had to develop to get by in many respects, but he is also the most generous, giving person I have ever come across," says Derek. "Money and possessions really don't mean a great deal to him, almost nothing. I have only had two arguments with him in all that time. It never turns into malicious confrontation, but the fact that Ian stands up for himself and takes no prisoners means I never have to stick my oar in at all. I can just stand back and chuckle and if it all goes a little bit awry, I will sometimes try to smooth it out, but he can look after himself. There hasn't been a person born yet that could get the better of him verbally, he is electric on the verbals.

"He is a notorious tough guy, but underneath that toughness there is an emotional side to him which can surface in a split second. In public he is very hard, but he's never annoyed for long. You think, Christ how is he going to come back from this, but just as quickly as he can get the hump, he can go the other way. I don't think Ian dwells on things too much, I don't think he's got enough time. Obviously he is very emotional about things at the time, but I don't think he can keep them as baggage. They are always there underneath and every time he talks about Betty, he will instantly be emotional, but then he will pull himself together. He is not ashamed about showing emotion either, he doesn't keep it locked away, in fact he is quite ready with his emotions."

Ian operated an open house policy at his ground-floor flat in Hampstead village, particularly on Sundays when he played host to friends. Here, he lived as he always had, playing his old records, smoking joints, drinking cups of tea and talking, always with an eye on the future. He kept in touch with most of his old friends from college and Kilburns' days and visitors included long-term cohorts such as Humphrey Ocean, Denise Roudette and members of The Blockheads. The phone and the door-bell rang constantly.

One afternoon towards the end of 1999, Ian picked up the phone and a voice said, "Paul McCartney would like to speak to Ian Dury." "Well put him on then," said Ian, to which the caller replied, "I am on, I'm Paul McCartney." The former Beatle and friend of Humphrey Ocean then asked if he could meet up with Ian, a clear indication of the respect he commanded in the music industry. The two later spent an afternoon chatting together at Ian's home. Cabinet Minister Mo Mowlam also spent a Sunday afternoon at Ian's after making contact with him and was a great admirer.

At the Q Awards in November 1999, Ian was given a standing ovation by guests at London's Park Lane Hotel, when he and Chaz picked up the Classic Songwriter Award. Madness frontman Suggs made the presentation and said Ian was a songwriter whom he had striven to emulate.

Speaking from his seat at the dinner table, Ian paid tribute to The Blockheads: "I just want to say I'm very honoured, very pleased and very glad to get a Q Award for Classic Songwriter, which Chaz and I have become over the years. Spontaneity is the watch word. Hard work is what makes it happen. Thank you very much, it's well appreciated. There's only one thing for me better than writing songs and that's playing them with The Blockheads and they're all sitting here, all of them."

Chaz added: "It's really down to the band as much as anything. They give the songs the character they wouldn't have if we'd just done them as a duo. Cheers guys."

Ian's personal life was always shaped by spontaneous impulse, rarely constrained by the kind of routine or social mores which govern most, and he surrounded himself with clutter. The front room of his home was covered with his two little sons' toys and a large children's playhouse took up a corner by the window. On the walls were some of his paintings from Walthamstow and the Royal College of Art and a large portrait of him in his twenties by Betty. On a shelf was a framed tapestry by 'Jemima Dury aged nine, 1978' quoting some of the opening lines of 'Sweet Gene Vincent'. Ian, Sophy and their two boys slept in the same room of the flat, which Ian, not wishing to disturb her spirit, changed little since his mother died.

Towards the end of his life he seldom ventured out, except for hospital appointments or strolls on Hampstead Heath, with Mickey Gallagher, his son Baxter or Derek providing a supportive arm. He didn't need to visit people. They came to him, like they always had.

In November 1999 I met Ian at his home. He knew all about my biography and had been happy for me to interview members of his group and other friends. However, his casual interest had been heightened when he received a telephone call from his childhood pal Barry Anderson whom I had tracked down in Switzerland and had given Ian's number. I was shown in by Sophy, made a mug of tea and was being entertained by Albert in their toy-scattered front room when a coarse voice uttered my name from behind the half-open door. I replied to the invisible speaker and Ian slowly emerged, directing an inquisitive gaze at me before clambering up on a seat and facing me – his entrance then complete. Ian had an aura that was intimidating and on first meeting anyone he would test them, putting them on the spot, while he checked them out. That way, he remained in control, pressing the buttons, triggering the reactions instead of giving them. He fired a volley of questions at me about my research, but was especially curious to discover how I had managed to trace his old Upminster friend. Ian smiled as I told him how a visit to the community hall in Cranham's Front Lane, where he once lived, and a chance meeting with a local woman had led me to Barry. We chatted for a while and he suggested other people I should talk to. Ian had already arranged for me to visit his friend Rainbow George, who lived nearby, and after he gave me directions, I left, while Sophy and Albert went off hand-in-hand to pick up Billy from school.

Rainbow George (George Weiss), the king of the Rainbow Dream Ticket Party, lived just a short walk from Ian's home. Cut from the same eccentric cloth as the late Screaming Lord Sutch, he struck up a relationship with Ian at around the time of the death of his neighbour and companion in Perrin's Walk, the comedian Peter Cook. The eternal idealist was often to be found sipping coffee and exchanging stories in Ian's sitting room. For some time, he badgered Ian to contribute to a Rainbow Dream Ticket Party CD, and in 1999 Ian finally acquiesced and recorded a spoken lyrical introduction entitled 'Rainbowland'. The party's aspirations for a world with "neither need or greed or any use for silly money" are reminiscent of the utopian dreams found in Ian's own song 'You'll See Glimpses'.

"Ian was someone I had wanted to meet over a period of years, but I actually didn't meet him until 1993 when Derek & Clive's [Peter Cook & Dudley Moore] video was released and Peter Cook threw a party and I met Ian there and we became pals," explains George. "Ian has more or less taken over Peter Cook's role in my life because I've spent the last 15 years trying to start a revolution and I was hoping that Peter was going to assist me in starting this revolution and I had similar hopes for Ian and similar frustrations. Back in the early Eighties, Peter knew that I had political aspirations and he had created a party called 'The What Party', which was to give everybody what they wanted within reason and he offered me the post of Minister for Confusion, which I accepted with some alacrity. He told me to go out and cause as much confusion as possible. But he never helped, he was a spectator and not a participant. He used to say to me, 'I'm your biggest fan', but my biggest fan didn't really open any doors for me and he could have done and Ian is very much the same. We made this record over two years ago and in all the hundreds of interviews he has done he has never given this record a single plug. He says to me, 'You've got my verbals, what more do you want?' and that's fair enough. He doesn't support the Rainbow Party in any way, shape or form, but he does this introduction on our record. So, as far as I am concerned, whether he admits it or not, he is leading the Rainbow revolution, and I have said that to him and there is not much you can say about that."

When Ian was at the Royal Free Hospital for Billy's birth in the early hours of January 2, 1995, Rainbow George was by his side. Within hours, George was back at the hospital because Peter Cook was dying. He too saw the sensitive side of the notorious hard man.

"Ian is a great inspiration because he doesn't believe in anything I believe in," he says. "He has no belief in an afterlife or anything on a religious basis, although having said that, he is quite superstitious about certain things and I'm not superstitious at all. So he does have a sort of conscience, but doesn't profess to having any belief whatsoever. In the way he is facing up to the condition he is in, he's very tough and forward-looking and wants to be involved in things and doing things and living.

"In the seven or so years I have known Ian, the events of his life have been very finely balanced. Really awful things have happened on one side and really nice things have happened on the other. He is a very emotional guy, he cries very easily. People think he's a real tough guy, but he's soft and he's nicest when he's vulnerable."

Ian & The Blockheads continued to play live after he was diagnosed with cancer and despite becoming physically more frail, Ian soldiered on. Several new songs were recorded ('Books And Water', 'It Aint Cool', 'Dance Little Rude Boy' and 'Ballad Of The Strangler') and following the release of *Mr Love Pants* changes were made to the band's line-up. Stephen Monti was replaced on drums by Dylan Howe, while accomplished jazz player Gilad Atzmon was invited into the fold following the expulsion of Davey Payne. Born in Israel, and trained at the Royal Academy of Music in Jerusalem, the 37-year-old played live with The Blockheads, but continued to tour with his own jazz trio and quartet. Ian's illness caused him to pull out of the Glastonbury Festival in the summer of 1999 and a subsequent event in Becton, east London, but he then rallied and played sell-out shows in Luton, Blackheath, south east London, and The Shepherd's Bush Empire, in April 1999, and in Cambridge, Croydon and Coventry during December.

He also linked up with Madness to sing on 'Drip Fed Fred', a song from their comeback album *Wonderful.* The collaboration resulted from a chance meeting with sax player Lee Thompson, as the group's guitarist Chris Foreman explains.

"Lee went to Holland to see Mike Barson, who lives there, and they were writing songs together," he says. "He'd written this song 'Drip Fed Fred' and was going back to his hotel and bumped into Ian Dury. Lee just thought Ian would be really good to sing it, although he thought it would probably never happen."

It did happen and Madness got to return the favour from 'Uncle Ian' by hosting a fund-raising night at Walthamstow Dog Track for Cancer BACUP, the charity which Ian supported after he was diagnosed. The 'Nutty Boys' headed up the event on November 30, 1999, raised £30,000 for its 'Living With Cancer Appeal' – on which Ian was a board member, along with comedian Phill Jupitus.

In February, 2000, Ian played live dates at the University of East Anglia in Norwich and The London Palladium. Audiences were lost in admiration of his resilience as he dug deep into his energy reserves to pull off two extraordinary performances within three days. Physically, he looked thin and weak, but perched on the edge of a box and pulling the microphone backwards and forwards by its cable, he still had the performance skills of old.

Displaying his customary tendency for coarseness, Ian told the audience about how, during his first visit to the UEA in 1977, "I looked up into the lights and saw this great lump of green and purple gob flying towards me . . . And do you know what?" he said, using his finger to trace the trajectory as the phlegm flew into his mouth . . . "It tasted of Tia Maria." The crowd roared its approval and Ian lapsed back into silence, giving way to The Blockheads.

Ian's illness without doubt helped reconnect him with many of his old fans and in 2000 his profile had never been higher. His work with

UNICEF, television commercials for the *Sunday Times* and the Halifax Building Society, and guest appearances on TV shows such as *Never Mind The Buzzcocks, Later With Jools Holland* and *The National Lottery Show*, on which he performed with Madness, also introduced him to the younger generation. In the audience at his live shows were people of Ian's own age group, thirty-somethings who bought his hit records, accompanied by their own children, and those who missed him the first time and were now discovering 'Clevor Trever', 'Sweet Gene Vincent' and 'What A Waste'. He was so much part of British culture that even those who had never bought a single Ian Dury record could instantly have identified the gruff voice that helped narrate Channel 4's recent celebration of *Top Ten Punks*.

Back in 1984, Ian said:[15] "Everyone imagines that people like me really want to be popular and really want to be famous. But I don't. I don't like being popular and famous. I like being a lurker, I like being in the shade, I like being naughty." But although he railed against the establishment, Ian Dury was proud of the respect he commanded in elite circles. He was thrilled when the former BBC director general John Birt personally came to shake his hand in the dressing room at the Shepherd's Bush Empire and he took great pleasure from his involvement in the 'luvvie' world of theatre. Ian always adored attention, but only later in his life did he come to terms with his fame. "It's always nice when a mover and a shaker comes along to shake your hand. Anyway I've always been a bit of a snob!" he said.[1]

Ian voiced discomfort that his illness helped generate the ecstatic greetings he received after it was announced that he had secondary cancer. The sight of him struggling on stage, his face drawn and pallid, understandably saddened his fans. But for whatever reason they were there, Ian's relationship with his audiences had always been a deeply personal one.

The show at the University of East Anglia was marked by displays of mutual affection. Before bowing to screams for an encore, The Blockheads surrounded him, hugging and kissing him as he sat beaming at the crowd. Overwhelmed by the delirious cheers ringing around the venue and his voice cracking with emotion, Ian acknowledged the devotion of all around him: "When we go home we will feel well appreciated tonight," he said. ' Thanks . . . you've given me another year of energy."

At the London Palladium two nights later Ian paid the audience the same compliment as he left the stage. Sadly, however, it was not to be. At 9am on Monday March 27, 2000, Ian Dury died peacefully at his Hampstead home. He had been surrounded by his family in the weeks leading up to his death and they were with him when the final moment came. He was 57 years old. I was at work when Mickey Gallagher telephoned me to tell me the sad news. I knew Ian's health had declined in the previous few weeks but it still came as a shock. About an hour later his passing was announced on the news wires and on radio stations.

Rainbow George was one of the first to hear that his friend had died: "Sophy phoned me up about lunch-time and told me the news and asked me to come over. I made my way over with quite a lot of trepidation because I didn't know what the atmosphere was going to be like in the house. I rang on the door and Sophy answered with Albert and Bill and they're both smiling and saying, 'Daddy's gone to heaven,' so there was a good atmosphere.

"I went into the bedroom and Sophy had dressed Ian up smart, with his flat cap and everything, and laid him out on his little bed and he looked absolutely fantastic. Then Bill got his guitar and Albert got his bongos and sat at the foot of the bed playing music – it was just a brilliant atmosphere in the place, but that's Sophy. Ian really didn't have any beliefs beyond this existence and it's nice that Sophy was able to get that sort of imagery into Albert's and Bill's minds."

He adds: "Ian had bought a computer about a week before he died. He bought a new Apple Mac and was going to start writing his autobiography and of course it never came out of the box. That was what was so wonderful about Ian – the way he kept going for things and looking forward. He was fighting right to the end and he died with a smile on his face."

Ian Dury was held in unusually high regard in Britain and the fact that he had reached all sections of society, young and old, was movingly reflected in the coverage of his death. The *Daily Telegraph* and *Independent* carried large pictures of Ian on their front pages, it was front-page news in the *Guardian* and extensive obituaries were published by all the quality broadsheets. The tabloids also ran prominent tributes. The high-profile BBC2 current affairs show *Newsnight* included a tribute in its programme that evening, while old documentaries were rebroadcast in the days following his death.

Musicians and figures from varying walks of public life paid their respects to a man who had struck a chord with so many people. Jools Holland, the pianist and presenter of BBC2's *Later With Jools Holland*, said: "I was made an honorary Blockhead, which is one of the proudest accolades of my life. He should be posthumously made our Poet Laureate." Annie Nightingale, the former Radio 1 DJ, described him as "the most cheerful genius I have ever met". Suggs from Madness added: "Ian really was the reason Madness started. He was still giving his all right 'til the end. He was will be greatly missed."

Mo Mowlam, who had come to know Ian personally, said: "Those who knew him as a performer and a friend know that the world will be a duller

place without him. We have all lost a wonderful man, a real human being."
Jo Bexley of Unicef, with whom he had travelled on polio immunisation
missions, said: "There is only one word which describes him – awesome. He
said there were three things on his agenda: his music, Unicef and cancer, the
disease to which he finally succumbed."

Ian had campaigned for the charity Cancer BACUP and throughout his
illness attempted to remove the taboos about the disease. A spokesman for
the charity said: "Ian was a tireless supporter. Even during his illness he
raised £100,000 for us. His energy and enthusiasm were an inspiration for
all cancer patients."

Baxter Dury, speaking on the day of his dad's death, told *The Times*: "I
and the whole family were with Ian when he died. It's difficult to say
exactly how we feel because none of us has had any sleep. All I can say is
that he did everything that he wanted to in his life and he even died when
he wanted to. He was very ill. For the last day and a half he could barely
speak. But he was himself – he was himself to the very end. He had all his
dignity intact, right to the last second."

Particularly moving was the book of condolences on Ian's official
internet website, where hundreds of admirers from around the world left
heartfelt messages and tributes to their hero. It was clear that all those who
contributed to this spontaneous epitaph had been personally touched by
Ian and his music; many spoke of treasured record sleeves and tee-shirts he
had signed, meetings they had had with him, or concerts they had enjoyed.
So full was the first list of condolences that his record company, East
Central One, opened another site to meet demand.

Bright sunshine bathed the courtyard of Golders Green Crematorium on
the morning of April 5, as Ian's kaleidoscopic circle of friends gathered
outside the west chapel for his funeral service. A glance at the faces of those
who had known him revealed a great deal about his universal popularity and
his flair for connecting with people from all walks of life. Celebrity, money
and material possessions meant nothing to Ian and he made people feel
valued and loved by appealing directly to their human side, communicating
in the same robust and ribald manner with one and all. The invited guests
included well-known figures: Mo Mowlam, former Radio 1 DJ Annie
Nightingale, Neneh and Eagle-Eye Cherry and Robbie Williams. Also
among the mourners were ex-managers, ex- girlfriends, former Kilburns,
art college friends, and stars from the heady days of Stiff Records, Nick Lowe,
Lene Lovich, Wreckless Eric and Madness. Press photographers perched on
the crematorium wall, training their lenses on the motley collection whom
Ian Dury had – like the Pied Piper – led into his distinct and unordinary
world. They were all there; friends with stripy woollen hats, 'Teddy Boy'

threads, shaved heads, mobster shades, camel-hair coats and trilbys, and others on crutches, sticks and carrying gold-topped canes. Ian loved life's curiosities and felt an affinity with people who, like himself, knew what it felt like to be on the margins or physically vulnerable. Despite varying degrees of material success, Ian's friends have remained true to themselves; continuing to paint, draw, play music, write songs and put their talents to creative use. There, in the early summer sun, they were united; those who had given Ian so much friendship and who felt they had been repaid in the most handsome way.

The cortege, led by a Victorian glass-sided hearse pulled by two bay horses with black plumes, came from the funeral home in Haverstock Hill, Belsize Park, having stopped outside Ian's home in Hampstead to pick up his family, band members and other mourners. Little Billy Dury waited in his cowboy hat, sheriff's badge and a Blockhead tee-shirt, while Baxter and Jemima wore grey suits and white silk scarves, tied in the way their dad always wore them. The procession snaked through north London, passing within half a mile of Kilburn High Road, towards Golders Green, NW11 – the final destination in the journey of a performer whose songs were like a poetic London A–Z. From Billy Bentley's adventures in the capital to Fulham Broadway Station ('What A Waste'), Lambeth Walk, Turnham Green and Harold Hill ('This Is What We Find') and all the stops along the 'Bus Driver's Prayer', Ian took his followers on a colourful London tour.

A respectful silence fell as the horse-drawn hearse appeared through the crematorium gates and around 250 people filed slowly inside. The same music that announced his arrival on stage – a strange mixture of sleigh bells, singing and yodelling – was played as his coffin was carried into the chapel by Chaz, Johnny, Norman and Mickey, along with Chris Foreman and Lee Thompson of Madness. A black cloth bearing the Blockhead logo covered the casket, and his old overcoat was draped over one end. Death, for a man who had lived so joyously and who always looked to the future, suddenly seemed desperately cruel and unjust. But this was no sombre occasion. Rather, it was a celebration of Ian's inspirational contribution to 'The Passing Show', a chance to reflect on the "counterfoil" he had left behind.

It was a humanist ceremony, in accordance with Ian's wishes, and there was music and laughter as tributes were paid. Annette Furley, the officiant, gave a summary of his life which prompted smiles and tears. His disability "never made life easy, but he never let it stand in his way," she said. "He felt that people could do what they wanted if they wanted to do it enough." She told how Ian had said that "a sure way not to die on stage is to be mag-nificent", something that he always achieved. "He was one of the few orig-inal personalities in the music business. He used to write music that made you want to dance and also made you laugh," she said. He enjoyed his acting and lapped up the mutual adoration of the theatrical world, "although he did admit, in his own words, that it was a load of bollocks". Ian saddened that he would not see his two youngest sons grow up, had faced his illness bravely and was cracking jokes on the day he died. "He inspired all those around him and changed people's lives. He brought out the best in people. Many people have said they did what they did because of Ian," said Ms Furley.

Laughter rang around the chapel as Ian's long-serving accountant Ronnie Harris shared his memories. Ian never had a bank account, dismissed credit cards as "modern" and the two of them had signed off cheques from a single account, he said. Jemima had told Ronnie how Ian had asked for a computer only a few weeks before he died, so he could write a book, something he had never before asked for. He revelled in untidiness and mess and resisted paying poll tax and rates. "When Ian first tasted success, he said to me, 'Maybe I should get all posh and move up town.' He got a flat in Baker Street, but he didn't like that. He liked to be untidy and he couldn't do that being posh. So he moved to Hammersmith, which he loved, although he hated paying water rates when the River Thames was flowing just beneath his front window," recalled Ronnie. In 1978 Ian had embossed a Union Jack on his teeth and then asked if it was tax deductible. "And," said Ronnie, "it was." When Ian released *Mr Love Pants* on 'Ronnie Harris Records', "it was his way of leaving me something that didn't cost anything," remembered Ronnie, who said he'd been a "boring chartered accountant" when he met Ian and that the encounter had changed his life.

Tears flowed when The Blockheads, seated around a music stand, played a song Ian had written only a few weeks before he died, 'You're The Why'. The words of his last composition would have moved even the hardest heart and the sight of his group performing without him epitomised the sense of loss. "I shuffled through the modes of bad behaviour/And hankered for the desolated dawn/I couldn't cope with yet another saviour/To steer me from the way that I was born," sang Chaz. "Then like a ton of bricks the dawn descended/Recalcitrance was hurtled to the floor/The citadel lay breached and undefended/You brought a love I'd never known before. I'll want you till the seasons lose their mystery/I'll need you till the birds forget to fly/I love you more than anyone in history/Wherever there's a wherefore you're the why."

When the service was over, the mourners moved past the coffin, some pausing thoughtfully to lay their hands lovingly on the cloth; jazz records and other favourites of Ian's played through the speakers as they did so.

Outside, family and friends admired the extraordinary display of flowers and wreaths which had been sent. 'Durex' read one from Kozmo Vinyl, 'Uncle Ian from Madness' spelt out some bright yellow flowers, while the floral tribute from his friend Jock Scott came in the shape of a pint of Guinness. 'Say hi to Don' read a card from the Cherry family, while other bouquets were sent by Paul McCartney 'and the kids', Charlie and Shirley Watts, Roger and Heather Daltrey, Chas & Dave and his former neighbours from Oval Mansions. One eulogy simply read 'Oi Oi'.

What was to follow at The Forum in Kentish Town, was the kind of occasion that Ian would have loved – a night of drinking, laughter, music and even some fighting. The venue itself was especially appropriate. It sits directly opposite The Tally Ho, the music pub where Kilburn & The High Roads served their apprenticeship, and the scene of the benefit concerts played by Ian and The Blockheads after the death of Charley Charles, who also died from cancer. A large photograph of Ian – used on the 1999 *Sex And Drugs And Rock'n'Roll* compilation – looked down from the back of the stage, as the booze and the stories began to flow. Ian's favourite jellied eels and pie and mash were served to those arriving from the crematorium and musicians paid their own spontaneous tributes on stage throughout the evening. Some were raucous, such as Wilko Johnson's pulsating R&B and Wreckless Eric's Stiff classic 'Whole Wide World', while others were heart-rending. Baxter was ushered on stage by Derek The Draw – a re-enactment of his father's time-honoured stage entrance – and he gave an inebriated rendition of 'My Old Man', reading the poignant lyrics from a sheet of paper as he tried to keep time with The Blockheads. Meanwhile, Humphrey Ocean, wearing a flat green cap and a coat adorned with coloured badges from the Stiff tour, led the audience in a sing-a-long of 'Hit Me' and 'Billericay Dickie' for which song sheets were given out. Chas Smash from the "Kilburns tribute band" Madness also drunkenly helped conduct proceedings. Saxophonist Gilad Atzmon, one of the last additions to The Blockheads, gave a breathtaking jazz performance, aided by Dylan Howe on drums and Ed Speight on keyboards.

Possibly the most moving contribution of all came courtesy of Ronnie Carroll. He stunned the party into silence when he shambled towards the microphone in his buttoned-up overcoat to deliver an unaccompanied, note-perfect rendition of 'Danny Boy' (The Londonderry Air), changing the words to 'Ian Boy'. For those few minutes, the image of Ian above him seemed larger than ever and a peacefulness descended. It was indicative of the emotional ebb and flow of the occasion; moments later, figures could be seen brawling on the balcony. As the music ended, the crowd called for more, with Chas Smash reminding the guests that The Blockheads had just lost their "best friend". Somewhat curiously, the wake was reviewed in *The Guardian* two days later, with critic Robin Denselow grading the event, awarding it four stars no less, as if it was a paying gig. The review prompted a letter to the paper the following week to the effect that Ian's wake was probably the first in history to be classified in this way. Ian would have laughed his socks off.

Music has lost a one-off. Some of his lyrical gems now seem doubly sorrowful, but contained within them are the positive messages that will continue to inspire those who hear them. "But when we're torn from mortal coil/We leave behind a counterfoil," he sang in 'The Passing Show'. "It's what we did and who we knew/And that's what makes this story true." Ian thrived on the kind of advice for life advocated in his songs from "Get your teeth into a small slice/The cake of liberty" ('Sex And Drugs', 1977) to "You'll have time to regret it/If you don't go and get it" ('Cacka Boom', 1998). He took control of his own life, casting obstacles aside in the belief that he could not only achieve success for himself, but give inspiration for others. Ian Dury – "young and old and gone" – but his legacy will endure.

Bibliography

Books

Upminster: The Story of a Garden Suburb, Tony Benton with Albert Parish Britton & Walland Printer Ltd, 1996)

A Summer Plague: Polio And Its Survivors, Tony Gould (Yale University Press, 1995)

The Polio Story, PJ Fisher (Heinemann, 1967)

Punk Diary 1970 – 1979, George Gimarc (Vintage, 1979)

Stiff: The Story Of A Record Label, Bert Muirhead (Blandford Press, 1983)

The Guinness Book of Hit Singles, Jo and Tim Rice, Paul Gambaccini, Mike Read (Guinness, various dates)

Rock Family Trees, Pete Frame (Omnibus Press, 1993)

Elvis Costello, Krista Reese (Proteus, 1981)

Elvis Costello: A Biography, Tony Clayton-Lea (Andre Deutsch, 1998)

The Who Concert File, Joe McMichael & 'Irish' Jack Lyons (Omnibus Press, 1997)

A Dictionary of 20th Century World Biography (BCA, 1992)

The Oxford Companion to English Literature, Third Edition, compiled and edited by Sir Paul Harvey (Oxford University Press)

The Sound Of The City, Charlie Gillett (Souvenir Press)

The Wee Rock Discography, M.C. Strong (Canongate Books 1996)

The Encyclopedia of Popular Music, Ed. Colin Larkin (McMillan/Music, 1998)

Time Out Film Guide (1997)

40 Years Of New Musical Express Charts, Dafydd Rees, Barry Lazell & Roger Osborne (Boxtree 1992)

Sources

Comments made by Ian Dury which appear in this book have been taken from the following sources:

1. *On My Life*: A BBC2 documentary on Ian's life, screened on September 25, 1999.
2. Radio 4's *Desert Island Discs* with Sue Lawley, broadcast in 1996.
3. *A Summer Plague: Polio And Its Survivors* by Tony Gould.
4. *The Independent*, Deborah Ross, August 17, 1998.
5. *Penthouse*, Steve Fuller, 1973.
6. *Daily Telegraph*, Neil McCormick, July 16, 1998.
7. *Vox* magazine, October 1991.
8. Sleeve-notes for *Reasons To Be Cheerful*, a compilation CD released in 1996, written by Chris Welch.
9. *The Guardian*, Simon Hattenstone, June 19, 1998.
10. Radio 1 documentary entitled *From Punk To Present*.
11. *Hot Press* magazine article on Stiff Records by the author, 1996.
12. *Sounds*, Vivien Goldman, published on October 15, 1977.
13. *The Sunday Times*, Yvonne Roberts, May 21, 1978.
14. BBC Radio 2 documentary, presented by Richard Allinson, May 8, 1999.
15. Channel 4 documentary, producer Franco Rosso, 1984.
16. *The Observer* (Section 5), Marek Kohn, September 1989.
17. Q magazine, Adam Sweeting, February 1987.
18. *The Guardian*, Murray Armstrong, September 28, 1989.
19. *The Times* magazine, October 17, 1998.

Other sources:
New Musical Express, August 1975.
Melody Maker, Allan Jones, November 19, 1977.
New Musical Express, Monty Smith, December 24, 1977.
The Face, Mike Stand, September 1981.
Q, Phil Sutcliffe, June 1991.
Q, December 1992.
The Independent, Janie Lawrence, March 4, 1998.
Mojo, Will Birch, December 1998.
Mojo, March 2000.

Discography

KILBURN & THE HIGH ROADS

Singles
Rough Kids/Billy Bentley
Dawn-Pye (7") Nov 1974

Crippled With Nerves/Huffety Puff
Dawn-Pye (7") Feb 1975

Billy Bentley/Pam's Moods
Warner (7") 1978

Albums
Handsome
The Roadette Song/ Pam's Moods/ Crippled With Nerves/ Broken
Skin/ Upminster Kid/ Patience (So What?)/ Father/ Thank You Mum/
Rough Kids/ The Badger And The Rabbit/ The Mumble Rumble And
The Cocktail Rock/ The Call Up
Dawn-Pye June 1975 (Re-issued on Pye in 1977)

Wotabunch
The Call Up/ Crippled With Nerves/ Patience (So What?)/ You're
More Than Fair/ Upminster Kid/ Billy Bentley/ Huffety Puff/ Rough
Kids/ The Roadette Song/ The Badger And The Rabbit/ The Mumble
Rumble And The Cocktail Rock/ Pam's Moods
Warner Bros October 1978

EPs
The Best Of Kilburn & The High Roads:
Father/ Thank You Mum/ Upminster Kid/ Rough Kids/ The Mumble
Rumble And The Cocktail Rock
Bonaparte 1978
Upminster Kids PRT (10" EP with 8 tracks) 1983

IAN DURY

Singles
Sex & Drugs & Rock'n'Roll/ Razzle In My Pocket
Stiff (7") August 1977

Sex & Drugs & Rock'n'Roll/ Sweet Gene Vincent/ You're More Than
Fair
Stiff (12" – French release) August 1977

Sweet Gene Vincent/ You're More Than Fair
Stiff (7") November 1977

Sex & Drugs & Rock'n'Roll/ Two Stiff Steep Hills/ England's Glory
Stiff (7") December 1977 (Freebie: 1,000 copies pressed for *NME*
Christmas Party and another 500 for *NME*/Blockheads competition)

Spasticus Autisticus/(Instrumental)
Polydor (7&12") Aug 1981

Profoundly In Love With Pandora/Eugenius (You're A Genius)
EMI (7", Picture Disc also issued) October 1989

Apples/Byline Browne
WEA (7") October 1989

Albums
New Boots And Panties
Wake Up And Make Love With Me/ Sweet Gene Vincent/ I'm Partial
To Your Abracadabra/ My Old Man/ Billericay Dickie/ Clevor Trever/
If I Was With A Woman/ Blockheads/ Plaistow Patricia/ Blackmail Man
Stiff September 1977

Lord Upminster
Funky Disco Pops/ Red Letter/ Girls Watching/ Wait For Me/ The
Body Song/ Lonely Town/ Trust Is A Must/ Spasticus Autisticus
Polydor September 1981

Apples
Apples/ Love Is All/ Byline Browne/ Bit Of Kit/ Game On/ Looking
For Harry/ England's Glory/ Bus Driver's Prayer/ PC Honey/ The
Right People/ All Those Who Say Okay/ Riding The Outskirts of
Fantasy
WEA October 1989

The Bus Driver's Prayer & Other Stories
That's Enough Of That/ Bill Haley's Last Words/ Poor Joey/ Quick Quick
Slow/ Fly In The Ointment/ O Donegal/ Poo-Poo In The Prawn/ Have A
Word/ London Talking/ D'Orine The Cow/ Your Horoscope/ No Such
Thing As Love/ Two Old Dogs Without A Name/ Bus Driver's Prayer
Demon October 1992

IAN DURY & THE BLOCKHEADS

Singles
What A Waste/Wake Up And Make Love With Me.
Stiff (7" – Only 5,000 copies of 12" version pressed) April 1978

Hit Me With Your Rhythm Stick/There Ain't Half Been Some Clever
Bastards
Stiff (7&12") November 1978

Reasons To Be Cheerful (Part 3)/Common As Muck
Stiff (7&12") July 1979

Inbetweenies/Dance Of The Screamer
Stiff (12" – French issue only) 1979

I Want To Be Straight/That's Not All
Stiff (7&12") April 1980

Sueperman's Big Sister/You'll See Glimpses
Stiff (7") October 1980

Sueperman's Big Sister/Fucking Ada
Stiff (12") October 1980

Hit Me With Your Rhythm Stick/ Sex & Drugs & Rock'n'Roll/
Reasons To Be Cheerful/ Wake Up And Make Love With Me
(Remixed by Paul Hardcastle)
Stiff (12") May 1985

Albums
Do It Yourself
Inbetweenies/ Quiet/ Don't Ask Me/ Sink My Boats/ Waiting For Your
Taxi./ This Is What We Find/ Uneasy Sunny Day Hotsy Totsy/
Mischief/ Dance Of The Screamers/ Lullaby For Francis
Stiff May 1979

Laughter
Sueperman's Big Sister/ Pardon/ Delusions Of Grandeur/ Yes & No
(Paula)/ Dance Of The Crackpots/ Over The Points/ Take Your Elbow
Out Of The Soup (You're Sitting On The Chicken)/ Uncoolohol/ Hey,
Hey, Take Me Away/ Manic Depression (Jimi)/ Oh Mr Peanut/
Fucking Ada
Stiff November 1980

Warts 'N' Audience (Live)
Wake Up And Make Love With Me/ Clevor Trever/ Billericay Dickie/
Quiet/ My Old Man/ Spasticus Autisticus/ Plaistow Patricia/ There
Ain't Half Been Some Clever Bastards/ Sweet Gene Vincent/ What A
Waste/ Hit Me With Your Rhythm Stick/ Blockheads
Demon April 1991
(Included free single: If I Was With A Woman/Inbetweenies – both live)

Mr Love Pants
Jack Shit George/ The Passing Show/ You're My Baby/ Honeysuckle
Highway/ Itinerant Child/ Geraldine/ Cacka Boom/ Bed 'O' Roses
No 9/Heavy Living/ Mash It Up Harry
Ronnie Harris Records 1998

IAN DURY & THE MUSIC STUDENTS

Singles
Really Glad You Came/ You're My Inspiration
Polydor (7&12") Nov 1983

Very Personal/ Ban The Bomb
Polydor (7") February 1984

Very Personal/ Ban The Bomb/ The Sky's The Limit
Polydor (12") February 1984

Album
4,000 Weeks' Holiday
You're My Inspiration/ Friends/ Tell Your Daddy/Peter The Painter/
Ban The Bomb/ Percy The Poet/ Very Personal/Take Me To The
Cleaners/ The Man With No Face/ Really Glad You Came
Polydor January 1984

IAN DURY COMPILATIONS

Juke Box Dury
What A Waste/ Reasons To Be Cheerful (Part 3)/ There Ain't Half Been
Some Clever Bastards/ Hit Me With Your Rhythm Stick/Razzle In My
Pocket/ Sex & Drugs & Rock'n'Roll/Inbetweenies/ Common As
Muck/ Sweet Gene Vincent/ I Want To Be Straight/ You'll See Glimpses
Stiff November 1981

Sex & Drugs & Rock'n'Roll
Hit Me With Your Rhythm Stick/ I Want To Be Straight/ There Ain't
Half Been Some Clever Bastards/ What A Waste/ Common As Muck/
Reasons To Be Cheerful (Part 3)/ Sex & Drugs & Rock'n'Roll/
Sueperman's Big Sister/ Razzle In My Pocket/ You're More Than Fair/
Inbetweenies/ You'll See Glimpses
Demon April 1987

Reasons To Be Cheerful
CD1: Sex & Drugs & Rock'n'Roll/ Wake Up And Make Love With
Me/ Hit Me With Your Rhythm Stick/ Reasons To Be Cheerful
(Part 3)/ I Want To Be Straight/ Sueperman's Big Sister/ What A
Waste/ Sweet Gene Vincent/ Profoundly In Love With Pandora/
Rough Kids/ You're More Than Fair/ Billy Bentley/ Pam's Moods 2/
The Call Up/ Crippled With Nerves/ The Mumble Rumble And The
Cocktail Rock/ Billericay Dickie/ I'm Partial To Your Abracadabra/
Blockheads/

CD2: Waiting For Your Taxi/ This Is What We Find/ Dance Of The
Crackpots/ Hey, Hey, Take Me Away/ Funky Disco Pops/ The Body
Song/ Spasticus Autisticus/ You're My Inspiration/ Really Glad You
Came/ Apples/ England's Glory/ Clevor Trever/ Plaistow Patricia/ If I
Was With A Woman/ Inbetweenies/ O'Donegal/ Poo-Poo In The
Prawn/ D'Orine The Cow
Repertoire 1966

Sex & Drugs & Rock'n'Roll
Reasons To Be Cheerful/ Wake Up And Make Love With Me/ Hit Me
With Your Rhythm Stick/ Clevor Trever/ What A Waste/ Sex & Drugs
& Rock'n'Roll/ This Is What We Find/ Itinerant Child/ Sweet Gene
Vincent/ I Want To Be Straight/ Blockheads/ Mash It Up Harry/ There
Ain't Half Been Some Clever Bastards/ Billericay Dickie/ Inbetweenies/
Spasticus Autisticus/ My Old Man/ Lullaby For Francis
1999

RE-RELEASES ON CD

Kilburn & The High Roads
Handsome
Sequel 1990

Handsome
Castle 1998
(Extra tracks: Billy Bentley [Promenades Himself In London]; Huffety Puff; Who's To Know?; Back To Blighty; OK Roland; Twenty Tiny Fingers)

Ian Dury/Blockheads
New Boots And Panties
Demon 1986
(Included Ian Dury interview which featured on a limited 12" with original album)

Do It Yourself
Demon 1990

Lord Upminster
Great Expectations 1990

4000 Weeks' Holiday
Great Expectations 1990

New Boots And Panties
Disky 1995

Do It Yourself
Disky 1995

Laughter
Disky 1995

Do It Yourself
Repertoire 1996
(Additional tracks: Hit Me With Your Rhythm Stick/ There Ain't Half Been Some Clever Bastards/ Reasons To Be Cheerful (Part 3)/ Common As Muck/ I Want To Be Straight/ That's Not All/ Reasons To Be Cheerful (Part 3) Extended Version)

SELECTED COMPILATION ALBUMS FEATURING
IAN DURY TRACKS

Stiff Live Stiffs
Billericay Dickie/Wake Up And Make Love With Me/ Sex & Drugs &
Rock'n'Roll
Stiff 1978

Can't Start Dancing (The Sounds Album Volume 3)
Sex & Drugs & Rock'n'Roll/ Razzle In My Pocket
Stiff 1978

That Summer
Sex & Drugs & Rock'n'Roll
Arista 1978

Concert For The People Of Kampuchea
Hit Me With Your Rhythm Stick
Atlantic 1981

Formula Thirty 2
Hit Me With Your Rhythm Stick
Mercury 1986

The Sound Of The Suburbs
Hit Me With Your Rhythm Stick
1992

The Sound Of The City
Reasons To Be Cheerful (Part3)
Columbia 1992

The Stiff Years
Sweet Gene Vincent
Disky 1995

A Hard Nights Day
Hit Me With Your Rhythm Stick
Universal 1995

A Pint Of Your Best Pub Rock, Please
Sweet Gene Vincent
Nectar 1997

1.2.3.4: Punk-New Wave 1976–1979
Sex & Drugs & Rock'n'Roll
Universal 1999 (5 CD box set)

Index

5/09 (169805)